# COLORIZATION

# COLORIZATION

One Hundred Years of
Black Films in a White World

# WIL HAYGOOD

 Alfred A. Knopf · New York · 2021

THIS IS A BORZOI BOOK
PUBLISHED BY ALFRED A. KNOPF

Copyright © 2021 by Wil Haygood

All rights reserved.
Published in the United States by Alfred A. Knopf,
a division of Penguin Random House LLC, New York, and distributed
in Canada by Penguin Random House Canada Limited, Toronto.

www.aaknopf.com

Knopf, Borzoi Books, and the colophon
are registered trademarks of Penguin Random House LLC.

Library of Congress Cataloging-in-Publication Data
Names: Haygood, Wil, author.
Title: Colorization : one hundred years of Black films in a white world / Wil Haygood.
Description: First edition. | New York : Alfred A. Knopf, 2021. | "This is a Borzoi Book
Published by Alfred A. Knopf." | Includes bibliographical references and index.
Identifiers: LCCN 2020056224 | ISBN 9780525656876 (hardcover) | ISBN 9780525656883 (ebook)
Subjects: LCSH: African Americans in motion pictures. | Race in motion pictures. | Racism in
motion pictures. | Motion pictures—United States—History. | United States—Race relations.
Classification: LCC PN1995.9.N4 H39 2021 | DDC 791.43/652996073—dc23
LC record available at https://lccn.loc.gov/2020056224

Jacket images: Gordon Parks. AP/Shutterstock; Oscar Micheaux. Schomburg Center
for Research in Black Culture, Photographs and Prints Division, NYPL;
Sidney Poitier and Harry Belafonte. NARA; all the rest courtesy of Photofest
Jacket design by John Gall

Manufactured in Canada

First Edition

For Pamela Oas Williams, who loves movies

# Contents

# COLORIZATION

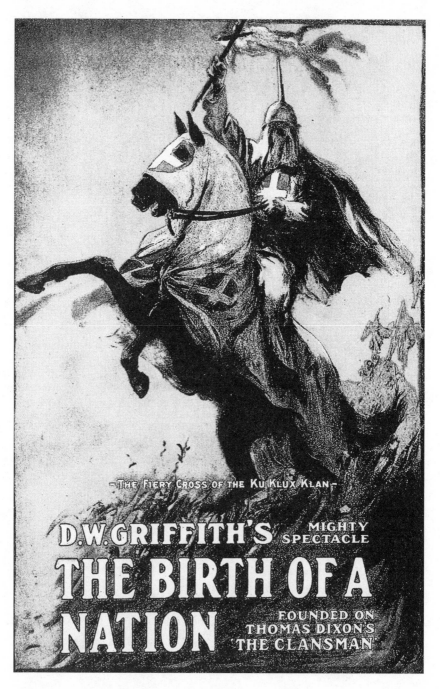

*The Birth of a Nation* (1915). The movie that started it all.

# Movie Night
# at Woodrow Wilson's White House

I N THE AFTERMATH of the Civil War, fathers throughout the Southern states—its landscape in ruins, the populace grieving—had to start imagining a future for their sons, who had either fought in the war or grown up around it. The Lost Cause of the Confederacy left the entire region in a state of near-shock. For families that still had money from cotton and plantation revenues, a college education for their sons was seen as a key to reclaiming a bright family future. No matter how smart the women in families were, or how intellectually gifted, it remained a patriarchal-led society.

Before the war, many moneyed families became attracted to colleges and universities in the North. Princeton University was a school that particularly stood out among Southern gentry. Fifteen Southern governors could count themselves as Princeton grads. It was not lost on Southerners that Alexander Boteler, Princeton Class of 1835, had helped design the Confederate flag. Boteler was revered throughout the South. In 1857, Rev. George Armstrong—Princeton Class of 1832—published *The Christian Doctrine of Slavery.* He argued that Southerners took better care of slaves than Northerners could imagine, though allowing, as he put it, for "some deprivation of personal liberty." Two years after Armstrong's screed, in 1859, a contingent of Princeton students from below the Mason-Dixon Line marched across their campus burning effigies of pro-Union Northern political figures. Alexander Stephens, who would serve as vice-president of the Confederacy from 1861 to 1865, proclaimed Princeton graduates to be "superior to those of any other school or college in the country." During the long and bloody Civil War, seven Confederate brigadier generals were Princeton men. Some saw fit to sing the Princeton fight song as they galloped in the direction of Union cannon fire.

Joseph Wilson prided himself on his Southern ministry. In his reading of the Bible, slavery was simply a necessity. He and his wife, Jessie, had moved around the South, from Virginia to South Carolina and on to North Carolina. Jessie Wilson tended wounded Confederate soldiers. In the aftermath of war's end, the Wilson family held on to endless grudges. They were especially pained with the onset of the Reconstruction era, when the United States tried to bring a measure of equality and opportunity to formerly enslaved Blacks. Their son Woodrow Wilson was born in Virginia and grew up in and around the South amid Reconstruction. Young Woodrow thought of Reconstruction as a terrible experience for his family and other Southern whites. His earliest school tutoring came from Confederate veterans; they were men he came to admire greatly, men who told him of the great battles they had fought to keep the South firmly in the grip of whites and away from Abe Lincoln, whom they called a madman, and whose assassination they did not bemoan. In 1875, Woodrow Wilson's parents—after he had spent a year at Davidson College—sent him off to a school they had heard a lot about because of its Southern pedigree: the College of New Jersey, the school that would become Princeton University.

Woodrow Wilson easily took to college life. He joined clubs and organizations. He honed a gift as a public speaker; his articles for the student newspaper were widely and favorably commented upon. Professors praised his serious approach to academic life. Wilson made friends with classmates who hailed from Southern states, all bonding together over their history and hometowns. One of the people Wilson would have come across on campus was a gentleman by the name of Jimmy Johnson. Johnson began work at the school as a janitor in the 1840s and would remain there for sixty years, later also selling snacks at a makeshift stand on campus. Jimmy Johnson was a runaway slave from Maryland. He was ever mindful of trips that ranged too far from campus, nervous about bounty hunters and slave catchers. The runaway slave never met any Black students at Princeton, because they were not allowed.

While on campus, Woodrow Wilson convinced himself he might prefer a career in law. He applied to the University of Virginia Law School and was accepted. Several years later, after undergoing an abbreviated law-school stint and passing the bar exam, Wilson was settled in Atlanta and practicing law. But he felt his chosen profession boring and began imagining instead a career in public service or academia. To make that happen, he was advised to seek a doctoral degree. He applied and was accepted to Johns Hopkins University, in Baltimore. He arrived on the campus in 1883.

A restless sort, Wilson sat through doctoral classes and concluded they were stuffy, and the professors too concerned with minutiae. The books assigned to him made him roll his eyes. So he began thinking of a book he himself would like to write. He began compiling notes about the inner workings of the United States government, and managed to get his book, *Congressional Government,* published in 1885. His professors were downright surprised. Some doubtless were also a little jealous. Wilson had dived into the gears of a churning government and explained its motions. There were six separate sections, all drawing the reader deeper into the arcane workings of the nation's political system. It was a dryly worded document, but enough critics thought of it as original scholarship to give it a shelf life. Woodrow Wilson was no longer just a doctoral student; he was a doctoral student who had published a book. Damn the traditional route to a thesis! The book gave Wilson a kind of celebrity around campus.

The young student author resided in a boarding house near campus, where he found the nightly dinners lively, with animated conversations. One guest who befriended Wilson was Thomas Dixon, Jr. Both men gravitated toward literature and writing. Both also hailed from and loved the South and had a sharp disdain for Negroes. "The only place in the country, the only place in the world, where nothing has to be explained to me, is The South," Wilson would come to say. Dixon was not shy in telling classmates he was going to write novels someday. He was also proud to tell them that his father had been a vaunted member of the Ku Klux Klan following Reconstruction. Dixon, however, wasn't long for Johns Hopkins; he left before the end of his first year, then bounced around in a variety of jobs—actor, minister, lecturer, finally writer.

The years ahead saw Woodrow Wilson settle into the world of academia. In 1890, he became a Princeton professor. By 1902, Wilson had ascended to the presidency of Princeton. Campus buildings were erected during his tenure; enrollment increased. During the same period, Thomas Dixon began to write a trilogy of novels that would avenge what he deemed the massive white suffering that had taken place during Reconstruction across the South. Two of Dixon's novels, both with baroque titles, became national bestsellers. *The Leopard's Spots: A Romance of the White Man's Burden* was published in 1902. Three years later, in 1905, came *The Clans-*

*man: A Historical Romance of the Ku Klux Klan.* His trilogy was complete with *The Traitor,* published in 1907.

New Jersey Democrats were closely following the rise of Woodrow Wilson. He had taken on snobbery at Princeton and appeared to be reform-minded. Political operatives imagined such traits could be attractive to voters. Wilson himself had always been enamored of those who succeeded in politics, so, when approached by politicians to run for governor of New Jersey, he accepted, launched a campaign, and won in 1910.

As the 1912 presidential election approached, many saw President William Howard Taft as vulnerable. Former President Theodore Roosevelt launched a third-party campaign; his lively supporters and followers became known as the Bull Moose Party. The Republican Party might now end up splitting votes, increasing the chances of victory for the Democratic nominee. Even though he had yet to complete his first term as New Jersey governor, Democrats nominated Woodrow Wilson to take their party into the fall elections. The Republican Party split did indeed prove disastrous: Wilson won forty states and he became the twenty-eighth president of the United States.

President Woodrow Wilson may have calmed the nerves of Negroes during his campaigning, but once he reached office, he enacted the kind of policies that convinced them they had been fooled. One of the early moves Wilson made was the resegregation of a previously integrated—at least in some departments—federal workforce. Congressional Democrats, with President Wilson backing them, began enacting measures to thwart Black achievement wherever they could. *The Chicago Defender,* one of the most widely read Black newspapers in the nation, wrote that Wilson's first year in office had been "politically the most disastrous year since Reconstruction." Wilson's record on civil rights remained shameful, but when World War I broke out, he did not oppose the formation of Black officer-training facilities. And, on occasion, he would speak out against lynching, though more often when the victim had been a non-Black immigrant.

The Civil War era was a period that continued to haunt learned men of the South. Sitting in the White House, relaxing on any given afternoon, Wilson was apt to start recalling how the demands of Reconstruction had hurt his family and other whites. In order for Southern states to be readmitted to the Union after the war, they had to agree to terms that involved voting rights for Blacks, new schools, and the celebrated "40 acres and a mule" decree. It was a shock to the system for many whites to watch Blacks striding into classrooms on previously all-white campuses, and a backlash rose quickly. Klansmen galloped through the countryside, terrorizing Blacks who had won the vote. There were hangings; Blacks were run off their own properties. The Reconstruction period—1865–77—ended after a little more than thirteen years. Federal troops, put in place to protect Blacks, were removed, as was any federal oversight. Local politicians and powerful landowners went about returning the South to its former state of affairs—Blacks as second-class citizens. A white professor who had left the University of South Carolina because of the presence of Black students received a letter from a white trustee who was trying to lure the professor back to campus. "Nothing could be farther from my thoughts than suggesting, in the remotest manner possible, that you should," the trustee wrote, "return here to teach negroes, or to connect yourself with any educational institution in which they are present or are likely to be present in social or other equality with our race."

At times it seemed as if Wilson and Thomas Dixon were racing against each other to see who could get the most words published in defense of their beloved South. Wilson was steadily at work on what would become a ten-volume chronicle, titled *The History of the American People,* with the maiden volume arriving in 1901. The volumes, cloaked in the respectability of academia, were an outright attack against the North and the Reconstruction effort that had taken place on behalf of Black Americans. Dixon's novels were more popular and drew the attention of Southern belles, Confederate veterans, conspiracy theorists, and book readers throughout the South. Dixon was steadily raising his profile by giving lectures that often turned into racist tirades against the North. The years had been kind to both Wilson and Dixon since they went their separate ways after Johns Hopkins, but no matter their good fortune, their animus toward the North remained feverish. Then, with publication of *The Clansman,* Thomas Dixon became an outright literary star.

*The Clansman* is a fulsome celebration of Ku Klux Klan brutality during Reconstruction. It portrays free Blacks running rampant throughout the South, raping white women and attacking their families. Its theme is that Blacks could not be trusted to handle the freedom they'd been given by the Emancipation Proclamation. Northerners tended to be repulsed by the novel's gruesome and stereotypical depictions of Blacks. White Southerners, however, turned the book into a bestseller: it surpassed the hundred thousand mark in sales.

David Wark Griffith was among the Southerners quite moved by Dixon's novel.

D. W. Griffith was born in La Grange, Kentucky. He grew up listening to his father, Jake, retell episodes of his so-called glory in the Civil War. The stories, delivered on the Griffith farm in Kentucky—and embellished with the aid of bourbon—centered on the belief that Reconstruction and Northern allies of freed Blacks had ruined the elder Griffith's homeland. When Jake Griffith died, the family lost its farm and its Black servants. They eventually moved to Louisville. Young D.W. began leaning heavily into books and hanging out with an artistic crowd. He eventually became an actor, and traveled around the country for more than a decade in stage productions—some of these low-rent vaudeville acts, others more professional. He discovered he had a gift for drama. When time permitted, he wrote plays. By spending so much time backstage, he became eager to learn all he could about directing even as he continued hustling for acting roles.

A consortium of inventors, working independently of one another, had been imagining that pictures could actually move if shown on a screen. Two film-equipment designers, Auguste and Louis Lumière, were working in France. Thomas Edison was headquartered in West Orange, New Jersey. One of the Lumière brothers had discovered the photographic plate; Edison had given the world the Kinetoscope, a forerunner of the movie projector. On April 23, 1896, during a vaudeville show at Koster and Bial's Music Hall on Broadway in New York City, the first of twelve short films were shown before an audience. The audience squealed with both delight and wonder: People were dancing on screen! Two comics were moving about while boxing each other! Movie venues—called nickelodeons, since they charged only a nickel—were soon multiplying. The filmgoing craze was taking off. Improvements in cinema inventions kept coming, enthralling the nation's populace.

D. W. Griffith found it difficult to make a name for himself as a New York actor. The years were rolling by, and he fretted about his future. His interest in directing became more intense. He began hanging out at the American Mutoscope and Biograph Company on East Fourteenth Street. (Biograph would join forces with the Edison Company to create the Motion Pictures Patents Company—the beginning of Hollywood.) He sold story ideas to executives at Biograph, the film company. One of his ideas was turned into a 1908 film, *At the Crossroads of Life,* in which Griffith also starred. That same year, Griffith got an opportunity to direct *The Adventures of Dollie,* his first film for the studio. Producers were impressed with his work habits, and Griffith was soon named general director of the Biograph studio. He would go on to direct scores of one-reel films in the coming years. He helped turn actresses like Dorothy Gish, Mary Pickford, and Lillian Gish into stars. He became notable for his vivid camera angles, crosscutting, the utilization of lighting, and close-ups, which had rarely been seen. D. W. Griffith was making a name for himself, and he left Biograph in 1913 to take a position with Reliance-Majestic, another film company, where he became head of production. A short while later, he formed his own company, the David W. Griffith Corporation. An ad trumpeting his new endeavor appeared in *The New York Dramatic Mirror,* proclaiming that Griffith must be given credit for "revolutionizing motion picture drama and founding the modern technique of the art."

With more independence than he had ever had, D. W. Griffith was now quite eager to shoot a large arrow right into the heart of American cinema. To do so, he needed a special project, something that would not only garner a great amount of attention, but also match his epic ambitions for what cinema could do. Griffith asked Frank Woods, a writer friend, if he knew of any project that had a large and challenging storyline. Woods quickly brightened. He had been working on trying to figure out a way to bring *The Clansman* to the screen. The novel had already been adapted for the stage and had made its backers plenty of money. The book touched Griffith on an emotional level as few other books had ever done. "It hit me big," he remembered. "I hoped at once that it could be done, for the story of the South had been absorbed into my very being." The more he pondered the idea of turning the novel into a movie, the more giddy Griffith became: "I could just see these Klansmen in a movie with their white robes flying."

———

Woodrow Wilson, sitting in Washington, was assuring supporters that he was doing as much as possible to keep Negro workers segregated in the federal workforce. This type of news was well received by Wilson's old Hopkins classmate Thomas Dixon, who had complained to Wilson that he and some friends were hearing that segregation—in some cases resegregation—was moving too slowly in the nation's capital. Wilson assured Dixon that effective efforts were being put in place so as not to "mix the two races." Dixon much enjoyed writing to President Wilson and receiving timely replies. The novelist wrote his letters on stationery in which the letterhead read "The Clansman" in a bold, fancy typeface.

Ensconced in a lovely home in New York City and happily married, Dixon felt the year 1914 was unfolding beautifully for him. His bank account from lecture fees and book sales was quite healthy. He had a friendship with the president of the United States. And now there was news that the great D. W. Griffith himself was going to turn *The Clansman* into a movie.

In the spring of 1914, Griffith began letting actors know he was going to undertake a massive project about the American South and the aftermath of the Civil War. "It hasn't been told accurately in history books," he felt. "Only the winning side in the war ever gets to tell its story." In Griffith's enthusiasm for film, he now saw himself being viewed as a visionary. Film existed, he thought, for the daring imagination. And his new movie would force him to dare. "Now," he mused, "I could see a chance to do this ride-to-the-rescue on a grand scale. Instead of saving one poor little Nell of the plains, this ride would be to save a nation."

The sets for *The Clansman* began to rise across various southern-California locations in the spring of 1914, and filming began on July 4. There was even a set built of Ford's Theatre to show the moments around President Lincoln's assassination. When it came to casting, Griffith felt comfortable relying on actors and actresses he had used before, among them Lillian Gish, Miriam Cooper, and Mae Marsh. The novel's setup highlights the stories of two Southern families, the Stonemans and the Camerons, and how each family dealt with the Civil War and Reconstruction. In both the novel and Griffith's telling, the Klansmen are heroes and the Negroes are sex-hungry villains who conspired with Northern carpetbaggers to destroy the South. "The Klan at that time was needed," Griffith once said of the Reconstruction era. "It served a purpose." The filmmaker was intent on making the kind of film that had never been seen before. Griffith filmed important battle scenes. He filmed the burning of Atlanta. He challenged his technical crew more than he had on any other film he had made. When Griffith ran out of money, he badgered investors for more, and they were confident enough to give it to him. The final figures showed he had spent $110,000 on his movie, making it at the time the most expensive movie ever produced.

Griffith had shot more film than he'd ever need, and the editing process proved arduous. He concluded that the film would need intertitles, popular descriptive explainers to be inserted into the film as it played across the screen, and he knew the exact source from which he would cull these words: the works of Woodrow Wilson, his Southern-born heroic president! The idea thrilled Thomas Dixon.

On February 3, 1915, Dixon paid a visit to President Wilson at the White House. "I told him that I had a Motion Picture he should see, not because it was the greatest ever produced or because his classmate had written the story and a Southern director had made the Film, but because this picture made clear for the first time that a new, universal language had been invented." Dixon invited Wilson to a screening at a Washington theatre. But Wilson told him that would be impossible, because the pall of his wife's recent death still lingered over the White House. Wilson then suggested something else: he'd host a showing of the film inside the White House. Dixon was elated, and his mind began racing. But, just as quickly, President Wilson told him that the screening must be kept private. "I assured him," Dixon later recalled, "that we would permit no announcement to be made, and no press reports to be sent out afterwards."

Dixon, who long had engaged in hyperbole about his career, wasted little time before letting D. W. Griffith know about his White House visit and what President Wilson agreed to do. "If we could get the backing of the President we would have a powerful weapon," Griffith replied.

President Wilson's daughter Margaret was put in charge of the evening. She set the date for February 18, 1915. (There had been West Coast showings of the film, and the reviews had been ecstatic, but the positive reviews hadn't saturated the East Coast crowds yet. And the important venues lay up and down the East Coast, the epicenter of the nation's media.) Nothing like this had ever been done before at the White House. Margaret Wilson, excited and wanting to make her father happy, designated the East Room for the film's showing.

Eyes were transfixed on the evening of the screening of *The Birth of a Nation* as the clunky projectors churned into motion. On-screen was a depiction of family drama bracketed by war. The two Southern families were at the center of the narrative as they became enmeshed in war and the battle to "save" the South from intrusion. That intrusion involved interactions with the Negro populace. The Black characters were white actors wearing blackface makeup; no Black actors were cast in major roles. The Blacks were portrayed as thieves, rapists, wild-eyed fools who had joined with Northern liars to wreak havoc upon the South. There were scenes

D. W. Griffith, 1915. He romanticized the Confederacy and harmed Black Americans.

to make any Southerner whoop with patriotic joy: A Confederate soldier plunging a flag into a Union cannon before dying; Reconstruction scenes depicting Southern legislatures becoming undone by the chicanery of Black lawmakers. The scenes cut right to the core of Southern emotion. Movies, as Griffith knew, need heroes. Griffith found his in the white-robed Ku Klux Klan, fiercely galloping across the screen to save the white race from Silas Lynch, the Black man who is portrayed as the personification of Black power run amok.

President Wilson may have had to squint a little, but there on-screen, spliced into the scenes, were words taken from his own books. He didn't stay through the entire White House showing—an unpredictable world crisis was looming, and every minute of his day was important. But the gathering inside the screening room applauded wildly and rose from their seats with looks of awe at the film's end—as if they had never seen anything like this motion picture, which, of course, they had not. The Black butlers concealed their emotions and went about their business in a stony silence. (Thirteen years earlier, in October 1901, Booker T. Washington had been the first Negro to dine at the White House, his invitation coming from President Theodore Roosevelt. When word leaked about the dinner, Southerners roared their disapproval at both Roosevelt and Washington. During his entire White House tenure, President Wilson would not invite a single Black to dinner.)

President Wilson surely had a lot on his mind. Europe had entered a war, and America would have to weigh in at some point. On the domestic front, women were becoming more politically active and demanding the right to vote. When it came to racial matters, Wilson exhibited a cold harshness that continued to unnerve Blacks. He had ordered the firing of many Black federal workers in the South. And now there was the matter of an incendiary movie he had hosted at the White House, a fact that the

White House decided had to be kept out of the press.

Griffith and Dixon were not yet finished with their private showings of *The Birth of a Nation* on the East Coast prior to its countrywide unveiling. Edward Douglass White was chief justice of the United States Supreme Court, as well as a Confederate war veteran. White accepted an invitation to see the film, as did many members of Congress. Dixon convinced the National Press Club to host the affair on February 19 inside the elegant ballroom of the Hotel Raleigh in Washington. The list of those receiving and accepting invitations kept swelling. It ballooned to five hundred guests. With a crowd full of Southern sympathiz-

President Woodrow Wilson, c. 1915–20. He would come to regret showing that movie at the White House.

ers, the three-hour film was rapturously received. Everyone had been asked to keep their attendance at the event secret. Just as at the White House gathering, those watching Griffith's film were awed by the storyline and the technical wizardry. Given that the event was hosted by the gossipy National Press Club, there was little doubt that news of the showing was going to leak, and it did. "There were 500 spectators who cheered and applauded throughout the three hours required to show the gigantic picture," *The Washington Post* told its readers. And with that, word began seeping out that the movie had also had a private screening at the White House. White House operatives remained silent, but their silence did nothing to deter Griffith and his publicity team from plowing ahead. "I was gratified," Griffith said about the White House viewing, "when a man we all revere, or ought to, said it teaches history by lightning." (After seeing the film, President Wilson allegedly said, "It's like writing history with lightning.")

Woodrow Wilson considered himself an astute politician. He had navigated the byzantine world of academia. And though he showed only antipathy toward Blacks and their plight, he would not have been so obtuse as to utter the quote that Griffith attributed to him. Some in the

White House, attuned to the film's fervent anti-Black slant, were upset at Griffith's linking Wilson to the quote. But the White House was also backed into a corner: to deny it, they would have also had to admit that Wilson hosted the movie, which they didn't want to do. It was going to be bad enough that Wilson's words were on-screen, adapted straight from his books. D. W. Griffith and Thomas Dixon, however, were not in the business of finessing White House political dynamics. They had a movie to market and sell.

Upon the national release of *The Birth of a Nation,* Black Americans recoiled from the brutish portrayals they saw on-screen. They began staging massive revolts against it. (New York NAACP officials had gotten word of the film's ugliness from their West Coast members.) It was, to them, nothing less than an anti-Black cinematic epic that had been made to undermine their dignity and freedoms. In New York, NAACP officials, among them W. E. B. Du Bois, went to City Hall to meet with the mayor and demand that city theatres not show the movie. Their efforts failed. When the movie opened in New York City, the crowds were huge.

The rollout process lasted ten months, creating a *Birth of a Nation* craze. Some communities got out in front and staged protests. Denver wouldn't show it, nor would Cleveland, Chicago, or Providence. The NAACP was successful in keeping the movie from showing in the state of Kansas. But many opponents of the film were realizing that, the more they objected to it, the more publicity it got, and that would only heighten interest in it.

Beginning midyear in 1915, *The Birth of a Nation* was causing the nation's first truly cinematic controversy. When Harriet Blaine Beale of Maine saw the movie, she was incensed. Beale was known in Washington social circles, a rich woman who was the daughter of the late James G. Blaine, a prominent Maine politician who had served in a variety of posts, including as onetime governor. In Beale's mind, the film was "calculated to arouse the worst form of race hatred and to send every ignorant white man away with a feeling that every negro should be lynched." Joel Spingarn of the NAACP said that in his memory nothing had done so much to "unloosen the energy and to stimulate the support of the colored people of this country as this attack on their character and their place in history." Griffith's personal Black maid had her own opinion about the film. "It hurt me, Mr. David," she told him, "to see what you do to my people."

The spreading contretemps put pressure on the White House. President Wilson realized he had to distance himself from the movie, and eventually did so.

Because of their history of abolitionist fervor and civil-rights protests, many looked to Bostonians to draw battle lines ahead of the movie's planned opening there in the spring of 1915.

It was a law—although rarely acted upon—in Boston that the city's mayor held decision-making powers over any controversial movie to play there. James Michael Curley, mayor of Boston, was a known liberal, and thought by many to be a friend of the Negro.

The controversy quickly landed upon Curley's desk, and he decided it best to hold open hearings to debate the film's fate. The matter brought D. W. Griffith himself to Boston. William Monroe Trotter, a well-known Black newspaper publisher who had previously pronounced himself and his publication to be foes of *The Birth of a Nation,* was already in town. Witnesses who had seen the movie elsewhere and opposed its being shown in Boston spoke with passion about their fears of the kinds of trouble the movie's showing might unleash.

Mayor Curley's convened meeting drew the known and the unknown. Mary White Ovington—one of the founders of the NAACP in 1909—told the gathering what she had heard some whites say after seeing the movie: "I would like to kill every nigger. I would like to sweep every nigger off the earth." It became apparent during the hearing, however, that Mayor Curley was equally worried about censorship and the concept of free speech, allowing that if Negroes were so aggrieved by the movie, then many ethnic people in the plays of Shakespeare could have grievances as well. His logic seemed to predict that this was a lost cause for the critics of the film. Following the three-hour hearing, Curley told Griffith to hold a showing of the film, and he would send city officials to view it. They would then determine if it crossed a "morality" line, and if it did, he would take action.

The announced screening was ostensibly supposed to be a private affair. But Griffith, who arrived early, obviously had sent out word-of-mouth invitations, because more than fifteen hundred people walked in to join him. All were quite eager to see what all the hoopla was about. By the film's end, the audience appeared wowed; so did the film critics whom Griffith had also been mindful to invite. Salita Solano, art critic for the *Boston Traveler,* wrote that the movie had been "most enthusiastically received" at the screening, and she was impressed with the technical craftsmanship of the movie. But she also wrote, "The more the pity that its lesson is so insidious." The *Boston American* critic expanded on the exuberant reception the movie received: "I cannot describe this picture in a half column, or a column; a page would not do it justice," Frederick Johns wrote. "It is impossible to keep from bursting into admiration at the marvelous way the author has woven the great incidents of the war into his film. He is an amazing impressionist; his scenes flash the story at you with never a rest." Johns offered that Griffith had dealt with Reconstruction "boldly" and in a necessary manner. "I am quite sure nobody last night left the theatre feeling inflamed against the respectable and industrious colored population of Boston." It might have been difficult to spot Mayor Curley himself in the crowd, but he was there, along with his censor-watching team.

The question lingered in the New England air: Would Mayor Curley allow *The Birth of a Nation* to open in his city? Not leaving anything to chance, Griffith and his allies quickly took out ads heralding the film, even mentioning—when they had clearly been told not to—that the movie had shown at the White House, a revelation that continued giving the film a unique cachet. Mayor Curley came down on the side of the film director Griffith and his partisans. So the much-contested film would play in Boston after all, in a city that had sent the famed all-Negro Fifty-fourth Massachusetts Regiment to fight in the Civil War, and that had played an illustrious role in the abolitionist movement. Curley's decision caused howling throughout the city's Black community. Many Blacks accused the mayor—who had such cordial relations with their community—of betraying them. Curley tried to soften the blow by revealing that Griffith promised he would cut a couple of scenes that had brought bitter complaints. One involved a white woman committing suicide before being abducted by a Black man.

When *The Birth of a Nation* opened at the Tremont Theatre in Boston on April 10, the lines stretched around the block. Day after day, moviegoers came to sit in the darkness for the three-hour film. More police officers had to be put on duty to keep the crowds moving.

One evening during the run, the police rushed to place plainclothes officers inside the theatre after a tip that there might be trouble from those who opposed the film. It happened to be on the very evening when William Monroe Trotter, the *Guardian* editor, was planning to attend. When Trotter reached the theatre, there was a large contingent of Blacks milling about in the lobby. One of the complaints by Blacks who wanted to see the film had been that some of them would reach the ticket window and be refused a ticket. Ticket vendors came up with arbitrary decisions on who would get in. Trotter had heard such stories before, and now intended to complain about the obvious discrimination. But shortly after he entered the lobby that evening, someone in the crowd shouted that a local Black minister had just been denied a ticket. And with that, the police, made nervous by the crowd and rising voices, demanded everyone leave. "We won't leave," Trotter cried out. "We demand our rights to buy tickets." His loud voice of protest was suddenly enough for the police to identify him as the ringleader, and they rushed to arrest him. But a contingent of Blacks surrounded him. A tough plainclothes policeman by the name of Dennis Harrington—dressed in undercover clothing—shoved his way up to Trotter and coldcocked him in the face. The punch stunned the onlookers. Other police officers quickly grabbed Trotter, who was demanding that the officers arrest the man who had hit him. With an edge in their voices, the officers told Trotter that the man who had hit him was one of them—a police officer! Outside, Trotter cleared his eyes and saw hundreds of Black people protesting against the film and, now, the ongoing police arrests. At the jail, Trotter's lawyer quickly posted bail. Then Trotter boldly raced back to the Tremont Theatre, where more Blacks had joined the demonstration. Inside the packed theatre, the movie, despite the mêlée on the street, was already playing. At one point, a Black man rose and threw an egg at the screen. Police rushed in and arrested him. A group of Black women started challenging the police, shouting that they were engaging in harassment. They, too, were arrested.

Later that same night, there was a racial clash not far from the theatre when some Blacks attacked a group of whites. The culprits were quickly arrested and charged with assault and battery. Other incidents broke out as well. "As a racial demonstration probably nothing like it has been seen in Boston since the Civil War," *The Boston Globe* reported. National wire services were now also feverishly covering Boston's *Birth of a Nation* story.

One of the reasons Trotter had gone to the theatre that night was that the two scenes—the white woman choosing suicide while fleeing a Black man and a biracial man wanting to force a white woman into marriage—which Griffith had promised Mayor Curley he would cut, remained in the film. It was painfully obvious they were not going to be cut. Griffith had changed his mind because he believed the large audiences justified keeping the scenes as he had filmed them. He blithely instructed theatre owners to beef up their security. The swelling publicity actually excited the director.

Anger kept rising among the Black citizenry. The titans of Black political action in America—W. E. B. Du Bois, Booker T. Washington, the NAACP—were all scrambling to stifle the movie's impact. Thomas Dixon figured that their collective efforts were foolish. He even saw the movie in political terms. "Within one year 20,000,000 people will see it," he crowed, and "before the next presidential election one-half of voters in the U.S. will have seen it." But Black protesters were not giving up. On April 20, not long after the movie had opened in Boston, a massive throng of more than five thousand people gathered at the statehouse to appeal to Governor David Walsh to stop the film. Walsh seemed attuned to their grievances and allowed that he would convene a meeting with Trotter's group. The day of the meeting was filled with tension from various quarters. As soon as the meeting got under way, it became clear what was at stake. Blacks were angry, and Walsh wanted to play peacemaker. "I sympathize with you tremendously," Walsh told the gathering. "I don't propose, while I am governor, to allow any movement arousing antagonism to any race of people in Massachusetts." At the meeting's end, the governor told the gathering that his administration would take their complaint to court, thus giving the antifilm crowd renewed hope.

There was a 1910 criminal statute in Massachusetts that zeroed in on immorality and obscenity as reasons not to allow any film to be presented to the public. The city of Boston was now formally charging that Griffith's film had instances of both. It would be up to Judge Thomas H. Dowd to issue a ruling. Dowd quickly convened his own hearing. On the appointed day, Judge Dowd listened raptly to arguments from both sides—Griffith's team, and the city of Boston, now speaking for Blacks and the growing number of whites who had joined their cause. A couple of hours into the hearings, Dowd abruptly ended the session, announcing he'd better get down to the Tremont Theatre to see the movie himself. That evening, he took his seat among another sold-out crowd.

Dowd returned to the courtroom in the morning and quickly told the gathering he saw reason only to insist that one "nauseating" scene be excised—the scene where the Black character Gus chases the white girl to her doom. The pained groans of the Trotter allies were audible. This was hardly what they had expected. Dowd actually had more to say. He thought the movie "a splendid thing, one of the best I have ever seen." There were those who now imagined that the forces aligned against the movie would have to retreat. Instead, they came up with another strategic move. They presented a new bill—the Sullivan Bill, named after Lewis Sullivan, a local politician—that would strengthen the 1910 obscenity statute and give it more teeth to actually censor a film. The bill began to wend its way through the legislature. The Griffith forces, however, did not sit idly by. They alerted film-studio heads and union lobbyists as to what the bill might mean if passed: the possibility of fewer movies, and thus fewer theatre jobs. Boston's newspapers were also nervous about the Sullivan Bill. *The Boston Journal* asked: "What should we think of a Southern city or State that forbade a film of *Uncle Tom's Cabin* to be presented? The suppression of *The Birth of a Nation* would be just such a narrow act of bigotry on our part." Other local newspapers expressed similar sentiments. The Griffith forces kept up the heat. They decided to invite members of the Massachusetts Legislature to a showing of the film—"not to accept our arguments or the argument of our opponents but to behold the proof firsthand." A local attorney aligned with the antifilm crusade wondered if Griffith's invitation to the legislators was an attempt at a kind of bribe. Griffith made sure, once again, that members of the press were told about the political screening. A reporter for the *Boston Evening American* who attended wrote, "There was general and vigorous applause when the Ku Klux Klan galloped to the rescue."

In May 1915, the politicos of Massachusetts—still quite aware that the nation was watching their every move regarding *The Birth of a Nation*—came up with a new censor law stating that any entertainment entity operating in the city be required to get a license, which could be revoked, ostensibly if the entertainment production caused racial strife or mayhem. This was seen as a good sign by William Monroe Trotter and his allies. However, the censor-law committee had to convene and actually vote on the contested movie in a formal manner. The committee met behind closed doors. The members all realized the gravity of the situation. Mayor Curley finally emerged to announce the committee's decision to Trotter and a group of anxious NAACP officials. He told them that the committee had "decided the license of the theatre should not be revoked or suspended." After eighteen mass rallies took place in the city to protest the movie, it had come down to this: *The Birth of a Nation* would continue playing in Boston. The Black citizenry listening to the announcement were now out of options.

"BIRTH OF A NATION WINS" came the blazing *Boston Post* headline.

Thomas Dixon was deliriously happy with how the long battle had ended. "Months of frantic agitation, scheming and shouting and feeble rioting had gone for nothing except to advertise the picture," he bragged. Griffith's so-called masterpiece would go on to play for more than six consecutive months in Boston. And audiences around the country flocked to see it multiple times. In November 1915, to herald the movie's openings around Georgia, the Ku Klux Klan celebrated with a ceremony at Stone Mountain, Georgia. A kerosene-soaked cross was set afire against the dark sky. William Simmons, a Klansman and a preacher who was in attendance that night, recalled: "Under a blazing, fiery torch, the Invisible Empire was called from its slumber of half a century to take up a new task and fulfill a new mission for humanity's good."

The controversy attached to the film showed no signs of abating around the country. In May 1915, a group of Black ministers in Chicago heaped scorn upon the movie. In February 1916, Iowa clergymen banded together and passed a resolution denouncing the movie. There were demonstrations in St. Louis.

Between 1915 and 1916, when *The Birth of a Nation* was filling American movie theatres, the nation's population was a little over a hundred million. Thomas Dixon had estimated that twenty million people would see the movie; his estimate turned out to be low. More than twenty-five million eventually saw the film during its initial run. A quarter of the population had it drilled into them from a movie screen that Blacks were criminal-minded, stupid, lazy, obsessed with white women, and malevolent. In some parts of the South, high-school teachers began using *The Birth of a Nation* as a text, indoctrinating students with D. W. Griffith's telling of history.

In the summer of 1919, four years after *The Birth of a Nation* had its official opening, a wave of race riots swept the nation. The episodes were beyond horrendous. Many stemmed from confrontations between whites and Black veterans of World War I. Other clashes erupted around crimes, or reported crimes. In June 1919, John Hartfield, a Black man, was accused of raping a white woman. He fled through woods outside Ellisville, Mississippi. Searchers on horseback with dogs scoured the woods, looking for him. After ten days, he was spotted, desperately trying to hop a train. He was shot, but survived. On June 26, a lynch party of upward of ten thousand gathered in the woods outside Ellisville, drawn there from advertisements placed in Mississippi newspapers. Hartfield was snatched from the hands of the doctor tending his injuries at the local jail. While he was still conscious, Hartfield's fingers were sliced off. Then he was lynched. Hilton Butler, a journalist who witnessed the hanging, would remember: "I had to drop from a tree behind him to escape bullets fired at his swinging body. Every time a bullet hit an arm, out it flopped like a semaphore. The legs didn't flop so easily. My newspaper account of it said that not less than 2,000 bullets were fired into his body."

———

On so many fronts, Black Americans were being beaten down politically and legally. And cinema had now achieved a new place in society with a nation-shaking film that Blacks found abhorrent. Their leaders and advocates could do nothing to halt the movie's ongoing popularity and social influence. *The Birth of a Nation* was big business in America. During its first run, the movie grossed between fifty and sixty million dollars. Men got rich; careers were indelibly made. *The Birth of a Nation* even helped change the dynamics of how America went to the movies! Theatre owners began keeping theatres open with longer hours. They started realizing, more than ever, the profitability of snacks at their concession stands and added even more goodies. But all of this had been done at a terrible price to Black America. It seemed as if Blacks had yet one more enemy: cinema.

If Black Americans were to fight back against what cinema had now done to them, they would need their own filmmaker. They needed someone to tell their stories, stories with nuance and honesty and respect and comedy and joy—all the things that this magical thing called cinema was offering to mainstream society. And if such a person were to emerge, he would have to possess fortitude, and a wide vision that would remain steadfast against the forces sure to rise and be arrayed against him.

# The Rare and Extraordinary Sighting
# of a Black Filmmaker

O NE OF THE MANY EVENTS that happened during the Civil War—and one that wasn't remotely alluded to in D. W. Griffith's fictional war-era movie—was the passage of the Homestead Act of 1862, which gave land in the West to those who desired to venture there and become homeowners. The Western part of the nation was known to be wild and certainly needed settlers. The legislation declared that applicants would have to farm the acres loaned to them for at least five years before the land would be given to them. There would be a small deed fee and taxes attached to the bequeathing of land. Though various politicians had tried to pass the bill for years, senators who hailed from slave states had constantly stymied its passage, fearful of a labor drain if it became law. But President Lincoln was determined to open the West. His young presidency had already been altered by war, but Lincoln still had to preside over a nation and think of its future. On May 20, 1862—having corralled enough politicians to support it—President Lincoln signed the Homestead Act into law. It took effect January 1, 1863, which was also the very day Lincoln signed the Emancipation Proclamation, freeing slaves. The new year was indeed having a grand and merciful beginning.

On paper, however, the challenge of becoming a settler in the West sounded far more glorious that it would be in practice. It took a sturdy and bold family to venture into Western lands, much of it still populated by Native Americans who were aggrieved at their own assaults by the American military government.

The Homestead Act did not discriminate by race: Blacks were welcome to participate. Of course, those held in bondage and just freed had no way of taking advantage of the land deal, because it required money and wagons and horses to travel. But the majority of Blacks who headed west to take advantage of the act had already been free and residing in Northern states. In time, though, former slaves who possessed the grit—and had accumulated resources—began their own journeys west.

Some did turn back during the trek, the weather and terrain simply too much for them. Others reached their destinations, enduring the hot summers, cold winters, and dangerous animals only to abandon their dream before reaching the five-year residency requirement. Most who went west during those early years of the Homestead Act were white families. Some of the landscape—like Nebraska—had not yet been designated as states. It was quite a rare sight to spot any Black man—rifle in hand and hatchet cinched into a belt loop for protection—waltzing around a cabin he had built for his family in Montana, Kansas, or the Dakotas.

Not long after the Civil War, Andrew Jackson Michaux, whose roots were in Illinois, journeyed west and arrived in Barton County, Kansas. Michaux became both a successful farmer and a savvy businessman. He acquired quite a reputation over the years and came to be known as "the richest Negro in Kansas and banker to the black community." Michaux wrote to members of his large family back in Illinois, telling them of his good fortune. A brother, Calvin, resided in Metropolis, Illinois. Calvin, a former slave—unable to read or write—was determined to lift himself into a better life. He married Belle Gough in 1875 and soon became a mighty proud Illinois landowner.

Calvin and Belle's son Oscar was born January 2, 1884. Little Oscar—he later added an "e" to his surname—was determined to take advantage of his own educational opportunities. He studied hard and without complaint. His mother particularly encouraged his reading habits. Teachers sometimes thought him too rambunctious. "About the only thing for which I was given credit was in learning readily, but was continually critiqued for talking too much and being too inquisitive," Oscar Micheaux would come to recall. His mind whirring at a heady clip, the young Micheaux convinced himself early in life that Metropolis was not going to be his final destination. Because of his imaginative mind, some classmates thought him odd, a strange dreamer, not eager to blend in with the society around him. Young Oscar decided he had had enough of school and quit before his high-school class graduated. Books had revealed a world beyond southern Illinois. In most directions he looked, Oscar Micheaux saw train tracks. The nation was growing, and the railways could take a young man a lot of places. Soon enough, Oscar Micheaux became a full-fledged Pullman porter for the Southern Illinois Railways. Many former slaves became Pullman porters. They lived mostly off tips as traveling waiters and saw the world inside the United States of America. For a young, snappy Black man, it was good work. Micheaux became fond of Boston, often there on a Pullman layover. "The mornings I spent wandering around the city, visiting Faneuil Hall, the old State House, Boston commons, Bunker Hill, and a thousand other reminders of the early heroism, rugged courage, and far seeing greatness of Boston's early citizens. Afternoons generally found me on Tremont or Washington Street attending a matinee or hearing music." With money saved up, Micheaux figured it was a good time to take a risk and find a place to stay put for a while.

In the summer of 1904, twenty-year-old Oscar Micheaux began studying a series of maps and surveys that explained and outlined farming conditions throughout the Western states. He was eager to join the exodus that had been staged by so many homesteaders before him, including members of his own extended family. The surveys and maps yielded plenty of information: one had to be wise in making a determination about where to go. Even in the best of circumstances, journeys could be fraught gambles. Micheaux was struck by a wide swath of available land in Gregory County, South Dakota, on the Rosebud Indian Reservation. He had hoped he'd get his land from a homesteading lottery, but failed to be chosen. Some homesteaders, however, had to relinquish their land after failing to meet government guidelines. Their land was placed in a status known as "relinquishment," meaning it was then available for purchase by another settler. Oscar Micheaux obtained 160 acres of South Dakota farmland through the relinquishment program. "Two hundred miles north, corn will not mature," Micheaux wrote about Gregory County. "Two hundred miles south, spring wheat is not grown; two hundred west, the altitude is too high to insure sufficient rainfall to produce a crop; but the reservation lands are in such a position that winter wheat, spring wheat, oats, rye, corn, flax, and barley do well."

The following spring, Micheaux set off on his journey. He stopped in Kansas to visit relatives from Illinois who had relocated there, and shared with them good food, laughter, stories about other homesteaders. Always an excitable and curious sort, Micheaux had a unique ability to inspire others to believe in him. He did not leave doubt in his wake. From Kansas, it was on to South Dakota. News of his arrival preceded him. "It had been reported that a colored man had a claim adjoining the town on the north,

Oscar Micheaux, center, date unknown (circa 1940–51). They had never seen a Black director on the plains of the American West.

so when I stepped from the stage before the postoffice, the many knowing glances," he would recall, "informed me that I was being looked for."

The presence of Blacks in South Dakota was quite rare. General George Armstrong Custer took Sarah Campbell, a fearless Black woman, with him into the Black Hills in 1874 as his cook. Campbell later settled on a ranch near the small town of Galena. Fort Randall had played host in 1882 to a regiment of Black soldiers formed by Congress following the Civil War. The soldiers escorted homesteaders through the territory and also fought during the Indian Wars. Those wars erupted from Manifest Destiny, when the American government took land from the Indians, sparking bloody conflicts. The Black military regiments would come to be known as Buffalo Soldiers, most of whom were former slaves. (The Indians so named them because of their curly hair.) Nearly two dozen of the Buffalo Soldiers received the Medal of Honor during the Indian Wars.

Oscar Micheaux did not worry unduly about landing upon the barren landscape of South Dakota. He made his way to his land, his very own purchased land, and it filled him with pride. He had to get wood and building supplies, sod and sand and tar paper, to construct his little home.

The work was arduous. "The fifth day I moved in," he would recall, "there was no floor, but the thick, short buffalo grass made a neat carpet. In one corner I put the bed, while in another I set the table, the one next [to] the door I placed the stove, a little two-hole burner gasoline, and in the other corner I made a bin for the horses grain."

The neophyte farmer was where he wanted to be now, beneath a roof he had constructed himself, standing upon the Rosebud Indian Reservation, a land full of blood and history, and sorrow from all those Indian battles. Whites from the town came out to get a glimpse of this strange man—a Negro, a Black man—working the land. Don Coonen, one of Micheaux's neighbors, got to know the Illinois transplant. "You can't find a better metaphor than a Pullman porter pushing a plow," Coonen would come to say of Micheaux. "He must have gone through the agonies of hell." If it was hellish, Micheaux never let on to those who saw him at work. He bent his back and kept plowing the land. Weeks and months began to roll by. As summertime rolled into view in 1905, Micheaux was beginning to feel fairly comfortable. Crops were coming up out of the ground, and his confidence was also growing. He owned horses, and land, and optimism. It was different from the rest of America, where racial tensions brewed seemingly everywhere. "At first I was regarded as an object of curiosity," he recalled, "which changed to appreciation, and later admiration." That admiration, however, didn't stop white prairie children from asking their parents if they could go out to the Micheaux homestead and look at him. More often than not, it was out of curiosity rather than mean-spiritedness. Though some Buffalo Soldiers had married Indians, the sighting of any Negro in the vast landscape was still quite rare.

When he had time to get away from his farming demands, Micheaux, a bachelor, moved coal around for some local businessmen, earning extra money, which enabled him to purchase even more land and get better farming equipment. Within two years of moving to South Dakota, Oscar Micheaux owned more than three hundred acres of land. During his downtime, he ventured back east, into New York City and Chicago, where his interest in theatre began to blossom. In Chicago, he visited the Pekin Theatre, the first Black-owned theatre in America that catered to vaudeville and musical comedies. The Pekin had been founded by Robert T. Motts, a Black businessman who made money with his lucrative saloon business. The Pekin had also formed the first all-Black acting company in the country, the Pekin Stock Company. Micheaux's eyes lit up brightly when he came into close contact with actors and their communities, in both Chicago and New York. He filled his bags with copies of plays by notable playwrights. He became a fan of Shakespeare.

Returning to his farm delighted Micheaux. He had been a lifelong reader of magazines and books, and it began to dawn on him that he was leading quite an adventurous life himself. He began keeping notes, jottings of his surroundings and the seasons that were passing by. The young pioneer also became smitten with a white woman of Scottish heritage who lived near him. They'd sit and read stage plays together. The romantic spark between the two began to frighten Micheaux. In 1908, South Dakota was debating a miscegenation law, stipulating that interracial marriage was a crime, punishable by either a hefty fine of a thousand dollars or ten years behind bars. As a result, Micheaux decided he did not wish to become a pioneer when it came to interracial marriage. The budding romance came to an end. In 1909, the South Dakota miscegenation law passed and went into effect.

The Black pioneer grew lonely. He had earlier met a young woman in Chicago, Orlean McCracken, who came from a well-respected family, daughter of a reputable minister. Micheaux ventured back to Chicago and began wooing her. They went on dates, evening excursions to see vaudeville shows, in many of which the actors were performing in blackface. The presence of blackface was a painful reminder to Blacks of the mockery theatrical productions shamelessly heaped upon them. Together, the couple saw Al Jolson, publicized as the greatest blackface performer on any stage. McCracken and Micheaux felt good enough in each other's company to discuss marriage. The idea intrigued her; Micheaux promised an engagement ring.

This romantic activity coincided with something else in Oscar Micheaux's life: he began to express himself through words, sitting down and writing letters and essays to the editorial departments of newspapers in hopes they would be published.

Micheaux's unique position in life—one of fewer than a dozen Black homesteaders in all of South Dakota—had filled him with the confidence that someone might take his offered opinions seriously. *The Chicago Defender*, in existence since 1905, was fast becoming one of the most respected publications in the nation aimed toward Negro society. The *Defender* garnered a lot of respect for giving space to Ida B. Wells for her crusading anti-lynching reporting. It also received attention—even if it did use wire-service reports—for covering the Jack Johnson–Jim Jeffries heavyweight bout on July 4, 1910, in Reno, Nevada. Jeffries, a former heavyweight champion, had been so incensed that Johnson had become the first Black heavyweight champion of the world that he came out of retirement to fight Johnson. He proclaimed he was doing it for the white race. Jeffries was embarrassingly outmatched. Johnson had him badly bloodied and bruised going into the twelfth round. Jeffries dropped in the fifteenth round, unable to rise back up. It was a proud moment for Black America, but disaster soon followed: there were vengeful attacks against Blacks throughout the country by white mobs enraged at Johnson's victory.

Oscar Micheaux had something on his mind about America and the tribulations of its Black citizenry, and he wanted to share his thoughts and suggestions. He thought the perfect organ would be *The Chicago Defender.* On March 19, 1910, Micheaux appeared on the front page of the *Defender* in what would become his first published piece. His article was titled "Where the Negro Fails." Micheaux implored black readers to venture west, just as he had done, and take advantage of land opportunities. "Isn't it enough to make one feel disgusted to see and read of thousands of poor white people going west every day and in ten or fifteen years' time becoming prosperous and happy, as well as making the greatest and happiest place on earth." He went on: "In writing this I am not overlooking what the Negro is doing in the south, nor the enterprising ones of the north, but the time is at hand—the Negro must become more self-supporting. Farm lands are the bosses of wealth." Micheaux's ardent advice may have been a bit too exotic for the average Black to swallow: there surely was no exodus into South Dakota by Blacks.

But Micheaux recognized what books and newspapers could do: they could shape minds and opinions. He knew that Americans loved to read, so he wrote at his homestead by candlelight. Some of that writing was in the form of letters sent back to Chicago and the home of Orlean McCracken. Micheaux wanted a wife and became convinced McCracken was the one. He went back to Chicago determined to ask for her hand. McCracken was both surprised and flattered at the sight of him. His wooing worked: the proposal and small marriage ceremony took place over a matter of days in Chicago. Rev. McCracken was still a bit suspicious of this Negro who wanted to whisk his daughter away from her family and out to the great barren plains of South Dakota.

Once the joyful aura of being newly married began to wear off in South Dakota, Orlean Micheaux had to face the reality of prairie life. Like many, she found it hard and demanding. The change in scenery—from urban Chicago to rural South Dakota—had been quite dramatic, and was soon unsettling to her. When she became pregnant, however, this brought immediate joy to the household. But the baby was stillborn, and that shattered the couple. Orlean's father blamed the harsh South Dakota landscape—and, by extension, Oscar—for his daughter's loss. He insisted she return to Chicago to recuperate, which she did.

When she had been what he thought was a long enough time away, Micheaux began writing to his wife, imploring her to return home. Her letters back to him were sporadic and often cryptic. He began wondering if she had abandoned him. "My head ached and my heart was wrung with agony," he would remember of the separation. But he was hardly ready to give up on his marriage. It was the early part of 1912 when he landed back in Chicago, but they did not have a happy reunion. There was screaming, accusations; the reality had set in of a husband and wife no longer in synch with each other. As well, Micheaux's father-in-law berated him unmercifully. When Micheaux departed Chicago, his marriage was over. The couple never saw each other again.

Back in South Dakota, Oscar Micheaux and other homesteaders were hit hard by a drought in 1912. Crops were lost. This only worsened his mood. Books kept him alert and hopeful. He became quite fond of a newly published and much-talked-about novel, *The Autobiography of an Ex-Colored Man*. Published anonymously, the novel was about the life of a man who had a Black mother and a white father. The story told of his boyhood, his pampered life in Connecticut, and his travels around the world. The narrator tells of a life lived in both worlds, white and "colored," and the unforgettable blows of racism he witnesses while "passing" as a white man. It all ends on a note of tragedy, as the narrator muses that he has sacrificed his life by pretending to be someone else and betraying Black people. The author had based the novel on people he knew in life and some of his own experiences. The reasons for the anonymity were political: In 1912 when *The Autobiography of an Ex-Colored Man* was published, James Weldon Johnson was a diplomat, having been appointed by President Theodore Roosevelt to a consulate posting in Venezuela. He thought the overall racial plotting of his novel might offend readers in certain political circles, inasmuch as he was a political appointee.

Born in 1871 in Florida, James Weldon Johnson had well-read parents, who were intent on their two sons' receiving good educations. Since the Black schools in Jacksonville stopped in the eighth grade, Johnson's parents enrolled him in Atlanta University, where he completed both high-school courses and college studies. When he graduated, in 1894, he became a grammar-school principal. In 1898, he took and passed the bar exam, becoming the first Black to be a member of the Florida bar. He had also become an accomplished musician. In 1900, Johnson and his brother, Rosamond, wrote a song, "Lift Ev'ry Voice and Sing," that became so popular in Black churches and meeting halls that it became known as the Negro National Anthem. Just before the outbreak of World War I, James Weldon Johnson became field secretary of the NAACP.

In Micheaux's forlorn and painful winter, when his farm was suffering and his marriage finished, James Weldon Johnson had given him—an ex-city slicker-now homesteader—inspiration to begin writing the story of his own life. Micheaux began thinking as much about writing as farming. All through the early months of 1913, he composed a memoir, though in the guise of a novel. When he felt ready, he took some of his chapters into the local town of Gregory, offering them up for sale to citizens in the hopes of hiking interest in the book to come. It was a small community, and most who did purchase chapters from Micheaux knew him by sight. He was the strange Negro, the oddball, the Black man out there on the dusty plains, moving his farm equipment around aided by the strength of his mules. He came up with a title for his finished book: *The Conquest: The Story of a Negro Pioneer.*

When he finished his autobiographical novel, Micheaux began trooping around to nearby small towns, smiling into the faces of his weather-beaten South Dakotans and talking up his book. He was encouraged by the sales. He made sure the local newspaper, the *Gregory Times-Advocate,* knew what he was up to. "The book has had a wonderful sale and is pronounced by those who have read it as being an excellent story," the newspaper wrote.

Micheaux actually told the factual story of his life from its beginning to the collapse of his marriage in *The Conquest,* all of which would be verified by future biographers, who confirmed his actions, events, and movements at the times outlined in his book. (There would be two more Micheaux memoirlike books, *The Homesteader* and *The Wind from Nowhere.*) The novice writer did not wish his book to be seen as just a vanity production; he wanted sales and reviews. So he crossed into Iowa and Nebraska, dropping off copies of the book in newspaper offices, running ads in newspapers; the boon in eventual book sales gave him confidence in writing as a career. He began moving about the country, living for a spell in Iowa, for a while in Atlanta, identifying himself as a writer and a salesman. He carved time into his days, wherever he happened to be, to write.

Oscar Micheaux did something else to fill his days on the road: he went to see movies. The theatres he went to in the South were segregated—"operated and owned by white men." The manner in which movies drew crowds fascinated and intrigued him. He wondered about advertising, about theatre owners—about the filmmakers themselves. Most movies, he realized, had sprung from a story that someone, somewhere, had written. And that someone, Micheaux knew, was white. The feverish excitement around *The Birth of a Nation*—which played in Gregory, South Dakota, in 1915—unnerved Micheaux just as it did so many other Blacks. "We are always caricatured in almost all the photoplays [that] we have even the smallest and most insignificant part in," is how he put it. And then, as fate would have it, one of Micheaux's books was spotted by George Johnson, a Nebraska postal clerk who did more than sort mail: he had a little side gig showing all-Black movies in and around Omaha, in its segregated theatres. Even more fortuitous was that Johnson's brother was Noble Johnson, a Hollywood actor.

Noble Johnson was born in Missouri in 1881. One of his childhood friends had been Lon Chaney, who would have a celebrated acting and directing career in 1920s Hollywood. Johnson left school at the age of fifteen to travel with his father, a trainer on the horse-racing circuit. Eventually, he was lured to Hollywood, where Lon Chaney introduced him around. Soon enough, Johnson began acting and made his film debut in 1909. From silent films, he went on to talkies. A Black man, he was light-skinned enough to play a variety of ethnicities on screen; he sometimes was cast as an Indian in cowboy pictures. It was obvious to Johnson, however, that, because of segregation and the social mores of the time, he would only be offered certain roles. Along with investors, his brother, George, among them, Noble Johnson formed the Lincoln Motion Picture Company. They opened their doors in Los Angeles in 1916 and began scouting for properties to shepherd to the screen. In 1918, Oscar Micheaux received a letter from George Johnson, saying that he thought his novel *The Homesteader* (Micheaux's follow-up to *The Conquest*) might be a book that the Lincoln Motion Picture Company could adapt as a vehicle for Noble Johnson.

It was in the early summer of 1918 that Micheaux and George Johnson had their first face-to-face meeting. Micheaux bragged to Johnson that his experiences as a homesteader were unique and ripe for cinematic treatment. The meeting went well enough, and there was ongoing correspondence. In that correspondence, concerns developed on the part of both men. Johnson wanted to inform Micheaux of the byzantine world of Black movies—the segregated theatres, the inside hustling, the scheduling, the deep South, the censors. Johnson also wanted Micheaux to know he would lose some of his authorial independence by signing on with the Lincoln Motion Picture Company, because that was the manner in which all studios operated: writers turned over their work, and the studios tended to ignore them afterward. In Micheaux's mind, he was the one who had braved the South Dakota winters, who had dared embark on the risky life of becoming a homesteader. To have his work—his stories, his life—taken and left to the creative devices of others was becoming impossible to fathom.

Oscar Micheaux had proved his resilience and mettle over eight years as a homesteader. He had been one kind of pioneer, and now he started to convince himself he could become another kind: a filmmaker. He decided to produce a film of *The Homesteader* himself! When they learned of Micheaux's plan, George and Noble Johnson thought him far out of his depth, engaged in little more than a pipe dream. Their assessment, however, didn't stop Micheaux from asking Noble Johnson if he would like to play the lead role in his movie. Noble said no.

Micheaux proceeded to set up the Micheaux Book and Film Company in Sioux City, Iowa. He let it be known that this was but a temporary location. "I expect to establish the main office in the business district of Chicago, get a Dodge Roadster, and make my home" in Chicago, he said. He set about finding investors, hitting up friends, acquaintances, family members. The plan was to sell stock in the company and raise even more money. He printed up brochures announcing his grand plan. The would-be filmmaker vowed he would be booking *The Homesteader* at "the largest theatres in the largest cities under the personal direction of Mr. Micheaux, whose long experience in publicity work and the sale of his books to individuals, bookstores, libraries, etc., has peculiarly fitted him for the work in hand." But one paragraph in Micheaux's brochure stood out particularly for its mix of ambition and bravado:

Aside from the general public, who themselves, having never seen a picture in which the Negro race and a Negro hero is so portrayed, and can therefore be expected to appreciate the photoplay as a diversion and a new interest, is the fact that twelve million Negro people will have their first opportunity to see their race in [a] stellar role.

Their patronage, which can be expected in immense numbers, will mean in itself alone a fortune. . . .

Micheaux was soon being spotted back upon the prairie lands of Iowa and South Dakota, hawking stock shares for his movie company. White farmers listened, and, bemused as much as anything else, began forking over money for shares. Micheaux raised five thousand dollars, then ten thousand. He also found Blacks to invest. Many of them thought he'd fail and seemed to be investing out of an appreciation of his pluck. There was also the issue of racial pride. In the fall of 1918, Micheaux had opened his production company offices in Chicago. He acquired film equipment; a script from his book was in the works. "Writing it caused me considerable worry, but I am mostly through and relieved," Micheaux said of the *Homesteader* script.

Since he was far away from the environs of Hollywood, Micheaux knew he had to recruit actors and production staff from the Chicago area. The city was home to both the Lafayette Players and the Pekin Stock Company, both reputable troupes, so there were many Black actors available. Some had experience in vaudeville shows; others had had small roles in so-called "race" movies, films that catered to the Black populace. Everyone who was hired was advised that it was a bare-bones production. (Micheaux's budget for his first film was fifteen thousand dollars.) But the actors and actresses who joined Micheaux on his maiden venture were, more often than not, simply happy to be part of something rare—a Black man producing and directing his own movie, from his own life! Everyone knew *The Homesteader* was but an extension and a longer version of *The Conquest*. So it would be a movie about a Black man going to the prairie, becoming a farmer, falling in love with a forbidden white woman, finally marrying a Black woman, battling with her family, divorcing her, and enduring the times that lay ahead. Micheaux wanted a good actor to play the villain role of Rev. McCracken, his former father-in-law. He chose Vernon S. Duncan, who had performed in many Chicago productions. As for the role of Micheaux's wife, based on Orlean McCracken, Micheaux chose Evelyn Preer. Preer was a member of the Pentecostal Church, quite beautiful, and with a voice that stopped Micheaux as soon as he heard it on a Chicago street corner. Who would play "the colored homesteader"—the starring role, the role of Micheaux himself? The director chose another Lafayette Players actor, Charles D. Lucas.

The filming took place in Chicago, and in various locations around Iowa and South Dakota. Micheaux could be seen in those places wielding a bullhorn and wearing a pair of jodhpurs. These appearances on his roving movie set suggest he was enjoying himself immensely. Not long after filming ended, it was announced that *The Homesteader* would premiere in February 1919. Oscar Micheaux, who had once sold his books door-to-door, had a movie he now had to market. He relished writing his advertising copy:

> Every Race man and woman should cast aside their skepticism regarding the Negro's ability as a motion picture star and go and see [*The Homesteader*], not only for the absorbing interest obtaining herein, but as an appreciation of those finer arts which no race can ignore and hope to obtain a higher plane of thought and action.

Enthusiasm started rising—particularly in the Black community—for the Micheaux-directed movie. The initial premiere showing was planned to take place at the eight-thousand-seat Eighth Regiment Armory, a Chicago facility that catered to Blacks. Micheaux wanted to make the evening extra special, so he invited members of a local regiment of Black soldiers, the Illinois Black Devils, who had seen action in World War I. A short documentary had been made about their exploits, and Micheaux arranged to have it shown preceding the debut of his own film.

On opening night, *The Homesteader* delighted the audience. They were seeing something original, the first feature-length film by a Black filmmaker. The movie played out with all the twists and turns and heartbreaking moments of Micheaux's own life. The audience cheered lustily, and when they left the armory they were full of praise. Of course, word reached the McCracken family: Micheaux's former wife and in-laws all played a part in the drama, although given other names. The family was not amused and, led by Rev. McCracken, filed a complaint with the local censorship board. Inasmuch as McCracken was a respected elder of the A.M.E. Church, his complaint was taken seriously. The board decided to halt showings of the film. Micheaux grinned: he figured he'd win his freedom-of-expression argument, and the brouhaha would only gin up publicity for the movie. He was right. The censorship board decided against McCracken, and the movie resumed its run. Micheaux ran an ad, quoting a minister who came to his defense: "I can see no just cause for the personal objection to this [photo] play," the ad blared. "Every race

1941, Chicago Theatre. Blacks were often limited as to where they could see movies.

has its hypocrites. Frequently they are found in the churches." When *The Homesteader* resumed showing, it played at the swanky Vendome Theatre in Chicago. The lines were long; the newspaper stories and headlines gushed with praise: "Every detail of the production has been given the most minute care," *The Chicago Defender* offered. "Many scenes," stated the review in *The Half-Century Magazine,* "rank in power and workmanship with the greatest of white western productions." Micheaux delighted in making appearances at the showings, surprising filmgoers.

———

Oscar Micheaux's first brush with filmmaking had proved successful. There had been good reviews and glowing crowds! So he embarked on a dream no Black man had previously dreamed: he was going to write and direct a string of movies, and he was going to market them, all in segregated America. He set about this unique undertaking by hiring a small staff. Needing product, Micheaux came up with a new script about a Black schoolteacher and her efforts to raise money for a Black school in the South. Micheaux had always been fond of the legend of Booker T. Washington, the great educator who had raised substantial sums of money for his Tuskegee Institute in Alabama.

Micheaux's new film was called *Within Our Gates,* and he filmed it in Chicago in 1919. Among its cast were two actors he had cast in his first film, Charles Lucas and Evelyn Preer: "Oscar Micheaux presents Within Our Gates With the renowned Negro artist Evelyn Preer," said an advertisement. The movie aimed to show Black uplift, dreams, and ambition. The script shows its heroine suffering through a series of setbacks in trying to raise money for the Southern Black school. The drama is played out against a backdrop of thwarted love as well as white tyranny—in the form of beatings and hangings—that is visited upon Black people. The vivid display of Black suffering and racism was Micheaux's daring cinematic answer to Griffith's *The Birth of a Nation.* Micheaux wrote most of his own advertising, and he began promoting his newest silent eight-reel movie as "the biggest protest against Race prejudice, lynching, and 'concubinage' that was ever written or filmed." Another ad stated:

*Within Our Gates . . .*
SUPPORTED BY AN ALL-STAR COLORED CAST . . .
"THE LYNCHING EVIL"

The opening of *Within Our Gates* explains on title cards: "At the opening of our drama we find our characters in the North where the prejudices and hatreds of the South do not exist, though this does not prevent the occasional lynching of a Negro."

Oscar Micheaux appeared genuinely determined not to let D. W. Griffith's cinematic diatribe go unanswered. He found support from the public. A Negro schoolteacher wrote a letter to *The Chicago Defender* about Micheaux's latest movie. "*The Birth of a Nation* was written by oppressors to show that the oppressed were a burden and a drawback to the nation, that they had no real grievance, but on the other hand they were as roving lions, seeking whom they might devour," she wrote. "Within Our Gates is written by the oppressed and shows in a mild way the degree and kind of his oppression. That he is an asset to the nation in all phases of national life, aspiration and development. Nothing like it since Uncle Tom's Cabin."

Artistic ambitions were one thing; the lack of a financial foundation quite another. Micheaux was piling up debts as he tried to turn his cinematic dreams into reality. Persnickety items about his financial fragility were appearing in gossip pages of the Negro press. He hoped that the addition of his brother Swan to handle business affairs would calm the financial waters. Micheaux set about making his next picture, this one about boxing and the underworld. It was called *The Brute,* and centered on a beautiful woman (played by Evelyn Preer, a Micheaux mainstay now) who falls in love with a vicious underworld mobster. Micheaux found a onetime athlete, A. B. DeComathiere, to play the boxer. Micheaux wrote a big fight scene into the script. To get a large turnout for the picture's epic fight, he posted an ad in *The Chicago Defender* urging Chicagoans to come and be part of the movie: "See Yourself in the Movies by Being a Spectator at the Ringside During This Mighty Battle."

George Johnson—who had failed earlier to get Oscar Micheaux to join his film unit—began doing work for Micheaux, finding and booking theatres for his films. In the world of Negro cinema, the production end was quite small. A typical letter arrived in Micheaux's Chicago office from Johnson about a booking arrangement: ". . . beg to advise that I have closed as per contracts herewith, a three-day booking on 'The Brute' at the Diamond Theatre, Omaha Neb for Wednesday, Thursday and Friday, Nov 3–4 . . . 1920 on a 60–40% basis with an admission price of 20¢ & 40¢ . . ." Early word on Micheaux's latest was positive. *The Chicago Defender* announced that *The Brute* was "creating a sensation and breaking attendance records at every place it is being shown." The *Defender*'s film critic heaped praise upon the movie: "There is a great prize fight and a world of comedy," the review noted. Micheaux had actually filmed one boxing scene for the movie, of his Black boxer defeating a white boxer, but censors made him cut it. In any event, he was quite proud of the film.

As a filmmaker, Oscar Micheaux was well aware of his sociopolitical surroundings. Chicago had been engulfed in the racial turmoil that had swept the country in 1919. There was still quite a bit of residue lingering from the weeklong riot that had taken place in the city that year. It all began at a segregated beach on the city's south side. A seventeen-year-old youth, Eugene Williams, had disobeyed the beach's segregated demarcation line, swimming into the white section of the waters. Whites reacted angrily and began throwing rocks at the Black youth. There was pandemonium and loud threats; the hurled rocks and looming clash alarmed Williams, who couldn't regain his balance and drowned. When they arrived on the scene, the police refused to arrest the white man who had been pointed out to them as having instigated the tragic episode. Instead of arresting the accused white man, however, the police arrested a Black man! His arrest ignited anger and confrontation between whites and Blacks. The clashes soon spread around the city. They were ferocious and lethal. Thirty-eight people died: twenty-three Blacks and fifteen whites. The headline-making riot made life for any Black businessman in Chicago more difficult. Oscar Micheaux believed that the aftermath of the riot and deaths had dimmed turnout for *The Brute,* which premiered a year after the riots. Chicago had turned into an unpredictable place for Blacks. Micheaux began looking for a new base of operations, someplace where a Black filmmaker might be more welcome. He was greatly inspired by the cultural movement taking place in the Harlem section of New York City.

The opening of housing availability in Harlem in the early 1920s turned that enclave of Manhattan into a haven for Blacks. Black writers, artists, and musicians soon ventured into uptown Manhattan. Among them were Alain Locke, Langston Hughes, Arna Bontemps, Augusta Savage, and W. E. B. Du Bois. Benjamin Brawley, the Harvard-educated author of *The Negro in Literature and Art,* thought the appearance of so much Black talent in Harlem should be saluted. A fancy dinner brought together some of the leading editors and publishers in Manhattan to hobnob with the Black artistic crowd. Carl Van Doren, editor of the much-respected *Century Magazine,* was at the dinner. "What American literature decidedly needs at this moment is color, music, gusto, the free expression of gay or desperate moods. . . . If the Negroes are not in a position to contribute these items, I do not know what Americans are," he said. Black artists, indeed, had begun seizing the moment: books and plays and Black films all flowed from a movement that would come to be known as the Harlem Renaissance. "In Harlem," the writer Arna Bontemps said about the renaissance, "it was like a foretaste of paradise. A blue haze descended at night and with it strings of fairy lights on the broad avenues."

Oscar Micheaux, certainly a man of gusto, decided to join the flourishing Black mecca of artistic creation. He loaded his film equipment and departed Chicago.

———

It took Oscar Micheaux little time to get himself acquainted with the environs of Harlem and New York City. He arrived on the East Coast with a reputation as a pioneering filmmaker. (Some of his films had already been shown across the pond, in the great European capitals.) The filmmaker made the rounds of the city, meeting influential denizens, excited by the buzzing nightlife. In 1921, among his many speaking engagements, he appeared before a conference of the Associated Negro Press. These were the journalists of the Negro newspapers in America, who gave far more attention to stories affecting Black people than the mainstream white press did. Micheaux thought his moment before them had been a long time coming. In addressing the press gathering, Micheaux had film on his mind. "Moving pictures have become one of the greatest revitalizing forces in race adjustment," he told the crowd, "and we are just beginning."

Because they rarely paid attention to Negro films, the white mainstream press largely ignored Black talent. An exception was the Black musician or comedian, such as Buddy Bolden, Bert Williams, or Duke Ellington. Oscar Micheaux, however, was constantly on the hunt for ignored or missed Black talent that he could match to his scripts.

There were abandoned studio lots in and around New Jersey, because so many film executives had taken their operations out to Hollywood. Micheaux set about filming his fourth film, *Symbol of the Unconquered*, in and around Fort Lee, New Jersey. The plot centers on Eve Mason, a light-skinned Black woman—played by Iris Hall—who arrives in the West to reclaim family land. The dramatic turns in the film revolve around a gentle and kindhearted neighbor, Hugh Van Allen, a Black man, who befriends Eve. Eve becomes aware that Van Allen's land sits atop a lucrative oil reserve and that townsfolk, among them members of the KKK, wish to drive the homesteader off the land. In this film, Micheaux once again does battle in a kind of cinematic warring against Griffith's *Birth of a Nation*. Whereas Griffith's Klansmen win their fierce battles, Micheaux has something else in store: "See the Ku Klux Klan in Action and Their Annihilation!" his ads crowed. Eve, the female protagonist, ultimately becomes a hero of the film, helping Van Allen stave off an attack from the Klansmen. Van Allen survives and keeps his land, all the while becoming a millionaire because of the oil. Van Allen and Eve eventually marry.

Micheaux released two films in 1921, another two in 1922, and two more in 1923. He had clearly become the forerunner of a unique movement, directing snappy Black dramas that were entrancing Black America. But one of those six films, *The Gunsaulus Mystery*, which was released in 1921, veered into new territory for the filmmaker. The film was about the infamous 1913 Leo Frank case. Some Micheaux chroniclers have placed him in the vicinity of Atlanta during the Frank trial, which doubtless inspired his desire to revisit the case. He had even written a novel, *The Forged Note,* that resembled aspects of the case. Frank had been charged and convicted of strangling to death thirteen-year-old Mary Phagan, whose body was discovered inside the National Pencil Company factory in Atlanta, where Frank worked. The Phagan funeral was attended by more than ten thousand people. Frank was Jewish, and in the aftermath of the funeral, Jewish leaders, decrying evidence of anti-Semitism, wondered if Frank would receive a fair trial. They soon had their answer. In a kangaroo court, Frank was sentenced to death. Doubts lingered about the proceedings. Two Black men, Jim Conley and Newt Lee, also had come under suspicion. Given the brutality of Southern justice when it came to Black men and the charge of murdering or raping white women, Conley and Lee knew their punishment would likely be quite swift, ending at the end of a lynch rope. But it was Frank who received the murder conviction. Conley did receive a year in prison for being an accomplice.

There was national condemnation surrounding the Frank trial and verdict. Pressure was put on Georgia Governor John Slaton to commute Frank's death sentence to life in prison. The governor did so. Frank began serving his sentence in the state penitentiary. In 1915, he was kidnapped from the prison by vigilantes, taken to the woods, and hanged. This horrific incident illustrated to the nation how quickly racial hatred could jump through the darkness into religious hatred.

Oscar Micheaux realized he had substantial material for his Leo Frank–inspired film, which he shot around New York. The stars were Edward Abrams, Evelyn Preer, and Lawrence Chenault. Myrtle Gunsaulus was the Mary Phagan figure. The janitor who finds the body is Black, and quickly charged. But at the trial, attention turns to Anthony Brisbane, the Leo Frank character, who is ultimately convicted. The film premiered at Harlem's Lafayette Theatre in 1921. A review in *The New York Age* allowed that *The Gunsaulus Mystery* "holds the interest of the audience from start to finish," and proclaiming it "one of the best pictures" Micheaux had directed. The Atlanta censors—rattled at the possibility of bringing more attention to the infamous case—pulled Micheaux's film from theatres there shortly after it opened. Micheaux took the setback in stride, believing any publicity good for his film.

To be Oscar Micheaux in 1920s America was not easy. He was running a business and making movies. He was also trying to stay away from the kind of physical assaults that could be meted out to any so-called uppity

Negro. While traveling around the South, he often came face-to-face with belligerent restaurant managers who refused to serve him. It was hard to find decent accommodations. Often he was saved by Blacks employed by the Negro theatres where his movies played, who would offer him a spare bedroom, treating him with dignity. Any Colored YMCA was also happy to host him. Sometimes, when he was lugging one of his movies to a city to show, Micheaux would have to find lodging not only for himself but for the actors he would sometimes bring along to heighten excitement. In addition to the normal hardships, there were always unforeseen woes. A 1922 countrywide flu epidemic harmed attendance at Negro theatres, even forcing some of them to close.

Owing to the fraught relationship he had with Rev. McCracken, his former father-in-law, it was inevitable that Oscar Micheaux might decide to direct a church-set drama. He had written a story about an escaped prisoner who makes his way to a small town in Georgia and reinvents himself as a minister, Rev. Isaiah T. Jenkins. He proceeds to trick a trusting congregation out of money. At that point in the script, the real drama is just unspooling. There is another member of the church community, Sylvester, who looks exactly like Rev. Jenkins! What Micheaux was aiming to do in this layered melodrama—there are flashbacks and dream sequences—was to expose the shenanigans that can go on in any congregation, but that were especially painful inside Black churches. Micheaux titled the film *Body and Soul* and began filming in the fall of 1924. Julia Russell and Mercedes Gilbert were cast as the two leading ladies. But attention landed on the actor Micheaux cast to play Rev. Jenkins. His name was Paul Robeson. And he was as bewildering to the white public as Oscar Micheaux himself happened to be.


Born in 1898 in Princeton, New Jersey, Robeson got good enough grades in high school to be awarded a scholarship to Rutgers College. He became a phenomenal football player, twice being named an All-American. His academics were sterling as well: he earned a Phi Beta Kappa key. After Rutgers, it was off to Columbia Law School. While at Columbia, he would also spend time studying acting at the Harlem YMCA. In time he was noticed by the playwright Eugene O'Neill, who pleaded with him to appear in *All God's Chillun Got Wings*. The reviews—with Robeson in the lead role of the 1924 play—were effusive. A short while later, Micheaux offered Robeson the starring role in his movie *Body and Soul*. Robeson, who had never been in a movie, accepted Micheaux's offer of a hundred dollars a week. "Michaux [sic] made storm scene out in Corona [N.Y.] today," Robeson's wife would write in her diary. "What with the wind machine, fire hose, etc., it was the most realistic thing I ever saw." Micheaux imagined the censors would come after him on *Body and Soul* because of his portrait of church life, not to mention the drinking, gambling, and wanton sexuality in the picture. And come after him they did: he was forced to cut and edit scenes in the picture several times before it met the demands of the censors. This all seemed worth it, because the reviews for the 1925 film were wonderful. "A magnificent combination of Negro brains and art," the *Baltimore Afro-American* would conclude. "Beautifully photographed, extraordinarily original, one of the most tragic yet sympathetic stories ever filmed," came the assessment of *The New York Amsterdam News*. One of the dazzling features of *Body and Soul* was its exuberant display of wardrobe and costumes. Micheaux may have been suspicious of church politics, but he respected the sartorial stylishness of the Black church and put it on full display in his film. Maybelle Crew, who wrote an entertainment column for the *Baltimore Afro-American,* declared, "Oh boy! If some of the Reverends could see how Micheaux pictures the harm done by that Jack-Leg Preacher, but of course, they wouldn't go near that den of iniquity, a theatre."

With another movie behind him, the filmmaker rolled on across the great racial divide of the American landscape. Sometimes it felt as if he were operating in the ether of D. W. Griffith. Now and then, Micheaux would arrive in a town and notice, on the marquee of the local white theatre, *The Birth of a Nation.* The movie seemed to be playing, year in and year out, on a kind of continuous loop in Southern theatres, as if placed there to boost and fortify the cultural dominance of whites—along with the denigration of Blacks—on a movie screen. The jangling profits from the showings kept theatre owners smiling.

Oscar Micheaux directed two movies in 1926. The following year, he directed and released four films. But the filmmaker was constantly blindsided by the economic turmoil attached to operating Black theatres, to which his movies were confined. *The Pittsburgh Courier* took note of the dilemma: "In Houston are two theatres run by white people for colored, and one other colored theatre. Also are white theatres which permit colored people to enter by the back and side door."

By 1929, America had a new president, Herbert Hoover, a former engineer. That was also the year when the American economy began to rupture. Car sales plummeted, and housing sales collapsed. Wall Street crashed, and for the next several years the nation remained in a full-blown economic decline. Buyers had purchased more than four million new cars in 1929; in 1933, they purchased fewer than half that number. Farmers lost their land; the streets of American cities were filled with growing numbers of the homeless and destitute. It was often reported who lost how much in the devastating crash: the entertainer Eddie Cantor lost two million dollars; the tycoon-led Vanderbilt family saw their fortunes drop by forty million; the theatrical impresario Flo Ziegfeld saw two million bucks float away. If the scene was dire for many whites, it was far worse for Blacks. As for Oscar Micheaux, his problems only seemed to multiply: he had a nasty breakup with his brother Swan, who was proving to be an inept manager of the film company. Oscar Micheaux was forced to file for bankruptcy in 1928. He got only a single movie, *The Wages of Sin,* released in the calamitous year of 1929. The stars of the movie were William Clayton, Jr., Lorenzo Tucker, and Bessie Givens. Also among the cast was Alice Russell, an actress from New Jersey whom Micheaux had recently wooed and married. He welcomed his new bride into his world, believing she would bring order and stability to his fast-paced life.

Oscar Micheaux was not above honoring the turmoil in his own life by transporting it to the screen. His estranged brother Swan would not have been happy with the plot of *The Wages of Sin.* The movie was about the breakup of two brothers, with the younger brother portrayed as a corrupt businessman, a shameless pursuer of women, and a drunkard! The plot is driven by the older brother (the character obviously modeled after Oscar Micheaux himself), who strives mightily to resurrect the business that has been destroyed. Lorenzo Tucker had a fine time making the film and watching Micheaux in action. "He could get down behind the camera, or on the side, and it was like the director with his baton," Tucker would recall. The reviews for *The Wages of Sin* were stellar. *The New York Amsterdam News* proclaimed it "one of the finest pieces of work ever produced by the colored motion picture makers." The *Pittsburgh Courier* review stated the movie was "well worth seeing."

———

Advancements were constantly being made in the world of cinema, and if Oscar Micheaux was to continue making films, he needed to enter the world of talking pictures. Silent movies were becoming passé. Micheaux entered that world, haltingly, in 1930 with two pictures, *A Daughter of the Congo* and *Easy Street*. The former is a slave-kidnap drama starring Lorenzo Tucker again, Kathleen Noisette, and Salem Tutt Whitney. (Neither picture was completely full of sound, allowing stretches of silence.) Micheaux was financing his movie projects from book sales, savings, and royalties from previous pictures. He usually wrote his own screenplays, adapted from his own source material. But *A Daughter of the Congo* was adapted from Henry Francis Downing's novel *The American Cavalryman,* published in 1917. Micheaux's adaptation showed a heroic military hero, Captain Paul Dale (played by Tucker), rescuing the kidnapped daughter of an American; the daughter had been bizarrely lost and left behind by her parents in the Liberian jungle during a trip years earlier. Micheaux could not be pigeonholed in his selection of material, but this escapist melodrama was pilloried by critics. They lambasted him for engaging in color casting his actors, making the heroes light-skinned and the villains dark-skinned. Just as with church politics, shades of skin color was a prominent concern to Blacks, stemming from days of slavery, when lighter-skinned slaves received leniency on plantations. The *New York Age* critic charged Micheaux with a "persistent vaunting of interracial color fetishism." His own skin dark, Micheaux simply ignored the critics.

With the 1930s upon him, Micheaux considered himself in a fight for cinematic survival. He intended to utilize every ounce of his pioneer grit.

Now anchoring himself mostly in the Black mecca of Harlem, Micheaux formed a partnership with two film impresarios, Frank Schiffman and Leo Brecher. Just as businessmen of Jewish background had begun to invent Hollywood, they also played a role in the movie-theatre scene of New York City. The new partnership was called Fayette Pictures. Schiffman and Brecher saw in Micheaux a wise business and creative opportunity: no Black director in the country was as well known as Oscar Micheaux! Word was soon sweeping the press—notably the Negro press—that, despite financial setbacks, Oscar Micheaux had a new business enterprise in motion. And his first production under the new banner would be *The Exile,* a story that would cover the Chicago and South Dakota terrain that he knew so well.

In *The Exile*—Micheaux's first all-talkie film and billed as the first all-Black sound film anywhere—there is a love story between Jean Baptiste (the Micheaux alter ego, played by Stanleigh Morrell) and Edith Duval (played by Eunice Brooks). (The billboards proclaimed: "MIGHTY

MODERN ALL TALKING EPIC OF NEGRO LIFE—THE EXILE.") The action and drama in the beginning is centered in Chicago's Black underworld, where Edith has inherited a dazzling mansion bequeathed to her by a white family. The Baptiste character is soon swooning over Edith, but becomes disappointed in her desire to turn the mansion into a nighttime speakeasy. So Baptiste flees to South Dakota and becomes a farmer. There he falls for Agnes, a white woman. The more the relationship evolves, the more he fears some kind of racial tragedy will befall him. He leaves South Dakota and Agnes, and returns, heartbroken, to Chicago. It is back in Chicago where real tragedy awaits: a former lover murders Edith Duval, and Baptiste is immediately arrested. But the truth is soon recognized that he had nothing to do with her murder. Baptiste is surprised by a visitor upon his release: Agnes has come from South Dakota to be with him. She also has a revelation to share with him: she is actually part Black, a family secret only recently revealed to her. The two hightail it out of Chicago, bound for South Dakota. The reviews delighted Micheaux. "Some good acting is done in this picture," proclaimed the *Baltimore Afro-American*. *The Pittsburgh Courier* thought that Micheaux had presented "a portrayal of Negro life in a city that no one but a Negro, who has traveled and lived in cities, could tell." Nor did it go unnoticed by critics that Micheaux's musical numbers in *The Exile* were lavishly staged productions. For so many years, Micheaux had been operating with shoestring budgets.

Oscar Micheaux was finding the environs of Harlem and New Jersey (his wife Alice's family had a home in New Jersey) far more accommodating to his work than other places he had lived. But he remained well aware that Harlem was an unusual slice of America. In reality, the threat of racial upheaval was constant, and it was little wonder Micheaux kept inserting the fear of racial tyranny into his movies.

In rural Alabama in early 1931—dovetailing with the release of Micheaux's *The Exile* into theatres—nine young Blacks had been riding a train with two white women. Ashamed to have it revealed that they had been with the Black youths, the white women told law enforcement they had been sexually assaulted. The Blacks were arrested and quickly charged with rape. Eight of the youths received death sentences from the all-white jury as a lynch mob howled outside the courtroom. News of the case spread around the nation, then the world. Lawyers for the nine appealed, and the case was heard by the United States Supreme Court, where their death sentences were vacated. Still, the unjust prison sentences were long.

The last of the "Scottsboro Boys" would not be released from prison until 1950. The two white women had long recanted by the time of their release. It was all a lie, a fever dream inside of a scary movie plot.

A story that kept tugging at Oscar Micheaux's conscience was the 1913 Leo Frank murder-kidnap drama in Georgia. Micheaux had, of course, already written a novel about the case and made his film about it. But he just couldn't let the story go, and decided to tackle the case yet again. He assembled a cast—among them his wife, Alice, along with Andrew Bishop, Clarence Brooks, and Alec Lovejoy. Micheaux again set the story in Harlem, but this time he wrote a script laden with direct quotes and insights from the actual trial transcripts of the Leo Frank case. Micheaux's drama—full of flashbacks—focused a lot on Jim Conley, the Black man linked to the crime. Micheaux couldn't resolve the crime in his script, but he could present to the public his cinematic notion that his Leo Frank–like character might not have committed the murder. Originally titled *Lem Hawkins' Confession,* the movie, released in 1935, got a new title, *Murder in Harlem.* The critics were not kind, one calling it "decidedly overdone."

It was quite difficult to make a living in 1930s America in any line of work. The Depression hovered over the land like a ferocious blanket. But Hollywood itself was growing, churning out fanciful musicals as escapist entertainment. Stars like Fred Astaire and Ginger Rogers danced across movie screens with jubilance and grace. The dreamland of Hollywood kept putting on a cheery face. But things were only turning darker in the cinematic ravine where Oscar Micheaux dwelled. During the 1930s, dozens of the estimated 390 black theatres in the nation folded. Micheaux released only one movie in 1933 and one in 1934. He got two films out in 1935, but it was back to a single film in 1937. His directing history and oeuvre meant nothing to the men who ran the Hollywood studios. They were not interested in cavorting with a Black pioneer. Madison Avenue, the height of the advertising world in New York City, also offered little that might lift the spirits of the nation's Black populace. Black life continued to be presented to society at large as a caricature. A 1937 issue of *Life* magazine featured a nameless Black man on the cover. The caption read "Watermelons to Market." The article inside the magazine was supposed to be about the popularity of eating watermelon. The white women seen eating watermelon are dressed in bathing suits and smiling, without a hint of sarcasm or mockery. There is a photo caption attached to the photo of Blacks: "Nothing makes a Negro's mouth water like a luscious, fresh-picked melon. Any colored 'mammy' can hold a huge slice in one hand while holding her offspring in the other. . . . What melons the Negro do not consume will find favor with the pigs."

In 1938, Oscar Micheaux decided to make a film that incorporated the psychology of "passing"—denying one's Blackness—with a greater depth than he had previously explored. He also was bold in announcing it would be his answer to Fannie Hurst's *Imitation of Life,* which he thought wasn't adequately gritty and authentic.

For his latest take on "passing," Micheaux chose a cast that included Carman Newsome, Jacqueline Lewis, Ethel Moses, Gloria Press, and his wife, Alice Russell, who wrote the script for what would come to be known as *God's Step Children.* The focus of Micheaux's film is Naomi, born Black but constantly wanting to be in the white world. When Naomi tries to attend a white school, she is rebuffed, and when she spits in her teacher's face she gets sent to a convent school. Back among people who know her, Naomi wishes to apologize to everyone for her past behavior. She falls in love with Jimmie, a local friend. But Jimmie is already married. He does offer to help Naomi by introducing her to Clyde, a possible beau. But Clyde is dark-skinned, still a no-no to Naomi. However, she soon relents and marries Clyde. She is not happy in the marriage. She comes to declare: "I'm leaving the Negro race. . . . I'm going away from all I ever knew, to the other side. . . . If you see me, you don't know me. Even if you pass me on the street, I'm a stranger." And Naomi vanishes. A few years later, she returns and sees her family without their noticing her, spying on them. The family has recovered from her absence. She takes to a bridge and jumps, drowning herself in a suicidal act. When *God's Step Children* began appearing in theatres up and down the Eastern Seaboard, there were protests. Some thought Micheaux had been too hard on the Black race and their conundrum in dealing with "passing." If Micheaux had sought to challenge the artistry of the original *Imitation of Life,* his film was a noble effort, owing to its texture and deeper dive into the realities of Black life. In 2008, a *Time* magazine film critic gave a salute to the movie: "We may come to sneer; but if we have any capacity to be touched by a naked cry of pain from 70 years past, we leave in awe."

Following the release of his 1940 film, *The Notorious Elinor Lee,* Oscar Micheaux disappeared from the filmmaking world for eight long years. The venues where he had so often shown his pictures kept vanishing. The realities of the economic terrain hurt him. He went back to writing books. "Publishing a book is . . . a simple procedure compared with making pictures," he explained. "If I make a picture it's got to be well and expensively enough made to be appreciated by at least Negroes when it reaches the screen. But regardless how well and . . . in the case of a Negro picture, expensively made, it couldn't get beyond being shown in about 500 theatres catering almost exclusively to Negroes."

So Oscar Micheaux wrote his novels. He mailed them out to newspapers, then bemoaned the white publications that wouldn't review them, imagining if he were a white director who had turned full-time to writing that he would have received more attention. By the time Micheaux's Civil War novel, *The Masquerade,* appeared, in 1947, he hadn't made a movie in seven years. The book received scant attention, unsettling Micheaux yet again.

In 1948, with the emotional support of his wife, Oscar Micheaux decided to return to the world of filmmaking. He went back to what he knew best, his own life story, once again adapting his first book, *The Homesteader,* and adding to it with new plot twists. In *The Betrayal,* there was a pioneering Black farmer, a white woman, tangled romantic infatuation, much criminal activity—all of it a replaying of past Micheaux dramas. The picture, which debuted in June 1948, was an overly long affair at three-plus hours. It hardly excited the critics. "A preposterous, tasteless bore," cried the *New York Herald Tribune. The Chicago Defender,* which had often praised Micheaux's work, called his directing of the film "faulty, to say the least."

The succeeding years were hard on the filmmaker, who endured financial woes and failing health. Now and then, Micheaux got out and about the country to sell and sign copies of his novels. In 1951, the ailing and forgotten filmmaker found himself in Charlotte, North Carolina. Whites had no idea who he was. It was there, on March 25, that Oscar Micheaux died, in a hospital, from an accumulation of ailments—the most severe being high blood pressure. Oscar Micheaux's final resting place was back upon the Kansas prairie, where the brave Buffalo Soldiers had once galloped.

The wonder of it all is that the moviemaking life didn't crush Oscar Micheaux. He had come into Black filmmaking when it hardly existed, creating much of its origins and giving it ballast and a heartbeat. What D. W. Griffith had drilled into the minds of white America—that Blacks were untrustworthy and devoid of humanity—Oscar Micheaux tried to undo. Micheaux directed his last film in 1948, and it was not until 1969 that a Black director in America was given the reins to direct a Hollywood motion picture. Gordon Parks's *The Learning Tree* would be highly lauded.

Of all the bravura elements of Oscar Micheaux's life, what he did for

Black actresses cannot be denied. He gave a bevy of Black women opportunities in his films, writing complex roles for them. He catapulted Evelyn Preer into becoming the first female star of silent Black cinema. Black women everywhere knew her name and image; Black men had a pinup queen. There was a feeling and a hope in certain entertainment circles that, if a Black actress was going to cross over into white mainstream movies from Black cinema, it was going to be Preer. That prediction was heightened when she appeared in a small role in *Blonde Venus,* a movie directed by the gifted Josef von Sternberg and released on September 9, 1932. The film starred Marlene Dietrich (who had been discovered by Sternberg) and a young, dashing actor by the name of Cary Grant. But Evelyn Preer never got a chance to build on her appearance in *Blonde Venus.* She died ten weeks after the movie's release, from complications of childbirth. Eagle-eyed viewers of *Blonde Venus* would have caught a glimpse of a young actress by the name of Hattie McDaniel, destined for *Gone with the Wind* fame.

It mattered not at all to white Hollywood how gifted or versatile a Black actress might have been. Hollywood's doors opened only so far for the Black actress, and when they did, she was ushered, time and time again, into a world of playing maids.

# The Imitation Game

S HE ARRIVED IN NEW YORK CITY IN 1910, convinced it was the city where she must launch her writing career. Her parents, back in St. Louis, worried mightily. They had given her money so she wouldn't be pressed for comfort or necessities. Fannie Hurst, as her parents knew, had been a fearless and headstrong teenager. After college graduation, she let her parents know she'd remain under their roof only a year longer; then she was going to strike out into the world. It was a new century, after all, and she wanted to go play around in it. It didn't take her long after reaching her destination to realize there was simply no other place she'd rather be. Manhattan was a metropolis full of writers and book publishers and artists. There were Negroes rushing about, blurry, like brown shadows, and they intrigued her.

Her aim was to poke into the mysterious and valiant corners of human life. Dreamers intrigued her, workers who needed every cent from their paychecks, those souls who borrowed money time and time again because they just couldn't get ahead. She wanted to get to know the people who cleaned homes, who polished hallways inside fancy business addresses, who did laundry for strangers. She aimed to re-create their lives in her writing.

Fannie Hurst rented a typewriter and started writing short stories, snapshots of holding-on souls. She mailed her stories off to magazine editors, then stared at the rejection letters; she'd read them over and over. She couldn't believe she was being dismissed so cavalierly! So she adopted a new tactic, personally showing up at editorial offices. Secretaries and publishing assistants smiled, but politely dismissed her, making up excuses why no editors were available to see her. She would remember the "long hours outside editorial doors; of solitary day-long tramps through streets that poured a hot lava of impersonal humanity; of writing, rewriting; of rejections and rejections." Undeterred, she kept writing, going into unfamiliar settings for background material. She went to night court, to churches that handed out free food, anyplace where she could study people who were scuffling on the margins of life. "There is nothing like the common people," an editor told her once; she took it as a sign of encouragement. In her letters back home, she avoided her real situation and said she was doing just fine.

Her breakthrough came when she attracted the attention of Robert H. Davis, chief editor for a consortium of magazines. In early 1912, Fannie Hurst's stories finally began appearing in magazines such as *Smith's* and *Cavalier,* stories about cashiers and social workers and working girls and hotel manicurists—common people. That same year, she also attracted the attention of *The Saturday Evening Post,* one of the nation's premiere magazines. They wanted to publish her. Fannie Hurst's rise was swift. Among her most talked-about early stories were "In Memoriam," about German Jewish immigrants; "Ice Water P1———," about boarding-house inhabitants; and "Sob Sister." Magazine publishers were now eager for her stories. She was earning $1,750 per story. Between 1912 and 1916, Hurst published forty-six stories, most of them in top-tier magazines. She was being spoken of with the likes of Booth Tarkington and Mark Twain.

William Schuyler had been an assistant principal at Central High School in St. Louis, where Fannie attended. He was bowled over by her rising national reputation as a short-story writer. "That picture of two simple souls at supper in the midst of the vicious and vulgar dissipation of fast New York is a remarkable piece of dialect," he wrote to her about one of her stories. He concluded: "You have the seeing eye and the portraying hand of the true artist and I expect the very best from you."


Perhaps it was her Jewish heritage that caused Fannie Hurst to pay homage to the lost, the forgotten, the bruised. She knew and appreciated the travails of ethnic America. In Manhattan, she ventured into Black neighborhoods to look around, to study the people and landscape. She heard the cacophony going on up in Harlem in the early 1920s, that nascent movement involving Black writers and artists. One of the backers of this movement was Charles S. Johnson, who edited *Opportunity,* a magazine that published many Black writers. The moment was ripe, Johnson reasoned, to bring all this Black artistic talent in Harlem together for an evening of celebration. An announcement soon went out that a gathering, the first of its kind involving Black literati, would take place on March 21, 1924, at Manhattan's Civic Club.

As the writers and artists gathered on the appointed evening, they spied the likes of H. L. Mencken, Eugene O'Neill, Oswald Garrison Villard, and W. E. B. Du Bois. Carl Van Doren, the editor of the esteemed literary magazine *Century,* was also there. The gathering appeared like a call to arms to invade the status quo. Contact information was exchanged; writers were introduced to other writers and editors. The evening was such a smash that Paul Kellogg, who edited *Survey Graphic,* another influential magazine, decided he would devote one whole issue to Black writers. Then he decided that the best articles would be awarded literary prizes.

Kellogg went about seeking submissions for his upcoming issue. Then he recruited judges to determine the articles and essays that would be awarded prizes. Kellogg then decided there must be a celebratory dinner! Among the judges he convinced to join the undertaking was Fannie Hurst, who had now been traipsing around Manhattan for a decade and a half, writing her fictional stories—and new books as well—about all those desperate people trying not to become buried beneath life's woes.

The much-talked-about literary-awards dinner took place on May 1, 1925. The well-dressed and racially mixed crowd took their seats with a feverish excitement. They were a part of something unique in American letters, a gathering called to highlight Black achievement. The attending whites who supported the reach of black artistic expressions—Alfred and Blanche Knopf stood out among them—were happy to be there and be witnesses to it all. Among those who won first-place prizes at the Manhattan gala were Countee Cullen, Langston Hughes, Sterling Brown, Frank Horne, and Zora Neale Hurston. Days after the event, the chatter about what had taken place remained electric. The *New York Herald Tribune* opined that America could be "on the edge, if not already in the midst, of what might not improperly be called a Negro renaissance." This "Negro renaissance" quickly morphed into being called the Harlem Renaissance.

Fannie Hurst was overjoyed by what she had witnessed at the Harlem dinner. She was particularly taken with the young writer to whom she had presented prizes: Zora Neale Hurston. Hurston actually took home two prizes, one for her short story "Spunk," and another for her play "Color Struck." She had swept into the Manhattan dinner full of animation, outfitted with a bright-red scarf, which she twirled to great effect. Hurston had been in Manhattan only a short while, having decamped from her studies at Howard University in Washington because of money problems.

Zora Neale Hurston was born in 1891 in Notasulga, Alabama. Shortly after her mother died, her father remarried, and Zora rebelled against her stepmother; there were loud and testy arguments. Young Zora left home in 1905. It was a bold move for a young Black girl living in the American South. She got intermittent work in small Florida towns as a maid for white families. She'd find herself, however, in dangerous situations, suffering from sexual abuse. Poverty pained her as well. "There is something about poverty that smells like death," she wrote. "Dead dreams dropping off the heart like leaves in a dry season and rotting around the feet; impulses smothered too long in the fetid air of underground caves. The soul lives in a sickly air. People can be slave-ships in shoes." Nevertheless, she was an exuberant sort when she had to be; Hurston performed with an acting troupe for nearly two years. By 1917, she had settled in Baltimore, where she found work as a waitress. She longed to continue her education, and in 1919 got herself admitted to Howard University.

At Howard, her spirits brightened. She majored in English and quickly displayed a talent for writing, impressing her professors. (Hurston shaved years off her age. Classmates and professors did not realize she was at least ten years older than many of her fellow students.) Hurston's stories in the campus literary journal, *The Stylus,* were the ones that got the attention of Harlem's literary doyennes, necessitating her attendance at the May 1925 awards ceremony. In what should have been her final year at Howard, Hurston once again fell upon hard times and had no means to continue paying her tuition. Figuring that her literary recognition in New York City might portend better days ahead, she ditched Howard and took off for Manhattan, arriving with suitcases and books as the year 1925 began.

In Harlem, Hurston befriended the rising lights of the Harlem Renaissance—Arna Bontemps, Nella Larsen, Countee Cullen, Carl Van Vechten, Charles S. Johnson, and the ferociously talented Langston Hughes. "Zora Neale Hurston is a clever girl, isn't she?" Hughes asked a compatriot. What Hurston also wanted to do as much as she wanted to write was complete her education. At the awards dinner, she had wowed not only Fannie Hurst but Annie Nathan Meyer as well. Meyer was a Jewish philanthropist who had been important to the founding of Barnard College twenty-six years earlier. She was currently a Barnard trustee. When Meyer heard of Hurston's desire to finish college, she suggested

Barnard, a school that had never had a Black student. Meyer surely wasn't aware of Hurston's actual age, but she sensed in her a certain maturity and bravery, traits that would be needed to break the color line at Barnard. Following an interview with the Barnard dean of admissions—and an obvious boost from Meyer—Zora Neale Hurston was admitted to Barnard. But, in what was turning out to be the usual ticktock narrative of her life, troubles loomed, once again around money. Soon into her new college phase, Hurston was broke yet again, having exhausted the funds she had raised from a few benefactors. Meyer suggested to Hurston that she contact Fannie Hurst: since it was Hurst who had given Hurston her literary prizes at the awards gala, perhaps she would be willing to help the college student. Hurst did better: she not only offered money, but she invited Hurston to come live with her and work as her secretary. It was an offer Zora Neale hardly believed could be true. Fannie Hurst was not only a Manhattan celebrity but also a bona-fide literary star.

By now, Hurst had achieved the kind of fame rare for any writer, let alone a female writer of that era. Though she admitted she wrote for a female audience, her stories and books had gained wide readership. Her book sales afforded her luxuries: a beautiful home on West Sixty-seventh Street in Manhattan, an expansive wardrobe, and even first-class attention for her dogs. Yet Hurst never took her eye off the "common people" who populated her stories. It was their perseverance that had ignited her writing and fueled her social activism. She kept in her home newspaper and magazine clippings about Negro life. Hollywood had already called upon Hurst, having turned her short story "Humoresque" into a 1920 silent film. Hurst's 1923 novel, *Lummox,* also found a legion of admirers, even if some critics mocked her as "Queen of the Sob Story."

Not only had Zora Neale Hurston integrated Barnard College, but, by moving in and working with Fannie Hurst, she also, in a sense, invaded the white world of book publishing. The two women got along swell. Hurst saw in Zora Neale a young writer who "lived laughingly, raffishly . . . with blazing zest for life." Something else also sparked feverish interest from the famous writer: Zora Neale Hurston had been a domestic, a maid, and, having been out in the world since the age of thirteen, she owned the kind of sob stories that would shock the senses. And Fannie listened to those stories. The cohabitation between the two writers, employer and employee, was short-lived, owing to the demands on Hurston's college life. Still, they stayed in touch, spending time together, sharing meals, and talking about life. Hurston had found yet another "Negrotarian," the word she used to identify whites who aided Blacks.

Hurst was working on a novel about two women, one Black and one white. In the novel, the white woman, Bea, takes the pancake-waffle recipe of her Black maid, Delilah, and markets it, becoming a wealthy businesswoman. A potent subtext concerns the maid's daughter, Peola. Peola, with a very light skin hue, grows up and sees the horrible treatment meted out to Blacks in everyday life. She decides she doesn't want any part of that life and starts "passing," presenting herself to the public as a white person. Hurst's working title was *Sugar House.* However,

Fannie Hurst, circa 1931. She was curious about Black life.

by the time it was completed, and published by Harper on February 1, 1933, the novel's title had been changed to *Imitation of Life*.

Mainstream and popular white novelists of the time rarely tackled race in their books. Hurst's racial subplot—Black maid and haunted daughter—caught the attention of the public and critics. If the nation had been avoiding the truth in literature of its ongoing racial nightmares—and it had—it could no longer do so, because Hurst's books, even when scoffed at by highbrow critics, commanded attention as bestsellers. The *New York Herald Tribune* book critic saw the novel as "a triumph of the black woman more than the white." *The Cincinnati Enquirer* deemed Hurst's portrait of the Black maid to be "one of the most magnificently drawn characters in all the great store of literature depicting Negro life." And the *Chicago Herald Examiner* critics gushed that *Imitation of Life* represented "one of the most human documents written on the race problem that is the penalty of slavery in a free country." In 1933, rarely seeing themselves portrayed in popular literature, Black Americans swooned over the book. Harlem bookstores sold out quickly; Negro-oriented publications around the country lavished attention upon the novel. Hurst did not expect that Blacks would be so touched by the book and its storyline; after all, they were secondary characters. But Blacks were so desperate for narratives depicting their lives that they pulled the Black storyline to heights it didn't quite have in the book. Here is an exchange from the novel, adorned with Hurst's Southern Negro dialect, between Delilah, the Black maid, and her self-hating daughter, Peola. Delilah is trying to explain to Peola what lies ahead in the world when it comes to being called a "nigger":

> *I won't be a nigger! I won't be a nigger!*
> *Got to, mah baby. The further long you go apin' white and plea-surin' wid dem, de more you're letting yourself in for de misery. . . .*
> *Won't! Won't!*
> *Then brace your heart, mah baby, 'cause breakin's ahead for it. Brace your heart for de misery of tryin' to dye black blood white. Ain't no way to dye black white. God never even give a way to dye a black dress white, much less black blood.*

All the publicity and acclaim echoed the public's deep desire for a Hollywood movie to be made.

Hollywood quickly circled the novel. Universal won the rights and hired John Stahl, a dependable studio director, to helm the picture. Stahl was known for directing so-called women's pictures, including *Back Street,* another Hurst novel; that adaptation had delighted Hurst. But Stahl and the studio had challenges when it came to the *Imitation* script. They would have to grapple with race, which was foreign territory for Hollywood's scriptwriters. Though the script was eventually credited to William J. Hurlbut—who had worked with Stahl on the 1933 Margaret Sullavan picture, *Only Yesterday*—other writers were brought in to help, among them the gifted Preston Sturges. Stahl settled on a cast headed by Claudette Colbert, Louise Beavers, Warren William, and Alan Hale, with Fredi Washington—a very light-skinned Black actress—playing the tragic daughter who passes for white. Before she had become an actress, Louise Beavers—chosen to play the Black maid—had been a real-life maid to the silent film actress Leatrice Joy. Beavers had already had a busy year of filming in 1934; taking on more than a dozen roles, she played a maid in half of them.

The movie began filming in the summer of 1934. But books-to-movies are hardly literal translations. The filmmaker and scriptwriters have to make adjustments. A novel is written; scripts are designed and structured to illustrate a powerful adaptation of an article or novel. Stahl's nervousness about the finished script could be felt on the set of the movie, where scenes were constantly being tweaked and rewritten. It was the matter of race that bewitched the filmmaker, who plowed into mostly unknown territory for a Hollywood picture.

When *Imitation of Life* hit theatres, critical reception seesawed between praise and outright derision. *The Crisis,* the magazine of the NAACP, opened its pages to allow its readers to comment on the film. One letter writer wrote that the movie was "so full of vicious anti-Negro propaganda" that it simply "deadens the discriminatory faculties of those who see it." It was one thing to read about characters in a novel, quite another to see their perceived cultural moorings on a big screen. Try as she did to humanize the Blacks in the novel, Hurst's characters appeared on-screen as stereotypes, with clipped and embarrassing speech patterns, and blatant inferiority complexes. Sterling Brown, the gifted Harlem writer, felt that the movie only magnified the "old stereotype of the contented Mammy, and the tragic mulatto; and the ancient ideas about the mixture of the races." Louise Beavers herself was somewhat defensive about the reaction to the film. She told the press that certain lines in the script had been offensive, and she refused to deliver them. "I knew that Negroes would not want to hear them. I have always tried to protect my people and to show directors that they are just as sensitive and particular about their race as whites are about theirs." When Fannie Hurst weighed in, her reactions were rather mixed. She admitted that the film had shortcomings, that at certain moments its intentions "fall short or deviate or even malign my original theme."

The 1934 movie did manage a Best Picture nomination (then known as "Outstanding Production") from the Academy of Motion Picture Arts and Sciences, but that nomination seemed a mere formality, an admission by the Academy—which was only seven years old—that popular movies with known stars must be on its twelve-picture list. The selections were also about which studios had the most energetic and muscular publicity mavens. In 1934, *Imitation of Life* was not an important film. Even though its source material—the novel—had been popular, bitterness and hurt feelings were left in the movie's wake.

But Hollywood was not finished with *Imitation of Life.*

————

If Zora Neale Hurston felt slighted in the role she had played in Fannie Hurst's imagined life of a Black maid, she uttered not a word about it. In the ensuing years, she simply remained grateful to Hurst for the early faith she had shown in her and her writing talent. That faith would prove to have been well placed. Hurston became one of the great writers and folklorists in American letters, writing fiction and nonfiction. Her magazine articles were published in leading periodicals, and she conducted groundbreaking research into Black life, searching out former slaves across the South for oral histories. Her most remarkable novel, *Their Eyes Were Watching God*, published in 1937—three years after *Imitation of Life* hit the screen—told the story of Janie Crawford, a Black woman making her way in a hard and unfair world. Fannie Hurst herself proclaimed Zora Neale Hurston's work "shot through with the lightning of an authentic talent."

The ensuing arc of America in the aftermath of the novel and film of *Imitation of Life* showed a nation grappling feverishly with its racial demons. Protests from Blacks took on a more dynamic posture during and after World War II. The military remained shamelessly segregated even as the fate of the nation was being challenged. Black soldiers went off to war. Singers, actors, and athletes well known in the Black community—Sugar Ray Robinson, Sammy Davis, Jr., Joe Louis among them—appeared in national Black publications and film clips in their sharp military dress, all praising patriotism across the color line. Those Black aviators known as the Tuskegee Airmen flew through the European skies and earned medals for their bravery. First Lady Eleanor Roosevelt, knowing the extra pressures they fought under, bragged constantly about their exploits and wartime missions. The Black soldiers tasted real freedom in Europe's towns and villages, where there weren't any signs telling them where they must eat and sleep.

When the war ended, Black veterans returned to their hometowns demanding equal rights, figuring it was the least they deserved for fighting so valiantly for their country's freedom. But America had different notions of how they should be treated. The case of Isaac Woodard made headlines. In the Pacific Theatre, Woodard won a medal for bravery. Following his service, he was discharged from Fort Gordon, in Georgia. He hopped a bus, still dressed in his natty military uniform, heading home. In Aiken, South Carolina, an argument erupted between Woodard and the white bus driver over Woodard's seating. The driver deemed Woodard an upstart for talking back, and called the police. Woodard was beaten so savagely about the eyes by police that he was blinded, and then jailed. He spent a month in a military hospital. The vicious attack reached the White

House. President Truman—who would be responsible for desegregating the military—was outraged, and wanted the perpetrators brought to justice. Leonard Shull was the police official identified as the main culprit who had struck the blows against Woodard. Newspapers and the radio carried wide coverage of the trial. Orson Welles brought more attention to the case on his radio show. The all-white jury quickly acquitted Shull. A series of protests and confrontations in the latter part of the 1940s portended dangerous times ahead.

In 1954, the United States Supreme Court ruled unanimously in *Brown v. Board of Education* that school segregation was unlawful.

Zora Neale Hurston in 1938. It was writing—and not working as a maid—that energized her.

The titanic ruling upended the vile 1896 *Plessy v. Ferguson* decision, which decreed that separate was equal before the eyes of the law. Blacks praised the new law, which mandated integration, but many whites throughout the South vowed the decision would never be implemented.

In the summer of 1955, Mamie Till sent her fifteen-year-old son, Emmett, to Mississippi for a vacation. At a small grocery store in the town of Money, he allegedly whistled at a white woman. That evening, he was kidnapped by two white men—one the husband of the woman he had supposedly whistled at. Till was later found murdered, having been shot and thrown into a river. Till was Black; the two white men charged with the crime were arrested, tried, and acquitted in a kangaroo court. The murder outraged many across the nation. Till's funeral was held in Chicago. His battered face was visible; his mother insisted on an open casket so the world could see what Mississippi had done to her only child. Civil-rights groups became more emboldened in their protests. The brutal murder of a child represented a demarcation line. Emmett Till seemed to be the genie let out of some kind of historical bottle hoarding all of America's racial tragedies.

Four months after the Till murder, in December, a seamstress by the name of Rosa Parks refused to budge from a Whites Only seat on a bus in Montgomery, Alabama. Her arrest sparked a boycott and catapulted a young, elegant minister, Martin Luther King, Jr., into the headlines. A wave of bombings and civil-rights murders throughout the South erupted in the wake of the *Brown* ruling, the boycotts, the ongoing protests. In 1957—on the third anniversary of the *Brown* court decision—the Prayer Pilgrimage for Freedom drew about twenty-five thousand people to the Lincoln Memorial in Washington to call for equal rights. Among the notables addressing the rally were Martin Luther King, Jr., A. Philip Randolph, and Congressman Adam Clayton Powell, Jr. Powell stole the show. "We are sick and tired of the two-party hypocrisy," he cried out, in an attack on both Democrats and Republicans. He thundered that America had lost moral standing because of its segregation and the racial murders that went unsolved. "Asia and Africa will never trust America, because they know we're ruled by a hypocritical bipartisan Jim Crow policy." Powell, who had leading-man good looks, understood and followed the entertainment world more closely than most politicians did. His former sister-in-law was Fredi Washington, who had played Peola, the daughter passing as white in the film version of *Imitation of Life.*

The civil-rights murders taking place around the country played a part in forcing President Eisenhower to introduce the first federal civil-rights bill since the Civil War. Lyndon Johnson, the wily Texas senator, propelled Eisenhower's 1957 Civil Rights Act through the Senate. His shepherding of the bill bolstered his reputation as a fearsome political leader. The new bill, which promised bolder voting-rights protections, was seen by many, however, as not being nearly strong enough, because it did not dismantle legal segregation. It created, within the U.S. Department of Justice, a sorely needed civil-rights division. The civil-rights protests hardly let up. In the fall of 1957, the nation suddenly had to turn its attention to Little Rock, Arkansas, where white mobs at Central High School were blocking nine Black children from entering the school to integrate it. Arkansas Governor Orval Faubus backed the mob; President Eisenhower thought Faubus had become mentally unhinged and threatened federal intervention. He delivered on the threat: when the bayonet-wielding National Guardsmen showed up, the mobs backed away, and the Black children entered the school. They remained under guard for most of the school year.

If Black Americans appeared on edge, and the political world looked unpredictable, a sense of optimism could be seen and felt in the world of entertainment and artistic expression. "Sammy Davis, Jr., was hot. Harry Belafonte was hot. Sidney Poitier was hot. And Josephine Baker was coming back to America," says Louis Gossett, Jr., a young actor at the time, appearing on the New York stage in *Take a Giant Step*. That play, written by Louis Peterson, is about a Black high-school student who feels estranged from his white classmates and who comes to learn about life and wisdom from a Black maid.

The film producer Ross Hunter could see what was happening in America on the sociopolitical front during the latter part of the 1950s. He'd been a schoolteacher who had turned to acting and, of late, to producing movies. Three of his recent films were *Magnificent Obsession*, about a haunted man remaking himself as a surgeon to heal the woman he blinded; *All That Heaven Allows,* concerning an older woman wooed by a younger man; and *My Man Godfrey,* a comedy showing the wisdom a butler imparts to a know-it-all family. Now Hunter thought it a ripe time to make a movie about race, something that would powerfully touch upon some of the current issues being played out in the country. He tracked down Fannie Hurst in Manhattan and took her to lunch. He told her he wanted to remake *Imitation of Life*. Hurst was flattered, but also well aware of the attacks the movie had received back in 1934. Hunter assured her that America had changed in the past twenty years. He promised Hurst he was going to make a much different movie from the original.

Finally, with Hurst's blessings, Hunter set about plotting a new version of *Imitation of Life*. He needed someone to update it and to make it palatable to a restless Black population, but also wanted to hold on to those fans who still admired Hurst's novel. Hunter had only one director in mind. Douglas Sirk listened to the pitch and was very intrigued.

He was born Hans Detlef Sierck in 1900 in Germany. In secondary school, he became interested in art and theatre. By his teens, he had convinced his family to allow him to study film. The early German films he made showed promise, and also a visual dexterity. He married a Jewish woman as the Nazi madness was beginning to take hold. He and his wife, Hilde, knew it was wise to flee, and so they escaped to Italy, and from there to America.

In Hollywood, Sierck—who arrived with a solid reputation from his

German films—felt it prudent to scrap his German-sounding name. He became Douglas Sirk. His earliest Hollywood films were silly comedies and melodramas that were soon forgotten. But it was clear he had style with the camera; he liked lushness twinned with drama. He made two films—*Lured*, in 1947, and *Sleep, My Love*, in 1948—which proved his cinematic mettle to American audiences. In 1954, he began his series of notable films: *Magnificent Obsession* followed a year later by *All That Heaven Allows*. Then, in 1958, came *The Tarnished Angels*. When Sirk's talent began to command respect, high-profile actresses—Barbara Stanwyck, Dorothy Malone, Jane Wyman, Barbara Rush—wanted to work with him. Sirk accepted Hunter's challenge to direct a new version of *Imitation of Life*.

Sirk realized the tricky terrain he was on. The director had told Hunter he had no intention of watching the original movie version, or even reading that production's script. He wanted to create a vivid and timely freshness for the project. He hired Eleanore Griffin and Allan Scott to write the new screenplay; Griffin was the better known of the two, having been co-winner of a screenwriting Oscar in 1938 for *Boys Town*. When Griffin and Scott delivered their finished script, it was dramatically different from the 1934 film. In the new version there is no pancake-waffle mix business leading to riches. Instead, there is an actress who becomes famous. Her live-in maid is more assertive and determined to do something about her daughter's feelings of shame about who she is. Casting soon got under way.

There were five major roles to be cast in the new film—two grown women, their respective daughters, and a male suitor. On April 4, 1958, at the same time Sirk was envisioning his movie, Hollywood was hit with a thunderbolt of a story. Cheryl Crane, the teenage daughter of the actress Lana Turner, stabbed to death her mother's boyfriend, Johnny Stompanato, as he was attacking Turner inside their Beverly Hills home. Crane, arrested, explained to authorities that she had heard violent arguing between Stompanato and her mother, grabbed a kitchen knife, and raced upstairs to her mother's side. She said that when she came upon them Stompanato was beating her mother and so, to save her mother, she plunged the knife into his midsection.

Anyone following casting news in Hollywood would have easily imagined that Lana Turner might be on Sirk's short list of actresses to play the role of Lora Meredith. But she now had serious family issues concerning the legal fate of her daughter. Turner herself was no stranger to heartache. She had been married and divorced several times. When she was but a nine-year-old in San Francisco, her father was robbed and murdered. Hollywood wondered if Turner would be able to recover from the new scandal. The recovery became more likely when her daughter was let off and the killing was ruled justifiable homicide. Sirk sent the actress the script. (At the time of the Stompanato murder, Turner didn't have another film role lined up. She had completed a British film, *Another Time, Another Place*; Stompanato had shown up on that movie set, believing her costar, Sean Connery, was having an affair with her. Stompanato pulled a gun on Connery, upon which Connery—the future James Bond—snatched the gun and slapped him around. Stompanato was thrown out of the country.)

When Douglas Sirk approached Turner for his remake of *Imitation of Life*, Turner quickly accepted. Her traditional movie fans—her white fans—were relieved she would soon be back at work. But another set of fans were also happy for Lana Turner. It was common knowledge in Black communities that Lana Turner had sympathetic feelings toward Black people. She had once had a romantic relationship with the boxer Joe Louis. Her intimate friendship with Black actor James Edwards was widely known. Her interracial relationships had caused Turner much suffering. Black women could identify with her plight.

In addition to Turner, Sirk's other cast members included Juanita Moore, Sandra Dee, Susan Kohner, and John Gavin.

Early in the filming of *Imitation of Life*, Sirk walked over to Moore, who was playing Annie, the maid. "If you're not good, the picture is not going to be any good," he told her. Moore allowed the comment to sink in. It made her both nervous and determined to do her best. "That was a heck of a weight to place on me," she would recall. Both Moore and Turner were quite aware of the shortcomings of the original movie. Turner took the role because she thought the updated script a vast improvement over the earlier film. Moore, though, while happy to be working, expressed misgivings about certain lines in the script. Hollywood screenwriters in general still felt beholden to stereotypical speech patterns for Black characters. When Moore complained about lines she thought demeaning, Sirk agreed with her and altered some of them. By the time filming was completed, anticipation for the new *Imitation of Life*—aided by Lana Turner and her daughter's headline-making drama—was quite high.

The new film had select openings on March 20, 1959. The opening song over the credits—tender and soft, a song about the folly of imitating and hiding one's self—sounded like the voice of Nat King Cole. But it was Earl Grant, doing a mighty fine imitation of Cole. Sirk's touch is immediately evident on the screen: what seem to be teardrops falling to the ground with Grant's opening song soon turns into diamond-shaped tears as they near the ground. The movie opens onto Coney Island, where the major characters are introduced: Lora (Lana Turner) is bustling among beachgoers looking for her daughter, Susie, who is lost. Susie is gently rescued by Annie (Juanita Moore) and her own daughter, Sarah Jane, who are whiling away an afternoon at the beach. The four are soon sitting together among other beachgoers. After small talk, it's revealed that Lora is an out-of-work actress; Annie is also out of work, and she and Sarah Jane are in need of a place to stay. Annie explains to Lora that Sarah Jane is having a hard time dealing with the limitations imposed on her because she is Black, a fact that surprises Lora, because she had assumed that the very light-skinned Sarah Jane was white and that Annie was her governess. It's an awkward moment that sets in motion the turmoil to come. Annie, hearing of Lora's own woes, offers herself up as maid to Lora and Susie. Lora is reluctant to accept because of her financial straits, but Annie's sincerity and charm win her over. Annie and her daughter are soon living with Lora and her daughter.

Days later, Annie visits the grade school Sarah Jane attends. She knocks on a classroom door—full of white students—and asks for her daughter. The teacher, responding to Annie's black skin color, and knowing she has no Black kids in her class, informs this parent she must certainly have the wrong classroom. The camera catches Sarah Jane slinking into her chair and hiding her face behind a book. The slowly building psychic pain of race that Sirk intended to expose happens—albeit thirty-two minutes into the movie. Sarah Jane, seeing the astonished looks on the faces of her classmates, who are suddenly aware she is the child of a Black woman—meaning she is Black!—flees the classroom. Her mother chases after her and comes upon her outside, where snow is falling. Annie wraps her arms around her anguished daughter. "Why do you have to be my mother? Why!?" Sarah Jane demands. Annie simply tries to comfort the child.

Back home, Annie explains to Lora what happened at the school. "Sarah Jane's been passing in school, pretending she's white." Sarah Jane blurts, "I am white! I'm as white as Susie."

The craftiness of "passing" was a wicked ruse that Black Americans knew of all too well. It often brought outright shame to the perpetrators from other Blacks if they were caught and exposed. Some of the most talked-about incidents happened in Harlem in the 1920s and 1930s. There were light-skinned women who left the world of Black Harlem to work downtown in Manhattan as secretaries, sure that jobs were easier to get if they concealed their racial identity. Philippa Schuyler was a child prodigy in Harlem. A gifted musician, she was often the subject of profiles in Harlem newspapers. But as she went out into the world, beyond Harlem, she was victimized by racism because of her Blackness. She grew angry and began passing herself off as Spanish or, at other times, Iberian. Blacks were much quicker to detect someone passing as white than whites were. In the 1930s, Walter White wanted to investigate lynching in the Southern states. His presence below the Mason-Dixon Line caused him no problems. White, however, was not white, but very light of skin. He actually lived in Harlem and was an NAACP official. He had "passed" for an acceptable cause—to expose evil: he sent his investigative reports on lynching to Congress. Sometimes those who "passed" did it for political purposes, to prove the wickedness of racism. But, more often than not, the practice was adopted out of shame; American racism had driven certain members of the Black race to run from their true lineage.

On-screen, when little Sarah Jane is asked what color Jesus is, she retorts, excitedly, "He was like me: white."

The years scroll by—1949, 1950, 1953, 1956, 1958—showing the passage of time. Lora becomes a successful actress. Now she has a beautiful and spacious home, a Black butler to work alongside Annie. She falls in love with Steve (John Gavin), a photographer. And yet the story, because of the weight and drama of race in America, can't stray from Annie and her daughter for very long. The racial backdrop becomes cinematically cosmic, something akin to the Southern "one-drop rule," which stated that if you possessed any African ancestry—even one Black forebear—you are considered Black. In movies, scenes of Black life gave a movie a jolt, a dose of reality—America was hardly an all-white landscape, despite the magazines and television commercials. Susie, Lora's daughter (Sandra Dee), has always imagined that Sarah Jane was happy being in this lovely house. They've grown up together! But there is a bold sexiness to Sarah Jane, a yearning, and now a sudden bluntness in her interactions with Susie. She confides that she is eager to get out into the world and escape the confines of living with her Black mother. Sarah Jane wants Susie to know she has aspirations about life and big dreams. "If I have to be colored, then I want to die. I wanna have a chance in life. I don't wanna have to come through back doors or feel lower than other people. Or apologize for my mother's color. She can't help her color, but I can. And I will." Susie is walloped by seeing who Sarah Jane really is. She is no longer Susie's "sister" behind these walls; she is a young lady trapped in a Black cocoonlike shell who will crack that damn shell open if it's the last thing she does. Susie listens, dumbfounded. Sarah Jane goes on, confiding to Susie that she has fallen in love and aims to get married, and her beau-to-be is white: "What do you think people will say if they knew my mother? They'd spit at me. And my children."

Much bolder and more aggressive than the original, the psychic drama of a human being imitating another life is now complete in Sirk's telling. If the director had been maligned for having made "women's pictures," he was shoving this one down the throats of the public. America was a scary and hypocritical place, and he had no intention of hiding that fact. The picture now only has one direction to go: deeper into the quagmire of race. The showdown comes on a darkened side street, when Sarah Jane tells her boyfriend, Frankie (played by Troy Donahue), that they should flee the town, but Frankie, cold and twitchy, with something obviously on his mind—has but one question for her. There's been gossip about Sarah Jane passing. He delivers his question menacingly enough to be an accusation as well: "Is your mother a nigger?" The word "nigger" is delivered like a knife plunged into soft flesh. He doesn't give her a chance to answer; instead, he beats her up and leaves her bloodied in a rainy splash of water in the alley, with trash cans noisily rolling about.

Back home that night, Sarah Jane is discovered bruised and crying on the steps. All three women in the house—Susie, Lora, and Annie—are at her side. Between sobs, Sarah Jane blames the beating on the discovery of her Blackness, crushingly implicating her mother in her destiny. If white audiences were paying particular attention to Lora and her acting journey in the film, Blacks were viewing the film with a completely different eye and understanding: this was American racism on trial on a sixty-foot movie screen. It was indeed a Lana Turner vehicle, but it was Annie and Sarah Jane's battle cry into a nation that harmed them in a variety of ways.

Eventually, Sarah Jane leaves home. Annie, pained about her daughter's absence, grows sickly, keeping the particulars of her illness to herself. Annie finally receives a letter in which Sarah Jane writes she is doing fine in her job at the public library in Manhattan. Yet, when Annie phones the library to speak with her daughter, she is informed that no one by the name of Sarah Jane Johnson works there. Annie retrieves the stationery Sarah Jane wrote to her on, and it says "Harry's Bar." Annie arrives in Manhattan and makes her way unannounced to Harry's Bar. Though she is a forlorn-looking Negro woman, just a maid, she is a powerful physical definition—no matter the color—of a mother's wide love for her child. Annie spots Sarah Jane singing a bawdy burlesque number on a stage and is appalled. After the song, she races to Sarah Jane and expresses her hurt about being lied to. The club host approaches and asks who the woman confronting her is. "I don't know," Sarah Jane snaps. "Never seen her before in my life." Minutes later, Sarah Jane tells her mother she'll be fired because she's now been exposed as being Black. She grabs a suitcase and rushes out of the club; Annie follows, telling her that she should come back to Connecticut, that she can go to the colored teachers' college there. "I wouldn't be found dead in a colored teachers' college," Sarah Jane hisses.

Back home in Connecticut—more time having now passed—Annie, walking slower, looking more sickly, receives another letter from Sarah Jane. In it, Sarah Jane tells her mother never to contact her again. Annie soon tells Lora she just has to see Sarah Jane one last time. A detective informs the family that Sarah Jane is working at the Moulin Rouge nightclub in Los Angeles. Ignoring her illness, Annie flies there and goes straight to the club. When she sees her mother, Sarah Jane's face becomes contorted with agitation. Face-to-face with her mother, she tells her she'll surely be fired again. "I'm somebody else. I'm white. White!" she thunders. Annie swallows every word in statuesque silence, as if taking in the bottomless hurt and pain for all of Black America. Annie tells her daughter she wants only one thing: If Sarah Jane should ever get in trouble or need anything, please to let her know. Sarah Jane begrudgingly promises to do so.

Death comes for Annie. The wailing gospel song "Trouble of the World" hums out over Annie's funeral, sung by the legendary Mahalia Jackson. Sirk's camera catches the forlorn faces of Annie's friends inside and then outside of the church. These are the Black people whom Annie's employer, Lora, never bothered to ask her about. Sarah Jane suddenly appears, stumbling into view, rushing to the horse-led carriage carrying Annie's casket away, crying, wailing, begging forgiveness in a loud voice—a heart-stopping coda. She's now a motherless child.

Sirk's new version of *Imitation of Life* caught Black America by welcome surprise. Never before had a film so starkly addressed racial hatred, and addressed it with a Black protagonist—even if Annie had to share the screen with Lana Turner's Lora Meredith. Sirk knew that a star of Turner's magnitude was needed to get moviegoers into the theatre, but he had foisted a Black mother's story onto white mainstream America. Black

Americans had been starved for the type of telling shown through Sirk's lens. In Harlem, at the Apollo Theater, the marquee screamed "IMITATION OF LIFE—STARRING JUANITA MOORE." "I thought Lana would have a fit if she saw that," Moore later said. Studios were in the habit of staggering first-run movies to Black communities; mainstream films would not reach Black neighborhoods until after they had opened everywhere else. But Universal—following advance showings in New York and Chicago—had such faith in the appeal of *Imitation of Life* that it opened the movie everywhere at the same time. The decision left Black communities with a feeling of pride and cultural ownership. *Variety,* the show-business bible, acknowledged in its review that the Black storyline now overwhelmed the film: "the secondary plot of a fair-skinned Negress passing as white becomes the film's primary force."

The movie, budgeted at two million dollars, became Universal's biggest hit of the year, with receipts exceeding thirteen million. It took a foreigner, Sirk, to tackle racism in America in such a bold—and commercial— manner on the big screen.

Sirk understood what many Blacks in America were trying to claim—an authentic stake in the nation's life. Before he married a Jewish woman, Sirk, unbeknownst to him, had fathered a child with a German woman back in Germany: he had fled the country before learning about the child. The woman who gave birth to the child was a Nazi. Her son possessed a creative gene—like his father—and became a Nazi child star in cinema. Sirk ventured to Germany to try to see his son, but the mother, knowing he had married a Jew, kept Sirk away from him. The only way Douglas Sirk was able to see his son was by sitting in a darkened theatre in Los Angeles and watching Nazi-made films.

Juanita Moore and Susan Kohner both received Academy Award nominations. But Moore's agent expressed little excitement, warning her that popularity and acclaim did not translate into more work for Black actors. It would be two long years before Juanita Moore found another big screen role, in the 1961 film *Tammy Tell Me True,* which starred the *Imitation of Life* stars Sandra Dee and John Gavin.

In the decades following its 1959 release, *Imitation of Life* would become the first interracial Hollywood film to take a place on movie poll lists as an important and groundbreaking film. It would also be the last Hollywood movie of Douglas Sirk's career. He soon returned to Europe. America had exhausted a filmmaker who hungered to deal in realism.

.    .    .

It is highly unlikely that Zora Neale Hurston—who had emerged out of the divine fires of the Harlem Renaissance, who had once been a maid, who found herself befriended by Fannie Hurst—had an opportunity to see *Imitation of Life* when it opened in the spring of 1959. She was living in Fort Pierce, Florida, and suffering from severe ulcers and gallbladder problems. Her weight had ballooned dangerously. Money woes bedeviled her to the point where she had to ask for handouts and food. A series of strokes sent her to the St. Lucie County Welfare Home. On January 28,1960, ten months after *Imitation of Life* opened in theatres, Zora Neale Hurston was rushed to a Fort Pierce Hospital where she was pronounced dead. She was buried in a segregated cemetery. It was difficult to find her gravesite, because for years there was no headstone—a lack of funds did not allow for one. The novelist Alice Walker finally placed a marker on her grave in 1973, by which time Zora Neale Hurston had been rediscovered. Her literary acclaim and reputation would come to far outrank Fannie Hurst's.

Zora Neale Hurston had long tired of white impressions and summations—cinematic or otherwise—of Black life. Years earlier, she wrote an essay, "You Don't Know Us Negroes," in which she chided white interpretations of Black life. She said it was hypocritical that those plays and movies and works of literature could claim to be honestly "holding a looking glass to the Negro," and went on to point out, "In fact the conflict between what [Negroes] wanted to do and what we were forced to do intensified our inner life instead of destroying it."

One must look back through the looking glass to see how America—and the origins of its cinema—had come to the point in 1959 where a suffering Black maid emerged as a hero to her people and forced a nation, across the color line, to watch and weep in darkened theatres, many of which were still segregated in the late 1950s. For, in practically all facets of entertainment—radio, television, the movie screen—the Black maid had fastened herself—in a potent way—onto the psychic landscape of cinema.

# · 4 ·

# A Most Peculiar Kind of Fame

S OUTHERNERS WERE ABLE TO JUSTIFY the fact they were holding tens of thousands of Blacks in slavery, referring to a "peculiar institution," imagining the odd phrase might lessen the bloody reality of slavery and how outsiders might look upon them. But, no matter what excuses plantation owners and politicians gave—economic vitality of the region; survival of the very people held in bondage; Biblical interpretations—the reasoning only sounded maddening to abolitionists.

Little wonder that those with creative yearnings began to find something in slavery that pulled at them. One such person was Harriet Beecher Stowe. Stowe's father, Lyman Beecher, was respected as a New England minister and abolitionist. His first wife died, but with a second wife there came to be twelve Stowe children. Harriet, born in 1811, grew up in Connecticut and studied at the Hartford Female Seminary, leaving the school with a voracious appetite for reading and literature.

When Harriet's father was appointed president of Lane Theological Seminary in 1832, Harriet followed him to Cincinnati. The city—an escape valve on the Underground Railroad—intrigued young Harriet. She met and heard the stories of runaway slaves—some had come from nearby Kentucky—and these stories overwhelmed her. She was aghast at such human suffering. When she got the opportunity, she traveled to Kentucky herself to get a look inside a slave state with her own eyes. The man she married, Calvin Stowe, made the decision along with her to start hiding runaway slaves in their Cincinnati home. Some of the men and women the couple met also told them about the infamous 1829 riots in Cincinnati, when Irishmen attacked Blacks. In the minds of the Irishmen, the barely free Blacks—desperate for any kind of paying work—would vie for their jobs. The uprisings forced many Blacks to abandon the city and flee farther north, to Canada. As she moved around Cincinnati, it was difficult for Harriet Beecher Stowe to listen to these gut-wrenching stories, but she could not turn away from them, either. These former slaves were eyewitnesses, not just figures from abolitionist journals and periodicals. She began taking notes, which she kept pressed inside drawers.

When Calvin Stowe got a teaching job at Bowdoin College in Maine, the Stowe family resettled there. While in Maine, the Stowes heard about passage of the 1850 Fugitive Slave Act. For Blacks, this was a lethal piece of legislation, giving slave catchers the right to enter states that had outlawed slavery and capture runaway slaves. Now, even in free states, full-blown terror was upon the Black man, woman, and child. The sounds of horse hooves proved frightening; "Wanted" posters were spotted on buildings. Not many months after the uproar began about the Fugitive Slave Act, Harriet Stowe suffered the loss of an infant child. That painful loss only deepened her disgust with slavery and the ripping apart of families.

Stowe was determined not to succumb to her pain. She wanted something to occupy her mind, and began sending in short fictional sketches to an abolitionist periodical known as *The National Era*. Her pieces were about Tom, an escaped slave, and all his small heroic acts in the face of white tyranny. She was writing and unspooling all the information she had gleaned from Cincinnati, from her trip to Kentucky, and from family members who were involved in abolitionist causes and shared stories with her. For much of 1851 and 1852, Stowe's intermittent narratives in *The National Era* drew extraordinary attention. Her editors, delighted with the fanfare, thought there might be a commercial angle. The idea of a book came up. And her pieces thus came to be published in book form in 1852. *Uncle Tom's Cabin* became a sensation. In the first week alone ten thousand copies were sold. At the end of its first year of publication, a total of three hundred thousand copies of the antislavery novel had been sold. Harriet Beecher Stowe became a literary phenomenon.

What Stowe had done was bring slavery out into the open—into the parlors, small homes, railway cars, and salons of American society. Polite white society simply could not avoid the brouhaha the book was causing. Though Frederick Douglass's memoir about his years in slavery had been published seven years before Stowe's book, and also drawn attention, it did not garner the kind of attention Stowe's novel did. Slavery had not had a literary touchstone written by a white woman. Now, suddenly, it did. Journals and publications that had paid scant attention to Douglass's book heaped fulsome attention upon Stowe's book. A novel was seen as softer than a hard-edged autobiography; a novel could be shared by an entire family; a novel could be seen as both real and imaginary. Stowe's novel—actually inspired by the life of Josiah Henson, a real slave—featured slave catchers and slaves. Its hero was a slave by the name of Tom, Uncle Tom, who was, against the fictional backdrop of the book, as colossal as Frederick Douglass had been in real life.

Northern reviewers saw a great talent at work in *Uncle Tom's Cabin*. Southern critics unleashed their vitriol. William Gilmore Simms weighed in from his perch at *The Southern Review*. "Mrs. Stowe betrays a malignity so remarkable," he wrote, "that the petticoat lifts of itself, and we see the hoof of the beast under the table." Stowe had given full flesh to her creations. Uncle Tom himself would rather die than divulge the whereabouts of two runaway slaves—and die he did, whipped to death by his slave master. The characters in Stowe's book were soon being seared into the mindset and imaginations of the reading public.

Here is Stowe describing the maid, Chloe:

> *A round, black, shining face is hers, so glossy as to suggest the idea that she might have been washed over with white of eggs, like one of her own tea rusks. Her whole plump countenance beams with satisfaction and contentment from under her well-starched checked turban, bearing on it, however, if we must confess it, a little of that tinge of self-consciousness which becomes the first cook of the neighborhood, as Aunt Chloe was universally held and acknowledged to be.*

The trick of the novelist was sometimes to set horror inside the commonplace—a cook, yes, but also a human being held in bondage. Stowe, continuing:

> *A cook she certainly was, in the very bone and center of her soul. Not a chicken or turkey or duck in the barnyard but looked grave when they saw her approaching, and seemed evidently to be reflecting on their latter end; and certain it was that she was always meditating on trussing, stuffing and roasting. . . . Her corn cake . . . was a sublime mystery to all less practised [sic] compounders; and she would shake her fat sides with honest pride and merriment, as she would narrate*

*the fruitless efforts that one and another of her compeers had made to attain to her elevation.*

Because of the seriousness with which large segments of the public accepted Stowe's novel—and her creation of its cast—her characters seemed to take on the dimensions of real human figures. In *Uncle Tom's Cabin,* Chloe resides as "Mammy," or maid, of the Shelby plantation. Inside the pages of the novel, Chloe was hardly a rebellious figure, but she had been created; she had been born; she was alive! She commanded the attention of readers. In the ensuing years, entertainments known as "Tom shows" began to appear across the country. These were new and wildly creative dramatic renditions of Stowe's novel. The vaudeville-like shows played mostly in antebellum territories, where they drew excited crowds. Tossing nuance to the wind, these Tom shows elevated the stereotyping of Stowe's characters and ludicrously softened the horrors of slavery. At one point, upward of five hundred troupes were traveling the country to perform these shows. White audiences bent over in uncontrollable laughter at the "Black" figures on stages, played by white actors and actresses in blackface makeup. Stowe herself was aghast that "Uncle Tom," in name, became something else: the very definition among Blacks of a kowtowing and weak figure in the face of white mockery.

When the technology was in place, silent filmmakers caught up with *Uncle Tom's Cabin.* Between the years 1903 and 1927, nine films were made of the novel. All of them portrayed Stowe's characters in stereotypical glory. The 1927 version featured Gertrude Howard in the maid role. She was as overweight—and dark of skin—as all the other maids who had been cast in film versions of Stowe's book. Charles Gilpin had been originally cast as Uncle Tom in that version, but the producers cast a wary eye at Gilpin during early filming. In their minds, he was playing the character of Uncle Tom with a little too much rebelliousness. He could not—or would not—tone the portrayal down, so they fired him. Gilpin was hardly a stranger to racial hurts. He had been seen on Broadway in 1921 portraying the title role in *Emperor Jones,* the Eugene O'Neill play that had been awarded the Pulitzer Prize. Some thought Gilpin the best Black actor in America. One day, out of costume, Gilpin sauntered up to the box-office window of the theatre where he was performing. He wished to buy a front-row ticket; perhaps it was for a friend or a family member. The ticket agent informed Gilpin that Blacks could not sit in the front row. In a manner of speaking, Gilpin could not have gotten to see himself. In 1929—two years after being fired from his role as Uncle Tom in *Uncle Tom's Cabin* for changing lines to avoid racial slurs—Gilpin suffered a nervous breakdown. Friends took note of his heavy drinking and disenchantment with his chosen profession. The gifted thespian died a year later.

What others did with Harriet Beecher Stowe's novel was much beyond her control. Even though the public embraced the novel, those who dramatized it in its various incarnations had created Mammy—a maid—lifting her not only from the novel itself but also from stereotype, folklore, lies, and exaggeration. In the minds of much of America, the Black Maid had no interior life; she was content and fairly happy. The fierce momentum of her mockery went on unabated, ignited by those endless traveling shows, yet more and more books, and the casual gossip of white Southern belles—Northern women as well—who offered utterances about either how efficient or inefficient their maids happened to be. Yet another cruel cultural appendage was looming for the Mammy-Maid from *Uncle Tom's Cabin:* she would, in time, have company, compliments of an American product soon to be seen in kitchens all over the country.

This new product sprang from the world of minstrel shows. In 1875, one of the more popular songs on the minstrel-show circuit was "Old Aunt Jemima," an ode to a fictional Black Mammy. A couple of Missouri men, Chris Rutt and Charles Underwood, came up with the idea of creating a pancake mix and naming it after "Aunt Jemima." The sketch of Aunt Jemima they devised showed a heavyset, dark-skinned woman wearing an apron and a kerchief bow-tied atop her head. But Rutt and Underwood were not savvy enough to make the business work and sold it a short time later to the R. T. Davis Milling Company, also located in Missouri. The executives at the Davis Milling Company had an idea in mind: they were going to hire a real-life "Aunt Jemima"! They found her in Chicago. Her name was Nancy Green, and she was a former slave. The opportunity to be part of a business excited her. When the Davis execs told Nancy Green they planned to set her up in a booth at the 1893 Chicago's World Fair to give cooking demonstrations about their Aunt Jemima product, she was excited. The gatherings around her booth grew into crowds. The word-of-mouth about the taste of the pancakes was fantastic. Nancy Green, aka Aunt Jemima, kept smiling, and smiling. Her appearance and Mammy renditions had been a boost for the product. Soon enough, boxes of Aunt Jemima pancake mix could be seen in kitchen pantries all throughout the country, a Black woman smiling from the cover of the box, while outfitted in a kitchen costume, which, to some, hewed too close to plantation dress. The narrative of suffering Black women in the South was now being challenged by advertisers. Aunt Jemima, in the minds of many advertisers, was the happy Black woman come to life! It was also being ingrained into the minds of America that Black women, especially southern Black women, were not only maestros in the kitchen, but also gifted at keeping a house orderly and keeping it running smoothly. On-screen, on the radio, or on the cover of a box of pancake mix, the Black woman could be seen as Aunt Jemima.

Southern politicians in Washington couldn't understand what all the intermittent fuss was about concerning Blacks and their civil rights. Their maids were happy and beloved! They were like family! Their maids were perpetually smiling—just like Aunt Jemima! The noise of discontent annoyed Southern politicians so much that, in 1923, they came up with an idea to do something about it. They would have a monument constructed showing how much they adored their Southern maids. It would rise in the nation's capital, and it would be gigantic. It would actually be near the Lincoln Memorial, which had been dedicated in 1922; a statue and man that Southerners had hardly made peace with yet. North Carolina Congressman Charles Stedman, a Confederate war veteran, led the fight for the maid monument. "They desired no change in their condition of life," Stedman proclaimed of former slaves and maids. "The very few who are left look back at those days as the happy golden hours of their lives." Stedman and his allies decided on a stone monument of a single Black woman holding a cooing white baby in her arms. Because most political committees in Washington were controlled by Southern Democrats—powerful men who were called barons—they easily got the authorization for funding. When the plan was announced, it was stated that the monument would be "in memory of the faithful slave mammies of the South." *The Washington Post* followed legislative doings quite closely in the capital, and soon printed a story explaining that the U.S. Senate had voted to approve the construction of three monuments. One was going to be in honor of America's favorite pastime, baseball. Another would be to celebrate a former D.C. commissioner. And, finally, there would be a monument erected for "faithful colored mammies."

The legislation became known as "the Mammy Monument Bill," and it had to get past the House of Representatives. By the time the bill reached the House, however, Blacks had risen up in protest against it. Vice-President Calvin Coolidge received a petition signed by two thousand Black women in protest of the monument. Negro newspapers printed editorials condemning the plan. The *Baltimore Afro-American* had an idea for the wording of such a monument. They imagined a Black lady sitting at a washtub, with this inscription: "In Grateful Memory to One We Never Paid a Cent of Wages During a Lifetime of Service." The protests never died down until the Mammy-Maid monument plan itself was allowed to die without action by Congress.

In February 2021, the Quaker Oats company finally deemed it was time to vanquish the Aunt Jemima brand name, citing its racial connotations. The name and logo are now referred to as the Pearl Milling Company.

———

Carrie Holbrook was a Black woman living in Atlanta. She worked as a maid—the "Mammy"—for a white couple. She was known to be graceful, courteous, and quite protective of the lady of the house, whose name was Margaret Mitchell, and who was working as a magazine writer. Carrie Holbrook, whose friends thought she had quite an enviable job, did everything she could to keep "Mrs. Mitchell" happy.

Margaret Mitchell, born November 8, 1900, was the quintessential Southern belle. She was the daughter of two attorneys. During her childhood, male relatives who had fought in the Civil War, who had been in the thick of battle, would take her into the countryside, regaling her with war stories. The stories she heard as a little girl were sometimes so fanciful she thought the South must have won the war. Like so many Southerners, she grew up classifying Yankees as villainous invaders. Generals Ulysses Grant and William Sherman—especially Sherman, who flattened her Atlanta!—might as well have been sent by the devil himself. Young Margaret acquired an interest in horseback riding. She galloped past old plantations where Negro field workers, some who had been born in slavery, waved their straw hats in her direction. Books and reading also took up a lot of her time. One of her favorite novelists was Thomas Dixon, of *The Clansman* and *Birth of a Nation* fame. In school, she had even adapted one of Dixon's novels into a play.

In 1918, Margaret Mitchell enrolled at Smith College in Northampton, Massachusetts. It was her first experience living in a Northern setting. In one of her classrooms was Otelia Cromwell, the first Black student admitted to Smith. Mitchell, raised like so many Southerners to believe in a separation of the races, was alarmed by Cromwell's appearance. She had imagined her environment would consist of all-white classrooms, as at most all colleges and universities throughout her beloved South. Because of Cromwell's appearance, Mitchell asked to be transferred to another class. Then, just a few months after her enrollment at Smith, Mitchell's mother died. After completing her first year, Mitchell returned to Atlanta and remained there with her brother and father, never completing her college education. As for Otelia Cromwell, she would become the first Black to graduate from Smith. She would go on to earn a doctorate from Yale and become a distinguished scholar.

While she was back home, eligible bachelors began to call upon Margaret Mitchell. She married Berrien Upshaw, but it was a tumultuous union. Upshaw drank and became an alcoholic; the couple soon divorced. Another man who had his eye on Mitchell, John Marsh, a utility executive, had actually been best man at the Mitchell-Upshaw wedding. Mitchell's friends watched her settle into her second marriage, and she appeared to be calm and happy. The couple led a well-appointed Southern lifestyle. They had a Negro maid to keep their lives running in an orderly fashion. They had money and well-connected friends. They sipped mint juleps on fine autumn afternoons.

Margaret Mitchell had been writing for *The Atlanta Journal*'s Sunday magazine. She enjoyed writing so much that she began envisioning and shaping her very own novel. It became one of her main goals in life, to write a meaningful novel with scope and breadth, something people would be feverishly compelled to read. The novel-in-progress was about what she knew best: the South, the agony of Reconstruction, and the women who battled to keep the South alive after defeat in the Civil War. She really began working on the novel in earnest in 1926. Her husband was supportive; so was Carrie, her maid. Mitchell was even patterning a character in the novel, "Mammy," after various Black women who had worked for her across the years, Carrie among them.

The Mitchell family—there were no children—loved entertaining. When Harold Latham, a New York editor and an old friend of John Marsh, found himself visiting the Mitchell household, the conversation turned to her writing. (It is nearly impossible not to imagine that Marsh hadn't encouraged the visit, even if Mitchell chroniclers have made the visit seem coincidental.) Mitchell did not show Latham her manuscript during that home visit, professing shyness and a lack of confidence in what she had written. But just as Latham was about to leave Atlanta, she showed up at his hotel. She had changed her mind and was now willing to let him take her novel. The editor spotted her in the lobby—"a tiny woman sitting on a divan, and beside her the biggest manuscript I have ever seen, towering in two stacks almost up to her shoulders."

Latham proceeded to haul Mitchell's manuscript—more than a thousand pages—around on his train treks through the South. The story in those pages transfixed him. It was a sweeping saga about the Civil War and its aftermath, all set around a Georgia cotton plantation christened Tara. It involved Reconstruction, economic survival, and those damn sneaky, cruel Yankees. The characters—Scarlett O'Hara, Rhett Butler, Ashley Wilkes—all revolved around Scarlett's dreams and desires. There are also slaves—Prissy, Uncle Peter, Pork, nameless little children scampering about the plantation and derisively called "little pickaninnies" whenever they are called anything at all. But the one slave who stands out, who is closest to Scarlett, is "Mammy," her maid, ruler of the O'Hara household in the realm of cleaning and cooking. Of all the slaves, Mammy is truest to Scarlett, standing by her even as wreckage mounts up around them all. Not that wreckage hasn't been upon Mammy the whole of her slave life.

Scarlett O'Hara exhibits her indomitable will throughout the novel. The Yankees may have won the war, but she will not let them defeat her life's ambitions—to marry well and hold on to her grand plantation. When Harold Latham finished reading Mitchell's manuscript, he was so taken with it that he contacted Macmillan, his publishing house, and told them they must publish the novel. He confessed he had rarely been so excited about a book.

It was in the summer of 1936 when *Gone with the Wind* arrived in bookstores across America. Critics wasted no time in heaping praise upon the book. The sales were staggering. It didn't much matter that the nation was still in the aftermath of the Great Depression; customers were elbowing their way to the front of lines and forking over three bucks for Mitchell's book. By the end of the year, a whopping million copies of the novel had been sold. There were prestigious awards the following year: the Pulitzer Prize and the National Book Award.

What seemed to slip by America in the novel—by white America—was Mitchell's treatment of Black characters. They were referred to as "niggers," "black apes," and "pickaninnies" with a kind of relish and brio that echoed the work of Thomas Dixon's *The Clansman*. There were certainly utterances in the Negro press about the treatment of Blacks in the novel, but the commercial success of the book drowned out such criticism. In any event, the Negro press was all but ignored by mainstream society;

notable Black publications such as *The Chicago Defender, The Pittsburgh Courier,* and the *Los Angeles Sentinel* hardly landed on the front porches of white society. The lavish attention paid to Mitchell's novel guaranteed Hollywood's interest.

The early 1930s were good years for the film producer David O. Selznick. He had been in Hollywood since 1926, working on the production side of movies. In 1930, he married Irene Mayer, whose father was Louis B. Mayer—of Metro-Goldwyn-Mayer, known as MGM. Mayer was one of the most powerful men in Hollywood, dictating the direction of so many careers. As a producer, David Selznick was admired for his ability to spot and nurture talent, such as the director George Cukor and the actress Katharine Hepburn. By 1935, Selznick was overseeing Selznick International Pictures, an independent outfit, just in time to greet the publication of *Gone with the Wind.* The chess moves to land the cast for the major roles in *Gone with the Wind* were fierce. Topping everyone's curiosity was the question of the actor and actress who'd be chosen to play Rhett Butler and Scarlett O'Hara. Clark Gable quickly rose to the top of the list. Known reverently as "the King" in Hollywood, he had recently won an Oscar for *It Happened One Night.* Unfortunately, he was under contract to Louis B. Mayer. So Selznick simply set about brokering a deal with his father-in-law: he would grant Mayer the rights to distribute *Wind* if Mayer would allow Gable to play Rhett Butler. The sides struck an agreeable deal. Then the search began to find their Scarlett O'Hara. Many actresses coveted the role, and Paulette Goddard, Carole Lombard, and Bette Davis were in contention. But months stretched on without a decision: Selznick couldn't make up his mind. He was even bold enough to commence filming, on December 10, 1938, still without his Scarlett. The first scenes filmed were of the burning of Atlanta, and they took place on a Culver City studio back lot. The actresses who were in the filming sequence were told to hide their faces, since the real Scarlett hadn't been chosen yet. During the filming that night, the British actress Vivien Leigh visited the set. It was quite intentional; she badly wanted the role. She had become privy to the filming site because she was carrying on an affair with Laurence Olivier, and Olivier's agent was Myron Selznick, David's brother. When Leigh arrived, Selznick yelled over to his brother that surely he could see his Scarlett O'Hara standing right there, against the rising flames! Leigh got the role, though not without reading for Selznick some of the lines that Scarlett O'Hara would have to utter.

In the minds of Black America, the role that mattered, however, was that of Mammy, the maid in Margaret Mitchell's novel. Throughout Black communities, news of the actress to be chosen to play Mammy—her only given name in the novel—was being followed quite closely.

————

There was nothing fictional about the cruel and heartbreaking life of Henry McDaniel. He was born around 1838 into slavery on a Virginia plantation. Nine years later, along with his brother and sister, he was sold to a Tennessee slave owner. When news came in 1863 of the Emancipation Proclamation, McDaniel fled from his owners, running through woods and across dirt roads before landing in a so-called contraband camp in Tennessee, a place where once-enslaved Blacks could feel freedom for the first time surrounded by Union soldiers. McDaniel was eager to join Lincoln's Union Army and did so. Outfitted in Union blue and carrying an army rifle, he was now positioned to do battle with the very forces that had kept him in bondage. All Negro Union soldiers were quite aware of the penalty they would face if captured by Confederate forces: death. White captives would be taken to prison camps. Things, however, soon turned grim for McDaniel. He and his brother, Adam, were jailed by the Union military for unspecified disciplinary reasons. Eventually, they were both returned to active duty.

Henry McDaniel fought as bravely as other Union troops at the Battle of Nashville, but he emerged from it with nasty wounds: a busted jaw, ringing in his ears as an aftereffect of cannon fire. A short while later, traveling with fellow troops, he suffered frostbite on both of his legs and was hospitalized. After the war, McDaniel settled in Tennessee, where he barely eked out a living as a farm laborer. Klansmen, many of whom had fought for the Confederacy, terrorized the land, threatening free Blacks. McDaniel lived in constant worry. His wife, Louise, died in 1875. He married his second wife, Susan Staton, that same year. The family was soon on the move, first to Kansas. Henry McDaniel could not find steady work; his lingering war wounds limited his physical abilities. He filed a disability claim with the army, and it got turned down. He filed another one, and it got turned down, too, so he filed another one, and for a third time it was turned down—a common fate for Black soldiers. The family, despite their poverty, continued to grow. Etta McDaniel was born December 1, 1890. On June 10, 1893, Hattie McDaniel came into the world.

By the time of little Hattie's fifth birthday, the family had relocated to

Denver, Colorado. Susan McDaniel would give birth to thirteen children, only to see seven survive. Susan and her two sisters found work as maids. Henry McDaniel set about renewing his battle with the United States government for medical disability payments. Against all odds, he finally got it in 1902, eighteen years after his first request. The amount granted him was six dollars a month. Hattie McDaniel saw up close what America had done to her war-haunted father. She was determined not to be poor.

As Hattie began to grow up, her mother, Susan, sometimes took her to the white homes where she worked as a maid. Young Hattie started helping her mother—a kind of maid-in-training—and learned the ways and customs of white folks. But at least two of the sons of Susan McDaniel, Sam and Otis, harbored different ambitions in life from doing service work for white families. They heard the call of entertainment.

Sam McDaniel—outgoing, musical, gifted—began to get work with a circus band. His brother Otis made a mark as a local Denver comedian. Both young men, their popularity rising, caught on with the All-Star Minstrels, an all-Black troupe that had started getting fine notices in the Colorado press. All of the noise and attention around the McDaniel men rubbed off on Hattie. She began showcasing her own skills, in neighborhood homes, during school events. "I knew that I could sing and dance," she said. "I was doing it so much that my mother would give me a nickel sometimes to stop." By 1908, Hattie and her brothers were performing together with J. M. Johnson's Mighty Minstrels. Being out on the road only enlarged their scope. Otis McDaniel liked it so much that the experience furthered his ambitions. He soon formed his own stock company, and began bouncing around the Midwest. His sister Hattie's confidence was growing, and she started doing some solo engagements. When she was seventeen, she married a local pianist by the name of Howard Hickman. He supported her when she formed an all-female minstrel troupe. A review appeared in the May 1914 edition of *The Denver Star*, which singled out Hattie McDaniel:

> *Imagine a person with cactus hair, each hair sticking out independently to itself, fix in your mind a disfigured, clumsy, blackened, 200 pound woman whose color was a deeper black than ten midnights without a sun, then observe a misfit dress whose colors were those of the rainbow with the tango bloomers made of white sheetings which effect completely harmonized with her big, awkward feet filled with corns. When she batted her eyes it looked as if two white marbles were*

*placed in a bucket of soot and when she opened her mouth, it looked
like a bottomless pit.*

This was certainly a racially obtuse and mocking piece of commentary, but in Colorado at the time it was what passed as a positive review.
What Hattie McDaniel heard from the stage during performances of her
minstrel revue happened to be laughter, and it was laughter roaring from
the mouths of both Blacks and whites! And Hattie McDaniel wanted to
make people laugh. She wanted to entertain. The racial slurs were often
mixed with inklings of praise, but she didn't dare complain. Rather,
McDaniel dropped herself into the rabbit hole of portraying a signature
early-twentieth-century figure: Mammy. And she was going to keep on
letting Mammy put food on the table and feed and clothe her.

When Hattie McDaniel's husband died from complications associated
with pneumonia, she became depressed. At the tender age of twenty-one,
the rising comedienne had become a widow. For a while, she returned
to maid work. This quickly reminded her of the hard life she had tried
to leave behind, and it ignited another effort to restart her performing
career. She got back into the entertainment world by hustling up some
singing gigs in Denver jazz joints. Customers also wanted her to sing the
blues, and she found that easy enough to do. By the mid-1920s, she found
herself out on the vaudeville circuit in a duet act alongside George Morrison. That union coincided with a decision made by a group of white
theatre owners to form the Theatre Owners and Booking Association
(TOBA). The group was determined to buy up Negro theatres and keep
booking Black acts. If actors in general could be a complaining bunch,
Black actors—facing far more challenges—were soon wondering who
was benefiting from TOBA—them or the white owners. The white owners wanted the Black talent to feel that they now had more organization
and business savvy behind them. The truth proved more slippery in the
minds of both Black talent and the former Black theatre owners. The former owners began to realize that Negro independence—in the form of
ownership of theatres—was fading fast, even if they had been willing sell-
ers. In time, the Black entertainers began gossiping that TOBA might as
well stand for Tough on Black Asses. *Billboard* magazine decided to hire a
Black writer and dispatch him to cover TOBA and Negro vaudeville. J. A.
Jackson was happy to get the job, even if some ridiculed his position as

working the "Jim Crow beat." The *New York Amsterdam News* published a column defending Jackson:

> *We greet you brother Jackson of the Billboard and want to assure you that the position you occupy will occasion envy and malice in the hearts of the nincompoops as ninety-nine out of a hundred colored writers would welcome the opportunity to do "Jim Crow" work on any big white publication.*

Hattie McDaniel was happy to be working the Negro vaudeville circuit, joining other TOBA acts, including Ethel Waters, Bill "Bojangles" Robinson, and the Will Mastin Trio, which featured the young and precocious Sammy Davis, Jr. "Hattie McDaniel, blues singer, and Maxie of the team Maxie and Sumter were enthusiastically received," *The Chicago Defender* wrote in its April 23, 1927, edition. That review came before McDaniel had been forced to return to maid work for yet another spell, this time right there in Chicago. But she was happy that the "real" maid work—as opposed to her stage maid roles and impersonations—was only intermittent now. Still, it was frightening to her how unpredictable the singing work could be. She would be riding high one month, then diving downward the next. On one downward spell, she found herself working as a restroom attendant at Sam Pick's Suburban Inn, just outside Chicago. One night, the band found themselves without a singer. Hattie left the restroom area and offered up her singing talents. The crowd was wowed; the owner hired her on the spot, and she had a job there for the next two years. "I never had to go back to my maid's job," she said proudly.

There were few jobs in America for Black women with McDaniel's limited education. She had never trained for a job as a secretary, or any other job in a white-collar setting. She had made her choice in life, and it was going to be entertaining. Her physical looks—she tended to be overweight and was quite dark of skin—were traits that were rarely remarked upon favorably. Even Negro publications, espousing ideas of beauty, more often than not showcased their idea of beautiful Black women with pictures of light-skinned women with slim bodies. McDaniel took any perceived slights about her homey looks—and figure—in stride. And she boldly decided that the place for someone to go who possessed her kind of confidence and particular skills was Hollywood. In 1931, Hattie McDaniel, encouraged by her part-time actor brother, Sam, set out for Los Angeles by car.

If a Negro wanted a job in Hollywood at the time, it was necessary to present him- or herself to Charles Butler, who worked for Central Casting, a major talent agency that supplied Hollywood studios with actors and actresses. Butler, a Black man, had acquainted himself with Black churches and social clubs in the Los Angeles area—places he scanned for talent. The work he got for those actors was mostly "extra work," standing in crowd scenes in the rare movies where Black faces were actually seen. Butler was a slippery figure, and some Blacks suspected him of taking small bribes—charges at which he scoffed. Shortly after reaching Hollywood, Hattie McDaniel supplied Butler with enough evidence of her past work onstage, and he quickly signed her up.

Work for McDaniel came fairly quickly. They were tiny parts, but she was seen in *The Golden West* in 1932; in *Blonde Venus* in 1932, alongside fellow Black actress Evelyn Preer (the Oscar Micheaux discovery); in *I'm No Angel* in 1933; in the funeral scene in 1934's *Imitation of Life*. She was happy to get any work. The small roles kept coming. The pay for the extra work was $7.50 a day. If she could get a week's worth of steady work, it amounted to more than she could make in a month doing maid work, a fact she often bragged about to close friends. Those extra scenes, however, did not get her name in the end-of-picture credits. She got her first on-screen credit in *Judge Priest,* a 1934 picture directed by John Ford that starred Will Rogers. "There is a colored woman, Hattie McDaniel, who sings Negro spirituals as I have seldom heard them sung," the entertainment columnist Louella Parsons wrote of McDaniel's small role in the movie. "Rogers himself joins in with her and you'll love it." In 1937 alone, McDaniel appeared in fourteen films, all small and insubstantial roles, but it was work; she had become visible to segments of the acting community. And Charles Butler was quite happy she was being put on producers' radar. McDaniel was filming *Nothing Sacred* in 1938 when word really began heating up about *Gone with the Wind* and its looming shooting schedule. Butler began to plot to get McDaniel in front of Selznick and his team for an audition. Selznick already knew of McDaniel because she had played a small role (wife of a shoeshine man) in *Nothing Sacred,* which was a Selznick International production. Butler was keen enough to realize that Hollywood did not want to cast gorgeous Black women as maids, because, once they were on-screen, their beautiful looks could well detract from the as-yet-uncast white actress who would be playing the leading role.

At the time of the casting search for the role of Mammy, there actually was a young, beautiful actress rising on the East Coast. Her name was Lena Horne. She had just been cast in *Blackbirds of 1939*. Lew Leslie, the Broadway producer, was quite keen on her potential. He was also far more progressive than anyone in Hollywood. "In my opinion," Leslie said, "Lena Horne comes closest to the talented Florence Mills of any Ethiopian actress I have ever seen. She can sing, dance and read lines with great comic spirit. In addition to all of this, she has youth and beauty." Although it is true that Horne would very likely have outright rejected a role such as Mammy—she came from quite an enlightened and progressive Brooklyn family—the fact that no actresses with her type of beauty were even being approached for Mammy showed the mindset of Hollywood producers. (Horne was not Ethiopian; Leslie's comment seemed but an attempt to add exotica to her background, as if the misdirection might shield her actual American Blackness.)

Charles Butler had long been zeroing in on plump and dark-skinned actresses to dispatch on auditions for maid roles. Imagining what Selznick might be looking for as he cast Mammy, Butler sent Hattie McDaniel to an audition. McDaniel decided she would leave nothing to chance. She dressed up inside her home in a maid's Mammy outfit: apron, head scarf, wide dress. She looked downright frumpy, which was her intention. There were, of course, other actresses vying for the role. Georgette Harvey, who had performed overseas and played Maria in the original 1935 Broadway production of *Porgy and Bess,* auditioned for the role. Black actresses from the era of silent films implored Butler and Central Casting to get them an audition. The veteran actress Louise Beavers wanted the part. One woman wanted to play the role of Mammy so badly that she tracked Margaret Mitchell down in Atlanta. Mitchell was alarmed: the woman was white, and insisted she could play the role in blackface. But the screen test with Vivien Leigh and McDaniel went well, and at the beginning of 1939, Hattie McDaniel got the break she had long been praying for. She was chosen to play Mammy.

The cast of *Gone with the Wind* was set, with Clark Gable, Vivien Leigh, Olivia de Havilland, Leslie Howard, and, as Mammy, Hattie McDaniel.

John Ford was hired, then fired. So was George Cukor. Zanuck could be a mercurial sort. Victor Fleming then got the job to direct. He had filmed a movie—not yet released—called *The Wizard of Oz*, and Zanuck believed in him. Sidney Howard (no relation to Leslie) wrote the screenplay, though, as was often the custom of the times; other writers worked on it as well. Sidney Howard had been awarded a Pulitzer Prize in 1925 for his Broadway play *They Knew What They Wanted*, and had been a two-time Academy Award nominee for Best Screenplay. Howard was so admired that he made the cover of *Time* magazine on June 7, 1937. As attuned to American history as he professed to be—proclaiming to a critic of *Wind* that he had read W. E. B. Du Bois's work—Howard considered himself wise enough to tackle the racial dynamics of Mitchell's novel. The studio hired an expert on the history of the Confederacy. Selznick also had pondered hiring a Black scholar to gauge the script's portrayal of Black life, but then he abandoned the idea, satisfied enough that he had given Black actors work in the film.

Marcella Rabwin, Selznick's secretary, finally explained to another Selznick staffer that there would be no Negro consultant on the film because such a person "would probably want to remove what comedy we have built around" the Black characters. The portrait of Black life—Black slave life—in *Gone with the Wind* would, then, be left to Hattie McDaniel, given the largest Black role in the movie. And in McDaniel's mind, if David Selznick was hiring her to portray a Mammy—in what would likely be the most discussed motion picture of the year—then she intended to give him the best damn Mammy she could conjure, with the eye rolls and the broad stereotypical movements and tics she had been perfecting all these years.

Having adopted an activist posture with *The Birth of a Nation*, Negroes in America began arching their eyebrows in anticipation of the forthcoming *Gone with the Wind*. They wondered: Would the racial slurs from the novel appear in the film? Would Hattie McDaniel deepen the image of the stereotypical Black maids she had been playing with so much relish that it made many queasy? Selznick sent his vaunted publicity machine into action. He had emissaries talk to church groups and Black social organizations to calm them down. He let McDaniel know that this was her big break and she needed to help allay concerns, so she talked positively about the movie every chance she got. "I visualized myself as loving Miss Ellen, worrying over the willful Scarlett, respecting Gerald O'Hara, pinching and scolding the irrepressible Prissy," is how she put it, referring to key characters in the movie. At the filming's completion, Selznick and Fleming felt they had done quite well by Mitchell's novel.

Southern sentiments toward Hattie McDaniel would soon enough collide with her magnanimous attitude toward all things associated with *Gone with the Wind.* Word reached her that her presence would not be welcomed at the film's world premiere in Atlanta. Selznick and Clark Gable both disapproved of the wicked racial slight, but neither man could make Atlanta organizers change their minds. Nor did McDaniel's photograph appear in the special souvenir booklet printed for the Atlanta festivities. Hollywood—just as it had done twenty-five years earlier with *The Birth of a Nation*—was once again aligning itself with Southern disrespect toward Black life and offering a cinematic homage, against the backdrop of the Civil War, to white nationalism. McDaniel continued to follow Selznick's dictum and remained mum.

Two days' worth of events in Margaret Mitchell's hometown of Atlanta took place to honor the film. The night before the premiere, a Gone With the Wind Ball was staged at Atlanta's City Auditorium. Its master of ceremonies sought to fill the crowd with pride: "Tonight we want to give you a glimpse into the past—and visit an old plantation on a warm, fragrant June evening. Can you smell the wisteria? Can't you hear those darkies singing? They're coming up to the Big House." There was indeed a Black presence inside the City Auditorium, in the form of the resident choir from Atlanta's Ebenezer Baptist Church. The church's minister, Rev. Martin Luther King, Sr., was on hand; his wife led the choir as they sang spirituals for the lily-white gathering. Some of the choir members were outfitted in bandanas to resemble Aunt Jemima figures. (Little Michael King would be among the choir members; the world would come to know him as Martin Luther King, Jr.) The elder Rev. King was later berated for allowing the choir to participate in the segregated event.

Hattie McDaniel did attend the Hollywood premiere of *Gone with the Wind* on December 28, 1939. She smiled for the cameras, shielding any residue of hurt about the Atlanta festivities.

And the reviews of the film itself? They were full of praise from critics around the country. *The New York Times* and the *Los Angeles Times* wrote rave reviews. "It is the ultimate realization of the dreams of what might be done in every phase of film wizardry," is how *The Hollywood Reporter* felt about the movie. The important entertainment periodical *Variety* opined that the movie was "one of the screen's major achievements, meriting highest respect and plaudits." There were effusive predictions of Academy Award nominations. No movie had possessed a charged racial element like this since, well, *The Birth of a Nation.*

There was disenchantment, however, brewing beneath *Gone with the Wind* when it came to the Black populace. Hattie McDaniel—most agreed she played the role of Mammy to the hilt, but that was a dubious honor—had now taken a vaunted position in extending a stereotypical and painful image of Blacks on-screen. Like the comedians Stepin Fetchit and Amos 'n' Andy—famous for rolling their eyes and using mispronounced verbiage while playing comical foils to white performers—she had unwittingly deepened the hole that Black performers were already in.

It was a dinner affair at the Waldorf-Astoria where Walter White, the NAACP official, first met Wendell Willkie. Willkie, the progressive Republican defeated by President Roosevelt in the 1940 election, had plenty of contacts in the film industry, deepened by his career in politics and business. He knew of White's civil-rights work, and soon the two men formed a friendship. White was eager to discuss the motion-picture industry with Willkie. A lunch was arranged. "I pointed out," White recalled, "that the most widely circulated medium yet devised to reach the minds and emotions of people all over America and the world was perpetuating and spreading dangerous and harmful stereotypes of the Negro." White's concerns touched a nerve in Willkie. "Let's go out to Hollywood and talk with the more intelligent people in the industry to see what can be done to change this situation," he told White.

Willkie and White soon found themselves together in Los Angeles, sitting in the company of major Hollywood moguls and executives, telling them about the harmful effects of stereotyping Blacks in movies. The studio power brokers listened, smiling and nodding and showing concern. But then, yet again, they weaseled out of offering any concrete changes by blaming their positions on the men who ran the powerful boards of censorship throughout the Southern states. They were told that those men were resistant to change in movies, particularly when it came to Black-white interactions. The censorship boards generally took exception to overtly sexual displays and nudity. But Southern boards added race to the mix, threatening to yank films that they thought presented Negroes in any roles in which they were not accustomed to seeing them. At the meeting's end, the moguls escorted White and Willkie over to the swanky Biltmore Bowl dining room. But the two men decided that they were not finished with Hollywood. They came back in 1942, when White invited

Willkie to an annual NAACP gathering in Los Angeles. While in the city, the two men were also guests at a luncheon cohosted by Darryl Zanuck. Willkie was invited to address the luncheon. According to White:

> He reminded the audience that on his recent world tour he had found growing resentment, not only against the motion picture industry but against America itself, because American films almost invariably caricatured people with dark skins. . . . And then he bluntly pointed out that many of the persons responsible for Hollywood films belonged to a racial and religious group which had been the target of Hitler, and that they should be the last to be guilty of doing to another minority the things which had been done to them.

White, as the weeks began to pass, sensed that Willkie had made some inroads. Furtive discussions began to take place about improving the lot of Blacks in motion pictures. But Hollywood had always been resistant to change. And two years later, in 1944, the sudden death of Wendell Willkie from a heart attack seemed to bring all the racial dialogue in Hollywood to a halt. Willkie had not only been associated with Hollywood, but had served as White's entrée to the executive suites. Now White's point man was gone, and he grew leery of any possible forward motion. "But I am equally certain that the stereotypes about the Negro are so indelibly fixed in their minds," White said of producers in the aftermath of Willkie's death, "as well as a lot of other American white people that it is going to take a long time to eradicate them."

Margaret Mitchell realized that Blacks were never going to join in the acclaim heaped upon *Gone with the Wind,* but their resistance didn't seem to bother her in the least. She believed in segregation and could not envision the races coexisting on an equal footing. Her Atlanta remained devoutly segregated. (The local baseball team was the Atlanta Crackers, and Blacks were not allowed into the stadium to watch them play.)

The city's educated Blacks were trying valiantly to make inroads against the social order. Benjamin Mays, the esteemed president of Atlanta's all-Black and financially struggling Morehouse College, decided to ask Mitchell, one of the city's most celebrated citizens, for a donation to the school. Mitchell rebuffed him, and more than once following other pleas. But on June 29, 1942, President Mays received a surprising letter, accompanied by an eighty-dollar check, from Margaret Mitchell. "I am sorry that I cannot promise to make this an annual contribution," Mitchell told Mays, and also told him to keep the donation private. She did not want Atlanta's whites to know she had contributed to the Black school.

In the spring of 1946, Carrie Holbrook, Mitchell's longtime faithful maid, died of cancer. The loss stung Mitchell, who had run around Atlanta trying to find a hospital that would accept Holbrook during her final days. The Atlanta Urban League estimated at the time that there was only one Black doctor for every three thousand Blacks in Atlanta. Finally, Mitchell persuaded the Sisters of Our Lady of Perpetual Help hospital to take Holbrook in—and that was only after she donated money. Holbrook died just three days after being admitted. Mitchell genuinely grieved, telling her husband she was appalled at witnessing Holbrook's treatment, and the lack of good medical care available to her maid, all because of her race. On April 17, 1946, Mitchell wrote a letter to the chairman of the Board of Trustees of the Fulton-DeKalb Hospital Authority:

> Recently our colored laundress died of cancer. . . . I do not want ever again to go through the agonizing experience I had. . . . There just were no beds. . . . I do not think people who have not experienced so heartbreaking a time can realize the need for more beds for our colored population. . . . Atlanta is big enough now to have colored people in the white-collar class, and I wonder how many of them have been in the situation of our Carrie, willing to pay but being unable to buy a bed in which to die.

The Mitchell correspondence laid bare twin realities: Like most of the whites of Atlanta, Margaret Mitchell lived in her own world, removed from the anguish and horrible indignities constantly heaped upon Black people. But also, unlike most whites, she had an awakening, and sought to do something about it. Six months after her letter to the board chairman, President Benjamin Mays of Morehouse received another letter from Margaret Mitchell. This letter included a two-thousand-dollar check, which she wanted to go toward the training of a medical or dental student at the Morehouse School of Medicine—one of only a few Black medical schools in the nation. She also stated she was sending the money in the name of her deceased maid, Carrie Holbrook.

————

Of all the things the movie *Gone with the Wind* was about—romance, plantation life, deception—it most certainly was not about the deep horrors of slavery. And Hollywood moguls remained afraid of Southern censor boards, and thus of portraying Black life through an honest and nonstereotypical lens.

But seven years after *Wind,* another novel began making the rounds of Hollywood, giving studio executives a chance to proclaim their interest in a story that came with a racial angle. The novel, *Quality,* written by Cid Ricketts Sumner—like Mitchell, a white Southern woman—landed in bookstores in 1946. It revolved around the issue of "passing." In the novel, Patricia "Pinky" Johnson, the protagonist—who is very light of skin—has been living a life of comfort in the North and passing herself off as white. She had trained as a nurse. When Pinky returns to her Southern hometown, she admits her deception to Dicey, her Black grandmother, still working as a maid and washwoman. Pinky's Northern beau tracks her down in the run-down Southern town and tells her he wants to marry her. Pinky confesses the secret of her racial lineage. He still wants to marry her, but she is compelled to stay in the town to pay a debt to an elderly white woman who had bestowed kindnesses upon Dicey while Pinky had been away. Later, Pinky withstands an attempted rape by two white men, and news slowly seeps out that she is really a Negro. In this melodramatic stew, Darryl Zanuck, the Twentieth Century–Fox producer, saw film possibilities and acquired the rights.

Many Black actresses badly wanted to play the role of Pinky, among them Lena Horne, Dorothy Dandridge, and Fredi Washington. Horne and Washington, more than Dandridge, possessed the skin hue to play the film's titular role properly. Teddy Horne, Lena's father, was a slick man-about-America, a bon vivant who was proud of his daughter's budding career. Horne had gotten himself a meeting with the MGM studio chief Louis B. Mayer and proceeded to tell him of his disillusionment with Hollywood and the roles offered to Negroes. "The only Negroes I ever see are menials, or Tarzan extras," Horne told Mayer. "I don't see what the movies have to offer my daughter. I can hire a maid for her; why should she act one?"

Throughout the Black community, early speculation about the main role in *Pinky* began to focus on Fredi Washington. The reasoning went that Hollywood knew her, and she had a following—especially among Blacks. But Zanuck, and John Ford, who had been hired to direct, deemed they did not want a Black actress to play a Black woman who had been passing as a white woman. Instead, they chose Jeanne Crain, a white woman who would be playing a Black woman who had been passing as a white woman. Crain was known more for her beauty than for her dramatic talents. To Black America, the studio's casting a white woman to play a Black woman was illogical and insulting. Their complaints, however, drew no concern inside the offices of the producers. Others cast in the film were Ethel Barrymore, William Lundigan, and, as the grandmother and maid, Ethel Waters.

Darryl Zanuck did not like the way the early filming of *Pinky* was going, so he fired Ford. Rumors from the set were that Ford was spending too much time sitting around listening to Ethel Waters sing when she wasn't in front of the cameras. Zanuck hired Elia Kazan. Kazan had the right pedigree for a movie that would lean into race and ethnicity: he'd just won an Oscar for directing *Gentleman's Agreement,* starring Gregory Peck, a film about a writer pretending to be Jewish and becoming astonished by the anti-Semitism in his midst. Upon its release, *Pinky* presented Blacks with the awkwardness of watching and listening to a white actress on-screen portraying a Black person talking about the daily indignities they themselves were suffering in real life. And, despite the generally positive reviews, the movie showed a clumsiness in its execution. It all but snatched the blood and drama out of the story of race and miscegenation in America. Kazan would later bemoan Crain's inability to climb inside the mind of such a tortured character. The racial scenes in the movie only skirted the real racial horrors in the nation at the time; it was as if the filmmakers were either ashamed of American racism, or so mindful of Southern censors that they would only go so far in their portrait of a Southern town and bigotry. In the end, Pinky is told by Miss Em, the sickly white woman whom her grandmother had been caring for, that she must be true to herself and live as Black or white. When Miss Em dies, leaving her house and land to Pinky, bigoted legal forces in town charge that Pinky must have drugged the ailing lady—why else would she leave her property to a Negro? Pinky is forced to go to court to fight the contested will. She wins her case, and then turns the home and land into an orphanage; a gaggle of Negro students are seen inside the home during the last scenes of the film. In Sumner's novel, the home for Negro students was actually burned down by the Ku Klux Klan; Southern censors would likely have scorned such a segment in the script.

Although none of them won, all three actresses—Ethel Barrymore, Jeanne Crain, and Ethel Waters—received Academy Award nominations for *Pinky.* The most scintillating performance was given by Barrymore. Although bedridden throughout most of the film, she fearlessly played a bitter, racism-scarred Southern belle. But Ethel Waters did reap benefits from the movie. Three years later—with roles remaining difficult to come by for Black actors—Waters got a major role in *The Member of the Wedding,* a movie based on Carson McCullers's prizewinning Broadway play. Waters had also starred in the stage play, playing the role of a maid. This role, in both play and movie, might well have been marked for Hattie McDaniel. But McDaniel's career had gone stagnant in the aftermath of *Wind.* David Selznick had promised her he would find her better roles after that, but he never did. She was seen on-screen the year after the release of *Wind* in *Maryland,* a 1940 family drama about a mother and her son and their disagreements over his desire to participate in a local horse competition. The great character actor Walter Brennan played the horse trainer. Hattie McDaniel played the maid.

McDaniel could never understand why her news-making role in *Wind*—and her Oscar statuette—hadn't garnered her more work in Hollywood. "It was as if I had done something wrong," she said about her career. She soon found herself playing the role of Beulah, a maid, in both the radio and television series of that name, roles that once again drew barbs from many Blacks, among them NAACP officials. The *Beulah* television series premiered in 1950 and was the first TV series to feature a Black in a starring role; the radio show had premiered five years earlier.

In 1952, Hattie McDaniel, suffering from heart disease, fell ill. She never returned to work, and on October 26, 1952, she died, her legacy awash in reflective bouts of both pride and shame. Mammy giveth, and Mammy taketh.

# 5

# [An Interlude—1933]

## Baby Face and Chico

I F YOU WERE A NEGRO CITIZEN of the United States in the latter half of 1933 and got all dressed up to go out to the movie theatre, one of the movies that would have likely caught your attention was *Baby Face*. It starred Barbara Stanwyck and George Brent. But to Negroes the real star of the movie was Theresa Harris, who played Chico. Chico was best buddy to Lily Powers—the Stanwyck character—and, just like Lily, a prostitute. No matter their moral positions in life, Chico and Lily were one of the first, more honest Black-white friendships to be showcased on a major motion-picture screen. They were equals, and the reality of this at the time was its own kind of shock.

It all began in the mind of Cosmo Hamilton, who back in 1917 wrote a short story titled "Baby Face" that got published in *Hearst's International* magazine. The story centered on Lily Powers, abused as a teenager, when she was forced to sell her body to put food on the table. She grew up to turn the tables on men: she manipulated them, drove them crazy with her wanton sexuality, climbed into the corporate world, slept herself up, up, and away, all the while ruining men.

Barbara Stanwyck was a rising star when a young, successful screen-writer, Darryl Zanuck, met with her to begin developing the story. Zanuck had made a name for himself in his early twenties by writing several screenplays for *Rin Tin Tin* movies—all before he became a producer. Stanwyck loved the role. The movie's other female star, Theresa Harris, was a native of Houston who had studied at the UCLA Conservatory of Music, and had appeared in several pictures, playing the Negro maid. But *Baby Face* was her big break. She played a friend, a human being who did not have to serve another human being. The scenes between Lily and Chico are beautiful, almost sublime in their simple echoes of female friendship. They sip coffee together; they hop a train together. They dazzle each other by primping in their beautiful clothes. Only when they get to New York City—in order to remain close to each other—does Chico *act* as a maid in the company of Lily's lovers to throw them off the trail of Lily's true racial background. It's a subversive racial duet.

Why did Theresa Harris, a Black actress, get to play a fully dimensional film role while so many other Black actresses were denied the opportunity? The answer was that *Baby Face* had gone into production before 1933, and this was a pre-Code movie. The film didn't get completely away with its lurid storyline: Will Hays began battling once the movie came out, making so much noise that the studio mogul Jack Warner agreed to some cuts and alterations. Hays served as president of the Motion Picture Producers and Distributors of America. His mission was to guard against "immorality" in films—such as profanity, drugs, attacks against churches, and interracial mingling. In the narrow mind of the Indiana-born Hays, the whiter the movie, the better. But Harris's role was too big and central to the story for them to decimate her part. The reviewers were so perplexed by the appearance of a Black woman beside and equal to a white woman that they didn't know what to make of it, and thus simply ignored Harris's powerful presence. By the end of 1934, the Hays Code was in full effect, and its censorship added to the threat against Black actors. Theresa Harris would amass dozens more appearances in movies—more than 90 percent of those roles as a maid, the others as a background singer.

---

There were times in the succeeding years when the Negro maid almost disappeared as a presence in both literature and American film. That changed abruptly in 2009, when another white, Southern-born writer, Kathryn Stockett, published a novel, *The Help,* about Southern Black maids. The novel was a phenomenal success, spending months on best-seller lists. A film seemed inevitable, and it opened just two years later, in 2011. *The Help*—which starred, among others, Viola Davis, Octavia Spencer, Emma Stone, and Allison Janney—though a commercial success, did not avoid heated criticism. The Association of Black Women Historians issued a statement:

*Despite efforts to market the book and the film as a progressive story of triumph over racial injustice, "The Help" distorts, ignores, and trivializes the experiences of Black domestic workers. We are specifically concerned about the representations of Black life and the lack of attention given to sexual harassment and civil rights activism.*

For her role in *The Help*, Octavia Spencer received the Academy Award for Best Supporting Actress. It was impossible, at the moment of Spencer's win, not to think of Hattie McDaniel's fur-draped night in Hollywood in 1940, and the enduring emotions it had set loose.

Hattie McDaniel in *Gone with the Wind* (1939). They gave her an Oscar, but not a seat at the table.

# 6

# [Flashback]

## *The 1939 Academy Awards*

B Y THE MID-1920S, moviegoing had become the predominant cultural pastime in America. The movie chieftains who ran Hollywood realized it. They also began to sense they needed to band together and form an umbrella organization that would represent their rapidly growing industry to the world. Some of the earliest planning meetings of these film executives took place at the home of the studio chief Louis B. Mayer. Additional meetings would take place at other homes, with powerful men moving in and out of beautiful estates in and around Beverly Hills, homes with well-manicured lawns—and Negro maids and butlers attending to their needs. The meetings culminated on May 4, 1927, with the creation of the Academy of Motion Picture Arts and Sciences. Among its charter members were early Hollywood royalty: Douglas Fairbanks, Darryl Zanuck, Frank Lloyd, and Mary Pickford and D. W. Griffith, both indelibly associated with *The Birth of a Nation*. In 1928, a year after the Academy was formed, the population of the United States stood at 120 million; a hundred million people had purchased movie tickets that year. Everyone, it seemed, was going to the movies!

It was quickly determined by the Academy that they should honor the best in their profession. All agreed that an annual awards ceremony would be good for the organization and all those who worked so dutifully on films. The first ceremony was held on May 16, 1929, at the Hollywood Roosevelt Hotel to honor pictures from the previous year. The statuettes, which came to be known as Oscars, were gold-plated and made of Britannia metal. They were designed by Cedric Gibbons, an MGM art director. (There has long been debate about the origin of the "Oscar" name affixed to the awards; though the mystery remains, three people—Bette Davis, columnist Sidney Skolsky, and Academy librarian Margaret Herrick—would all garner some form of credit. There was little mystery to the first awards ceremony, because the winners had been revealed to the press weeks before. Emil Jannings won the Best Actor prize; Janet Gaynor was named Best Actress. The movies being honored from a year before were all silent films, so the ceremony was also an epitaph for that genre. There were two awards that year for film direction: Frank Borzage (dramatic direction) won for *7th Heaven,* and Lewis Milestone (comedy direction) for *Two Arabian Knights.* A special award was presented to Warner Brothers pictures for the first wildly praised talkie, *The Jazz Singer,* released in 1927 and which starred a white-gloved, white-lipped, blackface Al Jolson. The Jolson movie had garnered so much attention that the Academy felt they had to honor it in some way.

One look at the films Hollywood produced in 1939 showed a truly dazzling and phenomenal amount of talent behind and in front of the camera. Perhaps in no other year in the Academy's short history had moviegoers been treated to such a diverse slate of films. There was *Mr. Smith Goes to Washington,* starring Jimmy Stewart and Jean Arthur, a political confection about idealism, directed by Frank Capra; *Of Mice and Men,* originating from the pen of John Steinbeck and highlighted by Lon Chaney, Jr.'s best screen performance to date; *Ninotchka,* pairing Greta Garbo and Melvyn Douglas in a spy caper helmed by Ernst Lubitsch; the dreamlike fantasy of *The Wizard of Oz,* which made Judy Garland a star. Additionally, there was *Goodbye, Mr. Chips,* a U.S.-British production that featured Greer Garson—her big-screen debut—pulling a schoolmaster out of his shy disposition; *Stagecoach,* directed by John Ford and starring John Wayne, Claire Trevor, and John Carradine in a production that became the year's most talked-about Western; the William Wyler–directed *Wuthering Heights,* featuring Laurence Olivier, Merle Oberon, and David Niven. And, of course, Selznick's *Gone with the Wind.*

Her painful slights associated with *Wind* notwithstanding, Hattie McDaniel prided herself on her competitive spirit. She badly wanted MGM to nominate her for an Academy Award in the Best Supporting Actress category. A Negro had never been nominated for an Academy Award, nor had one ever been invited to the ceremony itself. (The Negro butlers and kitchen help didn't count as invited guests.) McDaniel realized her goal was an uphill battle. Friends in distant cities had sent her clippings from the Negro press about her being mentioned in so many of the *Wind* reviews, which she kept in a neat stack in her Los Angeles home. Every time she added to them, her determination grew. She needed to be proactive. And that meant getting an audience with David O. Selznick himself.

It was studio chiefs who decided which actors and actresses would be promoted for Academy Award nominations. The pressure from agents on behalf of their clients was intense. There were parties to go to and be seen at before the ballots were released; the all-important season of hobnobbing was in full motion on behalf of the 1939 films. But Hattie McDaniel wasn't invited to those parties. Instead, she went over to David Selznick's office—it was February 1940, a little before the ballots were printed up—and showed him all the clippings that had mentioned her role in *Gone with the Wind.* Selznick had already made up his mind he was going to nominate *Wind*'s costar Olivia de Havilland in the Best Supporting Actress category. To enter two names on the ballot in the same category was both rare and risky: each nominee very well could cancel the other out. But after his session with McDaniel, Selznick decided to take the gamble.

When nominations for the 1940 Academy Awards were announced, David Selznick was a very happy man. *Gone with the Wind* received a record-smashing thirteen nominations. Clark Gable and Vivien Leigh were nominated in the Lead Actor and Actress categories. But the history-making moment was Hattie McDaniel's nomination—the first ever for a Black performer.

When word reached her about the nomination, McDaniel was overcome with emotion. She allowed herself moments of elation, while managing to ignore the barbs still being directed at *Wind* by critics of the movie and its depiction of slavery. The other nominees in the Best Supporting Actress category—in addition to de Havilland—were Geraldine Fitzgerald for *Wuthering Heights,* Edna May Oliver for *Drums Along the Mohawk,* and Maria Ouspenskaya for *Love Affair.* It was a heady group that McDaniel was going up against. Ouspenskaya was viewed by some as a sentimental favorite. A Russian émigrée—as were many filmmakers in Hollywood—she had previously been nominated in the Best Supporting Actress category for *Dodsworth,* a 1936 film. But McDaniel had more immediate worries than her competition. She had to decide what to wear to the Academy Awards!

When Hattie McDaniel and her escort, Ferdinand P. Yober, arrived at the twelfth annual Academy Awards on February 29, 1940, the camera flashbulbs began popping. She was dressed in a flowing gown and an ermine jacket, with white gardenias pinned to her chest and her hair. The weight of racial history already trailed her with her nomination. It had not gone unnoticed that the academy, for the first time, had allowed Black actors to cast votes for nominees: that could charitably be deemed the Hattie McDaniel effect. McDaniel and her guest were not allowed to sit with the *Wind* cast; they sat at a table distant from the cast.

Bob Hope, the cherubic-faced comedian, was host of the ceremony. In previous years, the winners of Academy Awards had been announced weeks before the event took place. But beginning with the 1940 ceremony, a new rule was adopted: winners would be announced at the ceremony itself, a decision designed to add even more excitement to the star-studded affair.

The tables inside the Ambassador Hotel's Coconut Grove ballroom were filled as the ceremony got under way. Clark Gable looked suave; Bette Davis, confident; Olivia de Havilland, regal; and Greta Garbo, invisible, because, as expected, the reclusive actress was a no-show. It was customary that the previous year's winner in the acting categories would be called upon to announce this year's winners. Fay Bainter had won Best Supporting Actress a year earlier for *Jezebel,* an antebellum-set picture that, yet again, featured Blacks—this time in mostly offscreen roles—as slaves. Bainter stepped to the lectern and, before announcing the winner, uttered words that were wrapped in the knowledge of a nation long running on the fuel of racism and bigotry. She talked of "walls being moved back" and her hope that the about-to-be-announced winner would be embraced by all of America. She began: "It is with the knowledge that this entire nation will stand and salute the presentation of this plaque that I present the Academy Award for the best performance of an actress in a supporting role . . . to Hattie McDaniel." The applause was loud, so loud it seemed that those who had been tipped off from an early edition of the *Los Angeles Times* about the winners were still surprised at seeing what they had never seen before: a Negro rising to accept an Academy Award. McDaniel strode briskly to the podium. She seemed as nervous as she was thrilled. Leaning into the microphone, she said, "It makes me feel very humble, and I shall always hold it as a beacon for anything I may be able to do in the future." Then her voice began to quiver. Her Civil War veteran father was in the ground; her first husband was in the ground; she wasn't going to be allowed to sleep in the hotel where she was receiving one of the acting profession's highest awards. McDaniel continued, her voice now cracking all the way: "I sincerely hope that I shall always be a credit to my race and the motion-picture industry." As she turned to leave the small platform, the actress raised a white handkerchief to her eyes, sobbing.

––––––––

When Hattie McDaniel won her Oscar, it caught the attention of drama departments on Negro college campuses around the country. Her win ignited hopes and dreams that drama students on those campuses could start to envision careers in Hollywood. The drama dean at Howard University—the renowned Black university in Washington, D.C.—allowed the Howard Players, the drama group on campus, to host a luncheon for McDaniel on June 3, 1940. There was grumbling about the luncheon from some quarters. Howard School of Law students had picketed *Gone with the Wind* when it was released in 1939 in Washington's theatres, opposing its depiction of slavery and Black stereotypes. Nevertheless, the Howard luncheon was one of the few celebratory events held in McDaniel's honor. She never forgot the hospitality bestowed by the school, and she bequeathed her Academy Award to the university. Upon her death and the execution of her will, her Oscar was sent to the school and subsequently placed on display in a glass case in the drama department.

Theodis Shine joined the Howard faculty in 1961. A short while later, he was shown McDaniel's Oscar sitting in the glass case. "They said it was a 'Wartime Oscar,'" he would recall. "It was about six inches tall and looked like a plaque. . . . The thing that threw me was when they said Oscar. I thought of the tall Oscar. I was so amazed that it was a little plaque. I was very proud of it. . . ."

In 1992, an item appeared in *Jet* magazine revealing that Hattie McDaniel's Oscar seemed to be missing from the Howard University campus. Staffers ripped into old boxes; darkened storage closets were searched. No one could find her Oscar! University officials were embarrassed. The news made national and international headlines. *The Washington Post* and other publications launched investigations. Academic scholars weighed in. Theories abounded: a library official had absconded with it; it was junked during the 1960s Black Power campus uprisings when an Academy Award for an antebellum role had lost its luster; it had been secretly removed from campus and auctioned off by some unknown party. No answers were ever discovered. Nor was the Oscar.

Hattie McDaniel felt no need ever to apologize for playing the nameless Mammy in *Gone with the Wind*. Her "Wartime Oscar" was reflective of a larger reality: during her lifetime, it had always been wartime for the Negro.

# Dangerous Love

*Starring Inger Stevens, Sammy Davis, Jr.,*

*James Edwards, Ike Jones, and Dorothy Dandridge*

IN THE STILL-DARK MORNING HOURS of July 11, 1958, two police officers in Central Point, Virginia, climbed into their patrol car. It was a rural county, and they knew the landscape well, knew all the back roads, shortcuts, and wicked curves. Moonshiners could be such a nuisance in and around the county, but they were not going after moonshiners. They were headed to the home of Richard and Mildred Loving. And they were really hoping they'd catch them in flagrante, having sex, raw and naked in bed together. The officers had their weapons, flashlights, handcuffs at the ready. The car crept into the driveway of the small Loving home. Stealthily, they walked to the door. After a couple of knocks, they just broke right into the home. "It was about 2 a.m. and I saw this light, you know, and I woke up," Mildred Loving would recall. "There was this policeman standing beside the bed. And he told us to get up, that we were under arrest. . . . They asked Richard who was that woman he was sleeping with, and I said, 'I'm his wife,' and the sheriff said, 'Not here, you're not.'"

The Lovings had left six weeks earlier to marry in Washington, D.C., where it was legal for a white man and a Black woman to wed. But such a thing wasn't legal in Virginia, because of its Racial Integrity Act of 1924, co-written and drafted by Walter Plecker, a white supremacist, who served as registrar of Virginia's Bureau of Vital Statistics. There were similar miscegenation laws on the books in more than two dozen other states across America. Mildred Loving, five months pregnant, and her husband were handcuffed and hauled off to jail and kept in separate cells. When they finally had their day in court, on January 6, 1959, the judge sentenced them to a year in prison. Then he offered a deal: he'd suspend their sentences if they left Virginia for good. The couple reluctantly agreed, know-ing they'd have to leave family and friends behind, potentially forever.

The state of California's miscegenation law had been struck down in 1948 in a case involving a Mexican woman and a Black male. The couple were refused a marriage license and sued. Their suit went to the state Supreme Court; the favorable decision striking the statute, however, was close, four to three. The fear of Black-on-white sex so haunted America that few seemed surprised that the issue was still making headlines in 1959.

Hollywood had adopted a mindset in its entertainment community that echoed the nation at large. Black and white love was dangerous.

———

Sammy Davis, Jr.'s first love was Helen Gallagher. She was beautiful—and a blonde.

Sammy had been out on the road since the age of five, pulled from childhood into entertaining by his father, Sam Senior, and Will Mas-tin. They were two men rolling across the world of vaudeville, desperate to stay afloat during the Great Depression. The kid in the middle, little Sammy—who never attended a single day of school—gave the act novelty. At first, it was mostly comedy, but as Sammy grew up, the act became known as "the Will Mastin Trio Featuring Sammy Davis Jr." They played juke joints, lodges, nightclubs. Frank Sinatra noticed them—actually, he noticed young Sammy—and got them booked on a bill with him at the Paramount. The crowds swooned. With Sinatra's recommendation, other nightclubs began booking the Will Mastin Trio. One of those clubs was Bill Miller's Riviera, in New Jersey, across the river from Manhattan. A group of showgirls in plumes and sexy outfits were the signature attrac-tion at Bill Miller's place. They were, of course, all white, and known as the Riviera Beauties. Helen Gallagher was the most beautiful, or at least Sammy thought so. He invited her to a Broadway show, *Me and Juliet*, then figured it best also to invite her chorus girlfriends, too. They could serve as "beards," or shields, to throw off any ruffian who might become upset at seeing Black Sammy with white Helen. So there he was, passing out thirteen tickets to Helen's showgirl friends. He didn't care if people thought he was the chauffeur that night. It only meant, in that year of 1953, that the ruse was working. "He was good enough to perform at the hotels," Gallagher would recall, "but not to go into the dining rooms. It drove me crazy." Sammy phoned her from the road. There was talk of marriage. One evening, with Sammy back in town, the two scooted over to Brooklyn to catch Milton Berle's show. Berle was known to be blunt and had some advice for the couple: "She's a nice girl, but you two will never be accepted," Gallagher remembered Berle saying, "and she's going to ruin your career." The affair eventually fizzled, but not Sammy's infatuation with white women.

Sammy began wooing Peggy King, a Columbia recording artist. They'd go out, dine together in quiet places, talk all night long about music and their careers. King, politically adept, wondered if Sammy truly realized the risks he was taking in dating a white woman. He seemed to blissfully ignore her concerns. She saw the stares, even when he pretended not to. He got a kick out of telling her about his trips to Canada, where his father and Will Mastin dated white women. The revelation bewildered her: Canada was not America. Sammy's career could not thrive in Canada alone.

Will Mastin and Sammy Senior couldn't help worrying about Sammy and white women. Sammy struck his various conquests as sweet, naïve, kind. Sometimes Sammy—who had been in show business all his life—ratcheted up the gossip about him and white women himself. He once called some reporters and told them he was *not* having an affair with Marilyn Monroe—this following the release of some harmless photos of Sammy and Marilyn taken together. There was never a Sammy-Marilyn affair. She just giggled when he made such insinuations.

Sammy's publicists were warning him away from white women. And Mastin and the elder Davis sought to direct Sammy's mind toward other things. They treated Sammy to gifts—all with money, of course, that they would not have made were it not for Sammy himself. One such gift presented to Sammy was a gleaming lime-green Cadillac. Sammy loved cruising down Sunset Boulevard, waving to the pretty white girls. Many stared back quizzically.

One morning, November 19, 1954, Sammy was out on the road, having left Las Vegas and making his way back to Los Angeles. Charlie Head, his assistant, was with him, but in the back of the car, asleep. Sammy was a little drowsy, but felt he could make it into Los Angeles. On the outskirts of San Bernardino, a car passed them. The car seemed to be doing a U-turn up ahead, but it also seemed to be stalling a bit. Then Sammy was right up on the car, and just like that, boom, they crashed, sending Sammy's head down into the conelike knob on the steering wheel. Blood splattered; Charlie, asleep, woke up, screaming. The two women in the other car were rattled but not hurt. An ambulance arrived, and Sammy and Charlie Head were rushed to the hospital. An eye surgeon was most worried about the damage done to Sammy's left eye. X-rays were taken. Sammy was told the eye could not be saved.

The news of the crash was all over the media: it made the newspapers and hopped onto the radio. The wild rumors began—that the crash was an attempt to kill Sammy Davis, Jr.; that the two women who whizzed by him on the road and were involved in the crash were connected to the mob; that the mob was angry at Sammy because of his predilection for white women. An investigation revealed no such thing, no link between the elderly women in the other car and mobsters. It was an early-morning car crash and nothing else. But that wasn't good enough for Black America, where rumors and emotions—especially concerning interracial love affairs that had made the tabloids—could become elevated in a flash.

There was something about the women who appeared on the big screen in the 1950s that transfixed Sammy Davis, Jr. He sat wide-eyed looking at Rita Hayworth, at Janet Leigh, at Barbara Rush, at Deanna Durbin. At Kim Novak. Novak had come onto the scene in a big way in 1955, when she appeared opposite Sinatra in *Man with the Golden Arm*. Next, she was the Kansas girl who got romanced in *Picnic*, the screen adaptation of William Inge's play. She was tall, feral, and sexy. In quick order, there were magazine covers, gossipy rumors of boyfriends. Harry Cohn, the head of Columbia Pictures, became her benefactor. He was intent on guiding her path to stardom. Cohn was a charmless and threatening figure who bragged about making—or breaking—careers.

In 1956, *The Steve Allen Show* premiered on NBC. The network wanted interesting names for the premiere episode so that the public would tune in. Among those tabbed for the maiden show were Vincent Price, the comedian Wally Cox, Kim Novak, and Sammy Davis, Jr. Sammy—peering hard through his one eye—fell hard for Novak. "The white woman thing," mused Cindy Bitterman, a longtime friend of both Sinatra and Sammy, "was his way of saying, 'I'm just a little shorter than Sinatra.'"

Richard Quine directed the 1954 film *Pushover*, and cast Novak as a gangster's girlfriend, her first major leading role. On the movie posters, she was sultry in a red dress, her picture larger than that of her costar Fred MacMurray. Quine saw something in Novak—"the proverbial quality of the lady in the parlor and the whore in the bedroom."

Sammy and Kim wound up in the bedroom. Annie Stevens—the wife of Morty Stevens, who sometimes arranged music for Sammy—had befriended Sammy. She dropped by his place one day, unannounced. "Sammy and Kim had been in the kitchen, on the floor, making out." The couple were both single, but that didn't matter in race-obsessed America. They needed cover, friends who would protect them during their furtive outings. Janet Leigh and Tony Curtis were dependable friends. "They were very much 'together,'" Leigh would recall about Davis and Novak. "And very compatible." Then word of the affair began to seep out. Negro newspaper columnists chased down the gossip and uncovered solid evidence. Scandal was lively news in Hollywood, so white columnists also began dropping hints in their columns. Sammy was annoyed, but Harry Cohn, the man who felt he had "discovered" the actress, was furious. The funnyman Jerry Lewis adored Sammy. They'd known each other for years, crossing paths in East Coast nightclubs. Lewis, however, didn't think there was anything funny about the brewing fallout over Davis and Novak: "He was so enamored of her," Lewis would remember. "I said, 'They'll cut your knees off and you'll never dance again. Do you understand what you're doing?'" Sammy told Lewis what he told everyone else: he loved Kim Novak and she loved him; they were thinking of marriage; they'd make Hollywood history as the most highly visible interracial couple.

Alfred Hitchcock cast Novak in *Vertigo*, a twisty crime melodrama, opposite Jimmy Stewart. Filming took place in San Francisco. Sammy showed up on the movie set, ostensibly just as a Hitchcock fan, but really to ogle Novak. He told his friend Steve Blauner about the affair. Blauner worked as an agent at General Artists Corporation. "I grab him by the throat," Blauner recalled about Sammy's revelation. "I say, 'You stupid son of a bitch! How long you think it'll be a secret? They'll kill you.'" Sammy told Blauner he could take care of himself, and kept mentioning the guns he owned. Blauner wondered if Sammy was living in a dream world, disconnected from reality. His guns—six-shooters with which he would practice cowboylike fast draws—were too big and cumbersome to carry. Soon he began packing heat—a real gun, small enough to conceal.

Sammy's friend Cindy Bitterman worked at Columbia Pictures, in publicity. One evening, she was at a dinner gathering with Harry Cohn and other studio executives. "The names of Kim and Sammy come up," Bitterman would recall. "Cohn has no idea of my relationship to Sammy. He asked somebody at the table, 'What's with this nigger?' My stomach started cramping. 'If he doesn't straighten up,' he starts saying about Sammy, 'he'll be minus another eye.' I went to the bathroom and threw up. I threw up out of fear and greed and Hollywood moneymaking."

Cindy Bitterman wasted little time in letting Sammy Davis know that Harry Cohn could be dangerous. Cohn told Jess Rand, Sammy's publicist, that Sammy would never work in Hollywood or nightclubs again if the dalliance with Novak continued. "I know the right people," Cohn told Rand darkly. Jack Carter, a comic and friend of Sammy's, had his own take on the Cohn imbroglio: "Harry Cohn wanted him dead." Sammy felt he had to throw the wolves off. But how? Then his phone rang, an unidentified caller telling him to go to Las Vegas and meet with Loray White, a Black dancer, and that he should marry her, because that was the only way to pacify Harry Cohn. Sammy thought it was a crank call; Jess Rand did not. Sammy did indeed know White: she happened to be one of the very few Black showgirls in Vegas at the time. But they had no relationship. "The gossip," Sammy's friend Annie Stevens recalled, "was already backstage: Sammy has to get married—or he'll be killed." There had been mob killings on both the East and West Coasts, often over money and nightclub disagreements and contracts. Both Rand and Stevens imagined Sammy was putting his life in danger. Sammy raced off to Las Vegas and pleaded with Loray White to marry him, explaining to her the dilemma he was in. White, like most low-earning showgirls, could use extra money, and that's what Sammy dangled. She agreed, and the date was set for January 10, 1958. It was as if Sammy Davis, Jr., had to direct his very own movie quickly and cast it with friends who knew him and didn't want harm to come his way. He begged Harry Belafonte to be best man, and Belafonte agreed. Belafonte knew Sammy was in desperate straits: "Whites in the country were upset with his intrusion into their private realm—Kim Novak and all that," Belafonte said. The wedding went off as planned, a strange drama wrapped in a racial nightmare. Six weeks after Sammy Davis married Loray White, Harry Cohn died. And not long after that, Sammy abandoned the marriage and gave Loray White a nice little settlement. It was over. A wrap! Cut!

In the latter part of 1959—the byzantine Cohn–Novak–Loray White drama behind him now, since the Novak affair had finally ended—Sammy Davis found himself in Montreal, performing at the Bellevue Casino. There he met Joan Stuart, a lovely blonde ballet dancer. There were dinners, gifts given. Sammy was, again, in love. Plans for marriage were announced to the Canadian press. Her parents, however, nixed those plans. Sammy finally got his white wife in 1960, when he married the Swedish actress

May Britt. He ignored the death threats, though he did purchase a walking stick that had a poison tip attached to it. He told members of his entourage he'd stab any racist goon who tried to harm him or his wife.

Sammy Davis, Jr., had the wherewithal to survive the sexual and interracial-marriage paranoia against the backdrop of Hollywood and America, but Dorothy Dandridge, his *Porgy and Bess* costar, did not.

————

The sisters had come out of Cleveland, where they were guided by their mother, Ruby, into an all-sister singing act. The worshippers in the Black churches fell in love with them. Just as Gertrude Temple had told her daughter, Shirley, about the magic of show business—and possible financial rewards!—Ruby Dandridge made her Dorothy and Vivian believe in their vocal talents. The Dandridge sisters got plenty of publicity for their cute little Negro-girl singing act; when they became teenagers they added Etta Jones as a third member. They played venues around the country, getting work in vaudeville houses, and sometimes fancy nightclubs. One of their highlights was performing alongside Jimmy Lunceford, who had his own, highly respected orchestra. Ruby Dandridge was by now in Hollywood, playing maids in movies, telling anyone who would listen that her daughters were out in the world, singing, and were going to become stars someday.

All three of the singers were attractive, but something was becoming quite apparent: Dorothy was turning into a genuine beauty. She was tall and willowy and caramel-colored. Hollywood came calling, and the Dandridge Sisters wound up doing small bits in movies: *Easy to Take* was a 1936 comedy; *A Day at the Races* was a 1937 Marx Brothers vehicle. In 1942, Dorothy Dandridge appeared as a maid in *The Night Before the Divorce*. She was one of the prettiest Black maids ever to appear in a motion picture. Only eagle-eyed viewers would have spotted Ruby Dandridge, Dorothy's movie-star-dreaming mother, in that movie as well, playing an extra in a crowd scene.

In Los Angeles, Black entertainers stayed at the Dunbar Hotel on Central Avenue. One might see Duke Ellington in the lobby, or Cab Calloway, or crooner Billy Eckstine. Dorothy Dandridge could be spotted sometimes, prancing about. She wore ballerina shoes; she looked ethereal, divine. Harold and Fayard Nicholas, the famous tap-dancing brothers, introduced themselves to the Dandridge trio. The Nicholas brothers were roués, young Black men whose talent had given them an extra dose of freedom. The brothers had money. Dorothy Dandridge fell for the smooth-talking Harold Nicholas and married him. (Hattie McDaniel was among the wedding guests.) Nicholas came to feel that his wife was uppity and prone to asking too many questions about his late nights spent gallivanting around the Black quarters of Los Angeles. He had affairs, begun almost immediately after their marriage. They had a daughter, Harolyn; she was mentally handicapped, and it devastated the couple. Harold was never a homebody, given his work. The marriage dissolved after three years. Nicholas financially abandoned his ex-wife and their daughter.

Dorothy Dandridge went out on the road to make money so she could hire help for her daughter. She swore off any more romantic involvement with Black men and started dating white men, who were always mesmerized by her beauty. On the road, she sang Cole Porter, Gershwin. She told certain close friends she didn't like being Black. They thought it was just momentary anger and confusion, but she kept bringing her race into conversations, how the color of her skin had sabotaged her. Some of her friends thought it sad to hear such things. "She kept saying, 'If I looked like Betty Grable, I could capture the world,'" recalled Gerry Branton, her former sister-in-law. "She resented her blackness. . . . She wanted to have pretty hair, straight hair, blue eyes. . . . She didn't realize that part of her beauty was because she was brown. In Europe, they would turn over chairs trying to get a look at her."

In 1953, Dorothy Dandridge played her first lead film role, playing a schoolteacher in the low-budget *Bright Road,* an all-Black MGM production. The script, taken from a short story, focused on a young Negro boy's brooding anger over the death of a friend, and his schoolteacher, played by Dandridge, who tries to lift his spirits. The movie completely ignored racial issues, which critics found strange and unrealistic. "The whole thing has a prettiness about it, as though the people who made it didn't wish to open up any problems or tread on any toes," Bosley Crowther wrote in *The New York Times.* "Even the locale of the school is not mentioned, though it is plainly an all-Negro school." While doing publicity for the movie, Dandridge strangely allowed that she was happy the movie sidestepped race. Her comments hardly enticed Blacks to come to the movie, and whites all but ignored it. It was a box-office flop. One notable facet of *Bright Road,* however, is that it marked the screen debut of Harry Belafonte, who played the school principal. He was extraordinarily handsome, a nightclub-and-recording star, and proved himself a very capable actor. Hollywood took notice.

The film director Otto Preminger was looking for a beautiful Negro actress who had to be able to cause trouble between men. He was about to direct a film based on *Carmen Jones,* the all-Black musical opera that had opened in late 1943 on Broadway. The opera was set during World War II, and revolved around a female parachute maker tormented by two lovers, one of whom is an air-force officer, the other a boxer. Though Hollywood remained fickle about Black musicals since neither *A Cabin in the Sky* nor *Stormy Weather* had made big money, Preminger was an aggressive sort and convinced the producer Darryl Zanuck that he could turn a profit on the film. Zanuck liked Preminger's directing background and agreed to make the movie, but made Preminger agree to forfeit his salary agreements if it flopped.

Preminger knew that every beautiful Black actress in Hollywood would covet the role of Carmen. Eartha Kitt's sensuality put her high on the list, and she screen-tested for the role, but did not strike Preminger as the classic beauty he was looking for. It took Dorothy Dandridge two visits to Preminger's office to convince him she could play the role.

Once Preminger had chosen his Carmen, he needed a heartthrob to play the role of Joe—the air-force officer—in the film. The director went to visit Harry Belafonte at a New York nightclub and offered him the part on the spot. Pearl Bailey, Diahann Carroll, Brock Peters, and Roy Glenn were also cast. The names were known far more in the Negro press than in the white press. Belafonte was impressed with Preminger's enthusiasm: "He really was leading with his heart on this one."

When rehearsals got under way, Belafonte, who was married, was still under the Dandridge spell from having worked with her earlier. But she had sworn off Black men, no matter how handsome. They could not help her career inside the wicked world of show business. "What I wanted from Dorothy," Belafonte would lament, "was more than a quick fling—I really did adore her—but less, in truth, than full commitment." Preminger—whose looks teetered toward an overweight and fearsome-looking gangster—paid a visit to Dandridge's home one night, ostensibly to talk about the new movie. They began an affair. Preminger had clout in Hollywood and knew that vulnerable women who wanted to become movie stars could be pressured into sex. Belafonte knew as much, too: "Dorothy," he believed, "needed a special protector, someone with enough power in Hollywood to help pull her up, as a black actress, into the pantheon of white leading ladies."

By the time filming was completed on *Carmen Jones,* cast members knew that Preminger and Dandridge were having an affair. It would last four years and be the subject of incessant gossip. Sammy Davis, Jr., who would later meet Preminger on another movie set, knew how much of a cad Preminger happened to be. "All he ever wanted to talk about was broads," Davis realized. "As I could always muster up half-a-dozen good looking ladies with a couple of phone calls, I soon found I couldn't get rid of Otto even if I'd wanted to." Since he was both director and producer of *Carmen Jones,* Preminger weighed in on all decisions as the movie was readied for release. He made sure his paramour and leading lady was highlighted lavishly on the posters, and was delighted with the artwork done by Saul Bass. There she was: Carmen Jones, her hourglass figure, in an off-the-shoulder black blouse and white skirt, a lethal come-hither look in her eyes, her hands resting on the sides of her hips. And there she was, Dorothy Dandridge, the young Black woman from Cleveland, Ohio. Negro men walking by movie theatres all across America, where the posters were hanging behind glass, stopped in their tracks. The film opened October 28, 1954. The reviews were smashing, the lines at the theatres long. "Preminger directs with a deft touch, blending the comedy and tragedy easily and building his scenes to some suspenseful heights," *Variety* opined. "He gets fine performances from the cast toppers, notably Dorothy Dandridge, a sultry Carmen whose performance maintains the right hedonistic note throughout." In *The New York Times,* Bosley Crowther was even more rapturous, calling the film "a big musical shenanigan and theatrical tour-de-force." Carmen proved a hit and unqualified moneymaker. It grossed nearly ten million dollars on an eight-hundred-thousand-dollar budget.

With the success of *Carmen Jones,* Dandridge seemed to be everywhere. She was on television and radio, talking about her hit movie; she was flitting in and out of nightclubs, and more and more often was seen in the company of Otto Preminger. *Life* magazine contacted her. They had never had a Black woman on their cover, but they wanted her! The issue hit the stands November 1, 1954. She was turned sideways in the cover photo, looking over her left shoulder with a sunny smile, dressed in the red-and-black *Carmen Jones* movie-poster attire. She would ultimately be featured in several different versions of posters. Dandridge was nominated for a Golden Globe for Best Actress. Grace Kelly took the prize for *The*

*Country Girl,* but *Carmen Jones* won in the Best Motion Picture—Comedy or Musical category. The looming Academy Award nominations were on everyone's radar. A Black performer had never been nominated for Best Actor or Best Actress. On February 12, 1955, the Academy announced five Best Actress nominees: Grace Kelly, Judy Garland, Audrey Hepburn, Jane Wyman—and Dorothy Dandridge. It was the dreamiest of dreams suddenly come true. The first Black woman, and it wasn't for playing a maid!

On the evening of March 30, 1955, Dorothy Dandridge, accompanied by her agent, Earl Mills—who later became her manager—looked gorgeous as she entered the Academy Awards ceremony, hosted by Bob Hope. She was dressed in a long cream-colored gown; a piece of fur hung on her left arm. Often nominees are called upon to present an award, and Dandridge had the honor to present the award for film editing. She looked angelic, her caramel-colored skin tone gleaming as she strolled to the podium. "If I seem a little nervous," she began, bringing her hand to her face, "it's because this is as big a moment for me as it will be for the winner of this award." The depth charge of her comment washed over many whites who were watching, since they did not follow the cultural gyrations of Black America. But Blacks everywhere realized exactly what she was trying to convey. She opened the envelope and called the name Gene Milford, winner for *On the Waterfront.* Dorothy Dandridge's own name was not called that night. The Academy Award for Best Actress went to Grace Kelly. Mills consoled Dandridge by telling her that her nomination was surely going to alter her career and open opportunities for her.

At the equivalent moments in their careers, the likes of Elizabeth Taylor, Lana Turner, and Rita Hayworth were sent great scripts with major parts. It was three long years before Dorothy Dandridge got another role, and it was a supporting role at that. In 1957, Dandridge appeared in *Island in the Sun,* a tropical romance filmed in the West Indies that starred James Mason, Joan Fontaine, and Harry Belafonte. She played a pharmacy clerk; Belafonte a labor leader. In their roles, both Belafonte and Dandridge, respectively, are supposedly engaged in affairs—with white people. But there is no kissing, no touching, an element that scarred the movie with a sense of absurdity. Yet hate mail arrived from America to the movie set, directed at the white actors, berating them for even appearing in a movie that insinuated romance with Blacks.

Dandridge grew despondent. Preminger let it be known he was not going to leave his wife for her. Her agent, Earl Mills, fell in love with her, clouding his judgment when it came to her career. She made two dramatic movies in 1958, *Tamango* and *The Decks Ran Red.* Neither made any noise with the critics, or at the box office. In 1959, she appeared in *Porgy and Bess,* playing Bess in the antebellum-set musical. But the film was directed by Preminger, and because of their tumultuous breakup, there was a coldness between the two of them; she was even brought to tears on the set. Betty Grable kept getting roles; Dorothy Dandridge did not. Financial woes began to mount. Unable to keep up the expenses of private care for her mentally ill daughter, she was forced to put Harolyn in a sanitarium. She felt deep shame about having to do so. Friends noticed an increase in her drinking. There were affairs, all with deep-pocketed white men who appreciated and supported her lifestyle. Peter Lawford, a member of Sinatra's famed Rat Pack, was one of her lovers. Another was Giulio Ascarelli, who worked in public relations. Save for three appearances on *The Ed Sullivan Show,* she disappeared from public view. The friends who received wedding invitations were surprised by her announcement that she was going to marry Jack Denison, a maître d' whom she had met at the Riviera Hotel in Las Vegas. Denison, a World War II vet and ten years older than Dandridge, promised her he would put plans into place to improve her wobbly financial situation. Meanwhile, her daughter's health deteriorated; she was no longer able to recognize her mother.

The marriage took place on June 22, 1959. The bride wore a white mousseline-de-sole gown designed by Berman of London. There were upward of two hundred at the wedding. In the succeeding weeks, Dandridge had no intention of accommodating those in the Negro press who wanted to talk to her about her marriage to a white man. Even while imprisoned by race, Dorothy Dandridge was still blissfully ignoring it. Her sister, Vivian, allowed that Dorothy dated white men—and now was married to one—because there were only a precious few Black men who could afford her likes and her penchant for first-class travel, and all the ones who could seemed to be married.

Jack Denison's plans to strengthen his wife's financial outlook involved his decision to open a Los Angeles restaurant. It was, however, a losing venture, and painful to Dandridge, who invested some of her own money in the enterprise. Her mood darkened even more when it was revealed to her that money she had invested in Arizona oil speculation had been lost as well. Her heavy drinking became worse; her health declined. There were pills to help her sleep, and pills to ease her anxieties. When the phone did ring, it was for nightclub work and the occasional television offer. In 1962, NBC cast her in an episode of *Cain's Hundred,* a weekly mob drama.

It was her television dramatic debut. Her performance was fine; she sang in a nightclub. She hoped better offers would come from the appearance, but they did not, at least not in America. She was invited to Europe in 1962 to make a film with French star Alain Delon. But filmmakers didn't have the money to complete the film, and she returned to America.

Stateside, Dandridge's marriage only worsened. Denison became abusive. Finally, she had enough and filed for divorce. "The defendant [Dension] has a violent temper and has, on occasions, inflicted physical violence upon her, the last occasion being Oct. 23, 1962," noted the divorce petition.

She went through a long period of listlessness and holing up in her Los Angeles home. On the other side of the country, the big news in 1963 was the March on Washington. Dandridge had friends attending, among them Sammy Davis, Jr., Belafonte, and Sidney Poitier. But she couldn't be convinced to go. There were concerns closer to home: she worried incessantly about money. Earl Mills told her things would get better. She played herself in *Juke Box Jury,* a 1964 musical quiz show. Things did not seem to be getting better. Mills finally rustled up a film offer in Mexico, and Dandridge went there to sign the contracts. When she got back to Los Angeles, she began working out at a gym, wanting to be ready for the film work ahead. But during one of those workouts, she hurt her ankle. She didn't realize it at the time, but a small bone had broken. She'd need more of those pills she kept bedside for her sleeplessness and anxiety. The pain worsened, and she told Mills she should go to the hospital to have her ankle checked. He phoned to make arrangements to come pick her up. She didn't answer. "I thought that she might be asleep or in the shower," Mills recalled. He drove over to her home, and she still didn't answer when he knocked. He left, but returned a short while later. Using a spare key Dandridge had given him, he opened the door, but the security chain was still in place. Knowing she must be inside, he dashed to his car and got a crowbar. He broke in, and there she lay, naked, on the bathroom floor. Pills in a bottle were nearby. "When I touched her cold face," Mills later said, "I knew she was dead."

She was forty-two years old.

As news seeped out, Negro newspapermen—knowing their readers would want to know—began calling the L.A. Coroner's Office. It was all true. One of those Negro newspapermen was A. S. "Doc" Young, who had known Dandridge in her early Los Angeles years. He gave her credit in the aftermath of her death for having "borne the disappointments of love affairs with white men who dared not marry her" because of their public fear of an interracial marriage. In death, she became a symbol. In life, she was a cautionary tale. "No matter how well balanced a woman may be," Dorothy Dandridge once said, "too much sex and sin, even if it is play acting, is dangerous."

Some who knew them wondered why there never was a romance between Dorothy Dandridge and James Edwards. They were viewed as two of the most successful Negro actors in Hollywood. Their screen test together for *Carmen Jones* wowed Otto Preminger, even though the director did not cast him in the movie. He cast Harry Belafonte.

James Edwards had been one of the most handsome and well-trained Negro actors in Tinseltown. Those in the Negro press—and even some in the white press—wondered if he might become the first Negro male actor to cross over, bringing white audiences across the color line. He was Sidney Poitier before Sidney Poitier. By 1954, however, the beginning of the end of the Hollywood career of James Edwards had been set in motion.

———

Annie Mae Edwards was a Baptist minister, and her husband, James Valley Edwards, moonlighted as a religion instructor when he wasn't working as a laborer. The family, which included nine children, were avid churchgoers. James, who arrived March 6, 1918, was their firstborn. Though sharing his father's name, he never went by James Jr. By 1930, the Edwards family had relocated to Anderson, Indiana. Like most other Blacks in the community, they would have surely heard about the events that took place thirty miles away, in Marion, on August 7 of that year, proving that their surroundings were as unforgiving as any racially haunted locale in the deep South.

Thomas Shipp and Abram Smith, two young Negroes, had accosted a young white couple, Claude Deeter and Mary Ball, on the evening of August 6. They killed Deeter; Ball survived, but a rumor flew that she had been raped. There was little doubt that the accused, quickly arrested, were the murderers; a third member of their roving party, James Cameron, admitted as much. Tempers exploded among the white populace, as much because of the rumor of rape. A day after the jailing, a vigilante mob, swinging sledgehammers, broke into the local jail and dragged all three youths to a hanging party. Upward of five thousand had gathered. Abram Smith, as if he had some kind of superpowers, tussled and tried to free himself from the ropes. But where would he run? His actions only angered the mob more. So that there would be no more rope shenanigans, they broke his arms, and then commenced with the hangings. Cameron, the third Negro, sixteen years old, was on his way to the makeshift gallows in the dark woods. A voice, that of a white woman, shot out from the sweating and howling crowd. She began swearing that Cameron had had nothing to do with either the alleged rape or the murder. Cameron was spared a hanging and quickly escorted away. Lawrence Beitler, born in Marion, was in the crowd and carrying his cameras. He made his living as a studio photographer. He snapped pictures of the two hanged men, gruesome shots of snapped necks against the nighttime sky, cackling whites in straw hats gathered all around. After Beitler had his photos printed, he sensed he had something. They weren't art, but there was a ghoulish uniqueness at work in the photos—death before trial, a town's collective action, a moment in violent time. In the aftermath, when the lynchings had been exposed, the mob's leaders were indicted. Though the charges were dropped by the all-white jury, Beitler's photographs went all around the country. Decent folk were shocked by them. Abel Meeropol, a New York schoolteacher, wrote a poem about the photograph and titled it "Bitter Fruit." It got published, and he read it at labor rallies and civil-rights demonstrations. The photos came to be seen by singer Billie Holiday. They haunted her. She sang a song about men hanging from trees, called "Strange Fruit." She'd get high on drugs and listen to it in the quiet darkness.

James Edwards was an eleven-year-old Indiana schoolboy when the Marion hangings took place. By the time he graduated from high school, he wanted to fight. Boxing intrigued him, and he possessed skills, enough so that he fought Golden Gloves and eventually turned professional. Joe Louis, the Brown Bomber, the world champion, was giving young Negro boxers everywhere plenty of confidence. But the years out on the road were hard, and many other fighters were better than Edwards. He came to realize he would not become a great prizefighter. His mother had always wanted him to go to college, and he eventually enrolled at Knoxville College, in Tennessee, a small Negro school.

At Knoxville College, Edwards began taking to the stage. He was smart and handsome, took easily to remembering his lines, and was well liked by drama classmates. "When I was coming up," he recalled, "acting was unheard of—for blacks—except for Stepin Fetchit. . . . There was no chance and many of my friends thought me out of my mind." After college, he landed a couple of civil-service jobs. Then World War II came. Edwards found himself doing a tour of duty in the army. He wrote letters back to family in Indiana, expressing uncertainty about what he would do once he finished his enlistment.

After military service, Edwards headed for Chicago. Traditional nine-to-five jobs no longer interested him, and he began thinking, once again, of acting. In Chicago, he became a member of the Skyloft Players, a repertory ensemble founded by the poet and dramatist Langston Hughes. They put on several of Hughes's plays and listened proudly when Hughes visited, which he often did. Funding was always a challenge, but contributions came from the local arms of Delta Sigma Theta and Alpha Kappa Alpha, Negro sororities. Skyloft directors and actors were always telling Edwards, who was making a name for himself, that he had the potential to make it in New York City theatre.

In 1945, a groundbreaking play, *Deep Are the Roots,* directed by Elia Kazan, opened on Broadway. It revolved around a Negro family during World War II. In the play, Brett Charles is the decorated Black army veteran who returns to his Southern home. His mother remains the maid for a United States senator. But Lieutenant Charles, having been celebrated as a war hero in Europe and treated humanely, does not intend to play by the traditional rules of the still-Old South. He talks to his mother about freedom, and about agitating. The senator's daughter admires his courage, and the two begin an affair. Tension and high racial drama ensue. On Broadway, Gordon Heath played the role of Brett Charles. Heath had made a nice living in radio dramas—playing white men. Of course, on the radio, no one could tell his color; he was known to do a variety of accents. Heath had also played Othello and Hamlet and many other classical roles onstage. Still, no matter his talent, not long after his Broadway run in *Deep Are the Roots,* Gordon Heath concluded that a Black man couldn't make a living in theatre—or film—in America. He decamped for Paris, where he opened a restaurant and lived for the rest of his life. The producers of *Deep Are the Roots* had garnered so much acclaim that they decided to take the play on a national tour. James Edwards was chosen to play Lieutenant Brett Charles.

It was suddenly time for a renewed interest in what its proponents called social-activism theatre. Dramatists were writing and putting on plays that addressed racism and discrimination, a movement given urgency in light of the protests that erupted in the aftermath of World War II and the demands made by American Blacks. Edwards had begun appearing in an assortment of socially conscious plays. He drew raves and attention while touring in *Deep Are the Roots.* Producers sought him out. In early 1947, Edwards was seen in Philadelphia, appearing in Ben Bengal's play *All Aboard,* a drama about discrimination on a train heading South. Often at the performances—and before the drama got under way—a figure would appear onstage to talk about some newsworthy event that involved race or ethnic discrimination. A good number of Blacks and Jews were often in attendance. One evening, an Anti-Nazi League official appeared and read from a paper titled "The Klan Rides in Pennsylvania." Edwards and company took the play out to Los Angeles.

In L.A., Edwards drew the attention of Hollywood film producers. They began to cast him in small roles. In 1949, he appeared in two roles on-screen. His first came in *Manhandled,* a Paramount murder mystery. It was a forgettable role: he played the butler to a white homeowner. Most Negro butlers cast in white films were gray-haired, stooped men, but there was something different about Edwards's butler—he was regal, young, and handsome. Edwards also appeared in *The Set-Up,* which starred Robert Ryan as an over-the-hill boxer undercut by a deceitful manager. Edwards played Luther Hawkins, a wide-eyed boxer with potential. He had speaking lines, and was grateful he had been cast. While filming, he had been befriended by Ryan, another World War II vet. "He told me about the differences between stage and screen acting," Edwards said of Ryan. "On the stage you express emotion more or less with complete freedom; on the screen, mostly with the eyes with very little facial contortions." His third role was the one that would be quite different from all the others.

One of the Hollywood producers who now had an eye on Edwards was Stanley Kramer. Kramer had been in Hollywood since the mid-1930s, beginning as a researcher, then an editor, then casting director. By the late 1940s, he had formed a small production company to produce his own films. He was toying with a film adaptation of *Home of the Brave,* a play written by Arthur Laurents that had a brief Broadway run, opening December 27, 1945, but closing two months later. The play dealt with a Jewish soldier hospitalized during the war, and how he reacted to anti-Semitism. Kramer, however, had a radical idea: he thought the movie adaptation would be more dynamic and original if the protagonist were Black instead of Jewish. Carl Foreman, the screenwriter, agreed, and revealed he had watched the mistreatment of Blacks in his native Chicago and thought the big screen needed such a dose of reality.

Robert Stillman was a producing partner of Stanley Kramer, and Stillman's father, a wealthy businessman living in Florida, decided to help finance the film. Kramer wrapped a veil of secrecy around the movie and told the studio that housed his production deal that he was making a war picture indeed, but something called *High Noon*—not to be confused with the 1952 Gary Cooper Western of the same name. The ruse was to keep the studio from realizing what he was really making. Kramer assembled a small cast: Lloyd Bridges, Jeff Corey, Frank Lovejoy, and Steve Brodie. Then he announced he had hired James Edwards—but to work in a behind-the-scenes capacity on the project. Foreman, the screenwriter, knew what was at stake while writing. "This was breaking new ground, pioneering—and we had to be truthful and courageous. We didn't pull any punches."

Kramer and his producers worried whether the public would be ready to accept a picture about both patriotism and racism. So, before the release, Kramer plotted an aggressive marketing strategy, sending an emissary out across the country to chat up theatre owners. There was also a special marketing campaign geared toward the Negro press. There were conversations held with labor and civil-rights groups, explaining the film, preparing them for a type of movie that had never been shown in an American theatre. In big bold lettering, the ads proclaimed: "THE FIRST MAJOR MOTION PICTURE OF ITS KIND! And it's DYNAMITE!"

Hollywood clearly preferred—when they preferred to focus on Blacks at all—a movie that highlighted the travails of Black women as opposed to Black men. The poster of *Brave* showed four white soldiers stacked on the left side. On the right side, and at the bottom, was a picture of the James Edwards character. Such had been the dearth of Black men in major motion pictures that when *Home of the Brave*—after a slew of screenings—opened on September 14, 1949, it was shocking to see James Edwards at the center of action throughout the film. His character was part of a small reconnaissance team sent to a Japanese-held island. He was the only Negro among the group, and tensions arose as the men discussed their backgrounds. This is how Private Peter Moss tries to explain to his fellow soldiers what it's like being Black: "When I was six, my first week at school, a bunch of kids got around me, whites, and said, 'Hey, is your father a monkey?' I was dumb, I smiled and said 'No.' They wiped the smile off my face. They beat it off. I had to get beat up a couple more times before I learned that if you're colored, you stink." There are battles in the jungle, Japanese soldiers falling dead. During times of quiet, there is more talking among the American soldiers. There is a kind white soldier, Finch, whom Private Moss knew before the war, but the bigotry and meanness overwhelm Moss. When Finch dies in Moss's arms, Moss snaps. He loses movement in his legs. It has nothing to do with a gunshot; it is a mental breakdown, and he ends up in a psychiatric hospital. He tries explaining to the psychiatrist the relentless assault upon his racial background while he was in the jungle—fighting for his country. The psychiatrist concludes that his immobility is psychosomatic, nowhere but in his mind, and tries desperately to come up with remedies. Finally, the white psychiatrist is out of patience. "Get up and walk, you dirty nigger!" he screams at Private Moss. Moss, angered by the slur, slowly begins to rise. It is a scene both wretched and maudlin, a doctor falling back on a common slur, a slur that lifts Moss onto his feet.

There was great word-of-mouth about *Home of the Brave,* and standing ovations, especially in the Black communities. Black World War I veterans in good enough health insisted on seeing it. "Don't be discouraged by the lines and the SRO signs," advised *Color* magazine, which had a large Negro readership. Kramer and his team were excited about the reviews. "This comparatively inexpensive picture hits hard and with utter cred- ibility," wrote *Variety.* "Once customers are inside the theatre *Home* will have started a progression of comments that should win an accolade for the producer for having the courage to produce such a pic. And for doing it so well." Bosley Crowther, in *The New York Times,* admired the film and the performances. "In the role of the Negro soldier, James Edwards does a finely tempered job, revealing the man's inner torments from behind a frame of stoic dignity." The *Motion Picture Herald* weighed in: "It is hard hitting and tense; the dialogue is crisp; there are touches of subtle humor; the camera work and musical score are top shelf, and its moments of pathos will choke up the most calloused." And from *The Capital-Times* in Madison, Wisconsin: "It is something new and venturesome in our censor-ridden society as it deals, tellingly, with anti-Negro prejudices." Kramer worried about Southern critics, concerned that they might ignore the film completely. They did not, and their reactions surprised him. *The Dallas Morning News* wrote that the film "abashes the white man for both his habit of Negro prejudice and worse, his unconscious tactlessness." The Memphis *Commercial Appeal* review struck a similar note: "Let no smug section of the nation think [the Negro problem] is exclusively the South's baby. It belongs to us all." There was a worrisome note from the city of Houston. Theatre owners there would show the movie only at midnight screenings. Blacks came anyway.

The mission of cinema had always been to entertain, as Kramer and his team fully realized. But they also felt that socially conscious films could be thought-provoking and entertaining. They were hardly alone in such sentiments. "Home of the Brave has a lesson to teach," offered the *Baltimore Afro-American.*

Hollywood—the land of make-believe—had long steered clear of forcing America to confront racism and anti-Semitism. But cracks were beginning to appear. In 1947, both *Gentleman's Agreement* and *Crossfire* dealt with anti-Semitism. And in 1949, four movies dealt with racism against Blacks: *Lost Boundaries, Intruder in the Dust, Pinky,* and *Home of the Brave.* The moment did not go unnoticed. "Film's leading box office star for 1949," proclaimed *Cinema Journal,* "wasn't a personality, but a subject matter—racial prejudice—that until very recently was tabu."

With *Home of the Brave* continuing its long and profitable run in theatres, James Edwards became the most recognizable Black male actor in America. He was the buzz in his native Indiana. National Black publications wrote stories about him. If his career was to ascend, however, he'd need brave directors and studios to put him in their movies. He had clearly shown leading-man potential, but for months his phone didn't ring. He found comfort in the arms of women, often white women. His drinking had begun way back in high school. It began to escalate, though it didn't seem to affect his good looks. Lana Turner fell for him. She'd sneak into his garage apartment behind the Jungle Room, a nightclub on Jefferson Avenue. "Lana loved Black people, and Black people loved her," says the actor Louis Gossett, who was a friend of Edwards. Edwards didn't get any acting nominations for *Home,*

Lana Turner, one of the few 1950s white actresses who touched a nerve with Black America.

and Gossett believes it was because of an incident that happened between Edwards and Turner. Turner had shown up at Edwards's home one evening wanting to accompany him to a party. Edwards knew that such a public outing with a famous white actress would harm his career. Turner wouldn't accept his reasoning. Voices were raised. There was a commotion. Later reports said there had been a physical confrontation, and this got back to the studios. Turner was golden, not to be trifled with, and the insinuation was enough so that some studios began steering clear of Edwards. And that wasn't the end of unsavory gossip and reports connected to him and white women. Donna Rayburn, a white housewife, said Edwards had not only had an affair with her, but physically abused her. She told the press she was living "in terror" and afraid of the actor. No charges, however, were filed. Other women came forward, saying that Edwards had a temper. The drinking became more pronounced, so much so that he had to answer to it with the press. "It has been said that I drink excessively," he said. "To this I can only answer, 'Yes!' I like to drink now and then as does any man." Edwards would not admit he had a problem. Friends knew better.

James Edwards only had two small roles in films in 1951, so he went east, to New York City, and appeared in a play in Harlem about Nat Turner, the slave who launched an insurrection in 1831. Edwards had always been a voracious reader, and history fascinated him. One of the artist-performers he greatly admired was Paul Robeson, who had long been followed by the FBI for his pronouncements against racism, his visits to Russia, and his advocacy of socialism.

The House Un-American Activities Committee (HUAC) had been investigating unions and arts organizations for years, and throughout the 1940s directed a lot of their attention toward Hollywood. Congressman John Rankin of Mississippi took over the committee in the mid-1940s. He was a vile bigot and anti-Semite. Rankin proclaimed that Hollywood operatives were fostering "one of the most dangerous plots ever instigated for the overthrow of the government." HUAC had FBI agents going around the country, interrogating, among others, artists and actors about possible associations with communists. Those accused held up the mantle of free speech and the First Amendment. Ten Hollywood figures—among them Dalton Trumbo, Lester Cole, Ring Lardner, Jr., and Herbert Biberman—refused to "name names" and were sent to prison, with sentences ranging from six months to a year. It was all quite shameful, and supporters of civil liberties were stunned. Congressman Richard Nixon, and Ronald Reagan, who headed the Screen Actors Guild, supported the prison sentences. Following their release, the men were blacklisted and unable to get work in Hollywood for years. James Edwards would recall his own brush with HUAC: Three FBI agents—"well-dressed and well-poised gentlemen who had Harvard-Princeton-Yale written all over them"—visited him, seeking information about Paul Robeson. Edwards refused to say anything or name any names. The government wasted little time in alerting studios as to which actors had refused to cooperate with their investigations.

James Edwards made one movie in 1952 and one in 1953, neither role as involved as his role in *Home of the Brave*. Small roles in other movies followed, often as military men. He was a Negro actor and could hardly complain about being typecast, since the roles were so few. In the suites of Hollywood, producers were starting to talk about a young Bahamian actor by the name of Sidney Poitier. Poitier began to be offered roles that might have gone to Edwards. In between his all-too-rare film appearances, James Edwards paid his bills with the occasional television appearance, playing a boxer or a military figure in variety-sketch shows. He played military men in two 1957 movies, *Battle Hymn* and *Men in War*, the latter of which starred Robert Ryan. Ryan had put in a good word for Edwards.

For several years, Edwards had only intermittent work. He turned some of his attention to community theatre, teaching acting and directing plays at the Ebony Showcase Theater in Los Angeles, the kind of theatre that actors with Hollywood credentials avoided because it was far from the spotlight. But in the aftermath of the racially charged 1965 Watts riots, community theatre had become both a forum for artistic expression and an extension of political activism. For Edwards, it harked back to his earliest days, doing social-activism theatre around the country. "Of all the black stars he was the only one who was big enough and great enough to come back to the black community and work in black theatre," said Edna Stewart, who had long been involved with the Ebony Showcase Theater.

After a long absence from any major time on the big screen, James Edwards got another war movie, playing the military valet to George C. Scott's General Patton, in the 1970 release of *Patton*. He was fine and smooth in the role. The film won Scott the Best Actor Academy Award, but he refused it, telling the Academy beforehand that he didn't believe in competition among actors. The movie also won the Oscar for Best Picture. But by the time *Patton* was released in theatres, James Edwards was dead. He died on January 4, 1970, of a heart attack. He had been living in

James Edwards in *Patton* (1970). He perplexed Hollywood.

San Diego, in a small apartment. He was fifty-one years old. There was a sparsely populated memorial service, not in Hollywood but at the Ebony Showcase Theater, where the owners and others who had been in productions with him remembered Edwards: the Black movie star, covered in dust, hammering away at a prop on the stage, trying to fix it. "All young Negro actors today owe him a debt of gratitude because it was Jimmy Edwards," Sidney Poitier would say, "who started the employment situation outside the old stereotype with his performance in 'Home of the Brave'. As a matter of fact, the opportunities that came my way were a direct result of Jimmy Edwards' work in 'Home of the Brave.'"

Late in his life, George C. Scott began telling people he might have accepted his Academy Award for *Patton* if the Academy had nominated James Edwards years earlier for *Home of the Brave*. Scott had long thought the acting profession marred by grave pitfalls. "It is axiomatic that special talent suffers, and the result is that everyone around the talent also suffers," Scott once said. "It's a silly, unreal state of mind that produces cut wrists, pills, alcohol, jumping off cliffs. A survivor looking back over the shambles of his life as an actor is astonished he made it."

———

James Edwards first met Ike Jones in 1953 on the set of *The Joe Louis Story,* in which they both had small roles. They appeared together again in *Anna Lucasta,* a 1958 film that starred Sammy Davis, Jr., and Eartha Kitt. Jones, like Edwards, dreamed of becoming a leading man, but being a Black man hoping for such a thing in Hollywood became wearying. Years later, Sammy Davis convinced Jones to start thinking of producing, and Davis gave him the opportunity to coproduce *A Man Called Adam,* released in 1966. This was the first time a Black man held a producing credit on a mainstream Hollywood movie.

Most Black actors working in Hollywood were transplants, often having come to Los Angeles from the East Coast or the Midwest. Ike Jones, however, was a local native, born and raised in Santa Monica. A gifted high-school athlete, he attended UCLA, where he became a stellar football player. He was enrolled in the university's film-studies program, and became its first Black graduate. He got small acting roles throughout the 1950s; then disappointment over the lack of quality parts set in. Burt Lancaster hired him at his production company. Jones next went to work for Harry Belafonte's company. He finally joined Nat King Cole and produced his television shows. Jones kept his personal life quite private, and there was good reason. In 1961, he scooted off to Tijuana, Mexico, to marry an attractive blonde actress, Inger Stevens, who had become known for her appearances on episodic television. Jones and Stevens, given her burgeoning profile in Hollywood, both decided to keep their interracial marriage secret. The ruse depended upon subterfuge, and, most painful of all, living in separate residences.

When Harry Belafonte had formed his production company, HarBel, in the late 1950s, there was excitement in Hollywood. *The New York Times* opined that the venture "could turn out to be one of the most important developments in the American Negro's long and drawn-out struggle for representation on the nation's movie screens." Belafonte was intrigued with a 1901 novel, *The Purple Cloud,* written by the British writer M. P. Shiel, which had an apocalyptic twist: three souls, two men and a woman, are stranded in New York City in the aftermath of a global toxic catastrophe. This would make for drama and sexual tension. It would be Belafonte's company's first film, and he would be one of the stars. The casting of the female role was eagerly followed by Hollywood. Inger Stevens got the role. (Ike Jones had not yet started working for Belafonte's company.)

Mel Ferrer was cast as the third member of the trio. When executives at MGM saw the first daily rushes of the film, they decided the heat onscreen between Belafonte and Stevens was too intense. (It was also no secret that Stevens had a reputation for carrying on affairs with her leading men.) The studio demanded a rewrite that would lessen the simmering romantic stirrings between the two characters. Belafonte, incensed, threatened to abandon the picture, but his friend Marlon Brando told him such a move would be disastrous for his production company and his career. Reluctantly, Belafonte relented and stayed on the film.

Despite its daring premise, when *The World, the Flesh and the Devil* (Belafonte also didn't like the title change) opened in 1959, it flopped at the box office. Inger Stevens's career continued unabated. She starred in a television series, *The Farmer's Daughter,* that ran from 1963 to 1966. (The producer of that series, Peter Kortner, was a white closeted gay man who often acted as Stevens's "beard" on social occasions. Many people thought they were an item.) Her movie career flourished; she starred in films opposite George Peppard, Dean Martin, Robert Mitchum, Walter Matthau, James Stewart, Henry Fonda, Richard Widmark, and Clint Eastwood. But her secret marriage weighed heavily on her. America was not her native Sweden, where an interracial union might not have drawn so much attention. She was, however, in America, in Hollywood, places long bewitched by race.

On April 30, 1970, Inger Stevens was found dead in her Hollywood Hills home. She was thirty-five years old. She was discovered by her female roommate, who told the ambulance crew that Stevens had tried to mumble something when she discovered her, but the words wouldn't come out. The coroner later ruled that the death had been a suicide, an overdose of barbiturates. Ike Jones—because the couple had concealed their relationship so thoroughly—was forced to go to court to prove that the white woman he loved, had been married to, was truly his wife.

# The Pricey Black Movie That Vanished and How It Came to Be

T HE SAGA OF THE NOVEL *Porgy* and how it came to be the operatic juggernaut of *Porgy and Bess,* and how that opera swooped around the world, loosening thoughts of what Black America must be like, and how that opera finally morphed into a last-of-its-kind antebellum movie—with the greatest Negro stars of the day!—and how that movie ultimately vanished, unable to be seen, is a saga with a cast of thousands. Like so many stories that contributed to mid-twentieth-century Black cinema, the saga itself first stirred awake in the deep South.

During the long stretch of the struggle for Black freedom, South Carolina proved one of the most fearsome places to be held in bondage. The overseers appeared more wicked; the lynch rope yanked with more than the usual maniacal venom. During the summer of 1819, Denmark Vesey, a carpenter and free Black man living in Charleston, began plotting a revolt. Vesey had purchased his own freedom, but was finding it extraordinarily difficult to raise enough money to buy his family's freedom. Separated from them, he experienced unimaginable agony. Vesey convinced himself his only recourse was to kidnap them out of bondage and to encourage other slaves to join the escape. As ringleader, Vesey held secret meetings with others he recruited to the plot. Once freed, everyone would dash to the Charleston boat docks and take to the high seas in an effort to reach Haiti. In feverish conversations with his coconspirators, it all sounded doable. But Vesey didn't plan on informers and, ultimately, sabotage. The plot unraveled when several slaves grew skittish and reported Vesey's plot to their masters. Before any clashes took place—or shots were fired—Charleston officials formed a militia and began making arrests. It took less than two weeks for the 1822 trial to begin and conclude—and the hangings to commence. Vesey was among the first group of Blacks to be hanged. The whites of Charleston had sent a message: those who would dare challenge their slaveholding authority would be dealt with severely. Decades rolled over the land as bondage and lynchings continued.

————

Ever since he was elected on November 6, 1860, Abraham Lincoln had made Southerners nervous. They considered slavery their domain; Lincoln knew it was a moral sin and must be outlawed if the nation was to endure. Southern politicians began drawing lines and issuing warnings to Lincoln and his Cabinet that any attempt to free Blacks would be met with force. Lincoln's government considered it their duty to keep federal military installations in operation for the nation's safety. Fort Sumter, near Charleston, was one such installation. In April 1861, the fort was in need of supplies. A ship, the *Powhatan,* was dispatched to deliver those supplies, but before it was able to reach the fort, the South Carolina militia fired upon it. The shots meant that the American flag was under attack. And so the Civil War had begun.

The *National Intelligencer* was a Northern newspaper, fully aligned with Lincoln and his supporters. "Our people now, one and all, are determined to sustain the Government and demand a vigorous prosecution of the war inaugurated by the disunion," the newspaper intoned. "All sympathy with them is dead." Even Stephen Douglas, one of Lincoln's old foes, announced that he was prepared "to sustain the President in the exercise of his constitutional functions to preserve the Union, and maintain the Government." It took four years and more than six hundred thousand dead for the Civil War to come to an end. The assassination of Lincoln, on April 15, 1865, seemed to stand as a tragic postscript to the story of the dead and the dying.

For years after the Civil War, South Carolina remained deeply mired in the Lost Cause. The more any South Carolina politician denigrated and assailed Blacks and civil rights, the more that politician seemed to rise. Benjamin Tillman was an especially evil character. Elected governor in 1890, he sailed into office on a platform of white supremacy. He spoke out in favor of lynching. He seemed to loathe every Negro he set eyes upon.

Among his odd and seldom reviewed books, one was titled *Independence of Cuba: No Reconstruction or Carpetbag Government Under Pretense of Patriotic Motives*.

When DuBose Heyward, born in 1885, was growing up in Charleston, he heard plenty about Ben "Pitchfork" Tillman and others who promoted white supremacy. But Heyward's young mind was angling off into another direction. He was drawn to poetry and art. Afflicted with polio, he noticed that Negroes stared at him, and came to interpret their stares as harmless expressions of sympathy. As a young white man, Heyward got a job as an insurance salesman. The work required him to collect burial money, much of it from poor Black tenement dwellers. He sometimes found himself down near the Charleston docks, the same docks that Denmark Vesey had studied decades earlier while dreaming of freedom. In young Heyward's time, as in Vesey's time, Negroes populated the docks, working menial jobs. He watched and listened to the routines of their daily lives. It all fascinated him. As Heyward would recall: "Negroes in long lines trucking cotton on the wharves; dim figures in a deserted warehouse squatting over a crap game; spirituals bringing me up short to listen against the wall of a dilapidated church that I had to pass on the way to work." He befriended Negro stevedores, who came to find in Heyward someone who listened to their plight—and life stories—with consideration and respect.

Many of the Blacks in Charleston were descendants of the Gullah people, kidnapped and brought to the state under slavery. After emancipation, many of the Gullah remained on the islands around Charleston. Heyward's mother, a folklorist, had become so intrigued with the Gullah people that she began studying them. Heyward was quite interested in her work.

DuBose Heyward's insurance career was brief, and after a year at it, he started to write more seriously, with a dream to make his living as a writer. He began sketching the outlines of short stories; these stories were often about the Negroes of Charleston. He couldn't forget how they had made their own world, living in shantylike conditions, surviving on their own particular food, holding on to their customs. Heyward married in 1923, and Dorothy Heyward, also a writer, became as fascinated with Black life as her husband. Sometimes the white couple dropped by the Goose Creek Club in Charleston, where Negroes sometimes gathered to sing their spirituals. The Heywards would declare that they had never heard voices so beautiful.

Some in Charleston may have been interested in political or high-society news while reading their newspaper. But DuBose Heyward's eyes often rested upon stories that told of criminal activities and police pursuits. He noticed this item in the newspaper one day:

> *Samuel Smalls, who is a cripple and is familiar to King Street, with his goat and cart, was held for the June term of Court sessions on an aggravated assault charge. It is alleged that on Saturday night he attempted to shoot Maggie Barnes at number four Romney Street. His shots went wide of the mark. Smalls was up on a similar charge some months ago and was given a suspended sentence. Smalls had attempted to escape in his wagon and was run down and captured by police patrol.*

That brief item about the man Charlestonians referred to as "Goat Cart Sam" was all DuBose Heyward needed to ignite his fictional imagination. A crippled man; a woman; gunshots; a police pursuit and capture. This story melded with all he had seen while watching Negroes on the docks—working, sweating, singing, dreaming. He began writing. He wanted to feel Negro life springing inside his prose, to bring the reader into a whole other world. He was quite proud when one of his first pieces, "And Once Again—the Negro," was accepted for publication by the *Virginia Quarterly Review*. Emily Clark, Heyward's editor, understood his sensitive disposition toward the Negro, and how it separated him from many other Southern whites. As she explained: "For fear and suspicion of the African race, rather than affection and sympathy, are a part of the middle and lower class temper of the white South." In Heyward's own estimation, Negroes were but "an unfortunate race."

Heyward's short stories began getting published regularly and soon fused into the book *Porgy*, published in 1925. At the center of it was the love story between Porgy—who is crippled, scooting about atop a flatbed scooter—and Bess, beautiful but wicked, falling prey to drugs. Another figure, Crown, wants Bess for himself, and comes to abuse her. They're all struggling Negroes living on Cabbage Row in Charleston. (Heyward's debt to the life of Samuel Smalls, the crippled Charleston beggar, is obvious.) The book was populated with other Negroes—hard workers, gamblers, snake-eyed schemers, dope peddlers, all people not far removed from the residue of slavery. In his prose, Heyward adopted the Gullah dialect that South Carolina Blacks who lived on the sea islands were known for. "Hush, little baby, don' yo cry," he wrote. "Mudder an' fadder born to die." *Porgy* quickly became a publishing success, landing on bestseller lists, showing its universal appeal. The originality of the work surprised critics. "The best novel of the season by an American author," proclaimed *The Chicago Daily News*. It was quite an endorsement, inasmuch as there were new novels that season from F. Scott Fitzgerald, Ernest Hemingway, Sinclair Lewis, Anita Loos, and Gertrude Stein. "Of a beauty so rare and perfect it may be called classic," *The New Republic* offered about *Porgy*. Many wondered how the highly regarded Heywood Broun of the New York *World,* who had a syndicated column, felt about the novel. Readers got their answer when Broun wrote that "a literary advance in the South must be acknowledged when the writers of that land come to realize, as Heyward does, the incredibly rich material in Negro life which so far has been neglected. He leads the way with a magnificent novel." No other novel published that season by a white author concerned itself with Black life to the degree that Heyward's did.

The attention paid *Porgy* was enough to convince Dorothy Heyward that her husband's book could yield other creative opportunities. She began thinking of a dramatic play. DuBose was not convinced that white audiences would accept Blacks in straight dramatic roles. Dorothy kept insisting, and finally the couple set about jointly writing a play, hoping for interest from Broadway. The interest came quickly. The New York Theatre Guild came aboard as the sole producer of the play and wasted little time in forming a plan. They chose Rouben Mamoulian, an Armenian émigré who had trained at the famed Moscow Art Theatre, to direct.

During auditions for *Porgy,* Mamoulian began to sense the task faced by Black actors who had been accustomed to a world of minstrelsy and vaudeville, the only avenues of performance offered them. *Porgy* would be their introduction to straight dramatic plays—and to the discipline of traditional theatre. Not only did the actors have to learn their lines—no ad-libbing!—but they also had to learn the rudiments of straight drama. Mamoulian forged ahead, choosing a cast: Frank Wilson played Porgy, and Evelyn Ellis played Bess. Ellis had acted in Oscar Micheaux's 1924 film *Son of Satan.*

The Broadway production of *Porgy,* put on by the highly respected Theatre Guild, featured a sixty-five-member cast and opened October 10, 1927. The reviews were quite good. Brooks Atkinson of *The New York Times* called it an "illuminating chronicle of American folklore." Alan Dale, of

the *New York American,* was even more effusive: "To hear the spirituals sung as they were is worth twice the price of a seat.... There were
the fervor, the hysteria, the emotionalism, and the curious abandon that
must accompany such outbursts.... It was something new to most of
us—may I say to all of us." A unique feature of the Broadway play was
the participation of the musical band from the Jenkins Orphanage Home
in Charleston. The home had been founded to take in desperate homeless Black boys who had been roaming the streets of Charleston. The
white audiences introduced to *Porgy* were seeing something superior to
vaudeville and minstrel shows, which had always been rife with stereotyping. This was also the first time in theatrical history that so many Black
actors and actresses were called upon to act in a serious drama. Blacks
found themselves awash in pride that *Porgy* had made it to Broadway. "In
'Porgy,'" opined James Weldon Johnson, the first Black executive director
of the NAACP, "the Negro removed all doubts as to his ability to do acting that requires thoughtful interpretation and intelligent skill." Johnson
felt the play "loomed high above every Negro drama that had ever been
produced.... It carried conviction through its sincere simplicity." A bevy
of renowned white actors—Lynn Fontanne, Alfred Lunt, and Al Jolson
among them—became so enamored of the Black roles in Broadway's *Porgy*
that they expressed an interest in playing those roles themselves—albeit
in blackface, but the Heywards had no interest in mounting a blackface
production of their praised drama.

One of the unique features of *Porgy* was its renditions of folk songs.
Those rising Negro voices had seeped into DuBose and Dorothy Heyward
so much—and into the audiences as well—that the couple began wondering if the play might be successfully adapted into a musical. So it was
fortuitous when George Gershwin, rumbling around his Riverside Drive
apartment in New York City, happened to pull a book from a pile and
started reading it. He hadn't seen the book before. Theatrical types were
always coming and going from his apartment; someone had obviously
left it behind. Gershwin began reading *Porgy* and couldn't stop until he
finished it. He was enamored with the book.

If anyone was conjuring a musical or an opera in the late 1920s and
dreaming of a gifted composer, the name George Gershwin would have
certainly come to mind. His first song had been published when he was
all of seventeen years old. But it was the 1919 song "Swanee" that became
his first huge national hit. By 1922, Gershwin had already collaborated on
two Broadway musicals. But what he really wanted was to compose a great

and grand opera. "I'd like to write an opera of the melting pot, of New York City itself, with its blend of native and immigrant strains," he had confided. "This would allow for many kinds of music, black and white, Eastern and Western, and would call for a style that should achieve out of this diversity, an artistic unity. Here is a challenge to a librettist, and to my own name." Being in New York City when the Harlem Renaissance was flourishing had helped Gershwin appreciate Black music. The story of the lovers Porgy and Bess in Heyward's novel fascinated Gershwin so much that he sent Heyward a letter expressing his deep admiration of the book as soon as he finished reading it. The Heywards were stunned to receive a letter from the great George Gershwin. They had to confide to him that a dramatic play was already under way.

Years passed before Gershwin got back in touch with the Heywards. In 1932, he told Heyward, "It is still the most outstanding play I know about the colored people." Heyward, drawing on the folkloric gene from his mother, suggested to Gershwin that if he was truly interested in the characters in his book he should come to South Carolina and visit the native Blacks. Gershwin planned a trip.

Charleston and its environs were hot when Gershwin and an assistant arrived. The Heywards were delighted to see them, and to begin serious discussions with the composer about turning *Porgy* into an opera. Gershwin took a cottage on Folly Island and had a piano brought in. Word began getting around that the famous composer was in the area. He visited the homes of local Blacks, taking in as much as he could about the Gullah culture. His ease around Blacks impressed DuBose and Dorothy Heyward. When Black women started giving Gershwin friendly slaps on his shoulders, welcoming him into their world, it became obvious he was making quite an impression. Moving around the region, Gershwin heard their music erupt from church pews and church balconies. He listened to stories of their hard work. "I shall never forget," Heyward would recall of the composer's visit, "the night when at a Negro meeting on a remote sea island George started 'shouting' with them. And eventually to their huge delight stole the show from their champion 'shouter.' I think he is probably the only white man in America who could have done it." Photos that survive of the visit show the trim Gershwin standing near the water, often dressed in white linen slacks and poplin shirt. He was a continental figure, intent on trying as hard as he could to understand the Negro environment he was now in. Flies and mosquitoes seemed to be everywhere; now

and then, he spotted alligators gliding about the swamps. But the music
was beginning to form in his mind:

> Summertime, and the livin' is
>   easy,
> Fish are jumpin', and the cotton is
>   high . . .

In early 1934, the *New York Herald Tribune*, aware of Gershwin's
Southern sojourn, reported that the
composer was turning himself into
"an eager student of Negro music."
That very year, Gershwin summoned his brother, Ira, to help him
with the libretto for his planned
opera. Ira was nearly two years
older than George and a gifted lyri-
cist. Over the next twelve months,
the opera began coming together.
The brothers would toss songs and

George Gershwin, on Folly Beach,
South Carolina, June 1934. The
anonymous Black folk on the river
docks inspired his artistry.

lyrics back and forth to each other. Among the tunes they composed and
gave titles to were "Summertime," "It Ain't Necessarily So," "Bess, You Is
My Woman Now," and "I Loves You, Porgy." It was now time for George
and Ira, and the Heywards, to start thinking of a director and a cast. Gershwin didn't spend much energy on his search for a director. He went back
to Rouben Mamoulian, who had directed *Porgy* for Broadway. Since then,
Mamoulian had made a name for himself in Hollywood. But the possibility of *Porgy* as an opera greatly excited him. "I felt about Porgy, the play,
the way I imagine a mother feels about her first born," Mamoulian said.

George Gershwin realized it was going to be a challenge to find the cast
for his opera. Blacks had rarely been invited to join major opera companies around the country, and their lack of experience was a painful reality. But Gershwin was determined to find gifted singers, and he sent out
inquiries to both coasts. His actions started to pay off. He found his Porgy
on the music faculty at Howard University. Todd Duncan, a native of Kentucky, had graduated from Butler University and took a master's degree

from Columbia University Teachers College. He had sung in New York City with the Aeolian Opera, a Black opera company. When he found his opportunities gravely limited, he turned to teaching. But when Gershwin called, he auditioned and won the male title role. Anne Brown, at the age of sixteen, had been the first Black vocalist to be accepted into Juilliard in New York City. When she heard about Gershwin's planned opera, she wrote directly to the composer. He was so stunned by Brown's talent that he began inviting her to his apartment to sing songs from the opera with him. Gershwin offered Anne Brown the role of Bess and told her that the opera was being renamed *Porgy and Bess*—not only to distance it from the dramatic staging of *Porgy,* but to highlight her role, a distinction Gershwin felt was demanded by her talent. A onetime maid and housekeeper, Ruby Elzy, won the role of Serena. She had attended Rust College in her native Mississippi, washing dishes to help pay her way through school. While at Ohio State University, attending their graduate music school, she worked as a housekeeper for the chairman of the music department. After her stay at Ohio State, she studied acting and singing in New York City. She was one of the few who came to Gershwin with both opera and acting training, which aided her in winning the role. The roles of Sportin' Life and Crown—both nefarious characters in the play—were integral to the looming opera. John W. Bubbles had been a dancing star of vaudeville, and his popularity got him an audition with the *Porgy and Bess* producing team. He excited them because he could dance and had a magnetic stage presence; he worried them because he couldn't read music. They took a risk and welcomed him to the opera as Sportin' Life. Warren Coleman, a graduate of the New England Conservatory of Music, was given the role of Crown to play.

Neither George Gershwin nor Rouben Mamoulian was sure how the critics would react to an opera that displayed a melding of opera and jazz and blues. This brewing of musical genres had always been Gershwin's intent, but he also realized that the combination might well come under criticism from opera purists. The pre-Broadway opening was announced for Boston on September 30, 1935. Excitement and anticipation were noticeable, from Roxbury to Cambridge. A crowd of high-society denizens were in the opening-night audience, as were local university presidents and scions of wealthy blue-blood families. At the show's end, the applause went on and on, for an entire fifteen minutes, before it started to simmer down. Some had tears in their eyes. J. Rosamond Johnson, the assistant conductor of the chorus, had never seen anything like it.

"George," he whispered in Gershwin's ear, "you've done it—you're the Abraham Lincoln of Negro music." The local critics gushed rapturously. "When the cries of genius subside," wrote Ann Ames of the *Boston American*, "George Gershwin's Porgy and Bess will take its place indubitably as the 'first' American opera." Boston, of course, wasn't New York City's Broadway, where Heyward and Gershwin knew the critics would soon weigh in and have their own say.

It opened at the Alvin Theatre on October 10, 1935. And what happened on that starry Manhattan night was this: A brilliant composer shoved a folk opera down the throats of the American public. He said, in his own musical way, that America had ignored Negroes and their beauty and music and hurts for far too long; he said that a thing such as love, between man and woman, between Porgy and Bess, between Negro and Negro, was powerful and universal; he said that a nation seventy years removed from slavery should open its arms and minds to a different kind of artistic expression. The critics were critics—some kind, some bewildered—but all snapped to attention. John Mason Brown of the *New York Post* thought the opera too long, but conceded it was imbued with "one of the most notable feats in virtuoso direction our modern theatre has seen." Olin Downes, the music critic at *The New York Times*, questioned Gershwin's opera bona fides but couldn't deny the overall production itself. "He has not completely formed his style as an operatic composer. The style is at one moment of opera and another of operetta or sheer Broadway entertainment." Gershwin might have winced at that line, but Downes went on to offer genuine praise. "If the Metropolitan chorus could ever put one half of the action into the riot scene in the second act of Meistersinger than the Negro cast put into the fight that followed the crap game it would be not merely refreshing but miraculous." Joseph Wood Krutch wrote in *The Nation*—in what could be interpreted as a backhanded slap—that "admiring it will be one of the Things Being Done."

Gershwin realized he had broken ground on something new. He allowed that *Porgy and Bess* contained "elements that have never before appeared in opera and I have adapted my method to utilize the drama, the humor, the superstition, the religious fervor, the dancing and the irrepressible high spirits of the race. If, in doing this, I have created a new form, which combines opera with theatre, this new form has come quite naturally out of the material."

The play was not a huge commercial hit. It closed after a three-month run, on January 25, 1936. The cast gave 124 performances.

On July 11, 1937, the music world was stunned by the death of thirty-eight-year-old George Gershwin from a brain tumor. Three years later, on June 16, 1940, DuBose Heyward died.

———

Producers had expressed interest over the years in turning *Porgy and Bess* into a film, but nothing firm materialized. It became apparent that if the opera was to remain in the public mindset—especially given the absence of Gershwin and Heyward—it would depend on Negro singers and record companies. In 1940, Decca Records gathered members of the original cast and issued a two-set recording titled *Selections from George Gershwin's Folk Opera Porgy and Bess*. The recordings made such tunes as "Summertime" and "I Loves You, Porgy," and "It Ain't Necessarily So" part of the public's consciousness. In 1950, RCA Victor convinced Robert Merrill and Rise Stevens to record eight tunes from the opera. The response was so favorable that a year later Columbia Masterworks issued the first complete recording of the show, enlisting the talents of Lawrence Winters and Camilla Williams. The colorful *Porgy and Bess* album covers began appearing in record shop windows all around the country. Though it was hardly as famous as *La Bohème* or *Carmen* or *Don Giovanni, Porgy and Bess* was gaining a serious following. And Robert Breen meant to take advantage of that following.

Breen was born in Hibbing, Minnesota. In college, he had gotten involved in theatre, both acting and behind the scenes. After college, he roamed the country, putting on theatrical productions. Those who met him thought him charming and bustling with energy. He spent some time in Hollywood, but what he really wanted to do was take American theatrical productions abroad. To that end, he got appointed general director of the American National Theatre and Academy. It had government funding, and seemed expressly made for Breen's ambitions. He knew exactly the production he wanted to take across the Atlantic: *Porgy and Bess*. Breen knew he'd need help, in addition to governmental support, to mount a production, so he joined forces with Blevins Davis, a wealthy Missourian who was interested in the arts. Davis loved the idea of mounting *Porgy and Bess,* and was comfortable about leaving all of the artistic decisions to Breen. Negotiations with the heirs of the Gershwin and Heyward estates were mind-numbing, but Breen's infectious enthusiasm wore them all down. A new production of *Porgy and Bess* was announced for 1952.

It would start in Dallas and go to other cities; then the company would zoom off to Europe for engagements sponsored by the U.S. State Department. An opera that some had thought passé was suddenly in vogue again. Casting began right away.

A few very gifted Blacks—quite far from an avalanche, but noticeable—had come into the pool of mainstream entertainment by the early 1950s. Breen and his casting team could throw a wider net and feel confident that it would yield good results. William Warfield had received national attention when he made his recital debut at New York City's Town Hall in 1950. As well, his singing in the film version of *Show Boat* had drawn praise. When Warfield signed on, Breen had his Porgy. In the 1930s, Cab Calloway was one of the most electrifying nightclub performers in America. His single, "Minnie the Moocher," was the first recording by a Negro to sell a million copies. He led big bands and wowed high society at New York City's Cotton Club. Calloway hadn't acted onstage since an all-Negro production in 1929 called *Hot Chocolates*. Through telegrams and phone calls, Breen finally reached Calloway. The dancer-musician had reservations about jumping into an opera, but Breen convinced him, and when he came aboard, they had their Sportin' Life. As soon as Breen heard Leontyne Price sing in a small production of the opera *Four Saints in Three Acts,* he was wowed by her voice. He also liked her pedigree: she had studied at Juilliard. Price's audition consisted of singing "Summertime." Her rendition was beautiful, and when the twenty-four-year-old agreed to join the company, they had their Bess. The cast filled out; some performers came from Cleveland's famed Karamu House, which had trained many Black actors.

The year 1952 marked seventeen years since the opera of *Porgy and Bess* opened on Broadway. Breen was attuned to the new reality of racial dynamics. When a white stagehand in Dallas uttered a racial slur during a rehearsal, Breen wasted little time in demanding the crew member be let go. When the opera opened in Dallas, it became apparent that Leontyne Price was going to become a star, and that William Warfield's acclaimed reputation was going to keep rising. Price took Bess in another direction. "She gave it a gut-bucket quality, that just wrenched your heart," said Eva Jesse, the choral director, of Price. *The Dallas Times Herald* proclaimed the short run in that city "the box-office champion in the history of summer musical shows in Dallas." The reviews in Pittsburgh and Chicago were laudatory as well. The opening night show in the nation's capital drew government dignitaries as well as President Truman and his wife, Bess.

"A superlative cast sang the work to an audience which appreciated and understood its compassionate revelation of Negro life in this alien hemisphere," wrote Jay Carmody of *The Washington Post*. He thought the evening "one of democracy's . . . historic moments." The production prepared to move overseas.

The cast arrived in Vienna the first week of September, and wowed an audience of dignitaries, diplomats, and opera enthusiasts. "They kept up the applause for half an hour," recalled Ella Gerber, the drama coach for the production. "They had never seen anything in the theatre like it, the kind of blood, guts, and thunder Breen put into it." The critics in postwar Berlin—where a mere sixteen years earlier, Hitler had expressed his disgust with black skin by leaving the stadium when Jesse Owens won his Olympic medals—fell in love with the show. A *New York Times* correspondent sent a cable to his newspaper about the production: "One sits in the audience amazed, breathless, and again and again surprised how this graceful brown people moves around without any restraints and how completely they live their parts." It went on: "Tempo without pause, number after number, unbelievable precision, a feel for rhythm which borders on the fantastic, and voices—voices that take away one's breath with astonishment." There were champagne parties, galas, VIP affairs. The playbills and *Porgy and Bess* posters were so beautiful that many hoarded them as keepsakes. Europe hadn't seen this many Blacks in the field of entertainment since the aftermath of World War II, when Black musicians bebopped their way across France, Germany, and Amsterdam. In London—where the audiences had been impatiently waiting—*Porgy and Bess* opened, and later was named the "Best Musical" by the London Drama Critics. *Show Business Annual* deemed it "The Most Sensational Stage Offering of the Year." In Paris, there were moblike scenes outside the Empire Theatre. "It is life itself!" one French critic declared. The smashing press reports drew a lot of attention when they reached America. Hollywood took note.

A few years later, after he formed the Everyman Opera Company—an independent company that would give him more flexibility for booking his shows—Robert Breen's mind whirred off into territory that surprised everyone: He wanted to take *Porgy and Bess* to Moscow. To communist Russia! The negotiations between the American and Russian governments were laborious. But in December 1955, the *Porgy and Bess* cast found itself traveling on a train through Leningrad. Snow was on the ground. And Truman Capote was on the train, assigned by *The New Yorker* magazine to cover the excursion. A Southern-born writer, Capote had come to the attention of American readers with the 1948 publication of his novel *Other Voices, Other Rooms.* Then there was his play, *The Glass Harp,* which arrived on Broadway in 1952. John Huston employed him to co-write the script for *Beat the Devil,* a 1953 film that starred Humphrey Bogart, Gina Lollobrigida, and Peter Lorre. The cast of *Porgy and Bess* thought Capote—white, gay, Southern, sweet of nature—quite amusing. He wore colorful clothing and bragged about his gift of recall. "I admired his writing," the company member Martha Flowers would say of Capote, "but I did find him sort of weird."

Opening night in Leningrad—all the shows were sold out—was an illustrious affair, with the American ambassador and more than two thousand in attendance. The reviews throughout the run were glowing. "For fifteen years," wrote Leonard Lyons, an American syndicated columnist, "the Russians have been parched for contact with the Western world, and Porgy and Bess is helping to ease the drought." With Leningrad's audiences still sparkling from their performances, the company departed for Moscow on January 7, 1956, feeling like cultural conquerors. The *Newsweek* critic opined that the success of the tour thus far "came from its direct emotional impact, which transcends any obstacles of language." *Life* magazine readers were treated to a story and lavish photo spread about the tour: "RUSSIANS LIONIZE 'PORGY,'" the headline read. Among the highlights of the Moscow engagement—in addition to more rave reviews—was the appearance of Soviet premier Nikita Khrushchev himself.

When Capote's story appeared in the October, 19, 1956, edition of *The New Yorker,* it was a letdown. Perhaps exhausted—and receiving less pampering than he was accustomed to—he had abandoned the tour in Leningrad. Nowhere in the *New Yorker* story did there appear any insight about the presence of Black Americans in Russia. Rather, the story was full of decorative touches about pearls and fur coats and walks through palace courtyards and the wintry snow. There was precious little probing into the historical moment of classically trained Negroes breaking barriers in the midst of a dangerous Cold War while they were thousands of miles away from racially haunted America. What were they experiencing? How did it feel to be in a land that was barren, yes, but where they hadn't been met with racial insults all day long? What did the Black cast members think of the occasional Blacks (musicians, mostly, who had married Russian women) who came up to them eager for conversation? Capote completely ignored digging for such revelations.

All of the publicity throughout the mid-1950s about the world tour convinced one of the famed veteran studio moguls in Hollywood that now was the time for a *Porgy and Bess* movie. Samuel Goldwyn was convinced he could turn the opera into a hit onscreen.

––––––––

In the mid-1950s, several things on the political front happened across Negro America that began to shake the nation. In late 1955, a Montgomery, Alabama, seamstress, Rosa Parks, led a boycott of the city's segregated bus system. The boycott led to a victorious desegregation lawsuit, *Browder v. Gale,* that ruled the segregated bus system was unconstitutional. This momentous ruling ignited a more aggressive ministerial movement from the pulpit of Black churches across the nation. But Blacks everywhere realized that the first wave of this civil rights momentum concerned education and came to envelop the very South Carolina landscape used as the setting for *Porgy and Bess.*

In 1951, Oliver Brown, a Topeka, Kansas, parent, filed a lawsuit on behalf of his daughter, Linda, and the family's efforts to have her attend a white school rather than suffer travel hardships to go to her Black school. With guidance from the NAACP Legal Defense Fund—led by the cagey and brilliant attorney Thurgood Marshall—other jurisdictions around the country soon joined in, making it a class-action suit. In South Carolina, Harry Briggs was one of the first plaintiffs to sign the petition. He worked at a gas station. There were thirty buses to serve the white children of the county in which he lived, but not a single bus for Harry Briggs's five children and all the other Black children in the same county. For his nerve in signing a petition challenging the white educational power structure, Briggs was fired from his job—on Christmas Eve. His wife, Eliza, worked as a maid. She was fired, too. The case became known as *Briggs v. Elliott;* R. W. Elliott, the chairman of the school board, saw absolutely no reason Negro children should be provided with school buses. "We ain't got no money to buy a bus for your nigger children," Elliott told one of the parents of Clarendon County. These were the real-life Negroes of DuBose Heyward's novel *Porgy.* The Briggs case was folded into other desegregation cases, all eventually coming under the *Brown v. Board of Education* decision, delivered unanimously by the U.S. Supreme Court in May 1954, dismantling segregated education in America.

Practically every jurisdiction across the South refused to implement the 1954 landmark ruling handed down by the high court. In the spring of 1957, a group of Negro labor leaders and ministers—led by Adam Clayton Powell, Jr., A. Philip Randolph, and Martin Luther King, Jr.—planned a massive rally at the Lincoln Memorial to bring attention to the third anniversary of the *Brown* court decision. Congressman Powell was a liberal Democrat who had stung his party by backing Ike's 1956 GOP re-election, his major reason being that Southern Democrats refused to endorse the 1954 desegregation ruling. A Black and white crowd estimated between twenty-five and thirty thousand descended upon the Lincoln Memorial on May 17, 1957. Attired in a gray double-breasted suit and looking movie-star handsome, Powell thundered from behind the microphone: "We are sick and tired of the two-party hypocrisy!" He advocated more sit-ins and boycotts around the nation. "Asia and Africa will never trust America," he said, "because they know we're ruled by a hypocritical bipartisan Jim Crow policy." Three months later came the clash at Central High School in Little Rock, Arkansas. The aftermath of Little Rock saw white communities opening all-white academies and Christian schools around the country, a move that was a mischievous tactic to prevent Blacks and whites being educated together.

At the time of the Little Rock uprising, Samuel Goldwyn was taking in all the scintillating worldwide reviews of *Porgy and Bess,* and shared the clippings with other film executives. He did not bother to concern himself with the Negro citizens of South Carolina who had risked their lives to sign those petitions, nor did he concern himself with the demonstrations in Little Rock, and certainly not with those who had gathered at the Lincoln Memorial to highlight American hypocrisy. As well, Samuel Goldwyn most assuredly paid scant attention, if any, to the Negro criticism that had been heaped upon *Porgy and Bess* during its international tour. Much of that criticism came from the Negro press. James Hicks, respected columnist for the *Baltimore Afro-American,* referred to the opera as "the most insulting, the most libelous, the most degrading act that could possibly be perpetrated against the Negro people." Hicks bemoaned that the Black talent in *Porgy and Bess* was not being welcomed onto the opera stages of New York City in other productions: "Instead they are intermingled with the rattle of dice which roll across the stage throughout Porgy." William Warfield, who had been the *Porgy* star of the touring opera, had by now turned his attention to a solo concert tour. One of his songs from *Porgy and Bess,* "I Got Plenty o' Nuttin,' " was often requested by audience members during his solo tour. But now, with protests bubbling across the land, that song sounded too maudlin and weak. "The black community," Warfield said of his decision to forgo that song, "wasn't listening to anything about plenty of nothing being good enough for me. There was now another feeling in the community about being black—I'm a black man and proud. And with that attitude came a lot of negation and turning your back on things. Hattie McDaniel was accused of Uncle Tomism because of her playing . . . those servant roles in movies."

Samuel Goldwyn hadn't produced a theatrical-release movie since 1955's *Guys and Dolls.* Plenty in Hollywood were convinced his movie-making time had passed. To prove them wrong, Goldwyn successfully secured movie rights to *Porgy and Bess.* Like many in Hollywood, he remembered the excitement back in 1943 when two all-Negro musicals, *Stormy Weather* and *Cabin in the Sky,* had been released. (Both of those pictures had starred the luminous Lena Horne, made decent money, and, as important, introduced dazzling Black talent to moviegoers.) And there was also the colossal success of *Gone with the Wind,* another story shaved from antebellum America, and a movie whose release Goldwyn had helped orchestrate.

Samuel Goldwyn set about putting his *Porgy and Bess* creative team together. He thought either King Vidor or Frank Capra would be a smart choice to direct, but he could not make it happen with either, so he fell back on Rouben Mamoulian. N. Richard Nash was brought on to write the screenplay. Nash most recently had written the script for *The Rainmaker,* which starred Burt Lancaster and Katharine Hepburn.

If one was implored in the late 1950s to identify the small contingent of Negro stars—and up-and-coming stars—in the entertainment world, certain names would have popped to the top of that list: Sidney Poitier, Dorothy Dandridge, Sammy Davis, Jr., Pearl Bailey, Diahann Carroll, Harry Belafonte, and Brock Peters. Goldwyn secured the services of every one of them—save Belafonte, who turned down the role of Porgy. It was a coup, a lineup of Negro All-Stars, and it quickly proved to Hollywood that Samuel Goldwyn still had a lot of clout. But with Poitier, who was the biggest dramatic figure in the group, the negotiations were fraught. Poitier's agent, Martin Baum, had actually not confirmed to Goldwyn that Poitier would take the role. It was Lillian Small, a West Coast associate of Baum's, who had promised to deliver Poitier and even agreed to Goldwyn's offer of seventy-five thousand dollars for the actor's services. Small had waded into tricky waters negotiating for Poitier without Poitier's knowledge. Poitier had no intention of doing *Porgy and Bess,* which he, like Belafonte, believed was outdated and worn, and fostered stereotypes. "In a period of calm," Belafonte remarked at the time, "perhaps this picture could be viewed historically. But skins are still too thin and emotions still too sensitive for a lot of Uncle Toms in *Porgy and Bess* to be shown now." Poitier also happened to be sitting on another script, about two escaped convicts, one Black, one white, called *The Defiant Ones,* which the producer-director Stanley Kramer wanted him to do. Poitier believed *Porgy and Bess* was old Hollywood and hoped that *The Defiant Ones* might represent what could be the beginnings of a new Hollywood. "If I refuse to do Porgy and Bess," Poitier mused, "the town is going to know that I messed over Goldwyn, in which case, as I've been amply warned, the unwritten laws governing behavior in these situations will unquestionably wipe me out. But the other side of the coin, how can I do Porgy and Bess when I don't like it, don't want to do it, and have declared publicly that I have no intention of doing it?" Stanley Kramer, perhaps the most progressive-minded producer in Hollywood when it came to race, hinted to Poitier the folly of reneging on Goldwyn, even if someone else had made the commitment for him. Weighing his dilemma in a business in which not a single Black held real power, Poitier signed on for *Porgy and Bess.*

Dorothy Dandridge signed on to play Bess. Crown would be played by Brock Peters, who had distinguished himself in the same role in the *Porgy and Bess* touring opera. Pearl Bailey played Maria; the young Diahann Carroll was cast as Clara. The role of Sportin' Life was always a crucial one. Sammy Davis, Jr., badly wanted the role, but Goldwyn was already thinking of someone else, Cab Calloway. When Sammy Davis, Jr., heard that his friend Judy Garland was hosting a dinner party, and that Goldwyn would be attending, he had to be there. Sammy bounced into the party full of life, bestowing pleasantries and courtesies. When the time was right, he allowed Garland to implore him to sing something. Lee Gershwin, wife of Ira Gershwin, was also there. Something about Sammy's performance greatly annoyed her.

"Swear on your life you'll never use him," she whispered to Goldwyn.

"Him?" Goldwyn answered. "That monkey?"

Davis's agents grew worried when they heard nothing from the Goldwyn office. One of Sammy's William Morris agents, Abe Lastfogel, let him know that Goldwyn would be coming to the Moulin Rouge nightclub for dinner, and on an evening when Sammy was performing! On the appointed night, with Goldwyn in attendance, Sammy stopped and introduced Goldwyn to the audience. Flattery was an old show-business move that still carried currency, and Sammy knew it. He talked at the microphone about a wish of his, and that was to play Sportin' Life. Sammy had turned the nightclub into his office, a place to make a personal pitch to Goldwyn in front of a live audience. And then, as usual, Sammy Davis, Jr., put on a spellbinding show. At some point before the end of the evening, Goldwyn became convinced that Sammy Davis, Jr., might be a better Sportin' Life than Cab Calloway.

Filming of *Porgy and Bess* began in the summer of 1958. Just before that, Goldwyn donated one thousand dollars to the NAACP. This appeared to be a move to short-circuit any possible criticism. Still, unforeseen things began to happen. Pearl Bailey was in a snit, saying she didn't want to be in a film where Negro women wore Aunt Jemima–like bandanas on their heads, which she thought reeked of antebellum shamelessness. The bandanas stayed, though not as many. On July 3, flames tore through the *Porgy and Bess* set. No one was there, so no one got hurt, but the fire spooked many: could this be the work of angry Blacks who had nothing to do with the filming but were involved in the controversy that surrounded it? The official reason given for the blaze was a burning cigarette. Goldwyn shook his bald head and demanded that carpenters work fast to rebuild. The damage, however, required a two-month delay.

During the break in filming, Goldwyn concluded he didn't like Mamoulian's constant creative suggestions—a jazzier score, more script work!—and abruptly fired him. Mamoulian still received his full pay, but left in a fury. Next up for directing chores: Otto Preminger. Goldwyn liked the fact that Preminger had been around a large group of Blacks before, having directed *Carmen Jones*. But his past credits mattered little to Leigh Whipper, who had been in the original production of *Porgy* and was now summoned to attack Preminger on behalf of the Mamoulian camp. Whipper referred to Preminger, a man of Austro-Hungarian heritage, as "a man who has no respect for my people." The film's Black cast members, however, maintained a united front in support of the movie. Once the damaged set was reconstructed, filming resumed.

Goldwyn had a lot riding on this seven-million-dollar production, wanting it to remind everyone of his past successes, of his Oscar victories. He unleashed a bevy of press agents to trumpet the film. Two lavish and illustrated booklets were produced. One featured Poitier and Dandridge

on the cover, accompanied by a fine sprinkling of photos. The other featured printings of the sheet music from the movie. This was old-style
Samuel Goldwyn publicity at its best. The movie opened in New York
City on June 24, 1959, and in Los Angeles two weeks later. Both openings featured reserved seating only. Goldwyn was counting on spectacular
word-of-mouth. Cast members at the New York City opening arrived in
tuxedos and evening dresses. The sun was shining, and it was a beautifully
warm day. Sammy Davis, Jr., arrived with an entourage, his onetime showgirl mother, Elvera, by his side. The applause was loud and sustained for
cast members, but the reviews told their own story—they were decidedly
mixed. The complaints varied: The sound didn't seem right; it was obvious that some actors' singing voices (Poitier, Diahann Carroll) had been
dubbed by opera singers, and the synchronization appeared faulty. The
set of Cabbage Row looked clunky. "Choruses march and countermarch;
actors lumber woodenly about the stage obviously counting their steps,"
said the *Time* magazine critic. Writing in the *Saturday Review,* Arthur
Knight found plenty wrong with the production: "One can praise Irene
Sharaff's colorful, stylish costumes, but the question immediately arises
are they not perhaps too rich, too stylish for Catfish Row? Oliver Smith's
settings are eminently functional, but theatrical to such a degree that they
clash with an obviously real fishing wharf, an excursion steamer, and the
second-act picnic on Kittiwah Island. In addition, the interiors all tend to
look about six times the size of the exteriors that are supposed to house
them." Bosley Crowther of *The New York Times* wrote a favorable review.
Some of the harsher critics might have thought they'd seen a different
movie from Crowther, who then felt the need to write a follow-up piece,
supporting his initial review. In his second piece, he singled out Sammy
Davis, Jr., who indeed was the one performer who had seemed to escape
the dictatorial direction of Preminger. "He is a sneering, glinting spokesman for downright godlessness and a sly Pied Piper for licentiousness
when he leads the people in a wild dance at the end of the song," Crowther
wrote. "He has added a dimension to Porgy and Bess." Less-than-stellar
reviews were the least of Goldwyn's woes. Southern theatres were still
segregated and had no intention of lifting their bans to allow Blacks to
see the movie—a movie about Blacks! So Blacks in many Southern cities, alive now with protest fever, began to position themselves outside the
segregated theatres that were showing the film, carrying picket signs. The
adage that no publicity is bad publicity didn't quite compute when it came
to the combustible tandem of Black cinema and anger. Potential patrons

stayed away. Fearing protests, the white citizens of Charleston, where the opera is set, refused to show the movie at all. Goldwyn finally pulled the movie from all Southern theatres, announcing to the media he did not want racial confrontations.

Soon enough, Negro critics began making their own noise. A young playwright by the name of Lorraine Hansberry had plenty to say. "We object to roles which consistently depict our women as wicked and our men as weak. We do not want to see six-foot Sidney Poitier on his knees crying for a slit-skirted wench. We do not want the wench to be beautiful Dorothy Dandridge who sniffs 'happy dust' and drinks liquor from a bottle at the rim of an alley crap game." Hansberry had skin in the game: she had written a play that was, at the time, galvanizing Broadway audiences. *A Raisin in the Sun* opened on March 11, 1959—starring Sidney Poitier—and told the story of a Black Chicago family struggling to stay afloat. Black America, she clearly felt, was now more about *A Raisin in the Sun* than about *Porgy and Bess*. "We do not like to see our intelligent stars reduced to the level of Catfish Row when they have already risen to the heights of La Scala." A. S. Young, writing in the *Los Angeles Sentinel*, a Negro publication in Goldwyn's backyard, offered Goldwyn a rather novel suggestion: "If he will spend $7 million to make the story of Martin Luther King Jr. and the Montgomery walkers, and distribute this great progressive saga around the world, then I'll say, let him have Porgy and Bess." (It would take another fifty-five years for Hollywood to possess the nerve to make a motion picture revolving around a facet of the life of Martin Luther King, Jr. *Selma*—about his efforts to lead the Selma civil-rights march—premiered in 2014, to widespread acclaim.)

*Porgy and Bess* did receive four Oscar nominations, winning only one, for the musical score by André Previn and Ken Darby. Not a single actor was nominated. The movie vanished from the few Southern theatres that had decided to show it in the first place. Goldwyn's financial losses were significant. Against its seven-million-dollar budget—not accounting for additional marketing and publicity costs—the movie only made $3.5 million at the box office. Goldwyn would never produce another film. After airing only one time on television—and that wasn't until March 5, 1967, at the height of the civil-rights movement—the film version of *Porgy and Bess* vanished from sight.

What happened to *Porgy and Bess*?

.   .   .

It can be argued that if DuBose Heyward and George Gershwin had lived longer they might have made—the great songs aside—changes to the *Porgy and Bess* film, changes that could have lifted it from the antebellum amber in which it seemed frozen. What worked as opera did not translate to cinema against the backdrop of a changing nation—and a changing Black populace. The movie simply, and not so simply, came up against the end of a decade in which the high court had ordered schools integrated, in which federal troops swung bayonets at Little Rock on behalf of integration, and in which thousands had gathered in the shadow of the Lincoln Memorial on behalf of equal rights. In the same year, the recently formed United States Commission on Civil Rights issued a 686-page report chronicling the nation's ill-equipped battle against racism and inequality. The American government had never produced such an expansive document outlining the nation's ills when it came to race. "What is also sobering is the magnitude of the injury inflicted upon Negro Americans by the events recorded in this historical review," the commissioners wrote. "It is reflected in the poor education, low income, inferior housing and social demoralization of a considerable part of the Negro population. What compounds the problem is that these unfortunate results of slavery, discrimination, and second-class citizenship are in turn used by some more fortunate Americans to justify the perpetuation of the conditions that caused the injury."

James Baldwin couldn't stop himself from voicing his opinion about the film version of *Porgy and Bess*. Baldwin concluded it was "a white man's vision of Negro life." Baldwin not only thought that Preminger was the wrong choice as director, but that Dorothy Dandridge lacked the talent to play Bess. "Out of the Catfish Row or another came the murdered Bessie Smith and the dead Billie Holiday and virtually every Negro performer this country has produced," Baldwin wrote. "Until today, no one wants to hear their story, and the Negro performer is still in battle with the white man's image of the Negro—which the white man clings to in order not to be forced to revise his image of himself."

Both Goldwyn and Preminger may well have had good intentions, but they underestimated Black pride. When Preminger berated Poitier during the filming of *Porgy and Bess,* questioning his acting talents, Poitier calmly walked off the set. He sent word to Preminger that he would not return until Preminger personally apologized, which he did. Poitier had served notice: Negroes were rising up. That little Negro boy who had been singing in the church choir when *Gone with the Wind* premiered in Atlanta was now a grown man, and he was leading a movement. "History has thrust something upon me from which I cannot turn away," said Martin Luther King, Jr.

It was more than just the tide of the sixties that pushed the film of *Porgy and Bess* further away from public consciousness. Heirs and descendants of the Heyward, Gershwin, and Goldwyn factions began debating the quality of the film prints. According to Michael Strunsky, executor of Ira Gershwin's estate, both Ira and his wife, Lee, loathed the film. "They did something," Strunsky would recall, that "they had a right to do. After 20 years, they had the right to have Goldwyn call in all the prints and destroy them." Which he apparently did. But it wasn't a complete destruction. In 2007, Ken Kramer, a private collector who had a movie memorabilia shop in Burbank, emerged with his own 35mm print of *Porgy and Bess*—not revealing details of how he came across it—and gave a private screening for the philanthropist David Geffen. In 2016, the Cleveland Institute of Art received rare permission from the George Gershwin estate to show the film. They had to have a print imported from Europe. Dorothy Dandridge was a Cleveland native, and the art institute played up that angle. Otherwise, *Porgy and Bess* is a forgotten film.

# Two Cool Cats with Caribbean Roots
# Disrupt Hollywood

S IDNEY POITIER AND HARRY BELAFONTE altered both Hollywood and
America, arriving on the scene like torpedoes, gliding across New
York stages, into Las Vegas nightclubs, onto movie-theatre marquees, not
to mention racing around Mississippi together during the darkest days of
the civil-rights movement trying to stay alive. A decade before their cagey
1960s crossover leap into mainstream white America had taken hold, it
was unimaginable to think of two Black men who could attain their influence and clout. Paul Robeson and James Baldwin? Seen as too mercurial,
and far too honest about society. Joe Louis and Sugar Ray Robinson? They
were mired in a brutish sport that lessened the degree to which they were
viewed as intellectuals. Poitier and Belafonte stepped into another realm.
They got Hollywood to make movies with more diverse casts. They got
producing and directing jobs. They got Black stories up on the screen,
stories that had previously been ignored. They were summoned by White
House officials for talks. And they also made white men jealous because of
their looks and sex appeal. Little wonder that Black America looked upon
them as more than just actors. They judged the rise of Sidney Poitier and
Harry Belafonte against the progress of the nation itself.

———

The Poitiers of Cat Island, in the Bahamas, claimed Haitian and Caribbean roots. Reginald and Evelyn Poitier were tomato farmers, bending
for long hours beneath the hot Caribbean sun to clip tomatoes from their
stems and place them delicately in crates. They made the most money

when they took a boat and delivered their produce to Miami. There was a huge marketplace there known as the Produce Exchange. The place was always lively, the patois of the Bahamian farmers mingling with the voices of stern middlemen who'd try to get the best prices from the farmers. It was always a semi-comical battle of wit and wills as to the final purchase price of the goods the Poitiers had brought over from the islands. In the very early part of the winter of 1927, the Poitiers arrived in Miami on their usual produce trek. Evelyn was seven months pregnant. Her family had cautioned her to hurry back in case complications set in with her pregnancy, but she didn't make it back in time. Her seventh child, Sidney Poitier, was born in Miami on February 20, 1927.

Young Sidney grew up playing games, swimming, and fishing in the blue waters of the Atlantic. It takes a certain fearlessness to succeed as an actor, and some of Poitier's fearlessness was apparent in his childhood. He swam knowing that sharks and barracudas were in the same waters. "There was a very narrow tunnel in the rocks that would fill up with water with every wave," he would recall about Cat Island. "It was a death trap, but I kept on swimming through that tunnel for hours with no one else around. Just throwing myself into that tunnel." The family was working-class poor, but: "There was no juvenile delinquency, no marijuana, no gang member-ship, no drinking, and no prostitution," Poitier would later write of his near-idyllic childhood. When he was ten years old, the family left Cat Island and moved to Nassau. The change of scenery from rural landscape to city life shocked the senses of the Poitier clan. Nassau was big and noisy, and there was crime. By the age of thirteen—scrawny, taller, with a gregarious smile that often dominated his face—Poitier had quit school and gone to work in a warehouse. The family needed the money. He began hanging out with a wild crowd; there were run-ins with the island police. His father worried that prison might be in his son's future if he remained in Nassau. He suggested Sidney go to Miami, where the family had relatives.

In Miami, Sidney found work as a delivery boy. The city's raw segrega-tion unnerved him, the manner in which Blacks were treated, the parts of town to which they were confined. He had never seen anything like it—"Miami was awful—the white people were awful." He told himself he had to get out of the South, where so many things seemed to be conspiring against him. At the age of sixteen, Sidney Poitier boarded a bus bound for New York City. He had long heard about the skyscrapers, and Negroes, and opportunities.

It was a long bus ride, more than twenty-four hours, and he arrived in early 1943, exhausted. He didn't know a soul in the city, which didn't seem to frighten him. Within days he had a job, washing dishes, and, a short while later, a little room, on 127th Street, up in Harlem. This new beginning was starting to feel good. The bullet came out of nowhere, and tore into his leg. He got caught in a riot that had been ignited following a confrontation between a Black woman and a white police officer over her unpaid bill at Harlem's Braddock Hotel. She claimed the service was awful. When Robert Brandy, a Negro World War II veteran, came to the woman's aid in the lobby and took her side, the white officer grew incensed. A scuffle broke out between the policeman and the soldier. The policeman shot Brandy in the arm, then arrested him and the woman. Word of the confrontation swept throughout Harlem. By evening, with anger boiling among Negroes about the shooting and arrests, throngs had gathered. They began throwing rocks, breaking windows. There was the sound of gunfire—all while young Sidney Poitier was running, trying to get to his little apartment. "When I hear bang, bang, bang . . . I feel something cool on my foot," he would recall. "I've been shot. The slug has torn through the fleshy part of my lower calf and gone on out, leaving me with a bloody shoe and a painful gash, but not seriously wounded." Sidney Poitier had gotten a bloody taste of the racial convulsions ripping through America that summer.

The unpredictable city frightened this recent arrival. He thought joining the army was a good idea—a paycheck, food to eat. He lied about his age—said he was eighteen when he was only sixteen—and Uncle Sam welcomed him. He did his service Stateside, mostly out on Long Island, and mostly doing routine guard duty. But as the months passed, Poitier realized he was not suited to the monotony of military life. His mind began to swirl. He came up with a bizarre plan to get out of the army. He imagined that if he requested a meeting with a military-hospital executive, sat before that executive expressing dissatisfaction with the military, and erupted by throwing a chair in the direction of the hospital executive, it might get him labeled psychologically unfit for service, and they'd simply boot him out. But the army did not exactly work that way. Upon execution of his plan, Private Sidney Poitier was told he'd be seeing a psychiatrist, sure enough, but also that he could be court-martialed and possibly sentenced to a lengthy prison term for his eruption. The plan had backfired. The army psychiatrist, after listening to Poitier's honest explanation for doing such a thing, became interested in his patient. A touch of empathy set in. He told Poitier he was going to set up a series of appointments to talk about his life and background. If those meetings proved fruitful, Poitier was told, he'd recommend that he not be court-martialed. Poitier would come to admit he had acted out of pent-up anger: at the racism he had been subjected to and the fact that he had come from an environment in the Caribbean where such racism didn't exist. His honesty impressed the psychiatrist, who told military superiors that Poitier should not be court-martialed, and he wasn't. But he was discharged from the army after a year, under Section VIII.

It was back to New York City and Harlem, back to washing dishes. But an advertisement in the *New York Amsterdam News* caught Poitier's eye: "Actors Wanted by Little Theatre Group." The little theatre group was the American Negro Theater (ANT), which Frederick O'Neal, a well-respected actor, had founded in 1940. Poitier—with no photographs or anything suggesting he might have acting experience—went by the theatre. O'Neal was sitting with his small staff as they auditioned the hopefuls. As soon as Poitier was told to read a scene from a play that had been handed to him, O'Neal knew this was a gambit on Poitier's part: not only did he have trouble reading the lines, but his thick Bahamian accent could barely be understood. Poitier was ushered offstage and out of the theatre. The scene was embarrassing, but Poitier couldn't take such embarrassment without responding. For the next six months, he proceeded to lose as much of his accent as he could by listening to the radio. He began reading more. Finally, he was ready to go back to the theatre, where he successfully begged his way into the freshman acting program. In his second semester, he was cast as an understudy in the student production of *Days of Our Youth*. Rehearsals were fun; opening day approached. Then, much to the surprise of the acting class, an actor from outside their class was brought in and cast as the lead. His name was Harry Belafonte. He had been in some small productions and the ANT producers thought they needed an actor with experience. Poitier and other members of the acting class stewed a bit, but life in the theatre could be unpredictable.

So Sidney Poitier was now understudying this Belafonte interloper. When Belafonte missed a rehearsal one evening, Poitier had his chance. It happened that James Light, a Broadway director, had come to the theatre that day to offer notes as a favor to one of the troupe's officials. Light couldn't take his eyes off Sidney Poitier. This was talent, he told himself. Afterward, Light asked Poitier to come by his office.

Light told Poitier that he was mounting an all-Negro Broadway production of *Lysistrata,* the Greek comedy, and invited him to join the cast. This was a big break, and Poitier quickly accepted. "In one stupendous month of firsts," he recalled, "I signed my first contract for a Broadway play, promising me more money than I had ever earned in one week before, the first tangible indication that my still-embryonic self-improvement program, far from being a useless exercise, was in fact beginning to pay." The play opened and closed four performances later. The experience was both exhilarating and heartbreaking, but Poitier didn't have long to sulk. He had been noticed by John Wildberg, a Broadway producer. Wildberg was taking the play *Anna Lucasta* on a national tour, and offered Poitier a role as an understudy in that all-Black production.

Sidney Poitier began rolling across America as an actor. He remained on the road with *Anna Lucasta* for three years, staying in "colored hotels," watching an assortment of seasoned Black actors and actresses onstage as well as off. When they reached Los Angeles in early 1947, Lena Horne, along with the actor Canada Lee, hosted a soirée for the entire cast. In California, they cursed the movies coming out of Hollywood because they very rarely saw people in those movies that looked like them.

Back in New York City, his long road tour having ended, Poitier heard about a film that was being cast and seeking a few Black actors. He barely knew the plot, only the location for the audition. Though he didn't have an agent, he managed to fast-talk his way in. He got called back. Then called back again. And yet again. This was how Hollywood worked: they winnowed down the talent. It was ruthless. It was swimming with the barracudas. Finally, he was asked to come back one more time and take a screen test for Joseph Mankiewicz, who would be directing *No Way Out*, an urban drama. The plot of the movie involved two bank robbers, brothers, who've been shot. At a city hospital, one of the brothers is treated by Dr. Luther Brooks, the only Negro on staff. Brooks orders a spinal tap, and the bank-robber dies. His brother blames the "nigger doctor," and vows revenge. There is the threat of a race riot. Mankiewicz offered the part of Brooks to Poitier. Others in the cast were Richard Widmark, Linda Darnell, Stephen McNally, and Mildred Joanne Smith.

They filmed *No Way Out* on the Twentieth Century–Fox studio lot. The movie opened in New York on August 16, 1950, and marked the occasion of the first major role played by Sidney Poitier on the big screen. He was dynamic as Dr. Luther Brooks, a lithe figure working in an all-white hospital and having to suffer racial insults from two criminals. Mankiewicz, who had been a writer in Hollywood for more than a decade before turning to directing, knew how dynamic his racially charged narrative could be. Nonetheless, the improbability of the story did not lessen its effectiveness: In 1950, segregation was so entrenched in American life that it was unheard of for a Negro doctor to be working in a hospital unless it was a Negro hospital. "Sidney Poitier," the *New York Times* critic wrote, "gives a fine, sensitive performance as the Negro doctor and his quiet dignity is in sharp, affecting contrast to the volatile, sneering, base animal mentality and vigor that Mr. Widmark expresses so expertly as Ray Biddle." The Black press came alive with Sidney Poitier stories. Black communities coveted any news about him. "You're going to be awfully good in this movie," Mankiewicz had told Poitier before the film opened. "You're like a Roman candle."

Many Southern theatres, made aware that the film's protagonist-hero was a Negro, expressed their own sentiments about *No Way Out:* they simply refused to show it.

--------

Sidney Poitier—the poor kid from Cat Island—was suddenly being noticed. He made *Red Ball Express,* a 1952 World War II movie based on the exploits of a mostly Black army unit that had become known for its bravery in delivering supplies up the line in France to General Patton. Jeff Chandler got the starring role, and Budd Boetticher, a onetime bullfighter, got the directing job. Poitier played an officer battling discrimination. Things changed, however, from conception of the film to finished product. The movie focused mostly on Chandler's character and his battles with another white infantryman. The army itself was hesitant to support a movie about Black heroes. "The Army wouldn't let us tell the truth about the black troops because the government figured they were expendable," Boetticher conceded years later. "Our government didn't want to admit they were kamikaze pilots. They figured if one of ten trucks got through, they'd save Patton and his tanks."

In the year when *Red Ball Express* arrived on movie screens, a book written by Ralph Ellison, a Black Oklahoma-born writer, landed on bookstore shelves. It was a thick, rich novel about race relations in America. Its title: *Invisible Man,* and it would win the National Book Award. One of the signature lines from the novel: "I am invisible, understand, simply because people refuse to see me."

.    .    .

When Zoltán Korda, a Hungarian-born director based in London, asked Sidney Poitier if he wanted to go to South Africa to make a movie, the offer seemed too exotic to turn down. Korda wanted to film *Cry, the Beloved Country,* an adaptation of Alan Paton's prizewinning novel about a family dealing with racism and family heartbreak. Poitier would play a South African minister helping an older minister find his family, who are caught up in the country's turmoil. South Africa at the time operated under the apartheid system, a political regime far more restrictive even than the segregation laws in place in America. Canada Lee was also cast. He had been a boxer, a musician, and even a jockey in his younger years. In Alfred Hitchcock's 1944 *Lifeboat,* he played one of the stranded boaters, along with Hume Cronyn, William Bendix, and Tallulah Bankhead. He was the only Negro in the cast, and his picture was conveniently left off most of the movie posters. By the time filming had begun on *Beloved Country* in 1951, Lee was being hounded by the House Un-American Activities Committee because of his refusal to offer a public rebuke of Paul Robeson and his political views.

Korda and his producing team told South African immigration officials that Poitier and Lee were coming into the country to work as domestic servants. The deception was to avert any possible trouble about having two Black Americans there. Lee and Poitier were forced to stay in a Black settlement area, not allowed in the white hotels of Johannesburg. Some nights, following filming, Canada Lee would disappear. Poitier discovered Lee had a lover—a white woman. The revelation rattled Poitier, who imagined that if it were discovered harm might come not only to Lee but to him as well. "I will bend within reason to the madness that is required of us in this sick place," Lee told Poitier, "but I will decide what is 'within reason.' I will not twist my dignity out of shape to fit anybody's custom. I don't live that way in America and I'm not going to live that way in South Africa." Poitier was in awe of Lee.

Just before the cast and crew of *Beloved Country* arrived in South Africa, a free-speech demonstration by Blacks erupted. Eighteen Black protesters were killed by South African military police. Nelson Mandela, a young lawyer-in-training, had been part of the demonstration. He escaped the authorities by hiding out in a nurses' dormitory.

Poitier did not have a good time filming in South Africa. Making a film is hard enough. Being surrounded by death and dying radically multiplied the hardships. As the filming wrapped up, Poitier casually mentioned to a white South African on the film set the particular date on which he would be leaving the country. He later wondered if he should have revealed such information. When he told his security team, they immediately became concerned. On the day of departure, a member of the security crew handed Poitier a .22-caliber pistol. "Keep this in your hand," he said. "If anything goes wrong between here and the airport you may need it." The security force was arrayed in two cars. Poitier was in the front car; the second car was for rear-guard protection. Not long after they were out on the road, they noticed a sedan full of white men following them. All three vehicles began speeding up. The driver of the second car had been told not to let anyone get between him and the front car, the one that held Poitier. "We were doing about 110 miles [an hour] on that narrow dirt road, kicking up all kinds of dust," according to Poitier. The sedan following the second car kept trying to get around it but could not. Poitier's car crashed through a fence and kept speeding along. They zigzagged across a field, the sedan behind the second car roaring in their direction. Only when they neared the airport gates did the sedan finally slow and give up the chase.

The film release of *Beloved Country* got off to a wonderful start: it won the Bronze Berlin Bear at the Berlin International Film Festival. It also was featured in the 1952 Cannes Film Festival and awarded a BAFTA (British Academy of Film and Television Award) United Nations Award. The reviews were uniformly good. "Sidney Poitier is manly and striking as a young Negro preacher," noted *Variety*. Even though *Beloved Country* was set in a brutal political landscape, the movie itself turned inward, resting upon quiet interactions between characters. The *New York Times* critic took note: "The particular interest of Mr. Korda, working trenchantly from a script prepared by Mr. Paton, is the dark and terrible passage of two men through the valley of grief and distraction into which they are plunged by a mutually calamitous act." Canada Lee was singled out for fulsome praise in the *Times* review, but he never made another film. He died on May 9, 1952, of a heart attack. His widow and others who revered him believed he had been hounded into the grave by refusing to "name names" during the House Un-American Activities investigations. Canada Lee was forty-five years old.

Before he got approved for the role as the only Black student in *Blackboard Jungle*, a movie based on Evan Hunter's 1954 novel, Sidney Poitier was asked to sign a loyalty oath, a House Un-American Activities Committee piece of paper, denouncing both the dead Canada Lee and Paul Robeson. He declined to sign. He imagined he would be tossed from *Blackboard Jungle* even before filming started, but he was not. Richard Brooks, the film's tough, no-nonsense director on the film, vouched for Poitier as aggressively as he could. And the studio kept him on.

The novel told the story of a teacher trying to tame students at an inner-city high school. Hunter had once been a schoolteacher, and his novel touched on juvenile delinquency, a topic much discussed in America at the time. Among the cast were Glenn Ford, Vic Morrow, and Anne Francis. There are raw scenes in the movie—nasty fights, sexual assaults. A teacher is bloodied by a student in a brawl. Even though he had appeared in only a handful of films, Poitier's appearances were becoming more than acting assignments in the minds of many Blacks. Since whites rarely interacted with Blacks in American society, Black figures on-screen were often doing more than just acting—they were conveying the rhythms and presence of an entire culture of people. They were communicating with white America.

The release of *Blackboard Jungle* elicited a lot of talk about education in America; not so much talk, however, about race and integrated education. "I know much more than *that* about the public school system of New York," James Baldwin cryptically remarked about the movie. The movie did feature Bill Haley's "Rock Around the Clock," which had a lot of parents fearing the song was too sexually suggestive. But whether suburban parents wanted to acknowledge it or not, rock and roll was now swiveling in their direction, even faster than integration.

Sidney Poitier met Juanita Hardy in New York City before he went off to film *Red Ball Express*. She was a fashion model who had appeared on the cover of popular Negro magazines. Though she realized acting was an unpredictable vocation, she believed in the man who asked her to marry him. In short order, they had two daughters. And, with mounting responsibilities, Poitier's financial worries began to grow. There was not enough money coming in. He opened a restaurant, which took too much energy away from his acting, and which he and his co-owner soon abandoned. Despite his stage and film credits—and fine reviews—none of the big talent agencies had reached out to represent him. That changed when he got a phone call from Martin Baum, who had cofounded the Baum-Newborn

Agency. He had seen Poitier on-screen, was intrigued by him, and promised Poitier he'd set about finding interesting projects, though he admitted the task would not be easy.

Over the next few years, Baum found intermittent film and television work for Poitier, but nothing excited him like the film he heard producer-director Stanley Kramer was putting together. It involved two runaway convicts from a Southern chain gang, a white-and-Black pair of escapees. Kramer aimed to direct the picture. Elvis Presley and Sammy Davis, Jr., were approached. Presley was interested, but his manager decided he didn't want the singer handcuffed to a Negro for long stretches on-screen, because it might offend Presley's followers. Davis always had problems making commitments for lengthy film shoots because he had contractually committed himself to future nightclub engagements and so never entered negotiations. Kramer turned his attention to Poitier, and offered him the role of Noah Cullen, which Poitier quickly accepted. There was no shortage of white actors with A-list credits. But Marlon Brando, Burt Lancaster, Kirk Douglas, and Robert Mitchum turned the role down. Mitchum told Kramer he himself had served time on a Georgia chain gang and never saw Black and white cons chained together. Kramer ignored him and kept trying to put his movie together. Tony Curtis badly wanted the role of John "Joker" Jackson. He was just coming off fine reviews for *Sweet Smell of Success,* playing alongside Lancaster, but Kramer saw Curtis only as a pretty boy. Curtis trekked to Kramer's office and made an emotional appeal for the role. Kramer yielded. The two cons would be played by Poitier and Curtis. Once he was attached, Curtis became a producer on the picture as well.

In February 1958, Stanley Kramer and his cast and crew began filming *The Defiant Ones* around southern California. The idea of filming in the South, where the story is set, was never given serious consideration, because the Ku Klux Klan was too intimidating a presence. It was an arduous six-week shoot, slogging through swamps, falling down hillsides, hopping trains. Kramer began to feel—just as Joseph Mankiewicz had felt—that Poitier was going to become a star, the star that Kramer had hoped James Edwards, after *Home of the Brave,* would become. At the end of filming, Curtis told Kramer that Poitier's name should appear above the title, a move that would designate him a "star" of the movie rather than just costar. It would be a radical departure of Hollywood custom: a Negro's name had never appeared above the title of a mainstream film. Kramer was of a like mind.

The reviews for *The Defiant Ones*—which opened nationwide September 27, 1958—were superb. "Poitier captures all of the moody violence of the convict, serving time because he assaulted a white man who had insulted him," the *Variety* critic wrote. "It is a cunning, totally intelligent portrayal that rings powerfully true." Curtis was cited with fulsome praise in the same review: "He starts off as a sneering, brutal character, willing to fight it out to-the-death with his equally stubborn companion. When, in the end, he sacrifices a dash for freedom to save Poitier, he has managed the transition with such skill that sympathy is completely with him." The *New York Times* reviewer was equally effusive. "Mr. Poitier stands out as the Negro convict and Mr. Curtis is surprisingly good," Bosley Crowther wrote. Both Poitier and Curtis were nominated for Academy Awards. And though they didn't win, the screenwriters, Nedrick Young and Harold Jacob Smith, did win. Also, Sam Leavitt won for black-and-white cinematography. The picture would win a Golden Globe for Best Drama, while Poitier took home a BAFTA Award for Best Foreign Actor.

Kramer and Poitier vowed to work together again. But for his immediate future, Sidney Poitier was holding a stage play in his hands. The play greatly intrigued him.

————

Lorraine Hansberry grew up in a loving family in Chicago in the 1930s, surrounded by activists and so-called rebels, all friends of her parents. Carl and Nannie Hansberry were lawyers, ward leaders, writers, and poets. Her brother, also named Carl, fought in General Patton's army. In 1945, Carl Senior went to Mexico to make preparations to move his entire family there; America and its mistreatment of Negroes had exhausted him. But he died before the family could join him. "American racism helped kill him," his daughter Lorraine believed. She was fifteen at the time of her father's death. At the University of Wisconsin, she studied art and stage design. She also fell for the works of the Irish playwright Sean O'Casey. But she quit Wisconsin after two years and moved to New York City—young, savvy, beautiful, bisexual, and intent on becoming a writer. Paul Robeson, whom her family knew, had cofounded a newspaper, *Freedom,* with Louis Burnham, and she joined the staff. It felt great to write about political rallies and the oppressed. She met Robert Nemiroff, a songwriter, and they fell in love and got married.

There was a story, a play, brewing inside of Hansberry, and she started tapping out scenes on her manual typewriter. It was about a Black Chicago family dealing with the fallout over a family death and the repercussions of mismanaging a ten-thousand-dollar insurance policy. To make the play a reality, the producers raised money from 140 investors. *A Raisin in the Sun,* named after a line from a Langston Hughes poem, gathered a cast of theatre veterans, among them Claudia McNeil, Ruby Dee, Louis Gossett, Jr., Diana Sands, Ivan Dixon, and John Fiedler. And a young film star—Sidney Poitier. The rehearsals were tense. "Sidney, Claudia, and Ruby fought about who the play was about," recalls Gossett. "They wanted to outdo one another." Poitier felt the play should be centered around his character, Walter Lee Younger. McNeil felt the opposite, that it should be focused around Lena Younger, the mother. While staying at the Hotel Taft in New Haven, where the play was trying out before its Broadway debut, Hansberry wrote a letter to her mother:

> *Mama, it is a play that tells the truth about people, Negroes and life and I think it will help a lot of people to understand how we are just as complicated as they are—and just as mixed up—but above all, that we have among our miserable and downtrodden ranks—people who are the very essence of human dignity. That is what, after all the laughter and tears, the play is supposed to say. I hope it will make you very proud.*

When the final words of the play were uttered from Broadway's Barrymore Theatre on opening night, March 11, 1959, Sidney Poitier reached down and pulled Lorraine Hansberry up on stage amid the thunderous applause and tears and whistles. Word of the great reviews raced around the country, and the crowds—white and Black—kept coming; it was clear that something special in American theatre had happened: a play that cut to the bone of existence for a Black American family. Brooks Atkinson of *The New York Times* commented that the play "has vigor as well as veracity and is likely to destroy the complacency of anyone who sees it." Poitier and McNeil were singled out for praise: "Mr. Poitier is a remarkable actor with enormous power that is always under control"; Claudia McNeil "gives a heroic performance." *Raisin* would win the New York Drama Critics' Circle Award for Best American Play of the season, the first time a Black woman had won the award. It received four Tony nominations, but didn't win a single one, which seemed to many a miscarriage of justice. The play's long run was remarkable for a Negro production; it didn't close until

June of 1960. It made Broadway history on many levels: Hansberry, all of twenty-eight years old, became the first Black playwright to have a play produced on Broadway; Lloyd Richards, the director, was the first Black director of a Broadway play. James Baldwin, who had first met Hansberry a year earlier at the Actors Studio in Manhattan, realized the significance of what she had done. "What is relevant here is that I had never in my life seen so many black people in the theatre," he said. "And the reason was that never before, in the entire history of the American theatre, had so much of the truth of black people's lives been seen on the stage. Black people ignored the theatre because the theatre had always ignored them."

"I'm thrilled, and all of us associated with the play are thrilled," Hansberry gushed to Lillian Ross of *The New Yorker* about the play's success. "Meanwhile, it does keep you awfully busy. What sort of happens is you just hear from everybody!"

And everybody included Hollywood.

Columbia Pictures quickly purchased the rights to Hansberry's play. The studio signed Poitier to re-create the lead role of Walter Younger. Many members of the Broadway cast—McNeil, Ruby Dee, Louis Gossett, Jr., Ivan Dixon, and Diana Sands—were also cast. Daniel Petrie was hired to direct. Philip Rose and David Susskind signed on as producers. They both came from the world of television, which had been more daring than movies up to that point when it came to race. Rose and Susskind were two white men who were fierce in the face of discrimination. Susskind knew Hollywood would want bigger names than the Broadway cast members, but he rebuffed the studio. "We've violated every tenet of screen production," he said. "We took no screen tests, wrote no 'film treatment,' and we didn't consider Sammy Davis Jr. and Eartha Kitt for the leads." A strange thing happened—actually not so odd for 1960 America—when cast and crew went to Chicago to shoot some scenes in a white neighborhood. The whites who resided there thought the Blacks seen on the block were angling to buy property. They called the police and filed complaints. Cast and crew were happy to get out of there. When shooting moved to Los Angeles, Poitier complained to the press that he and his family were constantly being denied houses they wanted to sublet. The Poitiers finally decamped at the Chateau Marmont for the duration of filming. Before the premiere, a Columbia studio official said they would have to "write off most of the Southern market because of the Negro theme."

The reviews for *A Raisin in the Sun* were potent. *Daily Variety* praised the movie for its timing, given that race relations in the country were at "a critical juncture." Never before had a Negro family, its rhythms and very lifeblood, been seen by so many whites in American movie theatres. "Here, for the first time, is the new Negro on the screen," noted the critic for the *Saturday Review.* "Not a Negro fighting for his rights against the intolerance or injustice of society; but an entire family that has become aware of, and is determined to combat, racial discrimination in a supposedly democratic land." Poitier's portrait of Walter Lee Younger garnered him the best reviews thus far of his career. "Sidney Poitier . . . rises to new heights as the tormented, ambitious Walter Lee. . . . With never a false move, he projects all the pride, the hurt, the frustration, the dignity of a race-conscious Negro," the *Saturday Review* offered. "His is one of the few fully realized character portraits ever to come onto celluloid, and one of the most moving."

The release of *A Raisin in the Sun* in May 1961 coincided with headline-making news about the Freedom Riders, an interracial coalition of mostly college students. They sought to challenge Southern states that were keeping their buses segregated in violation of federal law. Things turned bloody when the Freedom Rider John Lewis was attacked in South Carolina. Other clashes followed. Sidney Poitier began hearing about Martin Luther King, Jr., and the Congress of Racial Equality (CORE), and the Student Nonviolent Coordinating Committee (SNCC). He began plotting ways to throw his growing artistic presence behind the civil-rights movement. The opportunity came from his association with Harry Belafonte.

Mass rallies for Negro freedom always got the attention of the white press. When A. Philip Randolph and Rev. Martin Luther King, Jr.—with a consortium of labor, Jewish, and other civil-rights leaders—began planning their March on Washington for August 28, 1963, it rattled the nerves of the Kennedy administration. President Kennedy and his brother Attorney General Robert Kennedy feared unrest and possible riotous behavior. King and the others, however, were determined to hold the march. Belafonte chartered a jet and asked his Hollywood friends to join him for the march. Some were skittish and declined, allowing that their agents told them it might harm their careers. Among the celebrities and movie stars fearless enough to attend on that sweltering, historic, peaceful, speechifying day were Burt Lancaster, James Baldwin, James Garner, Ossie Davis, Ruby Dee, Charlton Heston, Josephine Baker, Joseph Mankiewicz, and

Lena Horne. Thereafter, amid all the realities that Blacks were not turning back, ever, King was told by Belafonte and Poitier he could depend on them for future financial and moral support.

Hollywood had long been a land of timidity, with studio executives kowtowing before the Hays Committee. This committee, which went into action in 1934 and wouldn't dissolve until 1968, outlined "moral" guidelines for the making of motion pictures. These guidelines so often caused directors and producers to shy away from putting Blacks in films, to dismiss outright the idea of interracial romances. Martin Baum, Poitier's agent, knew his gut, and his gut told him that a script he had read—adapted from *The Lilies of the Field,* William Barrett's slim novella—could get around the Hays Committee, even if it did involve a Negro and white women. The Negro laborer in the novella has no intention of a romance, because all the women are nuns! And the nuns—not white American nuns, but East German nuns—just want him to build a chapel on their little piece of property. It's a kind of Bible-thumping fable. Ralph Nelson, who had won an Emmy directing television, had just become a Marty Baum client and wanted to direct. United Artists told Nelson they'd give him a budget of $250,000 to make the movie. This was an insult, a low and ridiculous sum; Poitier's salary would eat up half of that amount. (*Cleopatra,* starring Elizabeth Taylor and Richard Burton, had a production and marketing cost of forty-four million dollars, making it the most expensive-budgeted film till then.) Baum remained determined. He came up with a back-end sharing deal, advising Poitier to take a fraction of his salary and agreeing to take 10 percent of the profits. Everyone went off to Arizona and shot the film in two weeks.

Sidney Poitier and Harry Belafonte at the 1963 civil-rights march on Washington, D.C. The indisputable lions.

.　　.　　.

In 1963, a year in which Hitchcock's *The Birds,* George Sidney's *Bye Bye Birdie,* Otto Preminger's *The Cardinal,* Stanley Donen's *Charade,* and Joseph Mankiewicz's *Cleopatra* (which was a colossal flop) were released, no one expected much of Ralph Nelson's *Lilies of the Field.* But, stunning both the critics and Hollywood, it became a genuine success, grossing more than three million dollars at the box office against its tiny budget, and garnered worldwide praise. "Many factors combine in the overall success of the film," *Variety* noted, "notably the restrained direction by Ralph Nelson, a thoroughly competent screenplay by James Poe . . . and, of course, Poitier's own standout performance." *The Hollywood Reporter,* however, mentioned that the awkward issue of race was absent from the picture. "The element of racism is only once overtly made; in the rudeness of a native American to Poitier," *The Hollywood Reporter* reported. The biggest news from that film, however, was Poitier becoming the first Black to win an Oscar for Best Actor. This surprising victory seemed to welcome Black America, at long last, into the respectability of modern-day filmmaking.

There was a distinguishing feature of the Poitier style on-screen: his diction was beautiful. There was just the tiniest inflection remaining of his Bahamian accent, and that remnant gave his dialogue a kind of majestic—but not imposing—elocution. His walk also commanded attention. He walked swiftly in his scenes; his back was always straight, as if he were wearing a back brace. The combination gave him the appearance of total confidence. This was an actor made for the screen. And Black America was falling in love with him. White Americans lived at a distant remove from Black Americans; they used Poitier as a yardstick to gauge race relations. In 1961, Poitier starred in *Paris Blues* along with Paul Newman, Diahann Carroll, and Joanne Woodward. It was about two jazz musicians in Paris who woo two American women. Poitier and Newman wanted the relationships to be interracial, but the movie studio balked at the idea, fearing it would upset American audiences.

There were more Poitier movies in the ensuing years—*A Patch of Blue; The Slender Thread; Duel at Diablo; To Sir, With Love; Guess Who's Coming to Dinner;* and *For Love of Ivy.* But America had turned dark and menacing. Movies—including Poitier's movies—hardly reflected reality. "The industry is compelled, given the way it is built," James Baldwin wrote in the summer of 1968 about Hollywood, "to present to the American people a self-perpetuating fantasy of American life." In *Guess Who's Coming to Dinner,* which starred Katharine Hepburn, Spencer Tracy, Katharine Houghton, and Poitier, there was a single kiss—more a love tap—shared between Black man and white fiancée. Baldwin knew the downside of such screen cowardice: "The next time the [genuine] kissing will have to start." Katharine Houghton, the fiancée in the film, knew the gravity of even that one small kiss. ". . . If you'd been on the set when we filmed the one kiss you would have gotten chills because there was such tension," she said. "Tremendous tension. You have a lot of people on a film, a lot of different political opinions. Not everybody is coming from the same point of view. I was too naïve to realize this was extremely upsetting to people. The whole plot was taboo."

Beyond the movie screen, the nation turned over onto the terror-filled year of 1968. King was murdered; Bobby Kennedy was murdered. The world looked at America and it seemed to be its own big, terrifying, and heartbreaking movie, one where Blacks were still fighting daily for rights, despite the civil-rights bills that had been passed.

By the 1970s, Sidney Poitier—remarried in 1976 to the Canadian actress Joanna Shimkus—began turning his focus to directing films, two starring the ferocious comic Richard Pryor. He even got Harry Belafonte, his old West Indian buddy from those early days in New York City, to appear with him in a couple of comedies. It was a treat seeing them on-screen together. Cinephiles as well as the civil-rights crowd knew their history. The names could be uttered by now seamlessly in tandem. The duo—Poitier and Belafonte—had become cultural icons, two handsome Black men, defiant soul brothers who claimed their stake in the air of American celebrity even as whites were still learning the cultural depth of the phrase "soul brothers."

———

It always opened up a tricky conversation, which could be heard in Black barbershops, Black fraternity houses, Black hair salons, and at Black political gatherings. Why did Black Americans so often look askance at West Indians? And why did West Indians so often look askance at native-born

Black Americans? There was cultural friction, and both Poitier and Belafonte would be forced to address the issue during their rise.

While slavery and colonialism had greatly harmed West Indians, the
ruling British government outlawed slavery there in 1833. As a result, West
Indians had a jump on freedom compared with Blacks in America, where
slavery would be only partially outlawed in 1863 and not fully abolished
until 1865. Caribbean and American Blacks had both battled deep poverty,
but Caribbean Blacks, once freed, didn't have to wage a constant legal battle for basic human rights. "The Blacks in the Caribbean were 'unbroken'
slaves," says actor Louis Gossett, Jr., who witnessed the friction between
ethnic groups in New York City during the fifties. "They were 'free' slaves.
When they got to America, their spirits were not broken. American Blacks
had been beaten down through lynchings and whippings."

It was raw poverty that drove Millie Love out of Jamaica and into New
York City, where she had relatives in Harlem. In Harlem, she met the
smooth-talking Harold Bellanfanti, also Jamaican, who worked as a cook
on banana boats. Their first child, Harold Junior, was born March 1, 1927.
(Sidney Poitier had been born nine days earlier in Miami.) Everyone
called the child Harry. Because his parents were illegal immigrants, little
Harry led a furtive life, dodging authority figures, never answering the
door when home alone. His father was an abusive man who beat him with
branches and belts and threatened further harm if he told his mother. In
Harry's neighborhood, Greek and Irish kids abounded, and he wanted to
play with them. Because of his very light skin, he decided to "pass," pretending not to be a Negro. His friends believed him. "By the time I started
ninth grade at George Washington High School," Belafonte recalled, "my
passing period had ended, not due to any dramatic turn of events, just
the inexorable drift toward kinship with black students rather than white
ones."

Like most others, he rode the New York City subways. He practiced
graffiti, albeit with a political bent, and he glared at all the advertisements posted inside the subway car. They always featured white people,
and what certain products—creams and lotions—could do for them. The
ads angered him, and he began writing over them. "How about Negro
hands?" he scrawled over an ad showing a pair of white hands. "There is
bigotry in America," he wrote over another advertisement. His girlfriend,
Marguerite, who sometimes rode with him on the trains, fretted he'd get

in trouble, but he never got caught. She began to notice a change in his disposition. She felt that "there was a storm within Harry."

Harry Belafonte took himself—and his storm—off to the United States Navy.

In the navy, he began to read seriously and voluminously. He was particularly entranced with the essays and books written by W. E. B. Du Bois; he started getting an education about American-born Negroes and America's haunting racial history. Since the military was rigidly segregated, Belafonte, like Poitier, saw that American military muscle was intertwined with a flawed execution of the U.S. Constitution. Harry Belafonte battled with military officers. "Why don't you go fuck yourself," he bellowed to an officer who caught him dozing on guard duty. The infraction got him two weeks in lockup at the Portsmouth Naval Prison.

By Christmas 1945, Belafonte was out of the military and back in Harlem, where he met Poitier. "Both Sidney Poitier and I were skinny, brooding and vulnerable within our hard shells of self-protection, and each was about as unlikely as the other to become a future star," he recalled. In 1946, Belafonte was cast in the lead role in *Juno and the Paycock,* a Sean O'Casey play. To many young actors at the time, O'Casey might as well have been William Shakespeare. One evening, before the curtain went up on the play, Belafonte heard that Paul Robeson—the very Paul Robeson who had stood against fascists in Europe, and sung on military bases to lift the spirits of Allied troops, and who had made State Department officials nervous because he had gone to Russia—was in the audience. Belafonte and the cast became giddy: Robeson was one of their heroes. After the play, they all gathered around him and listened to him talk about the need for the arts to be merged with the fight for justice. He talked about John Steinbeck and Clifford Odets and George Bernard Shaw. He told the young actors to read, and read some more, and care about the oppressed. Some got teary-eyed. "We listened in amazement, too thrilled to respond," Belafonte recalled of the evening. "What I remember, more than anything . . . was the love he radiated, and the profound responsibility he felt, as an actor, to use his platform as a bully pulpit. . . . That night, Paul Robeson gave me my epiphany: It would guide me for the rest of my life."

Belafonte knew that smart actors kept training. In 1944, he had gotten himself into an acting class at the New School for Social Research. His GI Bill money paid the tuition. In the class were a bunch of anonymous souls, all determined to become actors: Rod Steiger, Elaine Stritch, Walter Matthau, Wally Cox, and some brooding guy with obvious magnetism by the name of Marlon Brando. Brando missed quite a few classes because he was starting rehearsals in a Tennessee Williams play, *A Streetcar Named Desire*. The play launched him as the greatest actor of his generation. Most of the others in the class also found their own levels of fame and success, on television, in movies, or at comedy clubs.

Music, as much as acting, also drew Belafonte's attention. He found his way into jazz clubs and listened to Charlie Parker and Miles Davis and Lester Young. Young's bandmates were Al Haig, Max Roach, sometimes Tommy Potter, and sometimes Parker. Belafonte snapped his fingers and bopped his head, all while pondering his nascent acting career. His white acting friends kept getting jobs, but he did not. Belafonte—and here is where the psychological split with Sidney Poitier began to manifest itself—also began filling his time with political activism. He went to union rallies and sing-alongs. He hopped up on stages with folksingers such as Josh White and Pete Seeger. He handed out pamphlets for an assortment of progressive causes. Paul Robeson recognized him at some of the rallies; his ongoing chats with Robeson meant the world to Belafonte.

In early 1949, Harry Belafonte finally caught a break, though it wasn't for his acting career. Monte Kay, who managed the Royal Roost, a Manhattan nightclub, put him on at the intermission of a show in which Lester Young's band was playing. Something beautiful happened that night: While young Belafonte—with the bruised actor's ego but a sweet-sounding voice—stood at the microphone, getting ready to sing, Al Haig gingerly walked out. Then Tommy Potter. Then Max Roach appeared. They just had to stand in with the new kid. Belafonte got goose bumps. Finally, the great Charlie Parker strode out and picked up his sax. The place went wild. "I couldn't believe it," Belafonte said years later. "Four of the world's greatest jazz musicians had just volunteered to be the backup band for a twenty-one-year-old singer no one had ever heard of, making his debut in a nightclub intermission." The kid—as Young's band members referred to him—wowed the crowd, so much so that Monty Kay knew he had to bring him back. And he did, night after night, for several weeks. Deejays began talking about Harry Belafonte. He got a publicist. Little items about his performances began showing up in newspaper columns. He was finally pocketing some dough. Paul Robeson invited him to his home, where he met other singers and activists. Before the decade closed, Belafonte was recognized as a legitimate singer. He toured the country. In Miami, Blacks—and that included performers with their names on the nightclub marquees—had to have passes, authorization cards, to travel to certain parts of town. Belafonte hated that he was forced to walk around in an American city with a pass. When the nightclub manager asked him to extend his stay, he refused.

Back in Manhattan, Harry Belafonte fell in with the folksinging Greenwich Village crowd. There was something about folk songs that touched his soul—"raw, gritty, American songs of hope, heartbreak," as he put it. He sang on behalf of workers' rights and against discrimination. In the fall of 1951, he debuted at the Village Vanguard, quite an in-crowd spot. He was a sensation. His shows began selling out. Crowds lined the block. "One of the season's catches—Harry Belafonte!" crowed *The New Yorker*. His engagement lasted for three months. Then he moved uptown, to the Blue Angel, another hot club, and the crowds caught up to him there. Now Harry Belafonte was making some noise; now he was moving. He went into RCA Victor's recording studio in April 1952 and began cutting records. "Belafonte," noted *Variety*, "has emerged as one of the outstanding practitioners in the folk singing field . . . causing something of a sensation."

The competitive spirit in Harry Belafonte forced him to keep an eye on the doings of his friend Sidney Poitier. And Poitier, of course, had broken out in movies. So Belafonte felt mighty good when MGM asked him to star, alongside Dorothy Dandridge, in *Bright Road*—that strange film with two Black leads that never mentioned race and never had a chance at the box office. So it was back to clubs for Harry Belafonte. Only the clubs got bigger; he got booked into amphitheatres; his folksinging became a national craze. A Canadian producer, John Murray Anderson, had seen Belafonte onstage and decided he wanted him for his upcoming Broadway revue show, *John Murray Anderson's Almanac*. Belafonte didn't take long to make up his mind. And the reviews, especially for Belafonte, were wonderful; he won a Tony Award for Best Featured Actor in a Musical. Now it was time for Round Two in Hollywood.

After the Otto Preminger–directed *Carmen*, Belafonte's next film role came three years later, in 1957, when he starred in *Island in the Sun*. He was a romantic lead, opposite Joan Fontaine, a white actress. Fontaine was unnerved enough by the hate mail she received while filming that she turned the letters over to the FBI. The only thing that dimmed the movie's box-office success was the controversy—an interracial romance—that trailed it. But Belafonte had done something: he had been part of an interracial couple on-screen, cracking some of the fear that studios had of Black-white sex. Lovers make love, and in the movie Mavis Norman and David Boyeur—the characters played by Fontaine and Belafonte—are lovers! Unlike Poitier, Belafonte refused to hide his sensuality on film. He became a matinee idol—openly for Negro women; in private to a lot of white women. ("From the top of his head right down that white shirt, he's the most beautiful man I ever set eyes on," said the actress Diahann Carroll.) In *The New York Times,* however, the cautious hint of interracial romance was too bizarre for Bosley Crowther, who all but dismissed *Island in the Sun.* "As was the case with his production of 'Pinky,' Mr. Zanuck has really not compelled a frank, unembarrassed and conclusive grappling with the subject of race," Crowther concluded.

As groundbreaking as *Island in the Sun* appeared to be, it also made Hollywood executives nervous about its male star: white women fans—along with Negro women—might turn him into a big box-office draw, but not if Hollywood executives had anything to do with it, and of course they had everything to do with it. Belafonte did not have a Hollywood figure around him—as Sidney Poitier did with Stanley Kramer and Ralph Nelson—who could shepherd and promote his career. "Harry scared Hollywood," says actor Louis Gossett, Jr., alluding to his sexuality. Harry Belafonte made two movies in 1959—*Odds Against Tomorrow* and *The World, the Flesh and the Devil*—then disappeared from the big screen for an entire decade. And during that entire decade, Sidney Poitier kissed one white woman on-screen, and that was, of course, barely a kiss.

In the summer of 1958, one needed to be in Europe to catch the full glimpse of Harry Belafonte's race-defying popularity. His performances sold out all across the Continent. The stage would be completely dark. He'd walk on quietly. Then a spotlight would softly come. And there he'd be, amid the screaming: tall, caramel-colored, in tight-fitting pants and a light-colored shirt, the top two buttons open. And then the repertoire of songs: "Matilda," "Day-O," "Brown Skin Girl," "Jamaica Farewell," "John Henry." After the shows, there he would be, in short sleeves and sunglasses, outside the stage door, surrounded by Italian women, British women, African women. The paparazzi would be snapping away. *Time* magazine put him on its March 2, 1959, cover.

————

Neither Belafonte nor Poitier could help getting caught up in the grip of legal and social barriers that were harming American Blacks, and had them, as Belafonte put it, "under the hammer." Martin Luther King, Jr., knew well how hard and wide that hammer was swinging. Belafonte was elated in early 1956 when he picked up the phone at his home and King was on the other end. From that point on, until the end of King's life, Harry Belafonte was King's strongest celebrity ally. "I need your help," King told Belafonte early in their friendship. "I have no idea where this movement is going." Belafonte, in the years to come, proceeded to give money, raise money, lead marches, comfort Coretta Scott King when her husband was under siege or jailed, and serve as a conduit between Attorney General Robert Kennedy and King. Whether easing through the throngs at the March on Washington, or gliding and singing down those dusty roads that led over the Edmund Pettus Bridge in Selma, Harry Belafonte became the golden-boy figure of the King-led movement.

In 1964, three young men—Mickey Schwerner, Andrew Goodman, and James Chaney—went missing in Mississippi. Twenty-four hours earlier, they had left Oxford, Ohio, where a training session had taken place for civil-rights volunteers bound for Mississippi. The three young men had been arrested shortly upon arrival in Mississippi, but law-enforcement officials had released them. The news that they had vanished sent tremors through those back in Ohio, where other volunteers were preparing to go down south. Their mangled and murdered bodies were eventually found in an earthen dam. They all had been shot at point-blank range. James Forman, an official of the Student Non-Violent Coordinating Committee, feared that the other volunteers in Mississippi might leave. He would not blame them, but sensed it might embolden the KKK even more. If he were to keep the volunteers in place, Forman knew he needed money—money for food and transportation and lodging. He made an urgent call to Belafonte to say it would take fifty thousand dollars to keep the Freedom Summer drive alive. Belafonte promised he'd get the money. He hopped a plane and flew first to Chicago, then to Montreal, where he also had friends who helped raise money. With thirty-five thousand dollars in hand, he landed back home in New York City, determined to get the final fifteen thousand. His wife, Julie (white, Jewish, as committed to the cause as Belafonte), pulled together a fund-raising dinner party. In the end, Belafonte had seventy thousand dollars in hand. Knowing that he couldn't wire the money into Mississippi—whoever picked it up would be vulnerable to attack or robbery or both—he decided he'd have to deliver the money himself. But he needed a cohort. Belafonte phoned Sidney Poitier and laid out his plan to go to Mississippi and deliver the money. Poitier asked a lot of questions—mostly about security. Harry was in a rush; told him the White House had promised security; they had to get going! Poitier was suspicious, but eventually agreed to go. They landed at night in Jackson, Mississippi. Belafonte was carrying the seventy thousand in cash in a doctor's bag. At the Jackson airport, Poitier grew uneasy because he didn't see anyone who looked like they were dispatched by the federal government to protect them. They quickly boarded a small Cessna plane for the short flight to Greenwood, which was ground zero for the freedom workers. The Greenwood airport was just a single-floor, one-room structure. The pilot flew off as soon as he dropped off his two Black passengers. His quick departure rattled them, but they spotted a couple of Black men, James Forman and Willie Blue, from SNCC. Everyone climbed into a car. In the distance, some headlights suddenly popped on. They were from pickup trucks.

"That must be the federal agents," Belafonte told Poitier.

"Agents, my ass," one of the SNCC workers said. "That's the Klan."

They decided that if they sped up they'd be stopped and arrested, and then anything could happen. Poitier was boiling—this was South Africa all over again. Their car, on the road, was suddenly rammed, then rammed again. One of the SNCC men called ahead to local SNCC headquarters on a walkie-talkie and reported their desperate situation. SNCC staffers hopped into cars and roared off. Within minutes, they had a convoy on the road. When the Klan-filled cars spotted the SNCC convoy, they stopped their trucks, but not before one occupant fired off several rounds of gunfire. Finally, the SNCC convoy made it into Greenwood. Everyone was waiting for them inside the Elks Hall. Having heard the gunshots, they had feared bloodshed. "When Sidney and I walked in," Belafonte recalled, "screams of joy went up from the crowd. Sidney and I had heard a lot of applause in our day, but never anything like those cheers." Poitier looked around at the brave students and adults. "I am thirty-seven years old," he said, as a hush fell over the room. "I have been a lonely man all my life . . . because I have not found love . . . but this room is overflowing with it." There were smiles and tears. Belafonte broke out into "Day-O," his signature song.

It wasn't just that Hollywood was continuing to ignore movies that had Black-themed stories; they weren't even putting Blacks in their movies. Of the eighty Hollywood films released in America in 1966, only one featured a Black in a starring role: Sidney Poitier alongside James Garner in

*Duel at Diablo,* directed by Ralph Nelson, Poitier's old friend who had directed *Lilies of the Field.* Perhaps the most provocative film that year when it came to race was one that opened in Britain, *Dutchman,* based on Leroi Jones's one-act play, which had premiered in New York City at the Cherry Lane Theatre in 1964. It was an exaggeration, however, to label it a full-length movie: its running time was only fifty-five minutes. Anthony Harvey, the film's British director, was young, possessed of a filmmaker's derring-do. *Dutchman* told a story of a Black man, played by Al Freeman, Jr., and a white woman, played by Shirley Knight. She tries to seduce him on a New York City subway. It does not end well—for the Black man. In 1967, the film opened briefly in America before quickly disappearing. Bosley Crowther of *The New York Times* managed to catch it and was not impressed, calling it "a drawn out, rancorous gabfest in a sometimes empty, sometimes half-filled subway car between a clearly psychotic young white woman and a pleasant but gullible young Negro man."

In Harry Belafonte's mind, cinema was continuing to miss out on the rich history of the American Black—the art and music and jazz and the ferocious march toward freedom. He came up with an idea, but quickly realized that the men running Hollywood wouldn't care for it, so he went to CBS TV, which gave his project a green light. The idea sprang from the works of Langston Hughes: a salute to 1920s Harlem. Belafonte assembled an eye-popping, big-name cast: Sammy Davis, Jr., Joe Williams, Diahann Carroll, Nipsey Russell, Duke Ellington. And to play the narrator of this hip-swaying, head-shaking musical revue, he called upon his friend Sidney Poitier. Langston Hughes scripted the whole affair. "I found my own values in the Harlem ghetto, and I wanted somehow to show that—and with a touch of humanity," Belafonte explained. It was quite poignant during rehearsals to spot Hughes puffing on a cigarette; Duke Ellington grinning beneath those saggy eyes; Sammy jitterbugging; Harry and Sidney conferring in their own special language that stretched back to their youthful days in Harlem. "Never, not ever in your whistling lifetime," *Life* magazine said of the revue, "was so much big-time Negro entertainment talent crammed into so brisk an hour."

The Strolling '20s may well have reminded filmgoers that it had been a long time—seven years—since Harry Belafonte had appeared on the big screen, his last appearance having come in 1959's *Odds Against Tomorrow,* a crime caper. The next time they actually did see Belafonte on the big screen would be quite a sad occasion. He appeared as the narrator in Joseph Mankiewicz and Sidney Lumet's documentary film, *King: A*

*Filmed Record . . . Montgomery to Memphis.* It was a "one-time only" event on March 24, 1970, when certain theatres around the country premiered the film. The documentary began with Belafonte's presence and words: "Sometimes the good Lord closes his eyes and takes his own good time and makes himself a man. And sometimes that man gets hold of an idea. . . ." His voice is touched with deep anguish, his eyes seeming to stare off into the yonder. "That kind of man will do what he sees as justice. . . . Be thankful that the Lord let such a man touch our lives, even if it were only for a little while."

King was in the ground.

By 1974, Harry and Sidney were in the saddle, literally, in *Buck and the Preacher,* a caper about two Black cowboys, Poitier as Buck and Belafonte as the preacher, trying to save a convoy of Blacks from white outlaws. Ruby Dee, from their long-ago Harlem theatre days, was a costar. It was a hit, grossing ten million dollars.

As the years rolled on, Belafonte stayed close to the political heartbeat of the world. He helped raise money for the King Center in Atlanta; he rallied Americans to the anti-apartheid movement of South Africa; he went to talk to prisoners anywhere he could.

Sidney Poitier—although his acting career continued into the eighties and nineties—began that long season of being celebrated: honors and dinners and gala salutes piled up. They were two old pros, Belafonte and Poitier, two ageless Black men, the first of their kind, Hollywood pioneers. Poitier had seemed to own much of the 1960s when it came to a cinematic racial reckoning with such hits as *Lilies of the Field; In the Heat of the Night; To Sir, with Love;* and *Guess Who's Coming to Dinner.* "A lot of the films have lasted," he said, "which is the real test."

In 1976, Sidney Poitier sat on a California stage, addressing film students. As he looked out over them, he realized there was something important he wanted to share. "In the early days there was a man named Oscar Micheaux, a black moviemaker at a time when it's impossible to conceive of there having been a black moviemaker," he told them. "He did not ask permission for what to make. He did not get a collective democratic point of view on what he should do. He made his pictures and you know what he did? He put them in the back of a car and traveled the country." They were hanging on his every word. "If there's anything useful that I can tell you guys today as young filmmakers, it's that story. That's what you have to do. Not necessarily put your films in the back of your car, but you have to be true to your own vision and make those pictures that you want to make."

# [Flashback]

## The 1964 Academy Awards

THE ACADEMY AWARDS SHOW had to go on, even amid the nation-shaking agony four months earlier over the assassination of President Kennedy.

Kennedy had many friends in Hollywood, among them his brother-in-law the actor Peter Lawford, and Frank Sinatra. There had also been discreet relationships with many beautiful women—among them Marilyn Monroe. Hollywood—all that glamour, all that make-believe—was a Jack Kennedy kind of town. Five months before the fateful trip to Dallas, a Warner Brothers movie, *PT-109*, opened in theatres. It told the fact-based story of Lieutenant John F. Kennedy's naval exploits in the Pacific during World War II. He saved several of his men after their PT boat was capsized by a Japanese destroyer, and emerged from the war with a badly damaged back, a winning smile, medals attesting to his heroism, and political ambitions. Cliff Robertson played Kennedy in the war film. Ty Hardin and Norman Fell were among the film's costars.

Sidney Poitier was seated in the back of a limousine on the evening of April 13, 1964, en route to the Academy Awards ceremony. Martin Baum, and Baum's wife, Bernice, were with him. Poitier had left his lover, Diahann Carroll, behind. Both had split from their spouses, convinced that they would marry at some point in the near future.

As the well-dressed crowd made its way into the Santa Monica Civic Auditorium, they seemed to be in a bubble. Blacks were being arrested for protesting discrimination throughout the South—and in the North as well. American troops were dying in Vietnam in a war rife with riddles, mysteries, and governmental deceit. Black soldiers in 'Nam were hearing the news about the protests. Many vowed that, since they were putting their lives on the line for American freedom, they had no intention of returning home only to be beaten down.

The Academy had called upon Jack Lemmon to host the awards show. The nominees for Best Picture were: *Tom Jones, How the West Was Won, Cleopatra, America America,* and *Lilies of the Field.* The nominees for Best Actor were: Albert Finney in *Tom Jones,* Rex Harrison in *Cleopatra,* Paul Newman in *Hud,* Richard Harris in *This Sporting Life,* and Sidney Poitier in *Lilies of the Field.* Poitier thought Finney was a shoo-in for the honors. Anne Bancroft opened the envelope for Best Actor and said quickly: "The winner is Sidney Poitier, *Lilies of the Field.*" The applause erupted; Poitier leaped from his seat, pantherlike, and made his way quickly to the podium, his tuxedo tails flapping just a bit, the lush gospellike musical anthem of the film, "Amen," now filling the auditorium. A Black man had never won an Academy Award. The applause wouldn't stop. When it finally did, Poitier, at the microphone, took a deep breath. "Because it is a long journey to this moment," he began, "I am naturally indebted to countless numbers of people, principally among whom are Ralph Nelson, Martin Baum, James Pall, William Barrett, and members of the Academy. To all of them, all I can say is a very special thank you." It was a short speech, and a mighty loud moment.

The audience—filled with longtime movie stars—mobbed Poitier after the telecast. "I would like to think it will help, but I don't believe my Oscar will be a sort of magic wand that will wipe away restrictions of job opportunities for Negro actors in films," Poitier told the media. There were journalists from all over the world. In the days to come, the foreign press would try to make sense of this moment—a Black Academy Award winner, and Blacks out on the streets of America being arrested and killed, and even bombed in churches. "In the present rush of talented Negroes to demand more than a quota representation in plays, movies, television commercials, and general advertising," Alistair Cooke wrote in the London *Guardian,* "coloured people begin to pop up on the screen in jobs they would dearly like to land in life. Last night Hollywood gave a boost in this movement to help life imitate art by crowning a Negro, Sidney Poitier, as the best actor of the year." Many foreign journalists found the dichotomy of America bewildering. American journalists were quite accustomed to the legal segregation in America. It was little surprise when a wave of Southern newspapers criticized Anne Bancroft for being too enthusiastic when she presented Poitier with his Oscar. *The Dallas Morning News,* responding to Poitier's comment about Black actors and the future, wrote: "If the actor means that his prize should stimulate acting employment for other Negro actors, he is off his course."

# The Hustlers, Detectives, and Pimps
# Who Stunned Hollywood

THE MEN WHO RAN HOLLYWOOD were blindsided by the 1960s. A revolution was upon them, and it was being shown daily on television. This revolution of youthful and interracial uprisings stretched from Chicago to Berkeley, from Rhode Island to Delaware, from Virginia to Louisiana. The studio chiefs—who had no Black executives in their corridors—seemed frozen in place. They were also aging. In the 1930s, their concern was that families suffering from the Depression couldn't afford to go to the movies. But the country eventually turned the corner economically. War came, and people needed to be entertained. Now, decades beyond the golden age of film, there were physical uprisings on the streets. It all seemed so different. The very survival of the nation seemed at stake. In the summer of 1964, several months after Sidney Poitier's Oscar, the Civil Rights Act was passed. In certain communities, the white backlash—Klan rallies and white-supremacist gatherings—was frightening.

Hollywood tried mightily to avert the nation's attention with its cinematic offerings, but failed miserably. Many of their big-budget movies flopped. *Mutiny on the Bounty* (1962) was a painful failure, making a mere thirteen million against a nineteen-million-dollar budget. *The Greatest Story Ever Told* (1965) suffered a similar fate, making fifteen million against its twenty-million-dollar budget. These flops, along with the dismal fates of *Cleopatra* (1963) and *Doctor Dolittle* (1967) (seventeen million-dollar budget and nine-million box office) had studio chiefs scratching their heads and commiserating about their steep financial losses. (Sidney Poitier had been slated to appear in *Doctor Dolittle*, but his agent balked at the studio's low offer for his services, and the actor walked away.)

Mainstream movies were offering Black filmgoers—so often and so long ignored—very little in the way of variety. Poitier remained the best-known Black movie star, but there was something slowly, and perceptibly, beginning to creep upon his mystique. Some film critics now took a harsher view of his screen appearances, which, more often than not, presented him as the righteous moral foil to a white antagonist. "The caricature of the Negro as a Madison Avenue sort of Christian saint, selfless and well-groomed, is becoming a movie cliché nearly as tiresome and, at bottom, nearly as patronizing as the cretinous figure that Stepin Fetchit used to play," came the retort from Brendan Gill of *The New Yorker.* "Negroes must find it extremely irritating." In *A Patch of Blue,* released during the Christmas season of 1965, Poitier played Gordon Ralfe, an office worker. While strolling through a city park, he comes upon Selina D'Arcey, a young woman played by Elizabeth Hartman. Selina is scrambling to pick up jeweled beads that have fallen off a piece of string, and Gordon helps her. Selina is white, and also blind. Her mother, Rose-Ann D'Arcey (Shelley Winters) is a vicious drunk who abuses the girl. Gordon and the blind girl are soon drawn to each other, and Gordon wants to rescue her. Rose is also a bigot and soon reveals to Selina her friend Gordon's racial identity. But Gordon is relentless in his effort to save Selina. "The implicit moral is that affection between a Negro man and a white girl is all right so long as the girl is blind, ignorant, undeveloped and 18-years-old," wrote *Film Quarterly.* "We will have got somewhere when she's a bright 25-year-old who knows what she's doing." Even so, many Southern theatres that showed *A Patch of Blue* edited certain scenes in which it was felt that the Black-white relationship—as chaste as it was—was still too worrisome.

It was reported that by 1967 approximately 52 percent of the American population would be under the age of twenty-five. That age bracket turned certain movies—*The Graduate, Bonnie and Clyde,* even *A Patch of Blue*—into substantial hits. The bloated musicals and lily-white productions of the Hollywood past were not exactly what the youthful demographic now happened to be screaming for. Studio heads had to pay attention.

Aside from the youth revolution, there were myriad other problems that Hollywood had been forced to endure. In 1948, in a Supreme Court case, *United States v. Paramount Pictures,* the high court decreed that studios had to divest themselves of many of the movie theatres they owned. The court's position was that the studios had monopolized theatres because, by owning so many, they were booking only the films they wished to book. The antitrust ruling meant that studios lost their grip on theatre domination. Another problem was the issue of white flight. The inner-city uprisings—especially in the aftermath of Martin Luther King, Jr.'s murder—caused many whites to flee to the never-integrated suburbs. Shopping-mall owners wanted residents to spend as much time and money in the suburbs as possible, so they constructed theatres right in their malls, adjacent to the suburbs. Thus whites could continue to avoid the inner cities of America. The suburbs now had everything!

*Ebony* magazine took note of the nation's psyche behind the shrewd real-estate planning: "The city, state and federal governments cooperated in building super highways to transport the working suburbanites to and from jobs. Suburban living was within the price range of the white collar worker and upper level blue collar worker—so long as he was white. But the suburbs were no solution for the black man and for one reason—the new developments were as rigidly, if not more, segregated as the cities from which the white man was fleeing. Even if a black family could afford to move to the suburbs, they could not do so unless they were willing to face the court and public fight often necessary to force a developer to sell to them." The Fair Housing Act of 1968 was intended to stem the tide of suburban segregation, but its effectiveness was constantly curtailed by white real-estate agents intent on subverting the law. The population shift to the suburbs left inner-city theatre managers fretting about lost ticket revenue. The triptych-like setback for films and filmmakers—sharp decrease in theatre ownership; ill-advised 1960s films; drop-off in numbers of moviegoers—put studio moguls in a deep and ongoing tailspin.

Melvin Van Peebles was just another anonymous Black man who lamented that, while growing up during the Great Depression, he rarely saw anyone on a movie screen that looked like him. Born in 1932 in Chicago, he was an industrious sort all through school. After high-school graduation, he made his way to Delaware, Ohio, to begin college at Ohio Wesleyan University. He studied painting and astronomy, subjects that pointed to his growing eccentricities. He graduated in 1953. Afterward, he served a stint in the segregated United States Air Force. By the late 1950s, he found himself in San Francisco. Van Peebles fell in love with the city, which was one of the most progressive places in the nation. He got work as a cable-car

Jim Brown and Raquel Welch. *100 Rifles*. And 100 million reactions. (1969)

Chadwick Boseman in *Black Panther* (2018). Hollywood could no longer ignore Blackness.

Billy Dee Williams in *Star Wars: Episode V—The Empire Strikes Back* (1980). *Time* magazine called him "The Black Gable."

Lena Horne in 1946. Her father traveled to Hollywood and demanded better roles for her.

Diana Sands in 1963, star
of stage and screen, died at
thirty-nine—a terrible blow
to Black cinema hopes.

Dorothy Dandridge in 1954.
Her glamour was hardly enough
in segregated America.

Denzel Washington. He *became* Malcolm. (1992)

*Introducing*
*a new era in motion pictures!*

*Porgy and Bess.* Black stars—
and a disappearing act. (1959)

Richard Pryor in 1983. A ferocious talent trailed by demons.

Ossie Davis and Ruby Dee. The husband-and-wife acting couple were legendary activists.

"I Can't Breathe." The *Selma* cast made a defiant statement on the steps of the New York Public Library. (2014)

*Roots* (1977). It shook the nation when it aired as a television miniseries.

driver. While cruising up and over the hills of the city, the sensations and scenes inspired him. He bought a camera, and in his spare time took photographs. He began to write stories, many of them about his cable-car and taxi-driving experiences related to those photographs. His stories and photos eventually became a book, *The Big Heart*. In time, photography struck him as being akin to film and filmmaking. He spent long nights reading about movies and artists, and made a couple of very short films. Even what he didn't know about filmmaking seemed to excite him. "I thought they were features," he would recall about his very short films. "Each one turned out to be eleven minutes long. I was trying to do features. I knew nothing." Nevertheless, he kept asking questions and making mental notes. He was so naïve; it was charming to those who met him. He hopped down to Hollywood. They slammed the door in his face when he tried to show his short films in hopes of getting work. So he decided to ditch the West Coast for New York City. It was there that Van Peebles met Henri Langlois, who had cofounded the esteemed Cinémathèque Française in Paris. Langlois saw something in Van Peebles's short films and invited him to Paris to show them.

In France, he learned to speak French. There were financial woes, but he scraped by. Strangers were kind, women were kinder. Like James Baldwin and Richard Wright and other Black expatriate Americans inclined toward the arts, Van Peebles benefited from the racial openness of the French. He got a job editing a humor magazine, but what he really wanted to do was break into cinema. "I discovered there was a French law that said they'd pay a French writer to get a temporary director's card to get his own stories to the screen. You just had to write five novels in French. So I did and that's how I got my director's card." Van Peebles had also arrived in Paris at a fortuitous time, when the Nouvelle Vague (New Wave) movement was in motion. It was so named for a contingent of young, innovative filmmakers who sought to upset the old order of stodgy moviemaking. These new filmmakers told more personal stories; they let the camera move in dazzling and unexpected ways; they believed in poetry and an in-your-face style up on the screen. Among the filmmakers were François Truffaut, Éric Rohmer, Claude Chabrol, and Jean-Luc Godard. Among Godard's 1960 films, *Breathless* was about a romanticized Parisian hood (Jean-Paul Belmondo) and his American girlfriend (Jean Seberg), and it showcased a wide array of jump cuts made while utilizing a handheld camera. The style was kinetic and innovative. Van Peebles watched the films of the New Wave directors over and over, heavily influenced by their cinematic mannerisms.

With a generous French filmmaking grant, Melvin Van Peebles set about making his first full-length film. It took place in Paris, adapted from one of his own French-language novels, *La Permission*. It was the story of a Black American soldier, Turner (played by Harry Baird, a Guyanese actor), who gets a three-day furlough and proceeds to roam the streets of Paris. He meets a Frenchwoman, Miriam (Nicole Berger), and they have an affair. It is ultimately a rushed love story, with jump cuts on-screen and sensuous montages and jazzy music. There is also the weight of racial tension. The French were so impressed with the film—renamed *The Story of a Three-Day Pass*—that they entered it in the 1968 San Francisco International Film Festival. Van Peebles still had many friends in San Francisco, among them Albert Johnson, program director of the festival. His praise of a film tended to reach the ears of Hollywood. "Van Peebles," Johnson felt, "understands the attitudes of the expatriate African American as well as the objective wisdom of the French heroine, and the fluctuations between dream and reality are very much a part of contemporary life, with its painful contretemps, its bewildering disillusionments." It was a small film that played mostly in American art houses. (No one paid attention to the historical resonance at the time, but Melvin Van Peebles had become the first Black American to direct a film and have it released in America since Oscar Micheaux's *The Betrayal* in 1948.) Though the movie didn't get a wide release, it got the name Melvin Van Peebles mentioned in Hollywood circles. Columbia Pictures reached out to him. The overture convinced the filmmaker that his reception might be considerably different from the one he had received years earlier, when he first trekked to Hollywood.

Columbia Pictures was in possession of a script written by Herman Raucher that had gotten attention because of its ribald premise: a white suburban insurance man goes to bed one night and wakes up to find that he has turned into a Black man. What unfolds is a sometimes hilarious and mostly edgy account of the racism that has infected the country: the white man (inside the Black man) sees, for the first time, the differences in how whites and Blacks are treated. The premise itself harked back to a June 11, 1963, speech delivered from the White House to the nation by President Kennedy, in the aftermath of the University of Alabama's inability to protect two Black students whose admittance had been ordered by a district court. Kennedy was forced to send in National Guard troops. Staring into the camera, he said:

*If an American, because his skin is dark, cannot eat lunch in a restaurant open to the public, if he cannot send his children to the best public school available, if he cannot vote for the public officials who will represent him, if, in short, he cannot enjoy the full and free life which all of us want, then who among us would be content to have the color of his skin changed and stand in his place?*

Raucher allowed in interviews that he had written the script because he had many so-called liberal friends who expressed, quite casually, racist sentiments and were seemingly unaware they were doing so.

Columbia offered Van Peebles the opportunity to direct Raucher's script. Once the contract was signed, the studio mentioned they thought Alan Arkin or Jack Lemmon might be wonderful to play Jeff Gerber, the white-turned-Black. By the time Peebles returned from putting his own touches on the script, it had turned into something far more incendiary—a direct and piercing attack against racism, albeit still with jabs of humor. He also ignored the casting recommendations and cast Godfrey Cambridge—the actor who in the early 1960s had cofounded a group to investigate a lack of roles for Black actors. Estelle Parsons was cast as Mrs. Gerber. She had drawn attention for her impressive performance in 1967's *Bonnie and Clyde.* Also cast in the film was Mantan Moreland, who had come up through Black vaudeville and played the chauffeur in a host of Charlie Chan movies. His other films found him playing either a porter or a shoeshine man. His career had been emblematic of how Hollywood used Black actors in earlier decades, and Van Peebles's casting him was rather poignant.

At the time when Van Peebles was putting the film together, Godfrey Cambridge was working as a stand-up comedian. He tinged his jokes with racial humor:

*Tarzan is a fascinating cat. Here's a white cat living in the jungle who knows more about the jungle than the black cats who were born there! . . . I lost 170 pounds. And I hope Gov. George Wallace swallows every one of them!*

Van Peebles decided he wanted Cambridge to play the role of Jeff Gerber in whiteface during the first few minutes of the film. The comic in

Cambridge was quite willing to do so. While cast and crew were film-ing an early scene of the movie on the Santa Monica beach, the strolling gawkers couldn't stop staring. The impossible-to-miss whiteface makeup shocked them. Cambridge and Moreland sometimes looked at each other on the movie set and started chuckling. They just couldn't quite believe what they were witnessing: a cigar-chomping Black man, Mel-vin Van Peebles, still new to the American movie business, playing with all this money that Columbia Pictures had given him to make a movie about white comeuppance, all while commanding a mostly white film crew! Cambridge was particularly impressed with Van Peebles's ability to keep the Columbia execs at bay, keep Raucher from blowing up about the changes to his script, and keep the filming on schedule. "He can con anybody," Cambridge said of Van Peebles, by way of praise.

Of the many cultural things that caught Columbia executives—as well as Raucher—off guard was Van Peebles's selection of a title for the film: *Watermelon Man.* Given that watermelon had long been a fruit associ-ated with Black stereotyping, the title was jokey—and subversive. If whites wouldn't quite understand, Blacks needed only to see the comic Godfrey Cambridge's image and name on the movie posters to realize something unusual was afoot.

The movie was released May 27, 1970. The tagline on the movie poster read: "A very funny thing happened to Jeff Gerber. It won't happen to you, so you can laugh." Smack in the center of the poster was a head-shot of Cambridge, half of his face black, the other half white. *The New York Times* panned the film, proclaiming that it "falls crashingly flat on its black-and-white face." *Variety* wasn't much kinder: "Not much of a picture, but as a transient innocuous entertainment it is harmless." Black films had always been transient products in America, and Blacks ignored the barbs. They found the absurdities in *Watermelon Man* funny, and they helped turn the film into a modest moneymaker. The studio was so impressed that they offered Van Peebles a three-picture deal, but he imag-ined the studio would want to control too much of the artistic direction of any picture he would make. There had been heated arguments over the ending of *Watermelon Man.* In the final scenes, Jeff Gerber was shown doing vicious karate kicks, as if he were saying to America: Time for the Black man to kick ass! So there were conversations—billowing rings of smoke from Van Peebles's omnipresent cigar; exasperation from studio executives—and then a rescinding of the deal.

Van Peebles—ignoring his agent's calls—rode off into the California desert, a habit he had acquired to clear his mind. He took stock of his life: He had gone to France. He had made movies. He had gotten married—and divorced. He was an eyewitness—like so many Blacks—to the ongoing Black-white revolution in America. And he was an artist! Artists navigated their own road! Melvin Van Peebles decided it was time to get revolutionary with his cinematic dreams.

The script he began writing focused on a Black boy who grows up inside a brothel and becomes a southern-California pimp. He is surrounded by people trying to hustle their way through life and Los Angeles and all the strange and frightening danger associated with revolution, hippies, Blackness, the police state, the 1960s. The protagonist, called Sweetback—because of his sexual prowess—finds himself one night in a car with two crooked cops, en route to collect money. But there is another passenger, known as Mu-Mu, a Black revolutionary. Mu-Mu and Sweetback are strangers to each other. The police officers swerve the car off the side of a darkened road. Both Black men are ordered out of the car. The white officers begin beating Mu-Mu. Sweetback watches the beating in silent horror until he finally reacts by grabbing a pair of handcuffs and beating the white cops with them. With the cops now unconscious, Sweetback and Mu-Mu take off in different directions. The script has Sweetback in constant flight—running through the streets, through brothels, having sex, fighting, dealing with the Hells Angels, outwitting the white man! The script was a jangle of pages that Van Peebles kept shaping and rewriting as he puffed away on his cigar. At last, he was finished.

Movie executives like to hear a pitch that can be connected to another movie—preferably a financially successful one—so they can quickly explain the premise to others throughout their studio. But what Van Peebles began discussing around Hollywood had no precedent. There was no way to compare his film concept about a strutting Black lawbreaking pimp who goes on the run, stopping only to have more sex with white women—and then experiences a political awakening—to any film that had ever been made. The executives listened politely, then offered their collective decisions: No, no, no, no, and no. *Watermelon Man* was funny, they told Van Peebles; this pitch was not. It was downright strange. And far beyond their white upper-class grasp of life. The doors kept closing as Van Peebles went over his script again and again, wondering what he should change to make it more palatable. But he couldn't bring himself to change anything. It was exactly the script he'd wanted to write! So he told himself he'd raise the money independently. He'd line up financiers, give them his spiel, take their money, and go off to make his movie!

Rolling around town—sometimes with his two young kids in tow—Van Peebles met with deep-pocketed Los Angelenos. Money was promised; then the promises were broken. Money finally started to dribble in. Van Peebles started to put together his budget. There wasn't enough money to offer any prominent director the salary he'd expect, so he decided he'd direct it himself. He also realized that if he were to abide by Screen Actors Guild (SAG) union rules, even their minimum salaries, those salaries would bust his budget. When told that pornographic filmmakers did not have to abide by SAG guidelines, Van Peebles concocted a plan: he'd lie to SAG and tell them he was shooting a porn movie! The union fell for the ruse. Even though there was sex and nudity—and orgies—in the script, Van Peebles assured those whom he let read it that those elements simply served the revolutionary nature of what was happening in the film!

Word went out that the director of *Watermelon Man* was about to commence filming a new movie. Actors came in to read for the role of Sweetback. They were befuddled by the script; Sweetback spoke fewer than twelve lines in the entire movie, and actors wanted lines! Casting was not going well. Van Peebles, who had already hired himself as director, finally decided he knew just the actor to play the rambling, running, mustachioed stud known as Sweetback: Melvin Van Peebles! Other roles were cast with no-name actors. The cast and crew were multiracial—and low-paid. There was no money to hire stuntmen or stuntwomen, so the cast was informed they'd have to perform those duties themselves, clothed and unclothed. Everyone was game, despite the wildness and weirdness of it all—stepping over wires, watching boom lights being set up during filming, smelling the marijuana wafting about during breaks in the filming. Van Peebles hired some motorcycle riders from a nearby Hells Angels outfit to be in a scene. Some of them appeared testy and leery of taking direction, giving the film set a touch of menace; Van Peebles asked an acquaintance to bring him a handgun. The cameras kept rolling. (A couple of crew members were actual members of the union, but because they wanted to work on the film they concealed their identities whenever photos were taken.) The days—five, then ten, then twelve—began to fly by. The rushes—the daily footage one could look at on a monitor—didn't look like anything those on the set and working behind the scenes had ever seen before. That revelation delighted Van Peebles.

Then the money ran out.

Van Peebles had already poured a lot of his own money into the film. A total of $450,000 had already been spent and he was told he'd need another fifty thousand to complete filming. He didn't have it, so he went, hat in hand, to people he knew. He thought of his friend Bill Cosby. A few years earlier, Cosby had become the first male Black to costar in a weekly television series, *I Spy,* and his income had been growing. Cosby asked Van Peebles how much he'd need, and when Van Peebles told him fifty thousand, the comedian swallowed hard. But he consulted his wife, who was on board, and gave Van Peebles the entire amount. After a fierce nineteen days, Van Peebles completed his movie. He came up with a title: *Sweet Sweetback's Baadasssss Song.*

The postproduction process of editing and scoring the film got under way. Van Peebles didn't have money to have music composed in a traditional way, so he hired some musicians recommended by his secretary, who had come to Los Angeles from Chicago. They were into mixing jazz and funk and rhythm and blues, and seemed in touch with the times. Van Peebles gave them a check. The check bounced. The musicians wanted to break into film, so they stayed and scored the movie. They called themselves Earth, Wind & Fire.


It wasn't so much the strident Black-power affectations in the movie as it was the full-blown frontal nudity that earned *Sweet Sweetback* its X-rating from the Motion Picture Association of America. Hollywood was only a few years removed from the oversight of the Hays Code. The X-rated designation increased the challenge for Van Peebles of getting his film into first-run mainstream theatres. Nevertheless, he phoned distributors all around the country, making his pitch; as soon as he revealed to them that it had received an X-rating, the conversations usually came to an abrupt end. He finally found a company, Cinemation Industries, that signed on to help him distribute the finished movie. The company, six years old, dodging tax woes year by year, was based in New York City. Its highest-profile cinematic offering to date had been *Shanty Tramp,* which played in a lot of drive-ins and revolved around a backwoods minister, a poor white vixen in extreme distress, lurid crime, and incest. The movie poster's tagline: "A TEEN-STORY FOR MATURE ADULTS." It, too, had received an X-rating.

Cinemation finally informed Van Peebles they had gotten his film booked into two theatres. The first showing was scheduled to take place March 31, 1971, at the Grand Circus Theatre in Detroit. Van Peebles flew there nine days ahead of the scheduled premiere, with two goals in mind: to hold a press conference, and to talk to Black radio-station deejays.

Detroit's ethnic rivalries and large Black population—along with its white-dominated police departments through the years—presented a combustible brew. In the 1943 rioting that took place in the city, twenty-five Blacks and nine whites died. All of the Black deaths were at the hands of police officers. The legendary attorney Thurgood Marshall was asked to compile a report in the aftermath of the 1943 riots. "The certainty of Negroes that they will not be protected by police, but instead will be attacked by them is a contributing factor to racial tensions leading to overt acts. The first item on the agenda of any group seeking to prevent rioting would seem to be a critical study of the police department of the community, its record in handling Negroes, something of the background of its personnel and the plans of its chief officers for meeting possible racial disorders." Twenty-four years later, in July 1967, rioting and rebellion erupted again in the city. The statistics were grim and horrific: forty-three deaths were linked to the uprising, more than a thousand wounded. More than two thousand stores were torched or looted, oftentimes both. One of the searing moments had taken place in the early-morning hours of July 23. Three blacks were murdered in cold blood by Detroit police officers at the Algiers Motel. The officers would later be charged, only to be acquitted. Two years before the 1967 rebellion, the NAACP had issued a warning: "The Negroes of Detroit feel they are part of an occupied country."

Van Peebles arrived in a Detroit that was still showing signs of deep pain from 1967, as well as depthless hurt from the assassination of Martin Luther King, Jr., three years earlier. Storefronts in the city still looked as if they had been bombed out. Residents complained about the so-called recovery effort and how slow it was. Distrust of the police lingered. Van Peebles had with him a movie about Black empowerment and police brutality, which also had sex and hijinks and escapism thrown in. The zeitgeist was upon him.

First, the March 22, 1971, press conference.

The press contingent came as much out of bemusement as out of curiosity. They wanted to know if his movie really was X-rated. Van Peebles announced he had written a letter to Jack Valenti, head of the Motion Picture Association of America, from which he read aloud:

*As a black artist and independent producer of motion pictures, I refuse to submit this film, made from Black perspective for Blacks, to the Motion Picture Code and Administration for rating that would be applicable to the black community. Neither will I "self apply" an "X" rating to my movie, if such a rating is to be applicable to Black audiences as called for by the Motion Pictures Code and Administration rules. I charge that your film rating body has no right to tell the Black community what it may or may not see. Should the rest of the community submit to your censorship that is its business, but White standards shall no longer be imposed on the black community.*

The press gathering was now truly bewildered. Most had no idea who Jack Valenti was. (He had previously worked in the LBJ White House.) They also hadn't seen the movie, because there had been no advance press screenings. Van Peebles followed up the press conference with radio show appearances, during which he smiled as the deejays played songs from Earth, Wind & Fire's first album, which was just released and causing a stir. In between the songs and head bobbing inside the stations, he'd tell the listening Black audiences about his film, and its strangely hypnotic title. He made those audiences feel that they had invested—at least psychologically, because they were survivors in white America!—in his movie. It was really *their* movie, and they had to come out to see it!

The wide-eyed audience members who had walked into the Grand Circus Theatre and sat down with their candy and popcorn had never seen anything like it. At the beginning of the movie, in blazing red letters, were the words: "STARRING THE BLACK COMMUNITY." The audience whooped and hollered. And they hollered some more at the end of the movie, when they saw Sweetback himself—having escaped the police and possible death—hustling off into the yonder with more writing scrawled across the screen: "Watch Out. A Bad Asssss Nigger is coming back to collect some dues."

The applause and laughter and slapping palms echoed across the theatre. And the city telephone lines lit up in the ensuing hours and days. Detroiters spread the word along the grapevine that *Sweet Sweetback's Baadasssss Song* was a must-see movie. Patrons came back to see it a second time. The theatre managers couldn't believe the long lines or the telephone calls inquiring about the possibility of added screenings. "No one had the vision of what I could do," Van Peebles later said. In its first five days of showings, the Grand Circus Theatre broke a house record, amassing forty-five thousand dollars in ticket receipts. Simultaneously, at Friday- and Saturday-night house parties, they were shimmying to Earth, Wind & Fire. It was just the kind of merging—film and music—that Van Peebles had hoped for.

Melvin Van Peebles hopped a plane. Next up: Atlanta—the only other city with a theatre that had agreed to host the film.

For years, whites had thought of Atlanta as Margaret Mitchell land; it was their *Gone with the Wind* touchstone. But Black Americans, by the middle of the twentieth century, had a different take. The city's Black middle class had begun to emerge in the 1950s. There was growth inside the Atlanta-based Southern Christian Leadership Conference, propelled by its young leader, Martin Luther King, Jr. The big Negro Baptist church conferences brought in the cream of the ministerial crop. Atlanta was hope—that is, until the funeral, until all those mules clopped down the streets before the great minister who'd been murdered, his coffin lying inside an old farm wagon, a wagon that was emblematic of the long Black struggle fought upon the land. Thousands—on the day of the burial—followed behind the wagon with tear-streaked faces. Gordon Parks, the gifted photographer, covered the funeral for *Life* magazine. Sidney Poitier and Harry Belafonte were among those in attendance. Aside from taking photographs on that somber day, Parks also wrote a personal essay about King for *Life*. "No man spoke harder against violence. Yet few men suffered more from it than he. His worship of a higher law got him jailed, stoned and stabbed. He led us into fire hoses, police dogs and police clubs. His only armor was truth and love. Now that he lies dead from a lower law, we begin to wonder if love is enough. Racism still engulfs us."

King had seen the power of cinema, how the imagery could be so devastating to Blacks. He wasn't, however, above being seduced by the medium. He had listened to a movie pitch made to him by Otto Preminger, who wanted King to appear in one of his planned movies, playing a U.S. senator. King got a chuckle out of the proposed role, but ultimately declined.

Melvin Van Peebles strutted into Atlanta with his head held high. And by the time he finished his gabfests with Atlanta's Black radio deejays, talking up Earth, Wind & Fire and his movie ("Rated X by an all-white jury," blared the flyers about *Sweetback*), crowing about the big business the movie was doing in Detroit, talking politics with the college kids across the city, and joking with them that surely they'd be wily enough (wink, wink) to circumvent the age requirement attached to his film's X-rating; by the time he finished swinging in and out of the Black barbershops and hair salons and drinking establishments, handing out more flyers, the Black citizenry of Atlanta was beyond excited about this movie with the very strange title. And so Atlantans, mostly Black, started coming to the six-hundred-seat Coronet Theatre on Peachtree Street. The word-of-mouth lengthened the lines, and those lines began stretching down the street. The Coronet's managers couldn't have been more delighted, hustling to keep the popcorn maker going and the candy in stock. Filmgoers began bringing sandwiches in bags, staying to see the movie a second time. Buzz about the movie's day-to-day increasing popularity exploded on Black radio. *Sweet Sweetback's Baadasssss Song*—whose title, however, the *Atlanta Journal-Constitution* would only print as *Sweet Sweetback*—broke the house record at the Coronet. The film had now played in two theatres, and broken the house records at each. Van Peebles knew exactly why *Sweetback* was finding its audience: "It was beyond any thought that someone could defy white authority and live."

Movie theatres were in the business, of course, of making money, and theatre managers who had refused to show the film suddenly began requesting it. The film got booked into theatres all around the country. The Friday- and Saturday-night crowds in Los Angeles, Baltimore, Chicago, New York City's Harlem, Houston, Dallas, Philadelphia, and other urban centers stunned theatre managers. Those nattily dressed Black folk with their tickets in hand to see *Sweetback* streamed on in. The movie began breaking house records everywhere. (Little by little, the white audience also began to grow.) Black America had long lived in cinematic pain: Whatever happened to James Edwards? How come Hollywood won't give Lena roles she deserves? There were periodic bouts of joy: Look at Sidney! Look at Harry! But they were far too infrequent. What was happening now with Melvin Van Peebles's fever dream of a Black-oriented movie was different. By May 1971, *Sweet Sweetback* had jumped onto *Variety*'s list of the ten top-grossing films. Some weeks, it even outperformed *Love Story*, the popular Ryan O'Neal–Ali McGraw blockbuster. "As a businessman, Melvin is in a class with Jean Paul Getty and the Rockefeller family," opined Gene Wolsk, a New York stage producer. Van Peebles decreed the film to be about many things—politics, history, rebellion, and, not least, "the radicalization of a stud."

And the reviews of the film itself? They were, for the most part, downright awful.

*The New Yorker*'s review began: "Alas!—I mean hurrah!—there exists a furiously tasteless picture called 'Sweet Sweetback's Baadasssss Song.'" After acknowledging the movie as a fable, the reviewer adds: "It is also a boot in the face for the wishes of moderates, black and white, who are likely to come away reeling." *The New York Times*'s critic decreed *Sweet Sweetback* to be Van Peebles's "third and worst feature," and went on to call it "predictable formula material." (Predictable, however, it wasn't, and it certainly wasn't formulaic.) The *Chicago Sun-Times* believed the film—coming on the heels of Van Peebles's *The Story of a Three-Day Pass* and *Watermelon Man*—full of "shallow characterizations." For years, *Ebony* magazine had prided itself on reading the pulse of the Black community. The picture-laden monthly was read by the Black intelligentsia as well as Black common folk. With *Sweet Sweetback* breaking theatre records, *Ebony*'s editor, Lerone Bennett, knew he had to get a story into print, and decided to write it himself. He had long been considered something of a sage when it came to Black culture and history; his book *Before the Mayflower* was widely admired. Bennett's article about *Sweet Sweetback* was rather richly titled "The Emancipation Orgasm: Sweetback in Wonderland." Bennett proceeded to give *Sweet Sweetback* a drubbing, proclaiming the movie neither "revolutionary nor black." As he put it: "Instead of carrying us forward to the new frontier of collective action, [*Sweetback*] drags us back to the pre-Watts days of isolated individual acts of resistance, conceived in confusion and executed in panic." But the scorching reviews seemed only to increase the number of ticket buyers. The bad publicity, was, indeed, good publicity! Another review, from a white critic: "A technically fancy, absolutely mindless and dirty political exploitation film . . . almost psychotic."

———

Huey Newton wasn't a film critic. He was the Louisiana-born, beret-wearing cofounder of the Black Panther Party. He had also served time in prison for his involvement in a 1967 shooting of an Oakland, California, police officer who died. The premise of *Sweet Sweetback* touched Newton on such an emotional level that he decided to write his own review of the film. It was a gushing essay, so lengthy that it took up an entire issue of the Black Panthers' in-house magazine. The review was titled "He Won't Bleed Me: A Revolutionary Analysis of Sweet Sweetback's Badass Song." Newton felt the film was in synch with the anger long brewing in Black communities, calling it "the first truly revolutionary Black film made . . . presented to us by a Black man." In Newton's sentiments, the movie "presents the need for unity among all the members and institutions within the community of victims." As film criticism, it was strange. As prose showing solidarity with Van Peebles, it was hailed by those in Panther Nation as soulful and righteous.

Flying all around the country, bopping in and out of Black social gatherings, cornering Negro newspapermen, Van Peebles was, like Oscar Micheaux before him, hustling hard to keep his film in theatres. The mission—damn the reviews!—became easier by the week as the profits began to soar. The film was still playing when the snow began to fall in the Midwest in the early winter of 1972. By the end of the first year of its run, *Sweet Sweetback* had grossed upward of fifteen million dollars. It had quickly become the highest-grossing independent movie of all time. Hollywood executives may have been aware that Blacks made up only 10 percent of the American population, but it was absurd they didn't seem to realize—or appreciate—that Blacks also constituted 30 percent of the moviegoing public.

Melvin Van Peebles was now officially the bad Black hipster who had shocked Hollywood. He had his own motto, which he turned into one of his body tattoos: "Lynch me—if you can." The taunting filmmaker was laughing all the way to the bank-teller windows.

Hollywood, long in a financial tailspin, listened to the cash register. A Black-oriented movie could make money, and plenty of it. Because of *Sweet Sweetback,* Black Americans were awake to filmdom in a manner they had never been before.

———

Gordon Parks felt secure enough to leave *Life* magazine after the 1969 release of his first film, *The Learning Tree.* The film was adapted from Parks's own autobiographical novel and told the story of a Black boy growing up in 1920s Kansas. It took Parks years to convince Hollywood to make the film. One producer had suggested changing the characters from Black to white, a suggestion Parks scoffed at. The interracially cast film seemed a direct descendant of the kind of movies Oscar Micheaux had once made—set in the open and wide plains of the American Midwest. When *The Learning Tree* landed in theatres, the nation was on fire, and filmgoers seemed to have a lackluster appetite for a movie showcasing an adolescent Black protagonist. Reviews were so-so at best. "There is not a single memorable, or more than barely competent, performance," the *New York Times* reviewer wrote. Other critics felt that the movie, owing to Parks's skills as a photographer, leaned too heavily on lush vistas. But the film did get Parks another job. MGM hired him to direct *Shaft*, adapted from Ernest Tidyman's 1970 novel. The novel told the story of a Black detective prowling the streets of Manhattan in search of a Black gangster's daughter. Tidyman was no Raymond Chandler, but he seemed to know the detective-criminal milieu well enough. Shaft was described as "a black man made of muscle and ice." Parks was eager to direct the film, because he felt the movie "could give Black youth their first cinematic hero comparable to James Cagney or Humphrey Bogart."

Leading roles for Black men in films were so rare it was expected that the role of John Shaft would be widely coveted. But after an "exhaustive search," Parks was feeling dispirited that he still hadn't come across the right actor. His son David suggested he take a look at Richard Roundtree, a little-known New Yorker. Roundtree had been a cabdriver, but had been selected as a fashion model to go on the road with the Ebony Fashion Fair. That led to acting roles. At the time of his audition for *Shaft*, he was appearing in a Philadelphia production of *The Great White Hope*, playing the boxer Jack Johnson. The request to audition for Gordon Parks surprised Roundtree: he'd never been in a television show or a film before. He went into the audition with a lax attitude. "I just knew I didn't have a chance, so I really didn't give it a real try," he recalled. When Parks studied Roundtree before the audition, he thought he looked a bit young for the part. He put a mustache on the actor, strapped a holstered gun around his chest, and signaled for the tape to roll. Parks remained mostly silent, but secretly he liked what he was seeing. He didn't want to make a hasty decision, however, so he watched the Roundtree audition tape again the following morning. What he saw still excited him. He phoned Jim Aubrey, the head of MGM. "I think I've found him," Parks said. "I'm sending you several takes. Let me know what you think." After watching the tape, Aubrey phoned Parks. "You've got him. Sign him up."

Richard Roundtree could hardly believe he had been plucked from relative obscurity for such a big opportunity. MGM arranged a press conference at Sardi's, the hot entertainment hangout in New York City, to make the announcement that their John Shaft had been found. The location tickled Roundtree: he used to deliver passengers to Sardi's from behind the wheel of his taxi! The studio sent a driver to pick him up. "I'm dropped off in a limo and the paparazzi and the press is all there," Roundtree would recall about the day. "The whole world turned around."

Just days before filming was to commence in New York City, Parks was told the location was being switched to Los Angeles to save money. He was furious. "It has to have the smell of New York," he told Aubrey, who was not accustomed to being dictated to. But the studio head eventually relented. On the day filming was to begin—before the cameras started rolling—Parks spotted Roundtree holding a shaving razor. The actor told Parks he had been told by a member of the crew to cut off his mustache. Parks told Roundtree not to touch it. "Richard Roundtree," Parks recalled, "was about to become the first Black leading man who would wear a mustache on the silver screen. It was another one of those unwritten laws lurking within the minds of Hollywood's film barons. A mustache on a Black leading man was just too macho."

Parks and the MGM execs on site were impressed with Roundtree's comfort in front of a camera. The costume designer had outfitted him with a long black leather coat. He wore it like a panther in its own skin. The women on set were full of compliments. During filming, Parks had begun thinking of a soundtrack for the movie. He knew he wanted the music to move fast and have a soulful, rhythmic beat.

Isaac Hayes had made a name for himself in the gritty world of urban music that came out of Memphis and Stax Records. His audience had been mostly Black until he started doing some Burt Bacharach compositions—"Walk On By," "The Look of Love." The world of film scoring was new to him, but word had gotten around that he had done an impressive job with the music for *Maidstone*, an experimental Norman Mailer film. When offered the opportunity to score *Shaft*, Hayes jumped at it and went right to work. When Parks and others later heard Hayes's music for the film, they were thrilled. The opening score was a fast-moving and jazzy electric overture. There were guitar strings, violins, drums, a synthesizer, flutes, and horns. The verses that accompanied the main score were witty:

*Who's the black private dick*
*That's a sex machine to all the chicks?*
*Shaft*
*You're damn right.*

On the night of July 2, 1971, when *Shaft* opened, Gordon Parks's son David found himself in New York City's Times Square. In David Parks's mind, he personally had a lot riding on the film; after all, he was the one who had recommended Roundtree for a screen test. He watched the crowds emerge from the theatre, then watched another crowd line up to catch the next showing of the movie. The new ticket line kept stretching in length. Parks rushed to a nearby pay phone and dialed his dad. "Dad, you've got to get up and get over to Broadway! Right away." But it was late at night, and Parks was groggy. "Please! Get up, Dad!" David Parks kept urging. "You've got to see this to believe it."

Parks finally dragged himself over to the glittery bulbs flashing on Times Square marquees. Fans were waiting to see *Shaft*. A *lot* of fans. "The line was completely around the block," Gordon Parks recalled, "and growing."

What could be heard in theatres showing *Shaft* all around the country was noise, jubilant Black noise. John Shaft was the law, and John Shaft was also fighting the law! The Black populace of urban America well understood such a paradox. "And to kids," Roundtree himself opined, "Shaft is an idol. They say, 'Man, they finally have a guy who's real.'" *The New York Times* weighed in, allowing that the film "has a kind of self-generated good will that makes you want to like it even when for scenes on end you know it is doing everything wrong." *Variety* was one of the other publications that liked the film. "In his second feature film after a long career as a still photographer, Parks shows some excellent story-telling form, with only minor clutter of picture-taking-for-its-own-sake." Critics—no matter how hard they tried—could not dampen Black America's stampede to buy tickets for *Shaft*. Budgeted at $500,000, *Shaft* was on its way to a thirteen-million-dollar payday, a smash success at the box office. "Hollywood," *Time* magazine wrote of *Shaft*'s rising grosses, "finally took note of two basic facts: first, with movie theatres clustering in big cities and whites moving to the suburbs, the black sector of the moviegoing public was growing rapidly (an estimated 20% in the past five years). . . . Second, the black audience was hungry for films it could identify with, made by blacks, with black heroes, about black life."

To be a child of Gordon Parks, Sr.—photographer, filmmaker, boon buddy to Sugar Ray Robinson, bon vivant—was to exist in a world with advantages that many Black children of the late 1940s and early 1950s couldn't imagine. There was travel, tennis lessons, horseback riding, good schools to attend. The elder Parks had four children: Leslie, David, Toni, and Gordon Junior. The young Gordon Junior had varied interests—horses, auto racing, photography. It was photography that began to take hold. For several years, he used the name Gordon Rogers when angling for photo assignments; he wanted to feel he was earning his way on his own merits. As his photography work began to get noticed, it coincided with his interest in film directing. When his brother, David, came across a script written by Phillip Fenty about a street hustler wanting to escape the world of crime—after one final drug deal!—Gordon Junior felt he had found something he wanted to direct.

It mattered little that *Sweet Sweetback* and *Shaft* had made millions in profit. Black filmmakers still had to navigate and hustle to get into the Hollywood rooms where movie deals were discussed and finalized. Gordon Parks, Jr., quickly realized that Hollywood was not going to give him money to make his maiden movie. So he went to his father. The elder Parks rounded up several Black contributors and they came up with a $350,000 budget. As soon as Phillip Fenty heard the movie would be made, he got in touch with Ron O'Neal, a friend from his native Cleveland, whom he wanted to play Youngblood Priest, the lead role. The film now had a working title: *Super Fly*. In the Black community, the two words put together—"super" and "fly"—meant something great and nearly unassailable. O'Neal—who had quit college because of academic challenges—was a respected New York stage actor. He had also recently appeared in *The Organization,* a 1971 Sidney Poitier film. He quickly agreed to take on the role of Youngblood Priest.

Black filmmakers had become aware of how important music was to their films. They could not depend on mainstream white publications to do the same number of feature stories around a movie that they might do for white films. "You wouldn't see stories in the papers about upcoming Black movies," says Larry Young, who had been a classmate of Fenty's and O'Neal's in Cleveland. "You mostly heard about Black movies by word-of-mouth." A Black-oriented movie, however, that had popular music attached to it was sure to get added publicity on AM radio. And right alongside music was fashion; *Shaft* had caused a great many Black men to buy leather jackets, just as James Dean, in an earlier time, caused an uptick in white T-shirts and blue jeans. Nate Adams was the costume designer on *Super Fly*. He outfitted O'Neal in a dazzling array of clothes—long, flowing coats with wide collars, wide-brimmed hats, multicolored shirts and slacks. It was such an array of styles and designs that the clothing wouldn't have looked out of place in some of the fanciful Hollywood musicals of the 1940s.

For its music soundtrack, Parks turned to Curtis Mayfield, a Chicago native who had been in the music business since his teenage years. He joined with some friends, among them Jerry Butler, to form the Impressions, a rhythm-and-blues singing group. Their first hit, "For Your Precious Love," arrived in 1958. They melded their future songs to the civil-rights movement, and two songs—"People Get Ready" (1965) and "We're a Winner" (1968)—spoke to the throngs of Blacks on the streets marching for equality; they became some of the signature anthems of the movement. Mayfield had something unique in mind when he set about writing the music to *Super Fly*. He aimed to produce an antidrug album, using his own brand of sweeping lyricism and melodic phrasings. He did most of the recording in Chicago, where he also wrote every song that would appear on the soundtrack.

When his movie was finished and edited, and the music incorporated, it was time for Gordon Parks, Jr., to find a distributor. Warner Brothers took a look at *Super Fly* and liked what they saw.

In advance of the film's opening in the summer of 1972, singles from the Mayfield album, also titled *Super Fly*, began getting airplay on Black radio stations across the country. The first released singles—"Freddie's Dead" and "Superfly"—immediately started to climb the *Billboard* charts. Black America found the music a rapturous and spellbinding ode to street life. The album itself—welcomed by white America in later years, when it gained cult status—was a kind of lush prose-poem revolving around the ravages of drugs and drug dealing. The verses spoke of children robbed of childhoods, of dying drug dealers, of unrequited love, of the forlorn mysteries of drug addiction. When the movie landed in theatres in August 1972, urban America was primed and began lining up. A new cult figure was immediately born, seen on-screen sweeping through the streets and back alleys of Harlem, his hair flowing, his coke spoon dangling from the chain around his neck, a man desperately trying to get out of the treacherous drug business. The first-time director Gordon Parks, Jr., had made a fast-moving, dramatic film. *The New York Times*'s Roger Greenspun questioned his direction of the actors: "But he has gotten so many more important things right and, in his first feature, he has made such a brilliantly idiomatic film that it would be ridiculous to do less than praise him." *Super Fly* articulated a real facet of urban life in America, and spread and promoted a stylish fashion dynamic. Against its meager $350,000 budget, it grossed twenty-seven million dollars, a genuine and robust hit. If a movie took on a surprising cultural significance, *The New York Times* was apt to write about it beyond its initial film review. Vincent Canby at the *Times* offered his own feelings about *Super Fly*: "Its story of a successful addict-pusher who attempts to get out of the game is tough, unsentimental melodrama of the superior sort, that recognizes fate in circumstance, and circumstance in character. Priest (Ron O'Neal), the pusher, is no great thinker, but he's a man with style in a world where style is everything."

In a span of two short years, 1971 and 1972, three Black directors—Melvin Van Peebles, the Parks father and son—had made three movies whose combined budgets were $1.4 million and combined grosses were fifty-five million. Such profit margins had never been experienced in the history of Black-oriented film.

The three films filled seats in dying movie theatres, expanded Black radio listenership, opened new avenues of discourse about fashion and style, and allowed Blacks to dream about possible work in Hollywood. The close proximity of the films' release dates made it seem that an entirely new genre of film had been created, something akin to the New Wave French cinema. But none of that mattered to Junius Griffin. Griffin was president of the Hollywood branch of the NAACP. The trio of profit-making movies did not meet with his approval, and he had begun saying to other local civil-rights leaders how offensive and degrading the films were. "At present," he said to members of the media, "black movies are a 'rip-off' enriching major white film producers and a very few black people. These films are taking our money while feeding us a forced diet of violence, murder, drugs and rape. Such films are the cancer of 'blaxploitation' gnawing away at the moral fiber of our community." His comments were published in *The New York Times* and other publications. The black filmmakers behind the movies felt blindsided. Griffin—wittingly or not—had introduced a new word, "blaxploitation," into the public discourse, and the word came to have damaging effects as it fastened itself onto the landscape. Ron O'Neal, and Sig Shore, *Super Fly*'s producer, quickly told the press that Griffin, a onetime film publicist, was merely angry because he hadn't gotten the film's publicity account, which he had wanted. Griffin ignored both O'Neal and Shore and kept his attacks going.

In the 1930s and 1940s, Hollywood studios produced a wave of gangster movies. Audiences lined up to see Edward G. Robinson, James Cagney, George Raft, and Humphrey Bogart battling fellow criminals and law enforcement alike. Those films became widely popular, and there was no real movement judging their morality or their effect on society's youth. The Black propulsive cinema of the early 1970s became a source of pride but also a lightning rod. What Griffin and others didn't quite grasp was that this cinema had emerged from the ground up, plowing terrain that Hollywood had never plowed before. It was bound to be imperfect; a window had opened, and Black filmmakers rushed to react quickly with their creativity. These Black movies operated on small budgets and did indeed look scruffy, but they featured beautiful soundtracks and introduced new talent. Additionally, these movies portrayed a society that white America largely ignored, a Black world where poverty, crime, and the drug incursion were rampant and real. The Black films resembled a synthesis of French New Wave and urban documentary. Despite the critical attacks, for the time being, the films kept coming.

Many assumed Gordon Parks, Jr., would have a rewarding directing career in the wake of *Super Fly*. He did direct three more films: *Thomasine & Bushrod*, a Western; *Three the Hard Way*, a film about Black crime-fighters vowing revenge against white supremacists who infected an urban water supply; and *Aaron Loves Angela*, a tender romantic drama about a young Black–and–Puerto Rican couple. The latter happened to be his final solo-directed film. On April 3, 1979, Parks and three others took off in a small plane en route to a movie location site in Kenya. Parks had founded Africa International Productions and was in the country to shoot a film. The plane crashed shortly after takeoff. No one survived. Gordon Parks, Jr., was forty-four years old. They spread his ashes over Mount Kilimanjaro, a place he was known to love.

For years, Hollywood, when it deigned to put Black men in films, plucked them from the world of professional sports. The thinking went that the Black sports stars already had a built-in audience. Henry Armstrong, a championship boxer, starred in the 1939 film *Keep Punching*, loosely based on his own life. Jackie Robinson played himself in 1950's *The Jackie Robinson Story.* The films were terrible, and the acting was forgettable. Aside from Sidney Poitier and Harry Belafonte, Hollywood had not cultivated Black male stars-in-waiting. So, to satisfy the early-1970s appetite for Black action movies, Hollywood quickly turned to former professional athletes.

The film producer Larry Spangler had become entranced with the story of Charley Tyler when he spotted an item about him in the *Los Angeles Examiner.* Tyler, a former slave, had given up his horse to a white woman fleeing from an 1863 Indian attack along the Nevada-California border. The woman got away; the horseless Tyler did not. The newspaper story that Spangler spotted told of a skull, presumed to have been Tyler's, discovered at the scene of the attack. Spangler was eager to make a Black Western. He wrote the screenplay along with Martin Goldman and James Bellah. Then he hired Goldman to direct *The Legend of Nigger Charley.* Woody Strode, a Black actor who had been seen in John Ford Westerns—and was also a former college athlete—was cast as Nigger Charley. But something about the project began to bother Strode—possibly the title, which bothered many—and he dropped out. Spangler started looking at other actors.

Fred Williamson had been a professional football player, a bruising defensive back for, among other teams, the Kansas City Chiefs. On the field, he had been known as the Hammer because of his physical play. He walked away from football because "any dumb ox can go out on a football field and do what his coach has patterned and programmed for him to do. He needs no intelligence. I told the coach I was bored and I quit." Williamson made his way to Hollywood, now wanting to act, figuring he'd outwit the town by utilizing the psychology courses he had taken while an undergraduate at Northwestern University. He found small roles in episodic television, then was cast—small parts—in two feature films, *M\*A\*S\*H* and *Tell Me That You Love Me, Junie Moon.* Larry Spangler and his director, Goldman, liked what they saw of Williamson on-screen. They also figured that the Tyler-inspired role would require a lot of physical exertion, and Williamson certainly was capable of that. They offered the Hammer his first leading role.

Part of the filming of *The Legend of Nigger Charley* took place at the Shirley Plantation in Virginia.

Paramount won distribution rights to the Williamson film, and decided to release it as part of a double feature. Since there was much mystery around the life of Charley Tyler, the finished film could only be charitably described as a reimagining of his life. Allowing for wide liberties, the film revolved around a trio of escaped slaves who roam the West, kill racist white landowners, and rescue many Indian families from harm. The reviews were less than stellar. *The Boston Globe* lauded this rarity on the big screen—Black cowboys—but felt the actors "walk woodenly through their roles." *The New York Times* called the movie "fair," but singled out Williamson, saying he "shows definite acting flair." Larry Spangler was happy with the film's reception, estimating that "90 percent of the take so far has come from black patrons."

Williamson may not have had the smooth technical skills of screen acting down pat, but he had an ability to dominate scenes. The camera seemed drawn to him. He was smoldering, physical, rough, and full of on- and off-screen confidence. His next performance, *Hammer*—a riff off his football nom-de-plume—showed why the camera had taken to him. He played a boxer who becomes aware that his fate lies in the hands of mobsters. When he fights back, outside the ring, his girlfriend is kidnapped and his friends are hurt. It sends the action in myriad directions, all resulting in Hammer's seeking and getting revenge. The movie made a profit and assured the production of another Williamson movie. And his starring vehicles kept coming, sometimes multiple films a year: *Black Caesar, The Soul of Nigger Charley* (a sequel), *That Man Bolt,* and *Hell Up in Harlem* all came in 1973; 1975 was quite productive as well: *Bucktown, Take a Hard Ride, Mean Johnny Barrows,* and *Adios Amigos* all hit the big screen. None of them were classics, but all were profitable. Fred Williamson knew well the reason for his box-office popularity: "I'm a badass."

Williamson had company in the badass sweepstakes of Black male figures suddenly appearing on movie screens. Among them were Yaphet Kotto, Jim Kelly, Bernie Casey, Richard Pryor, and Calvin Lockhart. Most noticeable among them was Jim Brown, another football player turned actor.

At Syracuse University, Brown excelled in both lacrosse and football. When his 1956 football season ended, it was widely felt he was the premiere college player in the nation. But the Heisman Trophy—given annually to the best player—was awarded to Notre Dame's Paul Hornung. Notre Dame had won two games that year, losing eight. Syracuse's record was the inverse; they won eight games, losing only two. Blacks hissed that Brown had been egregiously overlooked in favor of a white player. (In 1961, Ernie

Davis, who played for Syracuse, became the first Black to win the Heisman.) From 1957 to 1965, Brown was a dazzling fullback for the Cleveland Browns, using power and balletic grace to dazzle Sunday-afternoon crowds. To this day, he is considered by many the greatest NFL player in history. But he was more than just a football player. He aligned himself with the Black social-justice movement, joining with other Black athletes to bring attention to discrimination. "[Cleveland] is the only city I've been in where I feel totally separated on a racial level—the whites on the West Side, the Blacks on the East Side," he reflected when he abruptly left the team—and the sport. There had been off-the-field turmoil, allegations of domestic abuse, court appearances, children born out of wedlock. He escaped to Hollywood, where he had gone during his football-playing days to make his first film, a Western, *Rio Conchos,* alongside Stuart Whitman and Richard Boone. The film centered on a quartet of men chasing down gun thieves: Brown played a cavalry officer. The reviews were decent; *Variety* opined that Brown "handles himself well." Like Williamson, Brown had a potent screen presence, and producers began sending him more scripts.

In 1966, Brown was cast in *The Dirty Dozen,* which starred Lee Marvin, playing one of an assortment of criminals given a chance at freedom by participating in a World War II secret mission. His dash across a courtyard to drop grenades down air shafts and upon Nazis was a heroic moment, and Blacks inside theatres yelped with delight. He was supposed to return to the Browns for the 1966 season, but filming ran late. Brown got into a war of words with the team owner, Art Modell, and then stunned the sports world by retiring while still in his prime. Many came to see 1969's *100 Rifles* because they were curious about the pairing of Brown and the screen beauty Raquel Welch. The posters that began showing up in theatre windows before the film's release showed Welch wrapping her white arms around the muscular Brown. Nothing could get the citizenry talking as much as the innuendo of white-Black screen sex. "We were trying to send a message to America," Brown warned. In the film, Brown played a sheriff sent south of the American border to retrieve an escaped prisoner, played by Burt Reynolds. He runs into Mexican bandits, a simmering revolution, and a rebel leader played by Welch. "The filming of our love scene was just like any other scene," Brown explained. "I just had to follow directions and remember to hit certain marks. . . . When I'm really making love I don't have to follow directions." The taboo of interracial sex on-screen had been trampled upon by the likes of Melvin Van Peebles, Fred Williamson, and now Brown. Kissing between whites and Blacks had slowly been introduced in movies in recent years, but nothing made studios more nervous than the idea of between-the-sheets sex between Black and white. In the minds of studio chiefs, it was their demarcation line. America was still a country where white protesters routinely showed up holding signs ("No Race Mixing") when blacks integrated certain neighborhoods. With the release of *100 Rifles,* and the studio eager for publicity, Welch and Brown posed for a photo—Brown shirtless, Welch behind him with her bare arms flung around his neck—that generated hate mail. The movie got mixed reviews, but Brown, yet again, escaped criticism. "The acting of Mr. Brown, a big, fine-looking chap, is strictly tentative but he does have presence," *The New York Times* wrote. By 1972, Brown was in full Black star-making mode, with his appearances in *Slaughter* and *Black Gunn.* In 1974, he starred with Williamson in *Three the Hard Way.* On-screen, at least, Black men were winning. And the theatres were full, because Blacks liked the look of victory.

The movies kept coming—comedies, romance, horror—Black movies with talent that white America had little idea existed. Those Black actors rarely got guest-star slots on TV talk shows, but the box office had spoken. "The eagerness of urban black audiences for movies with black casts, stories, and themes, and particularly for black heroes, exemplars of racial pride, has created the first situation of guaranteed profit for commercial film makers since the 1940s," *The Atlantic* realized. Mainstream publications found it difficult to look beyond Poitier and Belafonte—who had been beneficiaries of the studio system—when writing about these new films. A whole genre of film was growing up outside the white media, and they made only facile attempts to understand it. Black publications, however, were swooning. They had two stories to tell: the story of Black actors in this new genre, but also the story of the bevy of beautiful, karate-kicking Afro-wearing women appearing on the big screen. They were badasses, too!

# Foxy Brown Arrives, Vanishes, and Gets Resurrected

B LACK FEMALE BEAUTY had to invade white America, and it happened stiletto heel by stiletto heel. Oscar Micheaux, of course, had
showcased Black beauty, but those images might as well have been underground as far as the mainstream press was concerned. All throughout
the 1940s, 1950s, and most of the 1960s, the image of the beautiful Black
woman remained largely shielded from white America. Two of the most
alluring and attractive Black actresses to come out of the 1950s were Lena
Horne and Diana Sands, but the film world remained bewildered by both,
unable and unwilling to find suitable work for them.

Lena Horne appeared in two 1950s films, *Duchess of Idaho* (1950) and
*Meet Me in Las Vegas* (1956). In both, she played versions of herself, a
singer to jazz up the screen. She spent time in Europe during that decade,
entertaining in nightclubs, with visits back to America that sometimes
turned painful. As the year 1960 unfolded, Horne found herself in L.A.
One evening, she and her husband, Lennie Hayton, were at the Luau
Restaurant for dinner. A loud-talking, rude diner was seated near them.
Liquor had been consumed, and the loud gentleman was impatient to get
his food. The waiter explained to the man that he was completing an order
for Lena Horne and would be right with him. (Horne's husband had left
the table to make a phone call.) The waiter imagined such name-dropping
might calm the diner, but it had the opposite effect.

"Where is Lena Horne, anyway?" the liquored-up man asked. "She's
just another nigger."

Horne popped up from her seat, grabbed an ashtray, and cracked the
man over the head. Blood spurted. Diners shrieked and gasped; the man

spun in agony, howling. The maître d' hurried over; the bleeding man was rushed out of the restaurant. The story made it into the New York press. Friends around Manhattan saluted her. Black women greeted her with hugs. Horne escaped any charges.

That same year, Horne appeared on the cover of *Show* magazine. The caption read: "BREAKING THE WHITE BARRIER: LENA HORNE SPEAKS ON THE ARTIST AND THE NEGRO REVOLT." She made sure she was back in America for the 1963 March on Washington. It delighted her to see friends at the civil-rights gathering. There were TV appearances, but Horne appeared in only one film during the 1960s, cast alongside Richard Widmark in the 1969 Western *Death of a Gunfighter*. It was a moody film; Widmark playing an ornery sheriff battling his own townspeople, who wanted to fire him because he was aging out of the job. Horne played the madam of a brothel and Widmark's lover. Her racial background was not even a part of the plot. She garnered fine reviews, as the movie itself did, but only reminded many of how Hollywood had ignored Horne's luminous talents.

Lena Horne may have become exhausted by her struggle for any breakthroughs in the movie business, but such was not the case for Diana Sands. This actress was hungry and wanted to appear in movies. She had been a fierce presence on the New York stage, and had come to prominence playing Sidney Poitier's sister in both the stage and film versions of *A Raisin in the Sun*. She was awarded the Outer Circle Critics' Award for her *Raisin* stage performance. Her classmates at the prestigious Actors Studio thought she was nothing short of brilliant. Her performance—Tony nominee—in the 1964 James Baldwin play, *Blues for Mr. Charlie,* was highly praised. That year, she also appeared on Broadway with Alan Alda in *The Owl and the Pussycat,* receiving another Tony nomination. Hollywood came calling, and she listened intently but soon grew despondent, steadily declining the offers that came her way because the roles were subservient to whites and beneath her talents. In 1968, Sands played Joan of Arc in George Bernard Shaw's *Saint Joan* in a Lincoln Center production, the first Black actress to play the role on Broadway. Theatre work didn't pay nearly as well as film work, and she kept hoping the climate would improve out west. She got a nice role in *The Landlord,* a 1970 film that starred Beau Bridges and Louis Gossett, Jr. The movie revolves around a white rich kid who moves into a ghetto tenement and begins to fix it up while becoming involved with the tenants. Sands plays a woman he has a brief affair with; her performance, Roger Ebert declared, was full of "beautiful tenderness." In the end, it was a message movie: a rather liberal white kid being introduced to the world of Black America by way of a falling-apart building.

Sands—beautiful, with cinnamon-colored skin, a performer both versatile and regal—realized Hollywood was not going to embrace her. She began keeping company with a group of activist artists that included Ossie Davis, James Earl Jones, Rita Moreno, and Hannah Weinstein. They began discussing the idea of starting a film company. It sounded like a pipe dream, but the discussions went on and on. Weinstein and Davis emerged as leaders of the group. "Ossie was just dynamite," recalls Cliff Frazier, a part of that group. "Ossie and Hannah together made things happen." What once sounded dreamy started sounding more important and necessary than ever.

Hannah Weinstein was a Jewish activist who had been involved in New York City's leftist Democratic circles for years. She had worked on a mayoral campaign for Fiorello La Guardia. When the House Un-American Activities Committee starting hounding her because of her activism, she left the States and settled in London, where she became a prolific producer of television dramas. She returned to America when the political climate shifted and the country realized the destructiveness that the HUAC had caused.

She began inviting Sands, Davis, Moreno, and others over to her Manhattan apartment. They formed the Third World Cinema Corporation whose goal was to make films with Black and Latino talent. The films would be made independently but would seek Hollywood distribution. At a 1971 New York City press conference, Davis announced that Third World films would each be budgeted at five hundred thousand dollars—a figure he soon realized was unrealistically low. The company's bank account consisted of private funds and incoming federal grants. "If you do Super Fly, that's okay," says Frazier. "It provided opportunities for people to work. We wanted to do films that focused on Black families and Latino families and their children."

Third World Cinema was quickly up and running. Scripts were submitted and winnowed, and projects were chosen. A training program was put into action. "There are more than 40 trainees," Weinstein announced to the press. "Many of them may very well become union members before long and have the chance to work on Third World films. It's all very heartening."

The first film to go into production was *Claudine,* with a cast that included James Earl Jones, Diahann Carroll, and Lawrence Hilton-Jacobs.

It concerned the travails of a mother with six children trying to make it in Harlem. Jones was cast as Roop, the garbage-hauling boyfriend of Diahann Carroll's Claudine. A powerful plot point concerns the white welfare caseworker, who constantly tries to undercut the Roop–Claudine relationship by enforcing the rigid rules of the welfare system. It was Diana Sands who had first been cast to play Claudine. She filmed only a few scenes before becoming ill and suggesting Carroll for the role. Sands died while *Claudine* was in production, shocking the cast and crew. She was thirty-nine years old. The theatre crowd in New York took the news hard. The more prominent stories that circulated following her death were about how insistent she had been about color-blind casting, imploring directors not to stereotype her or other Black performers.

*Claudine* opened on April 22, 1974; Twentieth Century–Fox had come aboard for distribution duties. The reviews were glowing. "A gritty, hearty, heartfelt and ruggedly tender story of contemporary urban black family life avoiding blaxploitation genre," *Variety* wrote. "Claudine," stated *The New York Times,* "succeeds in being comic without denying the realities of ghetto life." In the *Los Angeles Times,* Charles Champlin wrote that the film was "an engrossing and effective movie which is somehow able to exist simultaneously as a high-spirited romantic comedy and as a fiction-alized documentary grim and angering in its implications." And *The New Yorker* review proclaimed it "a sweet-spirited film, saddened and rollicking, full of courage." It escaped reviewers that the film had been born out of frustration with Hollywood's refusal to tell richly drawn Black character stories. Given the level of poverty in so many Black communities and housing projects, the movie touched a nerve with the Black populace. It also featured a sensuous rhythm-and-blues soundtrack, courtesy of Curtis Mayfield and Gladys Knight. Against a million-dollar budget, the film grossed six million. It also garnered Carroll an Academy Award nomination. "It spoke with respect to people on welfare," Frazier says of the movie's success. "It was a Black family doing the best they could to make it. It didn't deal with perfection."

While *Claudine* was the first film to shine a light on the often disparaging treatment of Black families within the complex American welfare system, it also saw the unleashing of a ferocious stereotype. Stories soon appeared in both *Look* and *Reader's Digest* about mothers on welfare who were abusing the system. A term—"welfare queen"—was invented and entered the vernacular. These mythical welfare queens supposedly drove new Cadillacs and wore fur coats, all largesse from having scammed the welfare system. White politicians, among them California Governor Ronald Reagan, began mentioning welfare queens during political appearances. Crowds howled with anger. The term not only disparaged the welfare system—there were certainly some good and concerned people working inside of it—but it especially hurt and stereotyped Black women. The actual numbers of women abusing the welfare system turned out to be minuscule, but that hardly mattered to those who wanted to believe otherwise.

————

Third World Cinema had come out of the gate powerfully. The company also employed many minority members to work behind the scenes. Additional projects were announced, but it took time for Third World to get its second film into production. It finally came early in 1976, when Michael Schultz (director of *Cooley High*) signed on to direct *Greased Lightning*, a film about Wendell Scott, the first Black to win a Sprint Series NASCAR championship race. But from its maiden foray into filmmaking up to the production start of *Greased Lightning*, the political climate in America had shifted again. Third World was dependent upon government grants, and that money slowed during the Richard Nixon administration.

The ferocious comic Richard Pryor was cast as Wendell Scott, in his first leading role. Among other cast members were Beau Bridges, Cleavon Little, and Pam Grier. Upon the film's release—it was distributed by Warner Brothers—the public seemed confused, wondering, because of Pryor's presence, if the movie was comedy or drama. Though the reviews were respectable—"a pleasant, loose and relaxed comedy," noted *Variety*—the film flopped at the box office. The fortunes of Third World Cinema—always just a rebellious undertaking in the minds of Hollywood—suddenly began to decline. It never got another major film into production. "Money ran out," said Cliff Frazier, one of the company's officials.

The struggles of Black women in film might well have, to some degree, been alleviated had Third World Cinema stayed afloat. In any event, there were two cultural events that forced America to start paying heed to the beauty of the Black woman.

For decades in America—as Lena Horne and Diana Sands certainly knew—Black women were forbidden to participate in mainstream beauty pageants. Pageants were so often a portal into the world of entertainment. In the April 19, 1968, issue of *Life* magazine—which told the story of the assassination of Martin Luther King, Jr.,—there were plenty of pictures of female fashion models posing and presiding over consumer products. Not a single one of those models was Black.

In 1945, John Johnson and his wife, Eunice, cofounded *Ebony* magazine in Chicago. It steadily grew in popularity while highlighting Black achievement. The few Black actors and actresses who had broken through in Hollywood—in film or television—could count on the magazine to showcase them. Eunice Johnson paid particular attention to the fashion side of the magazine. She traveled yearly to the Paris fashion shows, expanding her tastes while being introduced to new designers. She'd return with bundles of couture clothing to be worn by her models in *Ebony*'s pages. When it was suggested to her that the models would look fabulous out on the road, in fashion shows, she hatched a plan. In 1958, a group of models were chosen, trained, and began traveling in buses around the country, putting on shows. The shows, known as the Ebony Fashion Fair, became yearly events, elegant, glitzy Black charity fund-raisers. The models wore American and European designs. Ultimately, there were sixty shows annually, stretched across the fall and winter seasons. They consisted of twelve female models and two male models and were quite theatrical, with music—jazz and bebop spilling forth—as the models shimmied and sashayed in colorful gowns, evening wear, and beach outfits to gasps of wonder from the audiences.

There was another cultural event that resonated through Black America—while drawing the attention of whites as well. On November 28, 1973, at the Palace of Versailles, just outside Paris, there was an international fashion show to raise money to restore the palace of King Louis XIV. Five American designers were invited to participate: Anne Klein, Bill Blass, Oscar de la Renta, Stephen Burrows, and Halston. There was a gala before the event; among those in attendance were the duchess of Windsor, Andy Warhol, Princess Grace of Monaco, Liza Minnelli, and Paloma Picasso. Josephine Baker and Rudolph Nureyev performed. So did Minnelli, outfitted in a Halston cocktail dress as she sang. Once the fashion extravaganza itself got under way, something happened, and that something was the appearance of Black models. Startling on the runway, they showered the royal setting with a Black-is-beautiful dynamism. The Black models were Billie Blair, Norma Jean Darden, Ramona Saunders,

Alva Chinn, Charlene Dash, Jennifer Brice, Amina Warsuma, Barbara Jackson, Bethann Hardison, and Pat Cleveland. Cleveland had been a member of the Ebony Fashion Fair. They strutted as if they had something to prove, not only to the French, but to their own America. Such fashionable Blackness had never been seen on an international stage before. The French patrons were wowed and full of glowing praise. These were the same Black models, however, who had to fight battles to get work back in their home country. In New York City, a mentor had once taken Amina Warsuma to meet Eileen Ford, who had her own prestigious agency. "Not yet," Warsuma was told by Ford about getting a job. "Give it a couple years." Well, a couple of years had now arrived.

Back in America, Black models began showing up in white fashion magazines. White America could no longer turn its face from the picture of Black beauty. And, finally, a conversation was forming about opportunities for that Black beauty.

———

In the early 1970s, a young college student entered the Miss Colorado Universe Beauty Pageant. Beauty pageants were often avenues that led to acting jobs, so Pam Grier considered it a smart move. She wanted to break into the movie business, and, though she didn't win that particular pageant, she did come in as runner-up. That was all the encouragement she needed to pursue her dreams.

Clarence Grier, Jr., Pam's father, was an air-force man, moving his family from military base to military base. Pam was born in 1949 in North Carolina, spent time in her youth in Ohio, then moved to other locales with the family. Her mother, Gwen, trained to become a nurse in those early years. The family finally settled in Denver. Young Pam was also happy when there was the opportunity to spend time with relatives on family farmland in Wyoming. The Griers had about them a touch of the homesteading spirit of Oscar Micheaux: Pam rode horses, rolled in lofts full of hay, grew fond of the outdoors, enjoyed playing with Rodney, her little brother. But she also suffered sexual abuse in childhood, assaulted in a relative's home while the adults were away. In the aftermath of the trauma, she grew sullen and often uncommunicative.

Clarence Grier was assigned to an overseas military base, and, in time, the family sailed for England; young Pam shrieked with delight during the ocean cruise. The Griers settled comfortably into an upstairs apartment. The white British women who sometimes watched over Pam when her parents were not at home shared stories with her about husbands who worked in mines, and memories of World War II. The white women were very curious about the mistreatment of Blacks in America, and especially about the news of racial murders that landed in their British newspapers. "These women impacted me deeply," Grier would recall. "I watched them having a ball and cooking dinner together while they danced and laughed. I listened carefully as they carried on deep discussions about power struggles between the genders and how to survive the oppressive and aggressive ways of their mining and military husbands when they got home from a grueling day's work."

After two years, the Grier family returned to America. Pam's life back in the States took a bitter turn when Gwen and Clarence divorced. Gwen, who had finally become a nurse, was intent on keeping her family together. Other relatives helped out while she worked her hospital shifts. Life for the teenage Pam revolved around school and church and physical activity, as she started taking karate lessons. She was blossoming physically, growing tall. In 1965, she was overjoyed to be on a bus with other members of a Denver church choir heading toward Los Angeles, where they were to perform in Compton and Watts. The Compton event went well. But the Watts uprising erupted on August 11, as soon as they arrived. There were shrieks and howls from inside the bus as bullets whizzed by. "Police in riot gear blocked the streets and we were rushed to a parishioner's apartment," Grier remembered. "All forty of us stayed in two apartments for the next several days, camped out all over the floor." The performance was canceled. Watts burned for five long days before it was safe to take the bus back to Colorado.

Following high school, Pam enrolled at the Metropolitan State College in Denver. Her goal was to study there for a couple years, save money while working a part-time job, then hightail it out of Colorado and transfer to an East Coast university to finish her education. While in college, she worked as a receptionist at the local KHOW radio station. Her looks began attracting attention, and a station employee suggested she enter the KHOW beauty contest. She was nervous, but did so anyway. She won. Pageants offered prize money, which thrilled the young college student. Soon enough, there was another contest, the Miss Colorado Universe

Beauty Pageant. She came in as first runner-up, seen as its own kind of victory for a Black girl in mid-1960s Colorado. Her prize: a thousand dollars.

David Baumgarten and Marty Klein—two Hollywood agents, always on the lookout for talent—were in the Miss Colorado Universe Beauty Pageant audience. Klein was the agent for the fashion model turned actor Richard Roundtree; Baumgarten represented a lot of young Los Angeles comedians. The tall, willowy Black girl who had been named runner-up grabbed their attention. "There are lots of opportunities for Black actors right now in music and film," Klein told Grier. She was quite intrigued but explained to him that she had no acting experience. He told her that she carried herself well on the beauty-pageant stage and he felt such composure could lead to good things in Hollywood. This was quite a lot to take in. Grier took deep breaths, and told Klein she'd have to talk it over with her mother.

Gwen Grier sat and listened to her daughter's recounting of the conversation with Marty Klein. She thought about her own life, having followed her husband all over the world, only to have him leave her. She told her daughter that she should give Hollywood a try, that it was good to dream, and that she could always come back home "if things don't work out." Not long thereafter, Pam Grier climbed into her blue Pontiac and pointed it in the direction of Hollywood. Both Oscar Micheaux and Hattie McDaniel had once lived in Denver. They, too, had ventured up and over the mountains of Colorado, full of desire and cinematic dreams. They also had been full of worry about how Hollywood would react to their ambition—and to the color of their skin.

———

It was 1970, and Los Angeles was teeming with hippies, protesters, Black activists—and paranoia. Much of the paranoia flowed from the August 1969 murders of the actress Sharon Tate, wife of the director Roman Polanski, and several others, a deadly rampage carried out by members of Charles Manson's crazed cult. Manson was a going-nowhere singer and a white supremacist with a bevy of young fragile women in his orbit. He strummed his guitar up in the hills while talking of race wars and murder. Pam Grier was just another pretty arrival in jittery Los Angeles that year. She was fortunate that she had family friends in the city who helped her find a place to stay. David Baumgarten, one of the agents she had met in Denver who promised to help her upon arrival in L.A., hired her to work as a receptionist at the Agency for the Performing Arts (APA), a talent agency on Sunset Boulevard.

One afternoon, Grier moseyed over to the UCLA campus, considering taking extension courses. She began hanging out with a circle of UCLA film students. They worked on experimental films. "We would stage scenes on Hollywood Boulevard and see what happened when we started shooting," she recalled. "It was so stimulating and creative, my interest in filmmaking was piqued even more than before."

It wasn't quite the improbable story of the famed actress Lana Turner, who was discovered at that soda fountain inside Schwab's Drug Store—which was all a made-up once-upon-a-time-in-Hollywood lie anyway—but it had its own kind of serendipity: APA was determined to find something for Grier in the acting world and told her about Roger Corman, a director-producer.

Corman—a one-of-a-kind eccentric with a driven personality—had gotten into the film industry at a young age. After working in the mailroom at Twentieth Century–Fox—even with his Stanford degree—Corman knew he was enamored with the world of film. He spent time in England for more study, then returned to L.A. and became a producer and director. His were low-budget films—*Swamp Women, The Oklahoma Woman, Teenage Doll, Attack of the Crab Monsters, She Gods of Shark Reef.* Many played in drive-ins; his detractors often referred to them as shlock. Not all of them were. In 1962, Corman's movie *The Intruder,* was released. An unknown actor by the name of William Shatner (a future *Star Trek* star) appeared as a bigoted agitator in a Southern town, rousing the white populace against school integration. Mainstream Hollywood thought Corman foolish for wanting to make such a film; he wound up putting up some of his own money to get it made. The movie is a scorching piece of drama, with Klan marches, frequent use of the word "nigger" flying off white tongues, cross burnings, and the old trope of a false allegation of rape against a young Black man. The advertisement for *The Intruder* proclaimed: "This may be the most shocking picture you will ever see. But you will know its truth and you will remember it always!"

The truth was that America—especially the American South—did not care to see Corman's movie. The movie got an anemic release—a few theatres, no publicity campaign—and subsequently flopped. (Years later, it was released in England, where it would reap a profit for Corman.) When it came to Black-white stories about race, Roger Corman was braver than most Hollywood directors.

When Corman met Pam Grier, he knew she was someone who could hold the screen. He immediately offered her a role in *The Big Doll House,* which he'd be filming soon in the Philippines. It was a female-prison movie, revolving around scantily clad prison inmates and their escape plan: more shlock. Grier was surprised to be offered a role without any audition. Feeling both giddy and afraid, she told herself she had to learn how to act, and quick! She went out and purchased books about acting techniques, she watched a lot of movies, she got scripts and began to analyze them. Then she flew off to the Philippines.

No one on the set of *The Big Doll House* mistook the undertaking for anything other than what it was—a B movie, of the grindhouse variety. The director, Jack Hill, had studied at UCLA's film school. (One of his classmates was a gifted student by the name of Francis Ford Coppola.) Hill's reputation, such as it was, came by way of codirecting Corman-like shlock. His solo directing effort, released in 1968, was a horror film, *Spider Baby.* Hill and his producers had fussed with the title, at one time considering *Cannibal Orgy* or *The Maddest Story Ever Told.* But *Spider Baby* won out. It was made for sixty-five thousand dollars, and caused squirming and derisive laughter from its drive-in audiences. Hill knew there were a lot of red-blooded young men back in the States who would salivate watching desperate women behind bars—with male guards and a sadistic female warden watching over everyone!

It was hot in the Philippines, and bugs were everywhere. The costume designer didn't have much work; the female inmates wore skimpy clothing, mostly just T-shirts. But Grier never complained, and Hill liked that about the novice actress. She also was physically fit, volunteering to do many of her own stunts. As soon as the production wrapped, Corman said he was so delighted he was going to stay and shoot another movie. He offered Grier a role, and she quickly accepted. In her second Corman movie, *Women in Cages,* she was back behind bars, this time playing a prison guard named Alabama. Inside the prison, once again, there was chicanery, lesbianism, more violence: again, more shlock. Gerardo de Leon directed this one. He had also made his reputation directing horror films. The Philippine in-crowd thought he was a genius. Both movies, *The Big Doll House* and *Women in Cages,* sailed blissfully by Stateside critics. But if anyone was pooh-poohing the films, it wasn't Roger Corman. Both of them were profitable. Against a two-hundred-thousand-dollar budget, *The Big Doll House* grossed ten million.

When Pam Grier landed back in the States, she saw her very own image—sexy, statuesque—on movie posters. Feature writers on Black newspapers had to hustle to find out who this alluring new actress was. She was asked to do some promotion for her two films, and when she showed up at the venues, long lines had formed, so many young Black men and women eager to meet her. Hill, the director, sensed the timing of the moment of Grier's arrival onto movie screens: "It was the age of 'Black power' and 'Black is beautiful'—and it was beautiful, and it was powerful." Hill enticed Grier to return to the Philippines to film *The Big Bird Cage*, another women-behind-bars movie. She played Blossom, a revolutionary on the outside plotting to break into a local prison and free inmates. The movie poster's tagline was in keeping with the blunt language that accompanied any Hill–Roger Corman production:

*WOMEN SO HOT WITH DESIRE THEY MELT THE CHAINS THAT ENSLAVE THEM—Lashed to a terrible machine that maims tender young bodies and cripples innocent young minds—THE BIG BIRD CAGE*

Once again, critics ignored the movie, which, once again, landed in a lot of inner-city drive-ins. And the drive-in crowds were having a ball. Upon entering the prison, Blossom lets it be known she means business.

"Which one of you dykes thinks she runs this place?" Blossom asks.

There are some hard, menacing stares. "All you have to know," Blossom announces to those doing the staring, "is that now I run this place. Any other questions?"

"Yeah," a white inmate asks. "Where do you want to be buried . . . nigger."

Grier's Blossom unleashes a furious round of body punches to the epithet-hurling inmate. Then Blossom's retort: "And that's Miss Nigger to you. Okay?"

An actor and a director choosing to work together over a period of time often do so because they have formed a cinematic bond. A type of chemistry begins to set in. John Wayne had it with John Ford; Alfred Hitchcock with Jimmy Stewart; John Cassavetes with his wife, Gena Rowlands.

The synergy applied to B-movie productions as well. "To me," Jack Hill remarked, "Pam has something magical; I can't put a name on it. Just 'It!' " Hill was convinced he should keep making films with Grier. They would have to be low-budget films; and the trailers on the sets—where the actors relaxed in between filming—would be small trailers; and the publicity budgets would be minuscule; and the screening schedules for the critics would be unpredictable. The goal was to get the movies up on the screens. Any and all screens!

Hill soon presented Grier with a script about a nurse who goes on a spree to avenge the hoodlums who got her sister hooked on heroin. This time, she was to be the lead, and she quickly accepted. The actress realized the script showcased a kind of Black woman rarely shown on American movie screens: a take-charge gun-toting vigilante bringing about her own brand of justice. Once filming got under way, Hill again depended on Grier—playing the character known as Coffy—to perform most of her own running and kicking stunts, which she was happy to do. Filming began in and around Los Angeles, and after only eighteen days, it wrapped. American International Pictures, which financed the five-hundred-thousand-dollar film, opened *Coffy* in Chicago in May 1973. ("They call her Coffy and she'll cream you!" the ads blared from posters and from voices on Black urban radio.) The reviews were mixed at best, but, no matter what the critics said, the public flocked to see Coffy—avenging the hopeless and looking hip and cool while doing so—kick ass. The film grossed upward of two million dollars. All of a sudden, there was a new kind of film heroine, one with an Afro, one thrillingly alive against the urban malaise of America, and one presenting a female hero to Black audiences. The Black press rushed to write more stories about Grier. She realized the deep degree to which *Coffy* had snared the urban audience. "It was common," Grier allowed, "for the persecuted female character, angry and less conflicted than her male counterpart, to destroy a white-based power structure that had caused pain and harm to herself and her family."

Jack Hill, Pam Grier, and American International Pictures immediately went to work on a sequel. Hill assumed that the budget for the sequel would be higher than the original. But because American International Pictures was a penny-pinching operation, the budget was the same—five hundred thousand dollars. The film also turned into a nonsequel. Grier was not going to play a nurse in *Foxy Brown,* and there were no references to the earlier film. Grier—playing Foxy Brown—was the tough girlfriend of a government agent who is murdered by operatives of a drug syndi-

Richard Roundtree in *Shaft* (1971). The counterpoint to Humphrey Bogart.

Gordon Parks, in director's chair (1968). In the footsteps of Oscar Micheaux.

cate. Foxy wants revenge. Posing as a prostitute, she talks her way into the modeling agency where an assortment of women "work," servicing members of the syndicate. Foxy Brown's Afro is high and wide enough to conceal small weapons. In her own unique manner and style, she begins dismantling the syndicate—after, that is, she is kidnapped, beaten, and sexually assaulted.

On April 5, 1974, *Foxy Brown* began its rollout across America. The

Curtis Mayfield in 1972. White America at first ignored the genius of his *Super Fly* soundtrack.

*Monthly Film Bulletin* quickly took aim at Hill's script: "*Foxy Brown* is in every way a far less interesting work than writer-director Jack Hill's previous film with Pam Grier. . . . Hill's colorless script does little for an actress who unmistakeably has, regardless of her material, all the strength and resilience of a Jane Russell." That assessment represented the high-water mark from critics weighing in. "*Foxy Brown* is selling Pam Grier's body just like it was sold a couple years ago in . . . Philippine women-in-prison pictures," wrote Gene Siskel in the *Chicago Tribune*.

And yet *Foxy Brown* proved to be yet another hit, amassing receipts of $2.5 million. Jane Russell—the 1940s starlet and sex symbol—would have admired that kind of profit.

With her back-to-back profit-making films, Grier had catapulted to the top of the heap of Black female box-office stars. Her box-office prowess commanded attention. Black women found her characters heroic; white women found her empowering. "To me," Grier remarked, "what really stood out in the genre was women of color acting like heroes rather than depicting nannies or maids."

By the early 1970s, no one could have mistaken Pam Grier for a nanny or a maid. She made three films in 1975. The first was *Sheba, Baby,* directed by William Girdler. Girdler was a journeyman director (drive-in movies, horror films) without the confidence or sure-handedness of Jack Hill. In *Sheba,* Grier plays a private eye forced to trek back to her hometown of Louisville, Kentucky, because thugs are threatening her father and his insurance business. There are shootouts and nick-of-time escapes. Grier once again shows her deftness with weaponry: she shoots a henchman with a speargun. In his review of *Sheba, Baby,* Roger Ebert appeared to be bemoaning the fact that Grier's movies were still playing before mostly Black audiences: "Although many moviegoers may not readily recognize her name, Miss Grier is one of the top three or four black movie stars, and (with Barbra Streisand) one of the two actresses whose name above the title can guarantee a profit on a film with the right budget. To be sure, most of Pam's movies seem budgeted at about 5 percent of what a Streisand epic costs, but they make money and they're entertaining." Ebert continued: "Howard Hawks, who had so much success directing strong women in the golden age circa 1940, might have had a lot of fun with Pam Grier."

In January 1972, a women's magazine called *Ms.* landed on newsstands. It was founded by a group of women—led by Gloria Steinem and Letty Cottin Pogrebin—with the intent of bringing to the forefront issues important to the growing feminist movement.

Pam Grier in *Foxy Brown* (1974). She drop-kicked her way— stylishly so—into movies.

The magazine represented a cultural gauntlet—like the Black-power and Black cultural movements that had swept from street corner to movie theatre—challenging the idea of continuing white male dominance. In its first year of publication, the magazine published the names of prominent women who admitted they had broken the law by having abortions. It was a sensational issue. A year later, in the landmark *Roe v. Wade* U.S. Supreme Court ruling, abortion became a legal right in the nation. The struggle and effort of Black women to gain rights and dignity in America had, of course, long predated the struggle waged by white women. The Black feminist community embraced *Ms.,* and eagerly waited for the magazine to have its first Black cover subject. This happened in August 1975. Pam Grier stared out from the cover: "PAM GRIER, super-sass." Even if mainstream America was not quite aware of Pam Grier—as Roger Ebert had intimated—the editors of *Ms.* magazine were. In a few short years, she had seemingly come out of nowhere, ushering in a new kind of Black actress, a ready-made sex symbol blessed with a feminist attitude. The cover photo of Grier was a head-and-shoulder photograph. She wore two necklaces and a modest amount of makeup, and she looked fierce and beautiful. Jamaica Kincaid's accompanying article said that Grier's movies "are the only films to come out of Hollywood in a long time to show us a woman who is independent, resourceful, self-confident, strong, and courageous. Above all, they are the only films to show us a woman who triumphs!"

Pam Grier's third film in 1975 was *Friday Foster.* It was, contractually, the final film she owed American International Pictures. The plot—taken from a 1970s comic strip—revolves around a magazine photographer, played by Grier, who sets out to thwart the planned assassinations of various Black political leaders. Deep inside the plot, there were also mobsters. The casting had a certain flair: Yaphet Kotto, Scatman Crothers, Eartha Kitt, and Godfrey Cambridge among others. Arthur Marks, a TV director known mostly for having directed over seventy episodes of *Perry Mason,* directed the film. *The New York Times* laughed the movie away: "This is one of those movies where everything and everybody looks a little too good—the clothes; the pimps; the hookers; the cars; the streets; the bosoms fleetingly bared; and even the blood, which looks as though it ought to carry a vintage." *Variety:* "Grier has some steamy sex scenes and a lot of rugged action, though she isn't totally macho and radiates a lot of traditional feminine charm along the way."

Despite the critics, Pam Grier was a key player in changing the dynamics of the Black actress in Hollywood. Vonetta McGee, a beautiful and

talented Black actress, had grown so weary of Hollywood that she journeyed overseas to act, where she found the environment more welcoming.
"When I came home on a visit after making this movie in Turkey," she
recalled, "I was delighted to notice that the United States had finally come
to terms with the fact that black Americans have all kinds of beautiful
features and complexions. It made things easier for me this time."

———

From 1970 to 1973, Black-themed films accounted for more than a hundred million dollars in box-office revenue. Movies headed by Black actors
were responsible for most of the revenue, but Black actresses were beginning to make noise. "Up until very recently, Lena Horne and the late Dorothy Dandridge were the only black actresses who could be legitimately
called movie queens," was the 1973 opinion of Bob Vincent, who wrote on
Black Hollywood for Texas-based *Sepia* magazine.

———

Hollywood rarely announced nationwide searches to fill a Black screen
role. It had, of course, been done for the part of Mammy in *Gone with
the Wind,* but that was hardly a proud moment for Blacks. In 1972, there
was a lot of buzz about a screenplay written by Max Julien, a dapper Black
man who had been acting in Hollywood since the mid-1960s. Director
Jules Dassin had cast him in *Uptight,* a 1968 film that focused on militancy
in the Black ghetto against the backdrop of the assassination of Martin Luther King, Jr. Dassin's film, highlighting Black pain, made whites
nervous, and few of them ventured into theatres to watch it. "A white
friend," the film critic Roger Ebert would write at the time, "tells me he
saw 'Uptight' the other day and was disturbed by the audience reaction:
'There was a cheer every time a white guy got hit.' This should have been
an educational experience, providing our side with the same sort of feeling that Blacks have had for years when a black guy got hit.' Or had to
shuffle." Despite his admired performance in *Uptight,* Max Julien did not
receive many acting offers after the film's release. To leverage his odds,
he began writing scripts. The idea of a Black-superwoman film came to
him in Italy. He named his heroine Cleopatra Jones, a Black woman who
drove fast cars, handled heavy weaponry with skill, and knew karate. She
was also an undercover U.S. Secret Service agent assigned to take down

a drug kingpin! "I conceived of Cleopatra Jones as a new and different image of the black woman for the screen," Julien said. "She neither suffers indignities in silence, nor does she put up a monumental struggle merely to survive—she fights and triumphs over an evil that afflicts all too many black ghettoes in this country."

Max Julien wanted Vonetta McGee, whom he was dating, to play the role. Warner Brothers, excited about the script, made it clear to him, however, that they would ultimately be picking the actress who would get the coveted role.

The studio announced a worldwide search for their Cleopatra Jones. Twelve finalists were selected, all of whom came to the Warner Brothers lot, where they were given screen tests. Tamara Dobson, a twenty-six-year-old statuesque fashion model from Baltimore, emerged as the winner. Warner Brothers executives thought it was a plus that Dobson was an unknown and felt that her selection added a dose of old-fashioned mystery and curiosity to the film. Dobson thought the film's antidrug message was potent. She also relished doing her own stunts. The actress let it be known she would not be going nude for any scenes in the picture. "Ladies don't have to take anything off to excite anyone," she said.

Also cast were the Academy Award winner Shelley Winters, the former professional football player Bernie Casey, the solid character actor Antonio Fargas, and the newcomer Brenda Sykes. Warner Brothers opened the film in the summer of 1973; the promotion focused on the Black globe-trotting super-agent angle: Cleopatra drove a Corvette, had innumerable gadgets, and blew things up. The tagline—"6'2" of dynamite"—splayed across the movie poster with the imposing Dobson in a short fur coat and holding a bazooka-like weapon. "Tamara Dobson," wrote *Variety*, "makes a smart starring debut, after fashion model and teleblurb work, as the title character, a sophisticated undercover agent working to stamp out the world drug trade." Vincent Canby of *The New York Times* didn't seem to care for it much: "The movie seems to want to be a James Bond sort of adventure in black drag, but it's more reminiscent of 'Batman,' especially with Shelley Winters having a high old time of it playing a character named Mommy, an underworld boss with a fondness for young girls and, apparently, for sweets." The reviews might have drawn snickers, but no one was laughing after *Cleopatra Jones* opened. The movie cost $1.5 million to make; five weeks after its opening, it was the number-two film in the nation, and went on to make eight million. Tamara Dobson became an instant cultural icon throughout Black female communities. A sequel, *Cleopatra*

*Jones and the Casino of Gold,* opened in the summer of 1975, but it failed to generate the profits of the original film.

A bevy of other Black actresses rode the 1970s populist cinema movement and made their way upon the nation's movie screens. Brenda Sykes, Carol Speed, Rosalind Cash, and Gloria Hendry may well have been, for the most part, beyond the sight and radar of white America, but in Black America, they were becoming known and widely discussed. Cicely Tyson starred in *Sounder,* directed by Martin Ritt, in 1972, playing the wife of Paul Winfield, a sharecropper sent to prison for stealing a ham. Both performances were lauded. The film—a rare crossover moneymaker—also became the first Black-themed picture whose studio, Fox, went about unleashing a vigorous screening campaign, showing it more than five hundred times before its opening in theatres across the country.

The climb of Black films, however, couldn't escape other forces, notably economic fissures. Samuel Arkoff, owner of American International Pictures, sold his company. He lamented that a lot of drive-in theatres—where many of his profitable films had shown—were beginning to shutter. At the beginning of the 1970s, Hollywood had been in financial trouble, the residue of the economic woes that had bedeviled the industry since the late 1960s. But those fortunes began to change when two Italian-themed films made the kind of profits that helped Hollywood recover from its financial hole—and all but begin to abandon the giddy energy that had propelled so many recent Black films to the screen.

———

In the latter half of the 1960s, Mario Puzo—who hadn't made much money on his first two novels, so he kept his job as a government clerk—began working on a new book. He told himself it was going to be ambitious. He wanted something that would sell and, he hoped, become a commercial hit. He had five children, so money was essential. But he loved the craft of writing, and his family, in spirit, supported him. He spent four years working on the new novel. The seeds of it were planted by stories his Italian-born mother had told him, stories about crime and family and loyalty. He embellished those stories with research into the Mafia. "My mafia is a very romanticized myth," he admitted. The novel, *The Godfather,* was published in 1969. It climbed onto *The New York Times* best seller list. Paramount Pictures purchased the rights. A screenplay was written, but Paramount was not happy with it. They had approached the famed director Elia Kazan to direct the picture, but he declined. They eventually offered the rewriting and directing job to Francis Ford Coppola.

Coppola was a San Francisco–based filmmaker who had won an Academy Award for his screenplay for *Patton*. He also had directed *The Rain People*, a 1969 movie about a pregnant woman who abandons her marriage to meander around the country. "When I realized I was actually going to make a movie out of The Godfather," Coppola would recall, "I sat down and began to read the book again, very carefully, my pencil poised. Upon that second reading, much of the book fell away in my mind, revealing a story that was a metaphor for American capitalism in the tale of a great king with three sons: the oldest was given his passion and aggressiveness; the second his sweet nature and childlike qualities; and the third his intelligence, cunning, and coldness." Coppola argued with Paramount over casting. He fought and won the battle to cast Al Pacino—a young actor known for his New York stage roles—to play the role of Michael, the "intelligent" son. In Puzo's novel, Don Vito Corleone was head of the Corleone crime family. Paramount had a slew of big-name actors they suggested to Coppola. The filmmaker, however, wanted Marlon Brando. Brando was a titanic talent but made the studio executives nervous: he was moody, independent-minded, and passionate about Black rights in a town that was not. Brando decided he wanted the role. He even auditioned for Coppola, spliced his audition onto a tape, and showed it to the powers at Paramount. The transformation from Brando to Don Corleone stunned the executives. Brando joined the cast.

The film opened in March 1972. The reviews were wonderful; the lines formed all around the country. To those who thought Hollywood was dying, *The Godfather* was the start of its reincarnation. Against a budget of seven million dollars, it made a whopping $287 million. Nineteen months after *The Godfather* opened, filming began on *The Godfather Part II*, which arrived in theatres in December 1974. The sequel grossed nearly fifty million dollars. This was far less than the original, but still a profit, and many considered the movie a masterpiece. Both films received multiple Oscar nominations. Just as important, they stymied talk of Hollywood's so-called collapse. The films proved that the movie industry had made a comeback! It was also estimated that 35 percent of ticket buyers for *The Godfather* were Black. With the coming of *Jaws* in 1975 ($470 million box office) and *Star Wars* in 1977 ($775 million box office), the shift of Hollywood's energy away from Black-themed movies had begun. By 1976, the era of Black-themed films was drawing to a close.

What of Pam Grier?

The actress who had been so visible during the heyday of the 1970s Black film mini-revolution all but disappeared from the big screen. White Hollywood continued to ignore her talents. There were occasional appearances over the following decade in supporting roles: among them 1981's *Fort Apache, the Bronx* and 1988's *Above the Law.* Mostly she paid the bills by doing a lot of television work. There was, however, one white filmmaker who had long been enamored of Grier's work and film persona. And he was determined to do something about her long absence from the big screen.

Quentin Tarantino was a film geek, Tennessee-born but living in California from the age of four. He had a job at Video Archives, a hipster film store in Manhattan Beach, and it delighted him no end. He described the job as if he were attending his very own film school. Some days, he'd bolt through the door, jabbering to the small staff about a movie he had watched the night before: Lubitsch. Hitchcock. John Ford. Ida Lupino. And when the store opened to the public for the day and the cinephiles started ambling through, he'd get to jabbering with them about every conceivable movie. He was antic and funny and smart and would tell stories about being in elementary school and going to East L.A. to see the blaxploitation movies. Not a lot of whites were going to those movies. "That was like a Black Hollywood," Quentin Tarantino recalled. "Every film was blaxploitation. I felt like I was in a Black world." Black life frightened many in the movie business, because most simply didn't have Black friends. But Tarantino had his own reality: Black life was hip, cutting-edge, cool, reverential, and full of astonishing music, history, drama, and intrigue. In his cinematic mind, Fred Williamson was iconic; Calvin Lockhart unappreciated; Pam Grier unforgettable.

Quentin Tarantino thought at first he might break into the business as an actor. It would not be easy. He found himself playing an Elvis impersonator on *The Golden Girls,* a television sitcom about three women of advanced age. Casting agents saw he had rather unique physical features, the kind that might lend themselves to character work, akin to roles played by Vincent Price, a famed horror-film star of the 1960s and '70s. Tarantino turned to writing. He received guidance at Robert Redford's Sundance film lab. He made connections with the right agents. He wrote the crime drama *Reservoir Dogs,* and also was hired to direct it. The 1992 film, starring Harvey Keitel, Steve Buscemi, and Michael Madsen, won acclaim, receiving nominations and awards. Quentin Tarantino was someone to watch. In 1993, Tony Scott directed his screenplay *True Romance,* which starred Christian Slater and Patricia Arquette. Then came the Cannes prizewinner *Pulp Fiction,* a 1994 drama that Tarantino wrote and directed. The film, a commercial success, resurrected the acting career of John Travolta. Tarantino was respected for being witty, charged, talky, fierce, and unafraid of dealing with race.

*Pulp Fiction* really introduced Quentin Tarantino to the American public. He went on radio and talk shows. There were newspaper and magazine profiles. Because the film also starred Samuel L. Jackson in a substantial role, it attracted many Black filmgoers. Tarantino may have been a film geek, but he was a hip one.

Pam Grier admired *Pulp Fiction.* She had seen Tarantino on talk shows. It was not easy to forget his look—tall, gangly, broad-shouldered, with stringy hair. One day, stopped at a light at Highland Avenue in Hollywood, Grier, in the passenger seat, peered through the car window and saw, on a street corner, a man she recognized from his photographs: Quentin Tarantino. "His long brown hair was unruly, he wore old sneakers, and he was talking to a gorgeous starlet-type young woman, all the while gesturing wildly," Grier remembered. At the same moment, Tarantino spotted Grier. He immediately walked over to the car. The two exchanged quick compliments, and what Tarantino said next was nothing to Pam Grier but a warmhearted lie to make her feel good: "I'm writing a movie for you," he told her smiling face. "It's based on *Rum Punch,* the Elmore Leonard book." He quickly mentioned that the movie was going to have a *Foxy Brown* vibe. There was more head nodding and chuckling, and then Tarantino backed away from the car as it rolled off, with horns honking.

Pam Grier chalked the Tarantino encounter up to just another oddly sweet encounter that had her on the receiving end of some lovely compliments. It was inconceivable that Tarantino was writing a movie for her! Only six months later, however, Grier received a package in the mail. It was a script, titled *Jackie Brown.* And it was from none other than Quentin Tarantino. She poured herself a cup of tea, sat down, and began reading.

The script, as Tarantino had earlier told Grier, was based on Elmore Leonard's novel *Rum Punch.* Leonard had been writing novels and short stories and getting them turned into films for many years. His short story "The Captives" became *The Tell,* a 1957 Randolph Scott Western; that same year, Glenn Ford starred in *3:10 to Yuma,* adapted from another Leonard short story. Leonard's most recent movie had been *Get Shorty* in 1995, a Hollywood-set crime caper that starred Gene Hackman, John Travolta,

Rene Russo, and Danny DeVito. Hollywood liked Leonard's work because he was really good at drawing up characters and giving them rich dialogue. *Rum Punch* told the story of a flight attendant who gets caught up couriering money for an arms dealer. To save herself after she is arrested, she becomes an informer. There is romance, as well as characters who shamelessly double-cross one another. Reading the script, Grier imagined Tarantino might want her to play Melanie, a strong supporting role. She phoned Tarantino's office and got him on the phone. She told him she was hoping to play Melanie. Tarantino ditched *Rum Punch* as a potential title. He was now calling his movie *Jackie Brown*.

"Bridget Fonda is playing Melanie," Tarantino informed her. "You're Jackie Brown, Pam. I told you I was writing a script for you. I loved Foxy Brown, and I wrote this in your honor."

*Jackie Brown* opened during the 1997 Christmas holidays. The reviews were better than good. "[Tarantino's] affection for Grier, and the maverick spirit she brought to films most critics wrote off as gory junk," *Rolling Stone*'s critic wrote, "fill every frame." Stephen Hunter in *The Washington Post* wrote that Grier had been "restored to star status under Tarantino's auspices." *Entertainment Weekly* may have been cool about the film but had this to say: "The picture is an homage to two of the pop phenomena that formed [Tarantino]: the crime fiction of Elmore Leonard and the underground stardom of blaxploitation queen Pam Grier, who, thanks to Tarantino, is now resurrected." Some tone-deaf critics opined that the movie would mainly play to Black audiences. Instead, *Jackie Brown* crossed over with style, grossing seventy-five million on its twelve-million-dollar budget. It seems especially sad that white critics mostly ignored the panache with which Tarantino assembled his soul-music soundtrack. "It's never too late," the *Salon* critic wrote, "to be transported by the Delfonics singing 'Didn't I Blow Your Mind This Time?' or for Grier to be treated like the star she is."

Pam Grier and Samuel L. Jackson were nominated for Golden Globes, and Robert Forster was nominated for an Academy Award. They didn't win, but they had made a film that would have a significant shelf life.

The Black-actress parts were now all frozen on screen: *Sheba, Baby; Claudine; Friday Foster; Coffy; Cleopatra Jones; Jackie Brown*. All those Mammy roles, avenged.

# [Flashback]

## *The 1972 Academy Awards*

I
N ITS LONG, HYPNOTIC HISTORY, Hollywood built a formidable image when it came to cowboys and Indians. The line was as clearly drawn as black and white: Cowboys good, Indians not so good. In Hollywood, cowboys rode stallions and fast horses. They roamed the West and settled scores in heroic fashion. They created—abetted by scores of dime novelists—brazen stereotypes about Native Americans. There were derogatory references to "redskins" and "squaws." From the earliest days of cinema, sharpshooting cowboys sent marauding Indians tumbling from horses. The directors of those films—John Ford, Howard Hawks, Budd Boetticher, Anthony Mann—enlarged the twisted cowboy-Indian narrative. "This is the West, sir," a character in Ford's *The Man Who Shot Liberty Valance* says. "When the legend becomes fact . . . print the legend." The actors who played cowboys—Tom Mix, Walter Brennan, Ben Johnson, Audie Murphy, Ronald Reagan, John Wayne, many others—achieved fame against the mythic backdrop of cowboys defeating all those Indians.

Hollywood movies very rarely told the true story of Native Americans—the broken treaties, the stolen lands, the bloodshed.

In the winter months of 1890, the U.S. Army issued an order that Native Americans on the Pine Ridge Reservation of South Dakota must turn over their weapons. On the appointed day—December 29, 1890—a group of them broke out in their spiritual Ghost Dance, communing with their ancestors. Their movements made the U.S. soldiers nervous. A single gunshot—perhaps from a tent, it was never determined—accidentally went off. Skittish army soldiers—who had already mounted a Hotchkiss machine gun nearby—then began firing. Mayhem ensued across the wintry landscape. When the gunfire ended, between 150 and 300 Lakota Indians lay dead. Half of the dead were women and children. Two dozen American troops were dead, with most of those deaths from so-called friendly fire.

A little less than eighty-three years later—February 27, 1973—a group of Oglala Lakota Indians, joined by others from the American Indian Movement, took control of Wounded Knee, South Dakota, in a mass protest against tribal corruption and American policies toward Indians. The protesters were demanding amendments to nineteenth- and twentieth-century Indian treaties, the American-devised treaties that downsized their land ownership. Because of the overwhelming presence of law enforcement—the protesters had taken many town residents hostage—the siege drew relentless national press attention. The standoff lasted for more than two months. Two Native American activists died. A federal agent was shot, but survived. The newsreel footage from South Dakota was often supplemented by historical analysis and commentary, some of it from Native American scholars. It was a shock to the system for many who had grown up on Hollywood's version of Indians and cowboys.

On March 27, 1973, it is unlikely that the Wounded Knee takeover begun a month earlier was much on the minds of those entering the Dorothy Chandler Pavilion for NBC's Academy Awards telecast. This was a night to celebrate the genius of American cinema! The two most talked-about films of the previous year were Francis Ford Coppola's *The Godfather,* and Bob Fosse's *Cabaret,* starring Liza Minnelli and Joel Grey. Many surmised that those two films would be competing against each other for Best Picture. There was also a feeling that Marlon Brando would walk away with the Best Actor trophy. Liza Minnelli and Maggie Smith (*Travels with My Aunt*) had both drawn praise on the awards circuit. Liv Ullmann and Roger Moore opened the envelope to name the Best Actor winner. When Brando's name was heard—that iconic music from *The Godfather* wafting across the music center—the applause was loud. It was quickly announced over the loudspeaker that Sacheen Littlefeather would be accepting for Brando. A slight woman in beautiful Native American dress, she announced, when she reached the lectern, that she had a statement from Brando, but had been told it was too long and she could not read all of it. She proceeded to tell the TV audience of eighty-five million that Brando was respectfully declining the award because of "the treatment of American Indians today by the film industry . . . and on television in reruns, and also with recent happenings at Wounded Knee." It was a stunning moment, echoing George C. Scott's similar stance years earlier. The audience, at first, seemed frozen by the rebuke, but then offered a generous round of applause. Brando had activist roots: he was one of the very few white actors to join the 1963 March on Washington for Black rights. He was biting the hand that fed him for political reasons. In the days after her television appearance, Sacheen Littlefeather received death threats.

The desire to win an Academy Award is powerful. But the creative team around *Sounder*—the Martin Ritt–directed movie—had to be satisfied with what they had accomplished that night. Paul Winfield, Best Actor nominee; Cicely Tyson, Best Actress nominee; and Lonnie Elder, Writing nominee, were all Black. They represented the largest contingent ever of Black nominees from the same movie.

Appearing on *The Dick Cavett Show* in the aftermath of the awards show, Brando was asked by Cavett if he regretted having sent Littlefeather to the ceremony. He said he did not. "I don't think people realize what Hollywood has done to Indians . . . and to all minorities" in film.

# Berry Gordy Dares to Make Movies

T HERE WERE MANY IMPORTANT ADDRESSES stretched out across America that linked to the modern civil-rights movement. In Atlanta, there was Ebenezer Baptist Church, where Martin Luther King, Jr., preached, at 101 Jackson Street Northeast; in Greensboro, North Carolina, sat the F. W. Woolworth store, at 132 South Elm Street, where college students staged lunch-counter sit-ins to integrate the Woolworth stores; in Birmingham, Alabama, there rose the 16th Street Baptist Church, at 1530 6th Avenue North, where four young girls were murdered on a Sunday morning in a KKK bombing; in Harlem, one couldn't miss the Abyssinian Baptist Church, sitting proudly at 132 West 138th Street, where the fiery Congressman Adam Clayton Powell, Jr., preached. The locations formed a geographical map of the unspooling of civil-rights protests. Another address that leaned into the consciousness of the nation and played its own unique role in the movement was 2648 West Grand Boulevard in Detroit, Michigan: the home of Motown Records.

Years before the epochal civil-rights bills of the mid-1960s became law, Motown had unleashed a phalanx of singers and songwriters onto the nation's airwaves and into its auditoriums and nightclubs. Those Black singers—guided by Berry Gordy, founder of the company—had created their own kind of legislation through music. It was sweet soul music, and it was as if a whole new art and musical form had cracked open before the citizenry. The music galvanized the nation. It inched whites closer than ever before to Black culture. And in due time—because he dreamed big—Berry Gordy would utilize his music company's success to propel himself into Hollywood, where the upper, middle, and lower echelons of its film industry were all-white.

His daddy, Berry Senior, whom everyone called Pop, worked hard at the family grocery store. The store had a history-soaked name: The Booker T. Washington Grocery Store. The elder Berry was a workaholic, and young Berry, born in 1929, knew there would be no loafing in the Gordy household. His seven brothers and sisters knew it as well. His mother, Bertha, was a schoolteacher, so attention must also be paid to schoolwork. Berry Junior was an active kid. He entered piano-playing competitions. He did some amateur boxing in his teen years. He put in time at a couple of automobile plants to earn cash. He cruised around the Detroit music scene on Hastings Street on weekends. His war was the Korean War, and after his hitch ended in 1953, he returned home to Detroit.

There, Berry Gordy started writing music. He wrote "Reet Petite," which got him taken seriously in Detroit music circles after the crooner Jackie Wilson turned it into a 1957 hit. Gordy also started thinking of himself as a budding promoter. He began keeping company with singers and songwriters. They'd meet up at the Flame Show Bar, or sometimes there'd be a crowd across the street at the Frolic Show Bar. The music was always lively at both places. One day, Gordy was at an audition with other talent scouts, watching a group, the Matadors, perform. Gordy thought there was something interesting about the group, and after the auditions he chased down its lead singer, a young kid by the name of William Robinson, whom everyone called Smokey. As Gordy recalled: "I said, 'Smokey, I really see a lot of potential in you, you're really great, but these songs, either they have a bad story and great lyrics, or great this and bad something else.'" Robinson confessed that Gordy "showed me that, for all my slick rhymes, I had no form. He explained that a song should tell a story with a beginning, middle and end. He rejected almost everything I had . . . but he set me straight." Gordy told young Smokey Robinson he wanted to sign his group up. He also gave the group a new name: the Miracles. The signing, and subsequent signings of other groups, convinced Gordy he should start his own record label. He pondered names. In 1957, *Tammy and the Bachelor* became a hit film. It starred Debbie Reynolds. (Louise Beavers, from 1934's *Imitation of Life*, played the cook.) The movie had a hit song, "Tammy," which reached number one on the charts. Gordy thought "Tammy" would make a fine name for a label, but it was already copyrighted. So he chose Tamla. He forked over twenty-five thousand dollars in 1959 for the simple house at 2648 West Grand Boulevard, which would be the company's headquarters.

But over the next few years, the music operation steadily grew to include publishing, touring (around the world!), opening business offices—and constantly birthing new soul acts. The national mainstream press—so often behind the Black press when it came to Black culture stories—began to pay attention. Lengthy profiles appeared about Gordy and the hits his company kept turning out. When it came to music, Detroit became Berry Gordy's town. His motor was running at a fever pitch. He renamed it all "Motown," even as his performers sometimes veered across his three record labels—Motown, Tamla, Gordy. Motown was more than just music; it was the whole cornucopia and a state of mind—sassy, sweet, and fearless, and aiming for the purse strings of not only Black America but white America, too. By the mid-1960s, Motown had more than four hundred employees. It quickly became the most high-profile Black business in America.

One of the company's first hits came courtesy of the Marvelettes, an all-girl group from Inkster, Michigan. Their song, "Please Mr. Postman," was a tender ditty about the hope that the postman will bring a letter from a lover. Tom Donahue, a San Francisco radio deejay, was wild about the song when he introduced it: "Your Big Daddy Tom Donahue at Channel 1260, where good things are happening . . . It's 28 minutes and 30 seconds after 12 noon Radio KYA time, and you have no fear because your Big Daddy is right back here. . . . And here's the prettiest sound you'll ever hear." The record zoomed to number one on the *Billboard* charts.

Berry Gordy was not sending his singers out into the cold with just their voices. The Motown women had been taught etiquette by Maxine Powell; the men had been schooled in choreography, and gentlemanly manners, by Cholly Atkins. The singers who came through Motown's doors and got record deals were Black; the marketing and promotional staff were white. It was part of Gordy's design: he needed white front men and women to go out into America to sell Motown, because America, when it came to business and sales, was white. Gordy's white promotional director was Barney Ales, a son of Italian immigrant parents. "When he came in," Gordy recalled about Ales, "he said he would build me a great team. I wanted to sell all music to all people: whites, blacks, Jews, gentiles, cops and robbers." Ales had worked for Capitol and Warner Brothers, white record companies. Motown struck him as a wonderful challenge.

"My parents," he said, "couldn't understand why I would leave Aurora [a record distribution company] to go with a black guy. The only black person my father knew was Charlie, the janitor at his shop."

If he was to succeed, Gordy knew he needed the support of Black radio deejays. They were the pipeline to inner-city America. He courted them and befriended the National Association of Radio Announcers, the first organized group of Black deejays. "In Cincinnati, [Berry] tested all of his acts with us," recalled Jockey Gibson, the renowned Ohio deejay. "We used to do a theatre show in the black community, five shows a day—that was four and a midnight wrap-up. We'd call the record company and let them know we were playing the hell out of their record and they would send the artist down to us."

It was not only the deejays who helped introduce America to the Motown sound. In 1957, a national music show went on television from Philadelphia called *American Bandstand*. The host of the show was Dick Clark. He was clean-cut, possessed a toothy smile, and seemed both square and hip at the same time. The show began attracting a large nation-wide audience, hosting such singers as Paul Anka, Frankie Avalon, the Beach Boys, and Peggy Lee—all white acts. Motown's the Marvelettes were among the first Black acts to appear on the show. (Blacks, however, were not seen in the studio audience in the beginning of the show's run, which angered the Black community. Clark and his producers had yielded to pressure from local advertisers, who didn't want Black teens to be seen dancing with white teens.) Still, what *American Bandstand*—which kept inviting Motown singers and acts to appear on the show—was proving to Gordy and his Motown staff was that white America, especially its gaggle of teenagers, was ready to finger-pop to Black soul music. In previous decades, white America had only embraced Black music in fits and starts, becoming interested in jazz in the 1930s and then blues music in the 1950s. But jazz and blues were not really danceable music. Motown shook loose the dancing energies.

Little Stevie Wonder, with his harmonica, came through the doors of Motown in the early 1960s. He was born in Saginaw, Michigan. Because of mechanical issues with hospital equipment when he was an infant, he lost his eyesight. He grew up phenomenally gifted in music. Smokey Robinson heard about him—and that harmonica, the way he blew it—and told Berry Gordy he just had to see this kid. Gordy liked what he heard, and signed Wonder to a contract. It wasn't instant success: the voice of a child singer changes, and the career, if promising, has to be nurtured. But Motown started issuing his singles, and they hopped onto the radio airwaves: "Little Water Boy" in 1962; "Fingertips" in 1963; "Castles in the Sand," "Hey Harmonica Man," "Happy Street," all in 1964; "Kiss Me Baby," "High Heel Sneakers," "Uptight (Everything's Alright)," all in 1965. Wonder was the first Motown singer to do an international gig when he played L'Olympia in Paris in 1963. Teenagers everywhere were accustomed to buying more singles than albums—they were inexpensive and easy to carry around. But Motown released some Stevie Wonder albums, too, and they helped solidify his rising musical stature. Among those albums: *Tribute to Uncle Ray* in 1962; *With a Song in My Heart* in 1963; *Stevie at the Beach* in 1964; *Down to Earth* in 1966; the seminal *I Was Made to Love Her* in 1967.

It was one thing to hear a Motown act on the radio, quite another to see that act in person. The Temptations were one of the most dazzling acts Berry Gordy had signed in the early years of the label. The young men had come from two separate local Detroit groups—the Elgins and the Pirates among them—before joining forces and presenting themselves as a five-member unit: Otis Williams, Melvin Franklin, Paul Williams, Elbridge Bryant, and Eddie Kendricks. They wore lovely suits with skinny ties and sang about broken hearts and gone-on-down-the-highway lovers. They had rich voices and took solo turns at the microphone, spinning to it and away from it in an eyeblink. They moved across stages as swiftly as ballerinas; they wore shiny patent-leather shoes.

In 1964, David Ruffin replaced Bryant; the group didn't miss a beat. Their singles appeared at a rapid clip and were like a new kind of coming-out party for Black male crooners: "The Way You Do the Things You Do" reached number eleven on the charts in 1964; "My Girl," the same year, rocketed to number one; in July 1965, "Since I Lost My Baby" reached number seventeen; "Ain't Too Proud to Beg" climbed to number thirteen in 1966; and "Beauty Is Only Skin Deep" reached number three that same year. The kids across the pond, in London, were listening not only to the Beatles; Motown also grabbed their attention. "Motown hadn't released any records in Britain but I'd heard them on tour in the states," said the singer Dusty Springfield, who hosted a London show featuring Motown music. "I wanted to use those influences in a country where they were still playing stand-up bass and the only black music they knew about was jazz."

Motown's Black stars were crossing over into the white medium of entertainment as never before. In 1963, Motown grossed four million dollars.

No other Black record company had ever made that kind of money. Berry Gordy pulled together a Black repertory company of singers and musicians, and his eye and ear were remarkable. He was suddenly looking like a genius. "We were convinced that our unique sound came from the way our voices bounced off the walls and the windows," said the young Diana Ross, one of Motown's rising female singers. "We recorded in every nook and crevice of that building: the hallways, the stairwells, next to the walls, and even the toilet." It signaled something powerful when the Motown acts kept being asked to appear on Ed Sullivan's variety show, proving the label's crossover momentum. It was a cool and lovely thing to appear on *American Bandstand,* which attracted a young audience; *Ed Sullivan* was a different and higher rung up the cultural ladder. The CBS show came on Sunday evenings, widely considered the largest viewing night for the American TV audience. Large segments of the nation were accustomed to watching the show, which had been airing since 1948. Americans trusted the straitlaced and avuncular Sullivan as an introducer of talent. A constant Monday-morning question at the water coolers across America was: Did you see the *Sullivan Show* last night?

Berry Gordy was quick to state that his performers weren't going to dilute any of their style for white audiences. "We here at Motown," he had told a mostly white business gathering, "are very proud to be one of the first companies to have incorporated the white element without compromising our standards of excellence." He understood that white youth were attracted to Motown *because* of its unique style.

Cars may have helped build Detroit, but Motown gave it its rhythm and a new kind of social pride and posture. Black Detroiters were thrilled to see Berry Gordy alongside Rev. Martin Luther King, Jr., when he visited the city. In Gordy's mind, music—and Black business executives—had a place in the world of social change. On June 23, 1963, King appeared at Detroit's Cobo Arena before a crowd of twenty thousand for a Freedom Rally commemorating the twentieth anniversary of the city's World War II race riots. (A street rally earlier in the day had drawn more than a hundred thousand.) King had something special on his mind when he stood before the crowd. He talked about dreams and mountaintops. Without realizing it, Detroiters were treated to a preview of King's "I Have a Dream" speech, which he would deliver in several weeks in Washington. Gordy had technicians inside Cobo Arena, and two months later, Motown released an album, *The Great March to Freedom: Rev. Martin Luther King*

*Speaks, Detroit, June 23, 1963,* for $4.98. Gordy, accompanied by Lena Horne, presented King with a copy.

———

The Temptations, the Four Tops, the Supremes, the Contours, Gladys Knight and the Pips, Eddie Holland, Stevie Wonder—all kept climbing the charts. The mainstream white press treated them with a completely different dynamic from the anemic attention they paid to Black film and Black filmmakers. Motown was becoming the lyrical megaphone of Black America—and white America was determined to stay close to the fun! Both Black and white radio stations were enjoying the constant hits coming out of Gordy's company. Motown had a kind of motto and credo, written by its marketing executives with Gordy's input:

> *Our youth are opting for reality. They seem better able to handle the pain of it than many of their elders. They are agreeing that you need to know where you are and who you are in order to know where you're going and what you can become. Motown is proud to communicate the message of humane profundity.*

Berry Gordy and his artists were creating a whole new genre of music, like rock and roll, like country music. A lot of the laurels being bestowed upon them highlighted the label's roster of four- and five-member musical groups. There were female lead singers with backup male vocalists, and male lead singers with backup female vocalists. There were teen groups, like the Jackson Five, siblings fronted by their youngest brother, Michael. Little Michael had a bubble-big Afro and the sweetest demeanor. When he sang "Got to Be There"—his first solo album, when he was thirteen—the nation swooned. That same year, 1972, he broke into Hollywood with "Ben," the Oscar-nominated theme song to *Willard.* The editors of *Jet* and *Ebony* magazines were deliriously happy with the wide array of Motown artists they could choose from to feature on their covers.

For all the genius of Motown, for all the panache of Smokey Robinson and the Miracles and Gladys Knight and the Pips; for all the horn blasting of Junior Walker and the All Stars; all the silky crooning of Marvin Gaye; all the guttural sounds of Edwin Starr belting out "War," his anti-Vietnam song; for all the soft-shoe stepping of the Temptations and the sweet, unbelievable sounds of Michael Jackson; for all the excited patrons crowding into the swanky Copacabana in New York City to catch yet another Motown act, it was hard for any of the performers to upstage a certain all-girl group on the label who many felt were the absolute darlings of the company.

Detroit always had plenty of jobs, but never enough housing for those working in its auto plants and factories. During World War II, the city began construction of the Brewster-Douglass Housing Projects on the city's eastside, low-income housing that drew a great many Blacks. Many of the occupants were families arriving into the city from Southern states. In 1958, Ernestine and Fred Ross moved into the Brewster-Douglass apartments. They had four children; Diana, fourteen years old, was their second oldest. She was skinny and had doelike eyes. When Motown began making noise in the city in the late 1950s, it ignited plenty of dreams among Detroit's Black youth. Teenage singing groups were sprouting all over the city. The groups rehearsed everywhere—in basements, in recreation centers, in their schools. They held talent competitions. They begged parents for money for outfits; those who had stitching talent designed their own. In high school, Ross was invited to join the Primettes, a group whose other members were Florence Ballard, Mary Wilson, and Betty McGlown. She enjoyed the group's camaraderie. They were energetic, giggly, and open to guidance. In 1960, they were invited to Windsor, Ontario, to participate in a July 4 Canada Day Holiday Weekend talent show. They came away with the winning prize.

Competition at Motown was tough, a kind of gladiator school for vocalists. Four young singers with a Canadian talent-show prize weren't going to impress Berry Gordy. And all the Primettes wanted to do was get into the inner sanctum of Motown. Smokey Robinson, a childhood friend of Ross's, finally got the Primettes some work doing backup vocals. "We kept hanging around Motown because it seemed so glamorous," Ross recalled. "There would be all these guys with flashy suits and big cars out front, and it was our idea of, well, Hollywood. Every day after school, we'd borrow bus fare from Mama, and if we didn't have bus fare we'd walk." Robinson was being cagey as he chaperoned Ross in and out of Motown, waiting for the right moment to get the group in front of Gordy. Finally, it happened. Gordy was moving around the offices one day and heard their sound. He stopped cold. Such harmony! He knew these were voices he

The Supremes in 1965. *Dianuuuhhhh!*

could work with. In January 1961, he signed the young all-girl group. But he didn't like their name, the Primettes. It made the singers nervous that they had to change their name, but Florence Ballard finally came up with a name everyone liked:

The Supremes.

The singers practiced hard. They learned new dance steps from the in-house choreographer, Cholly Atkins. They knew to be patient; strategies didn't evolve overnight. They let it be known that clothing meant a lot to them, but that seemed true of anyone inside Motown: they all wanted to dress with style and look great onstage. The Supremes first made it onto the rhythm-and-blues charts in 1962 with "Let Me Go the Right Way." It crested at number twenty-six. They were a little disappointed, but Gordy told them not to worry. Brian Holland, Lamont Dozier, and Eddie Holland were among the most gifted songwriters at Motown. The Hollands were brothers. "I'm putting you with my top writing team," Gordy told the group. "They're going to get you a hit." In late 1963, they popped higher on the charts with "When the Lovelight Starts Shining Through His Eyes." Nevertheless, Diana Ross was always worrying about other girl groups at Motown. "Barney," she asked Motown executive Barney Ales, "do you think we'll ever be as big as the Marvelettes?" Ross—and the nation—had that answer in 1964: First, in July, came the news that "Where Did Our Love Go" had zoomed to number one on the rhythm-and-blues charts. Three months later came "Baby Love," which also raced to the top of the charts. Blacks and whites were suddenly bouncing and swaying like crazy to the Supremes. Berry Gordy knew the significance of the moment. The Supremes—swishing down the sidewalks in those matching outfits!—and their sweet pop tunes were turning into romantic guides for the whole youthful generation. The requests for bookings poured in. "Listen, it's important that we keep The Supremes hot," Gordy told Eddie Holland, "because they've crossed over into the pop market so strongly. We must make them explosive, we must follow through." The following year—1965—they got booked into the Copacabana.

Even though the Copa only seated a little more than six hundred patrons, it was one of the most prestigious venues in the nation. The Supremes' show sold out quickly. On opening night, they offered a medley of hits—"Somewhere," "Baby Love," "Stop! In the Name of Love," "Put On a Happy Face," "You're Nobody Till Somebody Loves You." According to *Billboard,* the singers put on "a performance the likes of which the famed bistro has seldom experienced." And it wasn't just the Copa that the Supremes invaded in 1965. They appeared on *The Tonight Show,* they played Lincoln Center, they got booked into famed Madison Square Garden. Like Sinatra and Streisand, they were taking over Manhattan. And they weren't finished: they got booked on *The Ed Sullivan Show.* Mary Wilson knew what the *Sullivan* appearance meant: "It was like the first time you could see three beautiful black women on television."

The hits kept coming: "Back in My Arms Again" (another number-one hit in 1965); two number-one rhythm-and-blues hits the following year, in 1966: "You Can't Hurry Love," "You Keep Me Hangin' On." In February 1967, they had another number-one hit with "Love Is Here and Now You're Gone."

They began screaming her name—"Dianuuuuhhhh!"

She'd turn, and the cameras would flash, catching her movie-star smile. She had an ethereal look. Her shoulders were broad; her waist was so thin. And she looked dazzling in her clothes, as stylish as any Black fashion model on any runway. She was becoming a pop princess and a pop icon all at once.

Dianuuuuhhh!

They performed on the soundtrack for *The Happening,* a goofy 1967 counterculture movie that starred Anthony Quinn, George Maharis, Michael Parks, Milton Berle, and Faye Dunaway. Kids and guns and mistaken identities and hijinks. Their song, "The Happening," was yet another number-one hit. There were growing rumors that Ross might leave the group. To keep her in the fold, Gordy realized concessions would have to be made. So another name change:

Diana Ross and the Supremes.

Like most everyone, Berry Gordy loved the movies, but complained that Hollywood didn't understand the breadth and scope of Black stories, of Black storytelling. The blaxploitation movies, to him, were mere romps, geared toward Black audiences with hopes that discerning whites might become intrigued and add to the box office. His Motown was different; whites had waltzed into its web effortlessly and intended to stay. He had turned the label into a crossover juggernaut. Singers from his label—Michael Jackson, the Supremes—had already sung on white movie soundtracks, and their theme songs had become hits.

Berry Gordy, reclining in his Motown office chair, started thinking of Hollywood, a place where not a single Black executive had the power to green-light a movie. None of that mattered to him; he made up his mind he was going to get into the damn movie business! He wanted to make movies with Diana Ross, because Ross was more than just the supremely talented lead singer of the Supremes. She had become Berry Gordy's lover.

"Love Is Like an Itching in My Heart" . . .

———

She was both singer and junkie, and the whole story of her life is sad, horrifying, a little triumphant but mostly ruinous, and a lot of it brought into relief with her standing there, at the microphone, a gardenia in her hair, singing from her gut. Everyone wanted to tell her to stop abusing her gifts, but some fires just can't be banked. Eleanora Fagan, born in 1915, loved sneaking off to the movies while growing up in Baltimore. There was an actress, Billie Dove, a silent-film star (*The Folly of Vanity, The Lucky Horseshoe, American Beauty*) that she adored. Young Eleanora beamed while watching Billie Dove on-screen. It helped her keep at bay the darkness of her own little-colored-girl-lost life: Her mother had abandoned her when she was a child, hustling off to Manhattan, where she did maid work. In January 1925, there would be no more Billie Dove moviegoing for Eleanora Fagan, because she got sent to reform school, charged with truancy and being "a minor without proper care and guardianship." When she was released on parole after ten months, she moved in with her mother. It was her own mother who came upon the horrible sight of the neighbor raping young Eleanora. The man was sentenced to a mere three months; this was a Black-on-Black crime, and in many such cases the victim received far less than adequate justice. Before long, Eleanora was working as a maid at a brothel, cleaning, smiling at the customers—that is, until she began doing more than just smiling. She needed the money.

In 1929, now in Harlem, Eleanora Fagan started singing. She was fond of Ethel Waters and Bessie Smith. Maybe she could be like them someday. The more she sang, the more she was determined to find another name, a more stagy name. She thought of Billie Dove, the actress she so admired. Eleanora Fagan became, snap of the fingers, Billie Holiday. Her burgeoning singing career, however, was interrupted by the New York City police: Billie Holiday and her mother were arrested in a brothel. Holiday was imprisoned for a little less than six months.

It was 1933 when the record producer John Hammond discovered her in Harlem and got her into the studio. She became a sensation, performing with the likes of Teddy Wilson, Lester Young, and Ben Webster. Young began calling her Lady Day, and the nickname stuck. Holiday traveled and sang with the Count Basie Orchestra. She hated traveling through the American South: the dangers, the segregation laws, the hordes of poor Black folk. She left Basie (amid much later contention of who actually quit whom) and joined Artie Shaw's all-white band. Her best gig, however, was when the nightclub impresario Barney Josephson invited her to play Café Society in New York City's Greenwich Village. Her anti-lynching song, "Strange Fruit," became a sensation. She couldn't quit the drugs, though. In 1947, she was busted with heroin and sent to a West Virginia penitentiary, where she served just under ten months. Not long after her release, the New York Police Department took away her cabaret license, which meant she couldn't sing in clubs. "I have been caught in the crossfire of narcotic agents and drug peddlers and it's been wicked," she said. "One of the narcotic agents seemed determined to make me the means of securing promotion." She sued the NYPD, but a judge laughed at her. There were more arrests, from Philadelphia to San Francisco. She imagined that some of her punishment was due to "Strange Fruit" and its indictment of the American criminal-justice system. In the summer of 1959, she landed in a New York City community hospital. It wasn't the best hospital in the city. She was suffering from liver and heart ailments. Someone brought heroin to her room. Hospital personnel discovered it and summoned the police, and she was arrested in bed. A police officer was stationed outside her room. James Baldwin and some other notable Blacks claimed that the NYPD was harassing her. The police checked her food for heroin. The end came on July 17, 1959, her organs having collapsed.

Her memoir, *Lady Sings the Blues,* co-written with William Dufty, had been published in 1956. In her final years, Billie Holiday began telling people the book was filled with lies, and she regretted its having ever been published.

————

Berry Gordy had been accustomed to packaging things for years—solo acts, tours, singing groups. He arrived in Hollywood to begin assembling a movie package: he was going to produce a Billie Holiday movie, and it was going to star Diana Ross, and it was going to be based on *Lady Sings the Blues.* Lady Day said it was untruthful? Too bad: print the legend! A script was written; Suzanne de Passe (a Motown exec), Chris Clark, Terence McCloy all received credit. Sidney Furie, a native Canadian, wasn't an A-list director but had earned respect in Hollywood. In 1966, he directed *The Appaloosa,* which starred Marlon Brando; in 1970, there was *Little Fauss and Big Halsy,* a Robert Redford vehicle.

With Ross now preparing for her role, the search began to find the film's Louis McKay, Holiday's final husband. McKay had gotten quite an upgrade in the script. No longer was he the pimp and cad and untrustworthy figure he had been in real life; now he was a near-saintly figure, a handsome dreamboat. A lot of Black actors in Hollywood craved the role. Gordy considered Levi Stubbs, the lead singer of the Four Tops, but Stubbs didn't want to interrupt his singing engagements. Billy Dee Williams was called in for a screen test. A native of Harlem and a graduate of New York City's High School for the Performing Arts, he had made his motion-picture debut in 1959's *The Last Angry Man.* But it was onstage where he got wider notice. His breakout role came in 1961, when he appeared on Broadway in Shelagh Delaney's *A Taste of Honey* opposite Joan Plowright. "He was magic," recalls Louis Gossett, Jr. "If he'd've been white, he would have been Tony Curtis." Williams later appeared as one of the rotating actors in *The Blacks,* an Off-Broadway play that opened in 1961 and ran for nearly four years. The Jean Genet drama, originally written in French, revolved around a trial for the murder of a white woman. It was unlike anything Off-Broadway audiences had seen. The trial is actually a kangaroo court; some of the Black actors were called upon to whiten their faces for the roles. "The cast, all Negro, is masterly," opined *Cue* magazine. Williams's stage work got him noticed by TV casting directors. He trekked out to L.A. and for years appeared on episodic television shows—*The Defenders, The FBI, Dan August, Mission Impossible.* He played the football star Gale Sayers in *Brian's Song,* a 1971 acclaimed television drama, and received an Emmy nomination. Williams was delighted when summoned to audition for *Lady Sings the Blues.* Berry Gordy sensed the actor was nervous during the audition, flubbing his lines. Williams walked toward the door after the audition ended, believing he had blown the opportunity: "But Berry rushes over to me, he says, 'You're Louis McKay, you're Louis McKay. Don't worry about those other people [in casting]. You're Louis McKay." Among others in the cast were Richard Pryor (in a breakout role), James Callahan, Paul Hampton, Virginia Capers, and Jester Hairston. Hairston played a butler, working in the white household where Billie Holiday's mother does maid work. This was a familiar role for Jester: he had played a butler in Sidney Poitier's *In the Heat of the Night,* too.

As filming got under way on the Paramount lot, the Black actors were astounded by what they were witnessing: a Black man, Berry Gordy, calling so many of the shots, producing a big-budget motion picture! Gordy—short, bearded, voluble, bopping around the set like he had bopped around the offices of Motown—hardly seemed intimidated by the surroundings. But creative tensions began escalating as he clashed with Furie's direction of Ross. Furie threatened to quit; Gordy threatened to take over the directing. Other Motown execs were on set with Gordy, and the whispers began that Hollywood was what he always suspected it was: white men with paternalistic attitudes bossing people around—especially Black people. Not him! Not Berry Gordy! Furie and Gordy made up; argued some more; made up yet again. Finally—to everyone's relief—the film was completed.

The 144-minute *Lady Sings the Blues* was slated to open October 12, 1972.

It was jarring to witness the adult Ross playing a teenage kid in the early scenes, but thereafter, the film takes off. Ross and Williams exude a fierce and passionate chemistry; Richard Pryor is funny and tragic as the Piano Man, who risks a lot scoring dope for Holiday. He comes close to stealing the movie. America—especially Black America—kept rushing to the theatres. The reviews were strong. "The fact that 'Lady Sings the Blues' is a failure as a biography of legendary jazz singer Billie Holiday doesn't mean it can't be an entertaining movie," Gene Siskel would write in the *Chicago Tribune*. "And it is just that—entertaining—because of an old fashioned grande dame performance by Diana Ross, late of the pop-rock scene, in the title role." In *The New Yorker*, Pauline Kael offered, "When the movie was over I wrote 'I love it' on my pad of paper. . . . Factually it's a fraud, but emotionally it delivers. It has what makes movies work for a mass audience: easy pleasure, tawdry electricity, personality—great quantities of personality." In the mind of Vincent Canby of *The New York Times*, Diana Ross proved to be "an actress of exceptional beauty and wit, who is very much involved in trying to make a bad movie work." Canby had nothing good to say about the screenplay. *Variety* opined, "For the bulk of general audiences, the film serves as a very good screen debut vehicle for Diana Ross, supported strongly by excellent casting, handsome '30s physical values, and a script which is far better in dialog than structure." Charles Champlin of the *Los Angeles Times* gushed over the film, conclud-ing that Ross had given "one of the truly fine screen performances, full of power and pathos and enormously engaging and sympathetic." The film was not hugely profitable: it made nearly twenty million against a fourteen-million-dollar budget. More important, there were five Academy Award nominations—actress, art direction–set decoration, original song, costume design, and screenplay. It won none in that year of the *Godfather* juggernaut. Some wondered if Gordy's aggressive publicity on behalf of Ross and the movie (ten full-page show-business magazine ads!) were a little too much and simply turned off Academy voters. Liza Minnelli took the Best Actress prize for *Cabaret*. Motown also issued a two-album set in connection with the film—with gorgeous purple slipcover—of Ross singing Holiday tunes. The album and unusual recording, which included dialogue from the film, raced up the *Billboard* charts, selling a whopping two million copies. In May 1973, *Lady Sings the Blues* landed at the Cannes Film Festival. It played out of competition—meaning it wasn't eligible for awards—but it became a topic of international film conversation.


Diaaannnuuuhhhh!

Fans would see her in Manhattan—she liked staying at the ritzy Essex House—in her Pucci dress, high heels, sunglasses (incognito, ha ha ha), striding to the limo with her little Maltese puppy cupped in her arms. "Its very clear," Berry Gordy said, "why I fell in love with Diana—because she was my star, and she came from the bottom up."

Berry Gordy's *Lady Sings the Blues* had managed to elevate the idea of Black romance upon the big screen. Not only had Black-white kissing been taboo for decades; so had straight Black romance in mainstream movies. Blacks who saw *Lady Sings the Blues* had had only two recent Black movies that could be considered true romances: *Nothing but a Man,* a 1964 film starring Ivan Dixon (a Poitier protégé) and Abbey Lincoln, and *For Love of Ivy,* a 1968 film starring Poitier and, again, Lincoln. Blacks were starved for screen romances, and Williams had taken the character of McKay in a whole other direction, imbuing him with multiple degrees of depth and feeling. This was a man crying the blues to save the drug-addicted woman he loved! It was at odds with the truth of McKay's own life, but Williams created the Louis McKay legend.


Motown fans couldn't stop clamoring for more Diana Ross on screen. Gordy began telling other Motown execs that he aimed to find her a project in which she didn't have to sing. He wanted a straight dramatic picture, and so did Ross, who was intent on proving her range. It took two years to find a project. They settled on a script written by John Byrum about a Chicago fashion designer who goes to Italy to find fame, only to come up against cultural confusion, jealousies, and a bipolar, bisexual photographer. Gordy produced *Mahogany* under the Motown banner. Tony Richardson—a respected stage-and-film director—trooped to Bel Air to meet Gordy as the project was coming together. He thought the home of the Motown founder beyond opulent: there were llamas and armed guards. Richardson had won Best Picture and Director Oscars for 1963's *Tom Jones.* Gordy was impressed with his pedigree (an Oxford grad) and that he had worked with such esteemed actresses as Jeanne Moreau, Susannah York, and Vanessa Redgrave. This made him feel confident that Richardson would work well with Ross. Among other cast members were Beah Richards, Anthony Perkins (playing the mercurial photographer), Jean-Pierre Aumont, Nina Foch, and, to please fans, Billy Dee Williams, as Ross's lover, a community activist.

Gordy didn't need the Black entertainment magazines to tell him that America had found its first Black crossover superstar screen couple, but they told him anyway. The feature articles were omnipresent on the newsstands. Mainstream America had Tracy and Hepburn, Burton and Liz Taylor, Redford and Streisand. They also now had Ross and Williams. In Berry Gordy's mind, his forthcoming film would remind moviegoers of the epic romantic dramas that Douglas Sirk had made throughout the 1950s—films like *All That Heaven Allows, There's Always Tomorrow,* and *Imitation of Life.*

In November 1974, the cast and crew of *Mahogany* arrived in Chicago to begin filming. Trouble began brewing on the set right away. There were grumblings that Richardson, the British director, didn't understand Black culture. Some community activists began complaining to Gordy that both the script and Richardson's direction seemed tone-deaf. It didn't take long before the Gordy-Richardson conversations turned heated. Ross and Williams steered clear of the brouhaha. Paramount may have struck a deal to distribute the movie, but Gordy was financing it and lorded over the production. When he disagreed with some of Richardson's choices for small local background roles, an argument broke out. Richardson stood his ground. Gordy summarily fired him, stunning both cast and crew. Gordy then told Paramount he'd be directing the picture. Ross, a fragile actress who had respected Richardson, quietly grew nervous. When the production moved to Italy, it quickly became apparent that Gordy was in too deep. Running Motown was one thing; directing a major motion picture in a foreign locale with hundreds of actors and moving parts, quite another. Loud arguments erupted between Ross and Gordy. She thought he was disrespecting her—demanding multiple retakes of scenes—and harming her performance. With two days left in filming, Ross bolted the set and didn't return. She had only a few scenes left; Gordy was forced to hire a double and film those scenes from a distance.

Ross expressed hopes that fans would leave theatres "thinking of me as a total performer and not just as a singer-turned-actress." The advance test screenings, however, drew poor reactions, and Motown was rightfully nervous. The film opened on October 8, 1975. The reviews pointed to a film that had come undone, a picture that lacked both a solid script and smart directing. Roger Ebert referred to it as "an unholy alliance between daytime soap opera and Jacqueline Susann," a writer many saw as a campy romance novelist. *Time* magazine charged Gordy with "squandering one of America's most natural resources, Diana Ross." The *New York Times* review, though offering a smattering of praise for Ross's performance, concluded that the movie was "pretty silly any way you look at it." When it was revealed that Ross had designed most of the clothing in the film,

Berry Gordy. He used music to create his own film independence.

the hissing erupted that the whole thing had been but a vanity project. (Some of Ross's elaborate costumes did look a bit, well, campy.) Billy Dee Williams tried to explain the intended arc of the film: "We had this romantic situation, and then we had a conflict of interest in which Diana Ross is caught between two men and also sees her ambitions threatened. It's meant to entertain more than anything else." The movie cost $3.5 million; its grosses were five million dollars, a clear financial disappointment. The lone bright spot was Ross's recording, "Do You Know Where You're Going To," which spent seventeen weeks on the charts. The song also received an Academy Award nomination. Ross remained hurt by the critical drubbing. She blamed Gordy.

Film companies, of course, have hits and misses; it's all part of the business. In spite of the withering reviews for *Mahogany,* Gordy remained resolute about taking on Hollywood. He hired Rob Cohen to be his producing partner. Cohen had been working at Twentieth Century–Fox as vice-president of their TV-movie division. Gordy liked that he was quite young, in his mid-twenties, and that he seemed to understand and appreciate the depths of Black culture.

Berry Gordy's first two movies showed his drive and pluck. They had not made a lot of money, just enough to keep him in the Hollywood orbit. But there was a unique feature of his Hollywood presence, and Black audiences noticed it more than anyone else. Gordy had found, and promoted, a Black matinee idol. Women all around America had begun swooning at the sight of Billy Dee Williams. On a movie junket in Detroit, women actually fainted at the sight of him. In Savannah, Georgia, in 1975, the local police were summoned to keep things orderly when he showed up at an event. Williams was receiving several thousand letters a week from female fans—of all races and hues. "A star is what everyone wants to be, even Presidents," Williams confided. *Time* magazine compared

Williams to a screen icon from an earlier era: "The Black Gable," they called him.

———

Billy Dee Williams was a movie star. The camera adored him. He had proved he was more than just a handsome face. He could act; a lot of it was attributable to his stage training. Both Williams and Gordy expected he would now start to get wonderful offers from studios in the aftermath of his two Motown costarring roles and *Brian's Song,* still fresh in public minds. Williams seemed positioned to join other actors of his generation—Ryan O'Neal, Burt Reynolds, James Caan—in getting big-screen offers to play complex characters with depth. Perhaps the studios—aside from Motown—would realize his crossover appeal and pair him with white actresses in big romances. For years, Williams tried to make the leap from episodic television to film. But the years were lean. "It was Poitier, and that was it," he said. But Williams was now operating in a new decade, a supposedly more aware decade. He thought Hollywood was ready for him. "What I present on film today," he said, "is probably a step farther" than Poitier could go. "Audiences can accept a more complex black man, and I try to project an intelligent kind of individual with a certain amount of complications."

But the Hollywood studios did not begin clamoring after the services of Billy Dee Williams, so Berry Gordy stepped into the breach and signed Williams to a multi-year contract. One of the movies Gordy and his producer Rob Cohen had begun planning was an adaptation of *The Bingo Long Traveling All-Stars & Motor Kings,* a 1973 novel by William Brashler that told the story of a barnstorming team in baseball's Negro Leagues. The story, though fictional, had characters clearly drawn from the lives of famed Negro League baseball players, such as Josh Gibson and Satchel Paige. The script excited Williams. "When I was growing up in New York City," he recalled, "I used to go see those guys play in Central Park, the Negro league players and the Cuban players." Motown began assembling a cast: In addition to Williams, the cast included James Earl Jones, Ted Ross, Stan Shaw, Mabel King, and Richard Pryor. It was thought that George Roy Hill might direct, then that Martin Ritt might helm it. Neither could fit it into their schedules. A young director by the name of Steven Spielberg expressed interest, only to drop out when his movie *Jaws* exploded in theatres in the summer of 1975.

Michael Schultz heard about the search for a director for *Bingo Long*. He badly wanted the job. Schultz had just directed 1975's *Cooley High*, a charming comedy-drama set in an all-Black Chicago high school that presented a sharp, insightful contrast to the endless stream of all-white teen comedies. Schultz was an intriguing figure in Hollywood; many assumed, from phone conversations, that he was white because of his German surname. There would be double-takes when he showed up for meetings with white executives. Michael Schultz was quite proud that he was a Black man.

Due to the treachery of slavery, one Kentucky slave, George, had no last name. His owner was a Mr. Schultz. Upon Schultz's death, George was set free. Scuffling to make a living, he decided he needed a last name and decided to take "Schultz." When Schultz family members told him they opposed this, George reminded them he was now a free man and would no longer be mastered. So he became George Schultz. He loved saying the whole name, George Schultz: a man in full, a man with inalienable rights, a man with a first and a last name. He learned to write, and took pride in writing his full name down.

George Schultz's great-great-great-grandson was Michael Schultz, who was born in Milwaukee. Michael Schultz's parents, Leo and Katherine, had met in a nightclub, where Leo sometimes played in a band. They fell in love, got married. Michael dreamed of going to the Air Force Academy. When he didn't get in (he was listed as an alternate), he enrolled at Marquette University.

Schultz eventually made his way over to Marquette's theatre school. Father John J. Walsh, a Jesuit priest—he wasn't shy about letting folks know he knew renowned director Elia Kazan—ran the theatre program. "He delighted in shocking people," Schultz recalls about Father Walsh and the array of plays he allowed students to mount. "It was almost like being involved in an Off-Broadway situation." Father Walsh gave Schultz a job as lighting designer, and that helped the young student pay his tuition. Father Walsh also told Schultz he should go to New York City if he was really interested in theatre. Schultz took the advice. He had an aging Oldsmobile and gassed the thing up.

Michael Schultz arrived in New York City in 1964. He wound up doing the lighting for *Benito Cereno*, a 1964 play about the *Amistad* slave rebellion. Among others, it starred Frank Langella and Roscoe Lee Browne and won several Obie awards. From being around that highly praised production, Schultz caught the directing bug. At the McCarter Theatre in Princeton, New Jersey, he directed a production of *Emperor Jones,* which got great reviews. Back in New York City, Douglas Turner Ward, one of the founders of the Negro Ensemble Company, invited him to become a part of the company. He did all manner of jobs, learning as much as he could about all aspects of theatre. In 1969, Schultz was offered the opportunity to direct his first Broadway play, *Does a Tiger Wear a Necktie?* He cast a young actor by the name of Al Pacino in this play about young drug addicts. It drew raves and Tony nominations, winning a Best Supporting Actor award for Pacino. "My thinking at the time," Schultz says, "was that, if I can make a name for myself in theatre, someone will offer me a job in film."

As predicted, a producer offered Schultz a job directing *To Be Young, Gifted and Black,* for PBS Television. The teleplay adapted scenes from the works of the playwright Lorraine Hansberry with an interracial cast of actors. By 1974, Schultz was ready to venture out to Los Angeles. After his arrival, his theatrical background opened some doors, and he signed a contract with Universal Television. He did episodic television—*The Rockford Files, Toma, Starsky & Hutch.* A producer sent him the *Cooley High* script. "What I thought about the script was that no one had seen real love on screen between Black kids," Schultz recalls. "What I knew was, this was unique in terms of humor and tragedy and the strong bond between these Black boys. And if I could show these things—hijinks, heartbreak—then the movie could stick around for a long time." He went to Chicago for filming, having cast Glynn Turman, Garrett Morris, and Lawrence Hilton-Jacobs for major roles. The *Variety* critic felt a need to point out that "you don't have to be black to enjoy it immensely." On a budget of $750,000, *Cooley High* made thirteen million at the box office. It was a clear hit.

Schultz got word about Motown's planned Negro League baseball movie, *Bingo Long,* and tracked down Berry Gordy. But Gordy told him he had already settled on John Badham, who would be making his debut as a big-screen director, and who was white and British. Schultz was a bit despondent. But in the years ahead, Hollywood would hear plenty from Schultz. He directed several Richard Pryor films, as well as *Carbon Copy,* the big-screen debut of Denzel Washington. In his eightieth year, he was still directing, a survivor of Hollywood's long racial dynamic.

Filming on *Bingo Long* began in Macon, Georgia, in the summer of 1975. The locals were quite excited, especially Black residents of the city when told it would be a film about the Negro Baseball League. Macon was a Southern city that still held a powerful residue of segregation and racial strife. Former Governor Lester Maddox was still skulking around state politics. Blacks in Macon had hardly forgotten that Maddox, years earlier the owner of an Atlanta restaurant, had received national publicity for refusing to serve Blacks, in violation of the 1964 Civil Rights Act. Rob Cohen, the Motown exec, thought it a good idea to cast Macon Mayor Ronnie Thompson in a cameo role. Good civic relations! But an outcry immediately erupted from the town's Black populace. Thompson had been hostile to Blacks and civil rights: He once issued "shoot to kill" orders for suspected robbers, which local Blacks took as an edict directed at young Blacks. On another occasion, he purchased an army tank for the city and threatened to have it roll up on civil-rights demonstrators. A group of Macon Blacks sent a letter to Universal and Motown proclaiming that Thompson "has used the issue of race, in a negative way, to advance his political career." They opposed his casting, even for a tiny cameo appearance. The filmmakers withdrew the Thompson offer.

When filming was completed, Gordy, Badham, and Cohen were all thrilled with the result. Even reimagined as fiction, stories of Black sports heroes rarely graced the movie screen, and they thought they had something special. Billy Dee Williams and James Earl Jones gave magnetic performances. Richard Pryor gave a sly and comedic performance as a Black player masquerading as a Cuban, hoping to break into the all-white major leagues. Cohen took the movie to Universal, who would be distributing the picture. Watching it with a Universal executive, he was giddy, believing the movie would get a wonderful reception. "What do you expect me to do with this nigger epic?" the Universal executive asked Cohen after the end credits. Cohen was stunned. He told the executive he felt the film could not only find an audience, but could become a crossover success.

The rave reviews and box-office success of *Bingo Long* disproved any reservations Universal executives may have harbored. They also assuaged any hurt Berry Gordy still carried around about the reception for *Mahogany*. *Bingo Long* was an unqualified hit. Motown's biggest moneymaker, on a nine-million-dollar budget, it returned thirty-three million in box-office receipts.

Gordy and Williams wasted little time zeroing in on their next joint project. They both imagined a big-screen treatment on the life of the pianist and composer Scott Joplin. Like most others taken from the pages of Black American history, Joplin's story had been completely ignored by filmmakers. Born in 1868, Joplin had a rags-to-riches-to-rags life. By 1895, he was fully on the road, touring in saloons and writing ragtime music. His "Maple Leaf Rag," published in 1899, drew a lot of attention. After the turn of the century, ragtime—a highly spirited type of piano playing—became the musical rage across the nation and in Europe. One of Joplin's most famous tunes was "The Entertainer," a lively composition that made him a nice amount of money. But Joplin fell on hard times, contracting syphilis, losing a child, and going through a painful divorce. He was eventually committed to a New York mental hospital and died in 1917, destitute and forgotten. In the early 1970s, Joplin had a musical revival. His compositions served as the soundtrack—adapted by Marvin Hamlisch—for *The Sting,* the Oscar-winning 1973 Paul Newman–Robert Redford film. New editions of his music were republished and re-recorded. Berry Gordy took his Joplin project to Universal Studios—a natural fit, since Universal had produced *The Sting.* But studio execs—still leery of Black-themed movies—balked and suggested the Joplin picture be made as a television movie under their umbrella. Billy Dee Williams reminded Gordy that he no longer did television. Universal was steadfast about its ultimatum, however: Joplin as a TV movie or nothing. Williams finally acquiesced, and the studio threw out a bone: if it was good enough, they retained the option to release it in theatres.

The film *Scott Joplin,* directed by Jeremy Kagan, was released in 1977 as a television movie, but showed up in theatres (a very limited number of theatres) months later. This bizarre mishmash of a rollout served no one well, nor did the negative reviews. "Billy Dee Williams is effective as Joplin only when he's very happy or very angry," wrote Gene Siskel in the *Chicago Tribune.* "Unfortunately, most of the time in 'Scott Joplin' he's very depressed—just like the audience." *Variety* allowed: "Williams is fine, and the film has a lot of verve and intensity, but the story of Joplin's life is so grim it makes the film a real downer." Noting that the movie had been, oddly, released on television and theatrically, John J. O'Connor wrote in *The New York Times,* "The fact is it's not even a very good television movie."

Motown, once again, had to lick its wounds But setbacks only propelled Berry Gordy forward. He had tasted the glory of Oscar nominations with his first movie, and he knew that he could get there again. He once again summoned his go-to actress:

*Diannnnuuuuhhhh!*

Diana Ross was now being asked to play a young girl, and not just any girl but the iconic Dorothy of L. Frank Baum's classic *Wizard of Oz*. Motown had convinced Universal to join forces with them to make *The Wiz*, based on the all-Black Broadway musical that had enraptured theatregoers when it opened in January 1975. John Badham was hired to direct. But when he realized that Gordy was serious about having Ross, in her mid-thirties, play young Dorothy, he abruptly left the project. He felt that Ross was too old for the part, and badly miscast. The Motown version of *Oz* re-created Dorothy as a Harlem schoolteacher. Sidney Lumet came aboard to direct. Lumet was highly respected; among his recent movies were *Serpico* (1973), *Dog Day Afternoon* (1975), and *Network* (1976). The casting choices drew wide publicity: Michael Jackson would be playing the scarecrow, Nipsey Russell the Tin Man, Lena Horne Glinda the Good Witch, and Richard Pryor the Wiz. Ted Ross, as the Cowardly Lion, and Mabel King, as Evillene the Wicked Witch, would be reprising their roles from the Broadway show. Once again, Blacks—whose hunger for film representation was so large that any meal seemed almost a feast—grew giddy as the opening of *The Wiz* drew closer. Black radio began erupting with accounts of the production and highlighting the theatres at which it would be playing. Still photos from the set were showing up in magazines. Motown imagined the movie would appeal to its sweet spot: an audience of both Black and white filmgoers. "There is an almost apartheid policy in movie theatres," the producer Rob Cohen mentioned in a worried tone prior to the opening. "There is a Black audience and there is a white audience, and rarely do they mingle in the same theatre for the same picture. But when making a movie that's as expensive as this one, we've had to try to appeal to the entire audience."

There was no denying that *The Wiz*—which opened October 24, 1978—was colorful and at times spirited. But it also proved to be a critical and commercial flop. The reviews were often scathing; few, it seemed, could understand why Ross, at her age, had been cast as Dorothy. From *The New York Times*: "'The Wiz' is a mess due to the misguided efforts to turn the energetic, likeably dopey stage musical into what might pass for a ghetto fairy tale." Stanley Kaufmann, reviewing *The Wiz* in *The New Republic:* "It's torrentially syrupy, calculatedly simplistic, and the star is weak." (Kaufmann also took a swipe at the film's reported budget of thirty-five million dollars; other reports claimed it was twenty-seven million. It still was, at the time, the most expensive musical ever made.) "A huge budget corrupts hugely," John Skow wrote in *Time* magazine, adding that, by the end, "the viewer has realized that he can't win, he can't break even, and he must get out of the theatre." Movie-industry insiders had estimated that *The Wiz* would have to gross at least seventy million dollars to recoup its money and turn a profit. Motown-Universal had presold television rights to the film, which would soften some of the loss, but, still, the final receipts of twenty-one million represented a staggering loss.

Motown now had to consider if this gamble in moviemaking could be sustained. Berry Gordy had certainly raised the spirits of Blacks with his five films—*Lady Sings the Blues, Mahogany, Bingo Long, Scott Joplin,* and *The Wiz.* These were movies made with much bigger budgets than the blaxploitation movies, and it showed on-screen. He had hired Academy Award–winning talent. More than anyone had done before, he had treated Black audiences to the pleasure of big-time entertaining filmmaking with stories that felt relevant to their lives and their taste. There were first-class production values, prominent directors, and impressive casts. And he had gotten mainstream publications to take his movies seriously. But movies were far more expensive to produce than music albums; the losses and anemic box-office performances of the Motown films were more pronounced. Excitement and consciousness raising were fine, but Hollywood was a game of profit and loss, and the bean counters paid particular attention to loss. The top-grossing movie of 1978 was *Grease,* which hauled in $181 million. Just behind it was *National Lampoon's Animal House* at $141 million. *The Wiz* was number twenty-six in box-office revenue with its twenty-one million, far less than its explosive budget.

It was little wonder that Gordy slowly began turning his attention away from filmmaking. He had no intention of strangling his music business for the sake of pride in his Hollywood presence. Gordy made one more film for Motown, *The Last Dragon,* which appeared in March 1985. It was a ten-million-dollar martial-arts comedy; its grosses of thirty-three million were admirable. But critics savaged the film. Billy Dee Williams was not happy with Gordy's decision to abandon filmmaking. "The only guy who really knew how to present me was Berry Gordy," Williams said.

As Billy Dee Williams kept envisioning it, Hollywood would find a way to elevate him into the top ranks of his profession. He had become a matinee idol and had turned in textured performances. "I'm a leading man," he proclaimed. There was a strategic reason he had avoided blaxploitation movies: "If I'm trying to obtain a certain longevity in my career, to establish myself as a certain kind of star," he said, "I don't want that black exploitation image." In 1978, there were publicized reports that Williams and Diahann Carroll were going to team up for a big-screen remake of *Nightmare Alley,* a twisty, dark crime drama originally released in 1947 starring Tyrone Power and Joan Blondell. The project, however, never got traction. Movie directors were not offering leading-man roles to Williams. Frustrated, he slid away from the big screen down to TV. In 1978, Williams showed up on *The Jeffersons,* a sitcom, playing off his matinee-idol reputation. It was a spoof, but it still seemed beneath him. He starred in television films, among them *Christmas Lilies of the Field,* which was a veiled remake of Poitier's *Lilies of the Field,* and *Children of Divorce.* Television was income. But, still, it was hardly the way Williams had imagined his career progressing. James Caan, his *Brian's Song* costar, had solidified his big-screen staying power: in 1978, he appeared in *Comes a Horseman* opposite Jane Fonda; in 1979, Neil Simon's *Chapter Two* with Marsha Mason; in 1980, he both starred in and directed *Hide in Plain Sight.* And, of course, there was *The Godfather.* In 1980, Williams starred in *The Hostage Tower,* yet another television movie. Many in the fashion world and the Black community took it as validation of Williams's matinee-idol legitimacy when, also in 1980, he became the rare Black to appear on the cover of *Gentlemen's Quarterly* magazine. (Sammy Davis, Jr., had been the very first, in 1967.) Williams looked suave in a yellow leather jacket, his hair pressed back and his bronze face gleaming. In 1980, he was also cast in *Star Wars: The Empire Strikes Back.* He imbued his role with charm and flintiness, and the film was an enormous success, but his was not the lead role. He played second fiddle to Sylvester Stallone in *Nighthawks,* a crime drama. Williams missed Berry Gordy and Motown productions. In 1989, a story appeared in the *Chicago Tribune* with the headline "Billy Dee Williams Reflects on the Career That Got Away." The writer referred to his having gone from big Motown productions to "a kind of featured glamour man" in films. Williams was open about the issue of race and what opportunities it likely denied him. "Well, the unfortunate thing is, in this society, men of my hue and color, and if you're nice-looking on top of it, and you're a real person, a sensitive person—in other words you're not a comedian—it's very difficult." Gone was the optimism he had previously held. The Black Clark Gable was forced to face a harsh reality. He allowed that he had tried to jump-start his own projects. He wanted desperately to make a film about Alexandre Dumas, the part-Black Frenchman and author of many acclaimed works, among them *The Count of Monte Cristo* and *The Three Musketeers.* "A lot of people don't realize he was a mulatto," Williams explained. "But in France they said they didn't want a black man playing the character, so I said to myself, 'What do I do?' What do you do? It's like beating your head against the wall."

Hollywood careers are difficult to reignite, unless a specific role comes along that revives interest in an actor or actress, as with Brando in *The Godfather* or Travolta in *Pulp Fiction.* Billy Dee Williams continued popping up on television into the following decades. He went off to do occasional stage comedies. There were commercials. There were small roles in small films that went unnoticed. In 2019, he was back on the big screen in *Star Wars: The Rise of Skywalker.* He seemed to have fun making it. The television talk-show hosts clamored to interview him; they wanted to talk about the long career, about the Billy Dee–ness that had, once upon a time, caught fire. He went out with the cast on a worldwide press tour. He looked natty. He carried a walking stick. He was eighty-two years old. His fans were happy to see him. The producers had treated him with great respect during the making of the new *Star Wars* film, and he was always careful to mention their respect. Why, they had treated him the way the screen legend Clark Gable must have been treated on all his films.

# Kunta Kinte Seizes the Moment

THE SCENES CRIED OUT for cinematic treatment. And yet Hollywood routinely turned away from imagining such narratives. Perhaps it was because the scenes and stories would expose a nation, and the nation wasn't quite ready to grapple with so many extended truths. At least, not on a sixty-foot-wide screen.

Some of the scenes:

A man at an outdoor desk, surrounded by twenty or so other people, Black and white. Everyone is dressed in nice clothes, signifying the importance of the event. It is 1850, and they are gathered at Cazenovia, New York, for the Fugitive Slave Convention. They've certainly heard of escaped slaves being captured in the North and dragooned back below the Mason-Dixon Line. One wonders: Are there bounty hunters in the distance? Are they atop horses and galloping in the direction of Cazenovia in pursuit? The man at the left end of the desk is Frederick Douglass, himself a runaway slave. He is now a fiery orator and a hugely persuasive writer. The accompanying prose of this book called *Freedom* states of Douglass: "With the assistance of a free black woman named Anna Murray, whom he later married, he successfully fled the South in 1838. He soon began an extraordinary career as a public lecturer and political activist in the growing anti-slavery movement."

Another photo: a Black woman in a plaid dress with a white collar. The woman looks painfully thin; perhaps she is malnourished. She is, after all, a slave. She is holding a white infant in her arms. The baby has been born into a conflicted nation, but at least its freedom is not questioned. "For generations African-American women were the primary caretakers of well-to-do southern children," the text says. "The representation of the 'mammy'—the faithful, obedient domestic servant—became part of white southern folklore."

Moving on across history, a few years later, settling upon a cloudy day in Virginia in 1862. Oxen are trudging across the shimmering water. Runaway slaves are crouched atop the wagon and animals. It is a desperate scene. The caption reads: "Fugitives fording the Rappahannock River fleeing from General Stonewall Jackson's Confederate army, Virginia, August, 1862." Stonewall, of course, was out for blood. Even after the war, a version of bondage continued, with Negroes holed up on plantations, sharecropping all day long.

Another photo: eleven Blacks—two are children—somewhere in Mississippi. Half are standing atop a wagon. There is a white man behind them all; perhaps he is their overseer. There is a sternness about him. Not a single one of the Blacks is smiling; the two children look indifferent. "Beginning in 1890 in Mississippi, southern states prohibited nearly all Blacks from voting. Within several years, virtually all public settings—schools, churches, government offices, hotels, hospitals, public transportation, parks, and even elevators—were rigidly segregated by race under a system widely termed 'Jim Crow' after a minstrel show character."

The book holding these photos, *Freedom,* was published in 2002 by Phaidon Press, which has offices in both New York City and London. *Freedom* is oversized, hefty, more than five hundred pages. A good many of the photos had never been published. They'd be at home in an exhibit at some well-known museum. There are eight hundred or so photos gathered in the pages. The text is by two reputable scholars, Manning Marable and Leith Mullings.

Another photo, more a daguerreotype, sepia-toned and a little grainy: The location is unknown, though somewhere in the American South. There are five men in the photograph; four are white. The lone Black man has only a short time to live. He is on his way to be hanged. The crime is unmentioned. It likely involved a white person. Blacks were seldom hanged for crimes against fellow Blacks. From the caption: "Between 1882 and 1901, 2,060 African Americans were lynched in the United States. During the consolidation of the Jim Crow regime, southern whites devised a variety of methods to assert their social domination over black people. The most effective means was lynching—the use of extra-legal deadly force against a civilian population for the purpose of instilling widespread fear."

The years rolled by, with laws and institutions arrayed against a whole race of people. Unchained, they'd have to endure and survive and often even prove that they were worthy of existing laws that whites simply took for granted. Another photo shows a street parade in Harlem, 1925, everyone dressed to the nines. A convertible has turned a corner, and the big sign someone is holding inside the car can be seen from a distance: "THE NEW NEGRO HAS NO FEAR." But any Negro in those days could certainly be forgiven for having fear. It would be a natural reaction while living under tyranny. Flipping pages onward, you can see Zora Neale Hurston in a straw hat in 1935, in Florida. She's carrying a small purse that looks to be made of some kind of thin leather. She is preparing to set off on more journeys. She is looking for ex-slaves, all those ghosts behind her. She is documenting. It takes a great constitution for her just to hold herself together. She is flat-out brave.

This particular photographer must have been either in the balcony or on a stepladder. The view looks down upon a group of soldiers in uniform. All are Black men. They're in Alabama, at the Tuskegee Institute, training to be pilots. Seated in a big classroom, they are shoulder to shoulder. They're preparing to go get Hitler. Never mind that they aren't even totally free in their own country. They'll fight heroically for America anyway. They've come from all over the country. When the Negroes here in Alabama spot them in the local town, they'll beam with pride. They're already heroes. They're the fliers of the Ninety-ninth Pursuit Squadron. The caption says: "The squadron was stationed in North Africa in 1943, from where it flew bomber-escort, dive-bombing, and strafing missions in Europe." Some of the white soldiers called them "Eleanor's Niggers," a slur against both them and First Lady Eleanor Roosevelt, who championed their formation. They took it in jest, and on some of their planes penciled "EN": Eleanor's Niggers. Hitler, the biggest white supremacist of them all, never saw them coming.

Here's a couple—perhaps a Saturday or Sunday afternoon—climbing some cement steps. Their backs are to the camera. She's in a dress, and there's a light-colored sweater tossed over her shoulders. Her escort (husband? lover?) is wearing suspenders, white shirt, pinstriped pants, and a dress hat. The caption: "Colored entrance of a movie theatre, c. 1946. Although African American entertainers and artists had begun to achieve great popularity with white audiences, blacks continued to be forced to sit in segregated sections of movie theatres and other public venues." Who knows what movie might have been playing on the screen that awaited them up those steps and through the doors? Some of the popular films of 1946 were *Blue Skies, The Yearling, Duel in the Sun, The Best Years of Our Lives.* There weren't a lot of Black films in 1946.

It was obviously chilly in Montgomery, Alabama, on February 24, 1956. The suit jacket the young minister is wearing in this photo is thick and looks to be made of wool. He is seated on a wooden chair, and the police photographer is out of view, though a part of his—or her—camera is visible. There is a piece of cardboard hanging from a string around the seated man's neck, and his jail number—7089—is printed and quite visible lying against his chest. The minister stares straight ahead. He does not have a look of fear upon him. He looks to be a veteran of such events, and he is. He is just starting to burst upon the national scene. "Dr. Martin Luther King, Jr. is arrested for his participation in the bus boycott in Montgomery. . . . On 30 January 1956, Martin Luther King Jr.'s home was firebombed." Not many Americans, of course, lived in homes where they had to worry about being firebombed.

Four years later, in 1960—and several months after the sit-ins in Greensboro, North Carolina—there's yet another restaurant disturbance in Oklahoma City. It is all about dining. Some white patrons are being escorted into a local restaurant, while Blacks are forbidden, all under the gaze of police officers. Here's a Negro boy. One can bet he knows how to shoot marbles and how to fly a kite and how to bait a worm onto a hook and catch fish. Someone on this day, however, has put the fever of protest in him. The caption: "Sit-in demonstration in Oklahoma City, 6 August 1960. Under the leadership of sixteen-year-old Barbara Posey, the NAACP Youth Council initiated what became year-long demonstrations at several major eating places in downtown Oklahoma City."

So much of the news of the time kept returning to Alabama—it was such a hot spot of the times. Photographers took their bulky cameras and made a beeline for the state. It was as if Alabama wanted the world to know it had never conceded defeat, at least in spirit, in the Civil War. Here's Alabama Governor George Wallace, a runty little figure, on the campus of the University of Alabama. A lot of whites feel it's the best university in the state. Negroes wouldn't know, because they've never had the opportunity to attend. Wallace wants to be a powerful Confederate general; he might as well be atop a big white horse. He's representing much of the mindset of the whites throughout the state, throughout the South. The caption: "Wallace's conflict with the federal government over racial policy made him a popular national figure among white racists and extreme conservatives across the country almost overnight." A JFK Justice Department attorney stands in Wallace's face. The Kennedy government has started rolling, at long last, toward civil rights.

The images of marchers dominated the TV nightly news. White America began asking: What do those Negro people in those blue-jean coveralls want? For heaven's sake, why are those little kids marching?

And here he is again, that Alabama jail inmate number 7089, who sang as a little kid at the *Gone with the Wind* movie premiere back in Atlanta all those years ago. He stands at the Lincoln Memorial, his arm outstretched, his words sailing out and over the multiracial throng of thousands. A part of the caption about the August 28, 1963, address reads: "The speech carefully wove together appeals to classic American values of liberty and equality under the law that white Americans could accept. It spoke to a racially integrated future for the country, but in a language that was carefully crafted not to generate a racial backlash against the African American cause." So Blacks were not only the victims, but the moral guideposts, out to save themselves and a nation. The movies dared not touch this dynamic. Even if great and brave drama was everywhere.

There are so many jaw-dropping images, pressed between the hard covers of this handsome book. A great deal of detective work had to go into collecting such a treasure trove. It's a kind of kaleidoscope—the known and unknown, janitors and preachers, Adam Clayton Powell and Malcolm X, the comedian Dick Gregory and some crazed-looking bigots.

Here is Fannie Lou Hamer in Atlantic City, August 22, 1964, and she's speaking to the Democratic National Credentials Committee. She's wearing a print dress. A small microphone is pinned to the front of her dress, just below her neckline. She's wearing a name tag. She's here to protest the powerful sway—and she would know—that Southerners maintain over Democratic Party rule making: "Is this America, the land of the free and the home of the brave, where we are threatened daily because we want to live as decent human beings?" It's likely that most of those sitting before her don't know much about her life—that she started picking cotton when she was six years old, that she'd once worked as a timekeeper on a plantation, that she'd turned to activism and been beaten and jailed for trying to register Blacks to vote in Mississippi, and that she'd been removed from her home for doing such work. Visitors to Mississippi who were on the right side of history would always want to find her. They knew she could offer guidance and direction; she could tell them where the deadliest hot spots were. Some Southern sheriffs wanted her dead. Her most famous quote: "I'm sick and tired of being sick and tired." It was a lament geared to the whole of America—on behalf of Black folk. In February 2021—at long last—someone out in Hollywood announced plans for a Fannie Lou Hamer movie. Time will tell, of course.

More from *Freedom:* It seemed that the bullets were everywhere, constantly flying, slamming into heroic figures. Here's a thin Black man crumpling in agony to the ground. James Meredith has gotten shot near Hernando, Mississippi, in the June heat of 1966. He was on a one-man civil-rights march. He survived. A lot of people imagined he must have hated his home state with a vengeance. But home, even a bloody and wicked home, can come to have a powerful pull. In the years ahead, he'd come to write, and quite lyrically, about how much he missed Mississippi when he was away from it. The marching souls just wanted freedom.

All around the country, the twentieth century rolling onward, the battles continued: battles to move into mostly white neighborhoods; battles to break into corporate America; battles to integrate schools. As in so many other American cities, there was something wrong with the Boston public-school system. Despite the landmark 1954 *Brown* desegregation ruling, its school system was still profoundly segregated, denying Black children their right to a sound and equitable education. In June 1974, U.S. District Judge W. Arthur Garrity, Jr., weighed in on the Boston situation, issuing a ruling that forced the city to adopt a busing plan to integrate its schools. The clannish city erupted, with the protests most vocal among the city's Irish. There's a picture in the *Freedom* book taken in Boston during the school protests. A white man, holding a big American flag on a pole—holding it like a spear—has just rammed it into a Black man. The Black man, in suit and tie, seems stunned. At one of the Boston protests, someone held aloft a placard: "Bus Them Back to Africa." The imagery and placard were seen in newsreel footage all around the nation and the world. Bus them back to Africa. Therein lay the epic conundrum: "Them" and "Africa." Black Americans *were* Americans. It was their country, too, just as it was the country of all the immigrants who had come and laid a stake in it.

Even into the 1970s, the average white American still led a life—despite the racial-enlightening books and essays and documentaries—largely ignorant of Black culture. "Us ole Alabama boys don't care about niggers eating in hotels and cafes and such," an Alabama man by the name of Cecil told *Newsweek* magazine in 1970. "But they aren't setting down to dinner in our homes yet." Sports, of course, was an exception. Sports had long integrated, but sports happened to be about immediate victories. After the games ended, many Black athletes went home to their neighborhoods, many of which were still segregated. When it was publicly revealed that Gale Sayers and Brian Piccolo roomed together on the road in the late 1960s as Chicago Bears football players, Piccolo received a lot of racist hate mail. As for the movies produced by Hollywood, they lacked imagination and hadn't gone nearly deep enough regarding Black and white America. With each passing year, *Guess Who's Coming to Dinner*—no matter how well intentioned a film—seemed more and more dated.

Throughout the early 1970s, Alex Haley was at work putting the finishing touches on the manuscript he had been working on for years. It had something to do with a family, and Africa, and Black America, and, by extension, the whole of America. The searching out and threading together of the story—of slave ships and bloodshed and horrors—happened to be quite personal for Haley. The family at the center of his epic saga was his. Excerpts from the in-progress book had started showing up in magazines.

———

A good many Blacks of Ithaca, New York, in the 1920s worked as domestic servants in the fraternity houses near Cornell University. When those Black citizens sought news about other Blacks, they often turned to *The Monitor,* a local Black newspaper. Inside its pages were mentions of weddings and births and social goings-on throughout the Black community. Simon Haley and Bertha Palmer, two Ithaca Blacks, stood out in the community. He was in graduate school at Cornell, studying agriculture; she was studying music at the Ithaca Conservatory of Music. They met, fell in love, and married. In 1929, Simon Haley began teaching agriculture, moving from Black college to Black college in the South. The Haleys had three sons, Alex, Julius, and George. Growing up, the boys would spend their summer vacations with grandparents in Henning, Tennessee, fifty miles from Memphis, with a population of fewer than six hundred citizens. The Haley boys greatly enjoyed the rural landscape, where they could roam and fish. Their maternal grandmother, Cynthia Palmer, who had been born a slave, captivated them with stories of her history: stories about men who owned other men, who owned whole families; stories about escape attempts from slave plantations. They listened to sweet stories that told of weddings, slave weddings, in which a man and a woman would jump over a broom, an act cementing their union. They listened to stories about President Lincoln and the Emancipation Proclamation, and how that law meant freedom and jubilation. The boys' teachers never talked of such stories, of the most painful part of American history. A large part of their history had been denied them—until now. "Grandparents," Alex Haley would come to say, "will tell their grandchildren things they won't tell their own children."

Alex Haley, a precocious sort, graduated from high school at the age of fifteen and enrolled at Alcorn State University in 1936. After a year, he transferred to Elizabeth City State Teachers College in North Carolina. But college life proved difficult, and Haley left the school after two years. For a while, he seemed aimless and adrift. His father worried about him, and finally suggested Alex join the United States Coast Guard. The elder Haley knew that young men had long gone to sea in order to find themselves. The Coast Guard had been—albeit sparingly—allowing Blacks to join since before the Civil War. Those Blacks worked on ships as mates, the lowest of the menial duties. In 1939, Alex signed up for a three-year hitch. His job options hadn't changed all that much from what was offered Black enlistees during the Civil War era. His rank after joining was "mess attendant third class." Haley was assigned duty aboard the *Mendota,* a 250-foot cutter based out of Norfolk, Virginia. Coast Guard recruits mostly learned aboard ship, mentored by veterans.

Coast guardsmen, so often out on the water, did not have constant access to phone lines, so they tended to write a lot of letters. The guardsmen aboard the *Mendota* came to realize that Mess Attendant Third Class Alex Haley had a gift with language; he knew how to turn a phrase. This at first made his shipmates chuckle, then it made them envious, and with their envy they began pleading with him to dictate letters for them. Haley became a willing, smiling ghost writer. Just as he had done at his grandmother's knee back in Tennessee, he was also listening to some of the older guardsmen tell stories about hurricanes and squalls and death-defying voyages. He put some of their stories down on paper. There was a magazine, *Coast Guard Magazine,* and it was suggested to Haley that he might submit some of those stories. The idea excited him, so he started shaping his notes into narratives. Haley was told he had talent. He was transferred to another cutter, the *Pamlico,* based in North Carolina, in early 1940. Haley was there when World War II started. By May 1943, he was aboard the USS *Murzim* in the Pacific Theater. The idea of writing for publication was truly taking hold now. He wrote an article, "In the Pacific," that was published in the February 1944 issue of *Coast Guard Magazine*. He wasn't Hemingway, but it was war, and he was writing, and his stuff was getting published and drawing compliments from officers. Haley came up with an idea to start a newspaper aboard ship, called *Seafarer.* He wrote an editorial about how sad it was that many of the men never received letters—from anyone. This editorial tugged at the emotions. Newspapers on land picked it up and reprinted it. Soon enough, letters started pouring in to the crew—from cousins, sisters, ex-girlfriends, even strangers. It all had a touch of Frank Capra, the sentimental filmmaker. Haley had burnished his bona fides as a writer. After the war, in 1949, Haley was promoted to journalist, first class. Then he was named "chief journalist of the Coast Guard," the first such classification. He was transferred to land, to a New York City Coast Guard office. From a syndicated article that appeared in various newspapers at the time:

> You can call him "chief" now—the amiable, industrious and ever helpful Alex Haley, the man behind the public information phone at New York City's Coast Guard Headquarters. . . . When there's a ship in distress along the Atlantic coast, a plane down at sea, a fishing party marooned or on any one of a hundred other mishaps, Haley's the guy who feed[s] the newspapers and wire services the latest information.

The Negro press had a swell time writing about Chief Journalist Alex Haley. Haley finally left the Coast Guard in 1959, having put in twenty years. There was a pension, so he had a cushion, enabling him to write full-time. He had an overwhelming drive to retell some of the stories his grandmother had told him—stories about Africa and slaves and those ships landing in America.

Settled in New York City, Haley began getting freelance assignments. The editors at *Reader's Digest* liked his work. The country was becoming more aware of Elijah Muhammad, leader of the Nation of Islam. Muhammad used his reputation to vouch for a lot of prisoners, guaranteeing to parole boards that they'd have job opportunities when released. One such prisoner was Malcolm X—stoic, sharp of wit and mind—who began rising in the Muslim Brotherhood. Haley got an assignment to write about the Muslims. His piece, "Mr. Muhammad Speaks," appeared in the March 1960 issue of *Reader's Digest* and drew both interest and praise.

Haley later wrote a longer piece "Black Merchants of Hate"—co-authored with Alfred Balk—for the January 26, 1963, issue of *The Saturday Evening Post*. Muslims had begun playing a more prominent role in the struggle for Blacks to gain equal rights. Theirs was not a turn-the-other-cheek philosophy; it was self-segregation, and a vow to meet police brutality with confrontation.

Haley got an interesting assignment to interview the jazz trumpeter Miles Davis for *Playboy* magazine. The editors there liked the piece so much they began the "*Playboy* Interview," a monthly feature. Haley became the go-to interviewer, and he went on to interview such figures as Sammy Davis, Jr.; Quincy Jones; Martin Luther King, Jr.; the Nazi leader George Lincoln Rockwell; and Malcolm X. The nude pictures aside, a lot of enlightened folk read the "*Playboy* Interviews." The Malcolm X interview was such an eye-opening piece for both Black and white America that the two men soon embarked on a collaboration for Malcolm's autobiography. They spent hours and hours together, Malcolm speaking into a cassette recorder, Haley asking hundreds of questions. On February 21, 1965, Malcolm X was delivering a speech at the Audubon Ballroom in Harlem. Shots rang out. His assassination—three Muslims were arrested—further deepened the pangs of Black America. Doubleday was supposed to publish the Malcolm X autobiography, but canceled it after his death. The book was picked up by Grove Press and published in 1965, with both Malcolm X and Haley appearing as authors. The reviews were powerful: Truman Nelson, critic for *The Nation,* praised it for "its dead-level honesty, its passion, its exalted purpose, even its manifold unsolved ambiguities will make it stand as a monument to the most painful of truths." Writing in *The New York Times,* Eliot Fremont-Smith proclaimed it a "brilliant, painful, important book. . . . As a document for our time, its insights may be crucial; its relevance cannot be doubted." In death, Malcolm X rose as a multidimensional figure. And Alex Haley had established himself as an important literary figure.

There was enough money coming in for Haley to focus on the family chronicle he was working on. To construct any family history is an arduous task, but it was especially so for Blacks, because official documents about their past were not often kept by towns or cities. And—depending on plantation record keepers—Blacks were often not accounted for in census records. Haley found clues in libraries in Southern archives, and in Britain. In Gambia, West Africa, he heard the name Kunta Kinte, whom he identified as one of his main ancestors. He located records of slave auctions. His notes and folders stacked up—four years turned into eight, eight turned into twelve. His publisher, Doubleday, finally published Haley's book, *Roots: The Saga of an American Family,* in the fall of 1976. The praise it received seemed endless. Many other books about slavery had been written, but most were by white scholars. Here was a book written by a Black man, and one who could trace his ancestry to the particular slaves in the book. It seemed a feat of personal and heroic detective work. The book seemed to catch America—all of America—completely off guard. Haley had done something remarkable: He put slavery on America's front porch. He made it essential to discuss. It had forever torn at the heart and soul of the Black race. And too many whites, when they even deemed to discuss slavery, so often ran behind the ridiculous argument of states' rights and regional economics, ignoring the horrid brutalities. Jervis Anderson, writing in *The New Yorker,* hit upon the dissonance so many whites had with slavery:

> The condition of uprootedness, the pain of being an outsider in a strange culture and a strange land, has fascinated many American intellectuals for a long time—as well it should, in a nation made up so largely of the uprooted. In articles and books, in classrooms and drawing rooms, they have dwelt upon the tragic nature of that condition. But they seem to have been interested in the subject chiefly as it has affected immigrants; seldom have they been absorbed by the experiences of those who were hauled off and dumped upon this ground to serve as slaves.

James Baldwin weighed in, in a review for *The New York Times* on September 26, 1976. Baldwin much admired the book, but, as always with him, the article was more than just a review: "'Roots,'" he wrote, "is a study of continuities, of consequences, of how a people perpetuate themselves, how each generation helps to doom, or helps to liberate, the coming one. . . . It suggests, with great power, how each of us, however unconsciously, can't but be the vehicle of the history which has produced us. Well, we can perish in this vehicle, children, or we can move on up the road."

Hollywood was well aware of Haley's book. It held such high drama; it was a chronicle of high originality; it was, without question, cinematic. The top movie executives had long ignored slavery and deeply probing looks at race in America. This wasn't *A Raisin in the Sun,* which revolved around a contemporary Black family's inner turmoil. This was a Black family that had been kidnapped, enslaved, and ripped apart; this was America's original sin. Columbia Pictures stepped up to purchase the rights. Their burst of excitement told them it would make a grand movie. Perhaps it would be reminiscent of the lavish attention paid to Mario Puzo's *The Godfather,* another sweeping saga (though one, of course, that involved white Italians). But Columbia dithered, and Haley couldn't get clear-cut answers about plans for filming. He felt he was getting the runaround, that his book might get caught in so-called development hell—circulating among timid executives, only to be forgotten eventually. Haley bought back the rights to his book.

Blaxploitation aside, part of the mindset of mainstream movie execs in the 1970s remained tethered to the Hays Code, that guidepost implemented in the 1930s against film obscenity, but also against racially charged screen portrayals. Of all the films released in 1976—excluding the blaxploitation genre—only two featured blacks in substantial roles: *Silver Streak* had Richard Pryor in a costarring comedic role, and *Sparkle* featured three unknown Black actresses in a story about the travails of a singing group. For the Black community, the year when *Roots* was published had, once again, shown very little representation on the big screen. When turning the dial on television screens, Blacks saw slightly better representation, spotting Black actors here and there, although mostly in sitcoms like *The Jeffersons* and *Sanford and Son.*

———

David Wolper, who had made his name in TV documentaries, persuaded Alex Haley to let him buy the rights to *Roots.* Wolper envisioned a miniseries—a relatively new format, one that offered the potential for more depth and scope than a two-hour feature film—and convinced ABC honcho Fred Silverman to make it. Wolper's excitement quickly gave way to worry. The American television audience was 90 percent white. There were few major white characters in Haley's book. Wolper felt the only way he could mount a successful production, ratings-wise, was to cast some white TV stars in the miniseries. "If people perceive Roots to be a black history show," he said at the time, "nobody is going to watch it. If they say, 'Let me see, there are no names in it, a lot of black actors and there are no whites' . . . it looks like it's going to be a black journal—it's all going to be blacks telling about their history."

Television did not have much experience at all at the time in dealing with issues of race. In 1970, NBC aired *My Sweet Charlie,* an adaptation of a 1966 David Westheimer novel about a Black attorney, Charlie Roberts, who is accused of a murder in Texas. Charlie is forced to flee and comes to hide out in an abandoned house. A young white woman, Marlene, is inside the home, having run away because of the scorn heaped upon her when she became pregnant. The Black intruder shocks Marlene; her bigotry quickly becomes apparent. But as Charlie explains his civil-rights work to Marlene, she begins to soften and, for the first time in her life, begins to understand some of what it means to be Black and fight for justice. Marlene comes to respect and admire Charlie. Westheimer's novel was mounted first on Broadway, opening in 1966, and starring Louis Gossett, Jr., and Bonnie Bedelia. It closed less than a month after opening. The novel was seen as interesting, if risky, material for television, and landed at NBC. Network executives chose Patty Duke, a familiar name to television viewers, to play Marlene. Al Freeman, Jr., a highly respected stage and sometimes film actor, was chosen to play Charlie. During filming in Texas, white hooligans let it be known they did not appreciate the subject matter and threatened the production. The atmosphere became so charged and frightening that Texas governor John Connolly had to intervene. When the movie aired, it received fine reviews and multiple Emmy nominations, with Duke winning for her performance. Quite a bit of hate mail was sent to the network. Even a budding nonsexual friendship between a pregnant white woman and a Black man in a 1970 telecast was seen as groundbreaking.

David Wolper cast a bevy of Black actors for *Roots,* many of whom had become frustrated with their lack of work on the big screen. Among them: Louis Gossett, Jr., Ben Vereen, Maya Angelou, John Amos, Olivia Cole, Georg Stanford Brown, Leslie Uggams, Cicely Tyson, and Lynne Moody. "It was like *A Raisin in the Sun,*" recalls Gossett. "Wolper wanted the best Black actors in the [*Roots*] production." Wolper also cast Lillian Randolph as a slave. Her career had started in all-Black movies decades earlier. She had played a lot of maids. (Her sister, Amanda, who died in 1967, had also been an actress. She had appeared in several Oscar Micheaux films.) Wolper was desperate to find a young Black actor who could handle the role of Kunta Kinte, so pivotal in the book. After an intensive search, he cast nineteen-year-old LeVar Burton, a young Californian studying drama at

USC. Wolper, in hopes of luring a hoped-for white viewership, went about casting white veterans of weekly television shows: Chuck Connors, Vic Morrow, Robert Reed, Lorne Greene, Sandy Duncan, Ed Asner, Lynda Day George, Lloyd Bridges, and Ralph Waite. Wolper had to swallow the network's decision not to film in Africa, which would have lent the production verisimilitude but would have been extremely costly. Instead, the production filmed in California and South Carolina. William Blinn, who had written the teleplay for *Brian's Song*, served as script supervisor. Gilbert Moses was hired as one of several directors—and the only Black one—to work on the production. Moses was one of the cofounders of the Free Southern Theater, a group of Black thespians who went throughout the South during the height of the civil-rights movement putting on plays. It was brave work. Black farmers—most of them the descendants of slaves—came to see their performances in small country towns. Southern sheriffs often expressed their displeasure, and cast members were arrested for little or no reason. Moses himself eventually left the Free Southern Theatre, unnerved by the death threats he received.

ABC executives began fretting about scheduling after the production wrapped. They discussed airing it in February 1977, the all-important sweeps month, when can't-miss viewing equals robust advertising revenue. But that idea was nixed: a drop-off in viewers would be financially damaging. There was concern that Southern stations might not air the series and would preempt it with other programming! It was finally decided to air the first episode of *Roots* on January 23.

There were lavish promos on the network's shows; there were radio spots, and lots of print coverage about the coming telecast.

On January 23, 1977, from neighborhood to neighborhood, city to city, state to state, front doors were closed in Black homes and apartments, as whole families gathered around their TV sets. Children were hushed. And then it happened: a whole family unspooled, their journey beginning in 1750 in Africa, followed by the wrenching kidnapping to America—Kizzy and Fiddler, Kunta Kinte and Chicken George and Tom, Irene and Fanta, Omoro and Nyo. One night turned into two. Three became four. Four became eight. The ritual remained constant, Black families shoulder to shoulder, transfixed. This was wrenching viewing, a graphic depiction of how Blacks had been forced to fight for freedom and dignity within the borders of their own country. As the week went on, Blacks planned discussion groups to take place in the aftermath of the telecast. Local television crews rushed reporters into Black neighborhoods to do reports on the *Roots* phenomenon. Grown Black men admitted crying at scenes of slave auctioneering. Black heads of households called their older relatives, asking if they were okay, wondering if the emotion of watching *Roots* was too overwhelming.

White America also watched. The emotions in their households might not have been as gripping, but they were watching, and learning, and starting to arrive at a different outlook about Blackness and Black people. "They couldn't realize what they had done," Gossett says about whites who watched *Roots* unfold and reveal the scars of slavery. "The sun now shone on the entire situation. Whites had buffered their babies from this." After the wave of attention from the first night spread and cascaded, America seemed to shut down. Not for a natural disaster, but for a cultural awakening. "By the eighth and final night of 'Roots,' movie theatres in many cities didn't even try to compete," *The Baltimore Sun* reported. "They simply closed their doors." In 1977, the majority of critics (more than 95 percent) in American mainstream publications—reviewing for either film, television, or stage—were white. They had never been forced to digest—night after night—such a sweeping look at Black life. "Vistas of jungleland can't camouflage the intrinsic story of the struggles of the Blacks to preserve their own freedom and dignity," the *Variety* critic wrote. "It's a remarkable presentation." The New York *Daily News* called it an "absorbing, beautifully acted epic drama." *Time* magazine had some criticism, allowing that slavery was "a crime so monstrous that, like the Holocaust, it is beyond anyone's ability to re-create in intelligent dramatic terms." James Michener, a widely read novelist, was engaged by *The New York Times* to write about *Roots* shortly after its airing. " 'Roots' is best comprehended through two comparisons," he wrote. "It is this century's 'Uncle Tom's Cabin,' a long-overdue romanticization of a pressing problem. It is the black man's answer to 'Gone With the Wind,' which in its later chapters was sharply racist." Writing in *The Washington Post,* Sander Vanocur, a respected TV journalist, opined that what made *Roots* "so compellingly unique is that television is finally dealing with the institution of slavery and its effect on succeeding generations of one family in a dramatic form. That effort has been almost absent from our television screens."

*Roots* quickly became the most watched TV miniseries of all time. A year earlier, NBC had telecast *Gone with the Wind* in two parts. At the time, this established a Nielsen viewing record; *Roots* shattered that record. It was estimated that at least 85 percent of the people with television sets across the country, about 130 million Americans, watched some portion of the telecast. ABC's decision to run it on consecutive nights paid off royally; another popular miniseries, *Rich Man, Poor Man,* was broadcast the year before in weekly installments. But the *Roots* audience expanded night after night. Additionally, Haley's book was still in hardcover at the time of the telecast, something quite rare, and it became a number-one bestseller.

There were many Emmy Awards for *Roots.* Many progressive white mayors realized it was a good time to talk about slavery and the ongoing pain it had caused the nation. In many communities, interracial groups planned get-togethers to talk about the series. Interest in genealogical searches erupted across the country. The series also clearly illustrated just how anemic the film industry had been in taking advantage of Black stories. Now there was a sudden appreciation of the Black actors and actresses who had appeared in *Roots.* "American actors, whose brilliance is too often overlooked, prove to be equal to their BBC counterparts in this magnificent vehicle," *The Hollywood Reporter* wrote of the cast. The movie-theatre owners of America were so stunned and impressed by the success of *Roots* that they invited Louis Gossett, Jr., and LeVar Burton to their convention in Las Vegas. "They gave us an award," Gossett says, chuckling at the memory, "because we had kept people out of theatres for the week."

Many of the actors and actresses in *Roots* were certain they'd be receiving film offers. Absent that, they'd settle for more television work. "We were so fabulous I thought we would have jobs up the wazoo," Leslie Uggams said years later. "And there were no jobs. I didn't get another job until two years later. . . . We were very disappointed, because we had all these accolades; it was like we did our quota, and now that's it for the rest of time." Lynne Moody watched her white actress friends go on audition after audition, and has allowed that she fell into a "deep depression" when her career remained stalled.

Louis Gossett, Jr., was one of the few *Roots* actors who benefited in a substantial way from the show's success. The role of Fiddler—a slave and mentor to Kunta Kinte—was a tricky one. Gossett imbued it with a canniness and dexterity rarely seen. "I put my soul into the role of 'Fiddler,' " he says. He got more TV roles. A year after *Roots,* Gossett played the lead role of a doctor in *The Lazarus Syndrome,* a short-lived TV series. It was a rare occasion when a Black man played the lead. After that, he had a slew of TV movie-of-the-week appearances and the occasional big-screen role.

Haley's book remained on *The New York Times* best seller list for weeks. He won a "special citation of merit" from the National Book Award, and a special Pulitzer Prize. He became a multimillionaire. No other Black writer in history had ever achieved such fame in such a condensed period of time. And therein lay some of the problems that began to haunt him. Upon the book's publication, Haley announced that *Roots* was a combination of fact and fiction, calling it "faction." Critics raised their eyebrows. A great deal of research had obviously gone into the book; the work had taken up twelve long years of his life. But two writers swore they saw similarities to their own work. Margaret Walker sued Haley, alleging that he had plagiarized passages from her novel *Jubilee*. The case was dismissed. Harold Courlander claimed Haley had stolen from his book *The African*. That case went to trial in Manhattan. There were three passages from the Courlander book that Haley admitted made their way into his book. He said he had used student researchers. "Somewhere, somebody gave me something that came from 'The African,'" Haley admitted in court. "That's the best, honest explanation I can give." It was later reported that Haley had to fork over $650,000 to Courlander.

Haley was clearly embarrassed by both legal events. But they could not bury the singularity of his achievement. He had forced Americans—the world even—to look anew at slavery and what it had done to the country. Following Haley's death in 1992, the *Chicago Tribune* journalist Clarence Page wrote movingly of Haley, saluting him and concluding that he had possibly gotten "truths" and "facts" mixed up while writing *Roots*. But in Page's estimation, the truth of Haley's search—a family, slavery, American avoidance of the topic—had won the credit it deserved.

Alex Haley also forced large questions throughout Hollywood: Why had Blacks, for so long, been absent from the big screen? And why, for the most part, were they still absent? "Thank God for television," Louis Gossett, Jr., said. "They came to the plate earlier than motion pictures."

# Aiming a Camera in Brooklyn

A NY BLACK MAN who could get work in the 1950s and 1960s as a professional musician had something of an inroad to the American dream. It wasn't at all guaranteed, since segregation and other social ills lay hard across the land. But nightclubs were in all the major cities, and work was available if you were talented enough and could haul yourself and your instrument to some of those musical hotspots. The best venues were in Atlanta, L.A., Chicago, and New York City. Bill Lee, who played bass guitar, first had to get out of Snow Hill, Alabama, smack dab in the Bible Belt. Young Bill was far more fortunate than most Blacks in Snow Hill. He hailed from a family of educators with quite an impressive pedigree. His grandfather William Edwards had been an acquaintance of Booker T. Washington. In 1893, Edwards founded the local Snow Hill Normal and Industrial Institute, having convinced the owner of the R. O. Simpson plantation to grant him land for the school. Onetime slaves thought it was something of a miracle to watch their children troop off to the private institute. Bill Lee's father, Arnold, became bandmaster at Bethune-Cookman College in Daytona Beach, Florida, founded in 1904 by Mary McLeod Bethune. Its original name: the Daytona Literary and Industrial Training School for Negro Girls. Bill Lee's mother, Alberta, was gifted as well: she had trained as a concert pianist. Black audiences around Alabama were in awe of her playing.

Bill Lee got his B.A. degree from Morehouse College in 1951. Martin Luther King, Jr., was on campus at the same time, so they would have crossed paths. Bill also crossed paths with Jacquelyn Shelton, a young coed from nearby Spelman College, and he was smitten. After college—and marriage to Jacquelyn, now a schoolteacher—Lee bounced around a bit. He and his wife went to Chicago. Jazz was Bill Lee's métier, and Chicago had plenty of jazz clubs and patrons. He got a job at the Gate of Horn, a hip jazz-folk club situated in the basement of the Rice Hotel. Odetta and Oscar Brown and Josh White were just a few of the musicians who were making a name for themselves there. Lee, after a while, became the house bassist. Now and then, he'd hit the road with Odetta (born Odetta Holmes). On the road, Odetta sang her protest songs and Bill Lee strummed his bass guitar. A lot of Chicago musicians were talking about Manhattan, and its vibrant jazz scene. Lee himself kept thinking of New York, even when he and his wife found themselves back in Atlanta for a while. It was in Atlanta that Jacquelyn Lee gave birth to her first child, a boy, on March 20, 1957. They named him Sheldon Jackson Lee.

By 1959, the Lees had relocated to Brooklyn. (Five more children eventually followed Sheldon's birth.) Bill found plenty of work in clubs as well as on recordings with the likes of Harry Belafonte, Arlo Guthrie, Bob Dylan, and Aretha Franklin. Jacquelyn Lee began teaching school again. Her firstborn, Sheldon, gave her fits as he was growing up. Smaller than many other neighborhood kids, he acquired an obstinate streak, sometimes refusing to follow his parents' directions. His disposition was both ornery and comedic. It was as if he was always spiking instructions, directions, like one might spike a ball, just for the hell of it. His mother took to calling him Spike. "I was the firstborn, and my mother put a lot of pressure on me," he would recall. She also began taking him to movies: *A Hard Day's Night* and *Help!* and Sean Connery as James Bond. By the age of eight, he was starting to become visually in awe of movies. Jacquelyn also took him to see plays, and his father introduced him to jazz.

The Lees purchased a brownstone in the Fort Greene neighborhood of Brooklyn. Brooklyn in the sixties teemed. Protesters gathered in the big leafy green parks. Dylan's rich voice and canny lyrics floated from eight-track cassettes. Blacks were demanding fairer treatment by those in power. There seemed to be an ongoing teacher-student crisis in the New York City schools. Crime was up; minorities felt the police were too aggressive and unfair to them. Blacks would look anywhere for flashes of good news. So it came as a kind of celebratory event in 1965 when Shirley Chisholm, newly elected to the New York State Assembly in 1965, was able to get unemployment benefits for maids. There were an awful lot of Negro women rising in the morning and leaving Brooklyn to go into Manhattan, where they worked as housekeepers for well-to-do families.

At John Dewey High School in Coney Island, Spike Lee buzzed about like a summer insect. He walked in double-time through the hallways; he talked out of turn in class; his laughter could be heard at inopportune times; he was always thinking of the next Knicks basketball game he could get to. Come spring, he daydreamed about the Mets. Teachers scolded him about his lack of concentration. He became drawn to the arts. His favorite book was *The Autobiography of Malcolm X,* which he had read back in junior high. He could rhapsodize about jazz with anyone, because he had hung out with his dad at some of the coolest jazz spots in Manhattan. His schoolmates marveled at his energy, how wise he was about navigating through the tunnels of the New York subway system. But Jacquelyn Lee worried about her son. "Oh God," she wrote in a letter to her mother, "I hope Spike will amount to something, he is so immature. . . ."

There was little doubt where Spike Lee would be going to college. His father had gone to Morehouse; his father's father had gone there. The Lees were comforted by the fact that they still had relatives in Atlanta. Zimmie Shelton, Spike's maternal grandmother—and a 1929 Spelman graduate—lived a mere four blocks from the Morehouse campus. She assured her daughter she'd keep an eye on her grandson. It was thanks to Zimmie Shelton's foresight that Spike Lee had few financial worries: she had squirreled away her Social Security checks over the years to ensure her grandchildren's college educations.

The Atlanta that Spike Lee arrived into in 1975 was quite different from the one he had been born into eighteen years earlier. The city was forging a new identity as a liberalized Southern metropolis; in 1973, Maynard Jackson, also a Morehouse man, had been elected the first Black mayor of Atlanta—of any major Southern city—by building a coalition of moderate whites and get-out-the-vote Blacks.

Morehouse had a small campus, fewer than thirteen hundred students. Spike made friends his first year because he was sociable. Still, there were those who taunted him, calling him Half-Pint. He did not get along with his roommate that freshman year. He was paired with an upperclassman, which was unusual. "We got in an argument and he hit me, broke my glasses," Lee recalled. "[He] made my freshman year miserable." But his combustible introduction to college life was softened by Zimmie's presence. He'd stroll over to her house on weekends with his college friends in tow. She prepared big dinners for them all. Her loving ways filled him with confidence. He confided to her that he was still unsure of what field of study to pursue.

When he was home in Brooklyn on a holiday visit in 1976, a family member gifted him with a Super 8 camera. They heard he'd been hanging with Morehouse students who were interested in film; he'd already written a couple of screenplays. Back home again the following year—the summer of 1977—Lee roamed the city. There was a heat wave, and a July blackout that saw a wave of looting and mayhem. To add a film-noir–like aspect to it all, a crazed killer was on the loose. That August, the New York police arrested the man who had been terrorizing the city for a year. David Berkowitz, known as "Son of Sam" by the tabloids, was implicated in six murders; seven victims of his random shootings survived. Berkowitz proclaimed that a barking dog had been issuing orders for him to kill. Through it all, Spike aimed his camera everywhere. He began to feel like he had a calling in life.

When he returned to campus in the fall of 1977, Spike Lee decided he wanted to major in mass communication, which incorporated film and TV production. Morehouse, however, didn't even have a film program. Those few students interested in film could take courses across the street at Clark College. Herb Eichelberger, a Clark film professor, began mentoring Lee. "Film allowed him to be larger, externally, than he was in the everyday walk of life," Eichelberger felt. "He wasn't the most die-hard person to pick up a camera. But he always loved the editing process, and I used to have to kick him out of the editing booth. I told him, though, that a good editor would be a good director." Eichelberger found it difficult to convey to Lee and other film students how hard a road they'd have to navigate in the white-dominated world of filmmaking. He told them about Oscar Micheaux, Melvin Van Peebles, and Gordon Parks, and lamented that "such people were not really recognized." But Lee was determined. He directed a 1978 Homecoming production, held in Morehouse's Martin Luther King Jr. International Chapel. The event caused a stir on campus. Previously held in the school's gym, the student coronation turned into something of a fashion show, and a risqué one at that. Lee, with a director's confidence, announced a dress code: "We cannot have Black women in a chapel with their breasts and booties hanging out." The boyfriends of some of the girls didn't like his tone or ultimatum. They went looking for Half-Pint, the little filmmaker with the loud mouth and big Afro and eyeglasses who was always carrying that damn movie camera around. Monty Ross, a campus friend of Lee's, heard about the brewing trouble and came to his pal's aid, getting there just in time. "He ran all the way . . . to stop me getting my ass whipped," Lee remembered. Lee also concluded—as others did—that the Homecoming event was a wonderful success.

With a few student films to his credit, and his senior year nearing an end, Lee began to plot his future. His mother—who had passed away while he was in college—was no longer around to encourage him, and her absence was painful.

It was a hallowed and long tradition that, without connections or outright nepotism, the way to get work inside a big Hollywood film studio was to enter through its mailroom and work one's way up. But Lee figured there simply was "no way . . . a young black filmmaker could work his way up from the mailroom." He cast an eye toward graduate-school film programs. Both the USC and UCLA programs intrigued him, but the more he inquired, the more off-putting they seemed: their faculties decided which students got to make a film as part of their study. Since he had already made student films, Lee felt the possibility of *not* being allowed to make a film would be a step backward. He looked at New York University's graduate film program: "At NYU," he found out, "everybody got to make a movie." He was sold, applied, and was accepted. Once again, his grandmother generously agreed to take care of a large part of his tuition.

When Lee entered NYU's grad school, he was one of only two Black students in the film program; Ernest Dickerson, a Howard University graduate, was the other. The two quickly formed a bond. All students were required early on to start planning their first-year film. In order to stretch the students creatively, the requirement was that it be a silent film. The faculty, by way of pointing out technical wizardry in film, insisted the students watch D. W. Griffith's *Birth of a Nation*. The professors talked about Griffith's camera angles and split-screen shots. But Lee and Dickerson had quite a different reaction to the film from most of the white students. While they analyzed the film's technique, the two Black students could not ignore the movie's blatant racism. Lee decided his first student film was going to be a takeoff on Oscar Micheaux's initial film idea, which had been a response to Griffith's racist portrayals. Lee's film was about a Black filmmaker answering Griffith's cinematic diatribe. He went at the assignment with fervor. His sense of macabre wit is evident early in the film, when a Klansman—in full Klan regalia and carrying a briefcase—arrives to meet up with the Black screenwriter. There are overlays of Griffith's work throughout Lee's film. When they saw it, many of the faculty members were puzzled, and thought it nothing but a mockery of their admiration of Griffith's genius. Roberta Hodes, who was on the NYU film faculty when

Lee was at the school, recalled: "I don't think he was very much liked." Eleanor Hamerow was then head of NYU's film department. In her mind, Spike Lee was an overly ambitious student: "He was trying to solve a problem overnight—the social problem with the Blacks and the whites. . . . He was going to teach [D. W. Griffith] a lesson." Some faculty members wanted Lee tossed from the program, but they had already signed him up to serve as a teaching assistant for the following year: "So they wanted to kick me out," Lee concluded, "but they couldn't."

While they were at NYU, Lee and Dickerson watched and studied a lot of films by Martin Scorsese, Alfred Hitchcock, and John Cassavetes. They also kept their ears to the ground in anticipation of any favorable news about Black participation and improvement in the movie industry. Like any young Black cinéastes at the time, Lee and Dickerson were excited about an announcement from Columbia Pictures that the studio was entering into an arrangement with the comedian Richard Pryor to produce four films. The news helped encourage their own dreams.

Columbia was allotting the blazingly talented Pryor forty million dollars and giving him carte blanche over hiring and the selection of scripts. This was a tribute to Pryor's rising box-office clout, but it was still a rather curious investment given the actor's notable lack of discipline in his life. He had endured a wild past few years. In the early-evening hours of June 9, 1980, Pryor hosted a party at his home in Northridge, California. He was smoking crack cocaine, a powerful solution of burnt cocaine that causes dangerous flights of delirium. For some bizarre reason—his guests never figured out why, beyond the intake of the drugs—Pryor poured a bottle of rum over himself, then lit a match. The fire burst into flames on his clothing, sending Pryor bolting past startled guests, howling, to hurl himself through a window and out into the streets. When the guests ran to the door and looked outside onto Parthenia Street, Pryor was lit in flames. Two police officers grabbed him and tried to calm him, letting him know an ambulance was on the way. He was burned over 50 percent of his body and spent six weeks in a hospital burn unit. He would later blame his self-immolation on paranoia—and the guilt of having made it out of being raised in a whorehouse as a kid while so many others remained impoverished.

Nevertheless, Pryor seemed energized by the 1983 film deal, announcing it would bring more Blacks into the industry, behind as well as in front of the camera. Columbia Pictures, hoping his recovery had calmed him down, went ahead and signed the deal. Pryor took on the football legend and movie star Jim Brown to be the president of Indigo Productions. That, as well, was a curious choice: Brown lacked any significant movie-producing experience. Columbia thought so, too, because they soon fired Brown and other Indigo executives, citing an inability to do what they were hired to do: produce movies. The NAACP, which had expressed joy at the Pryor-Columbia deal, now was upset. "It's a slap in the face because we were working very hard with Jim Brown," said Willis Edwards Brown, president of the Hollywood–Beverly Hills branch of the NAACP. "Richard Pryor just couldn't fire Jim Brown by himself. I think they're using Pryor as a scapegoat, making everybody think he did this when in fact it was . . . Columbia making the move."

One of Pryor's more intriguing film ventures was an effort to acquire rights to *Cane River,* a Louisiana-set film, made in 1982, which, uniquely, had been financed by a well-to-do Southern Black family and featured an all-Black cast and crew. The story told the saga of a plantation and one of its previous owners who had been Black (she'd married a Frenchman)—and thus became part of a family that owned slaves. It also dealt with the issue of miscegenation in the Black Creole community. The movie was directed by Horace Jenkins, a young Black filmmaker who had worked on television programs such as *Sesame Street* and the news program *Black Journal.* In 1978, Jenkins—who had gone overseas to launch his film career; he had served as a script consultant on *Shaft in Africa*—won the Oscar Micheaux Award for his documentary *Sudan Pyramids: A Zandi's Dream.* He died when he was forty-two in December 1982 in New York City, of a heart attack, and *Cane River* was not released nationally. When Pryor saw the film, he thought it was astonishing and made an offer to distribute it. But the negotiations fell apart. And not long after Jenkins's death, the film itself disappeared; many wondered if the prints had been destroyed. But in 2018 prints of *Cane River* were located in the DuArt film-developing company in New York City. Film preservationists—aided by Sandra Schulberg's IndieCollect, the Academy of Motion Picture Arts & Sciences, and, among others, the Amistad Research Center at Tulane University—quickly began restoring the film. Oscilloscope acquired distribution rights, and in 2019 and 2020 there were screenings around the country. The reviews were laudatory. "It's a drama," Richard Brody would write in *The New Yorker,* "of remaking the present by reclaiming the past—not by bypassing or dismissing it but by revealing its silent presence and bringing it to the fore, as if with artistic X-rays, and by reimagining a personal past in the light of political and social history. In its modest, forthright warmth, 'Cane River' is a work of visionary artistry and progressive imagination.'"

Richard Pryor had seen what others would come to see in *Cane River*. But his Indigo Productions had a short life; its most popular film was his 1986 starring vehicle, *Jo Jo Dancer, Your Life Is Calling*.

At NYU in the early 1980s, Spike Lee's own life kept calling.

———

Spike Lee's master's-thesis film at NYU was about a barbershop and its owner's inability to avoid being drawn into the gambling racket. Lee's classmate Ernest Dickerson was the cinematographer. Zimmie Shelton, his grandmother, financed it. The film, *Joe's Bed-Stuy Barbershop: We Cut Heads,* is an urban parable, a forty-five-minute slice of Black life. In 1973, the American Academy of Motion Pictures inaugurated student-film awards as part of the Oscar prizes. *Joe's Bed-Stuy Barbershop* was entered for the 1983 competition. The Academy gave five awards that year, and Lee was one of the prizewinners, receiving a Merit Award. The award would have been a boon for any young filmmaker; for a young Black filmmaker, it was nirvana. PBS picked the film up. Lee got invited to the Rotterdam film festival and took off for Europe. The film also earned a slot in the Lincoln Center New Directors/New Film series.

Lee was bold enough to form his own production company. He pulled from Civil War history to name it 40 Acres and a Mule Filmworks. The majority of American Blacks had a vivid link to the American South, and Lee knew it. The "40 Acres and a Mule" reference had long morphed into another cruel joke swirling through Black history: The Union Army decreed that Blacks would get forty acres and a mule to help them start life in the aftermath of slavery. The program never was fully implemented, because President Andrew Johnson, who loathed Blacks, disbanded it. The story of that broken promise—which rarely showed up in school textbooks—was passed down by Blacks from generation to generation. Whites who saw the letterhead from 40 Acres and a Mule Filmworks may have had to do a little research, but Lee had no doubt Blacks would get the inside sarcasm.

Spike Lee sent well-known actors prints of *Joe's Bed-Stuy Barbershop* and had the chutzpah to include an accompanying note saying he would likely be working with them someday. Ossie Davis received the letter and chuckled, though he didn't throw it away. Those who knew Lee came to realize he possessed a roaring vision to match his outsized personality. He bopped around New York, making friends in the film community. He got backroom jobs in film companies. He rose before dawn, jotted down film ideas and scenes that were swirling in his head. He filled out applications for arts grants. He watched old movies. He saw the Italian troika of Scorsese, Harvey Keitel, and Robert De Niro out of the corner of his eye, but he couldn't get close to them. He did find a way to meet Ossie Davis and Ruby Dee. They filled him with the kind of history he loved digesting, stories about James Edwards and Canada Lee and Paul Robeson and Dorothy Dandridge, as well as Martin and Malcolm. He was becoming an encyclopedia of film knowledge.

Like most twenty-somethings, Lee was quite curious about and interested in sex. He wanted to make a movie about a female Black siren, a woman who determined her own destiny when it came to romping in bedrooms. Black sex rarely showed up on movie screens. Lee began his research by taking the Masters and Johnson approach: He commissioned a survey. Actually, he commissioned himself to do the survey. He wrote a list of questions and submitted them to Black female friends:

*What do you think about a woman who masturbates?*
*Have you ever OD'd on sex?*

Some recipients of the questionnaire—away from Lee's earshot—thought it was strange; some who knew him thought him prurient, a bantam-sized and nosy movie nerd. But he culled enough information from the questionnaire to forge ahead, believing he was on to something. He started writing a script. And bumming money; he also filled out grant applications and placed an ad in *Backstage* magazine looking for actors and actresses. Some thought he was putting the cart way before any horse might even come into view: ConEd was threatening to turn his utilities off. His Atlanta grandmother sent more money. Tracy Camilla Johns saw the *Backstage* ad and sent in a photo. She had no movie-acting experience, but there was a voluptuousness about her. She was invited to meet with Lee, and he chose her to play Nola Darling. Ernest Dickerson, again, was the cinematographer. The script's title: *She's Gotta Have It.* Lee got two prestigious grants—the New York State Council on the Arts, the Jerome Foundation—but it wasn't enough, so he kept asking friends to open their wallets. There was no money for insurance, so that got nixed. Authorized film-location permits? Also nixed. Lee hoped that a twenty-thousand-dollar American Film Institute grant he had received for an aborted film project could be transferred to *She's Gotta Have It,* but the request was turned down.

Nelson George was a young journalist who had moved to Brooklyn from Queens. He had recently written a book about the singer Michael Jackson, which sold so well he was able to buy a brownstone. "Spike lived around the corner, on Myrtle Avenue," George recalls. "It was a dangerous area. We called it Murderous Myrtle." George quickly became attuned to the growing "black bebop bohemian" movement flowering in Brooklyn, in which a coterie of writers and artists were constantly trying to inspire one another. He met Lee at a party, and Lee invited him to his apartment one evening. "At first I couldn't find it," George recalls. "He was living in a converted garage. All he had in his place was a bed, a Michael Jordan poster, lots of laser discs, and an editing machine with reels and reels of film." Lee needed more money for filming—and lab work—on his current film. George recalls: "I watched *She's Gotta Have It* for the first time there. I hadn't seen anything like it. He had all these different types of Black people in it. It felt very fresh to me. The film seemed to represent the next generation of Black culture." Lee—seeing that George was interested in the film—wasted no time in asking him if he would like to become an investor. "I had always heard about Black people needing to help Black people," George says. "It was time to put up or shut up." George not only invested thirty-five hundred dollars in the film, he hosted parties at his brownstone to get others interested in investing. "He was very, very visionary and ambitious," George says of Lee. "There was just no precedent for what he was doing. I knew a lot of independent filmmakers. It was just such a struggle. Most of their screenings would be held at museums."

In Lee's finished film, it was obvious that his cinematographer, Dickerson, had been influenced by Scorsese's *Raging Bull* and Jim Jarmusch's *Stranger Than Paradise,* both filmed in black and white—and convinced Lee to let him shoot their film that way. Lee cast himself in the movie as Mars Blackmon, a bike-riding would-be lover boy who chases after Nola Darling. In the script, Mars all but begs her for sex: "Please, baby, please, baby, baby, baby, please . . ." Other cast members—Tommy Redmond Hicks, John Canada Terrell, Joie Lee (Spike's sister)—were all unknown. Lee had no money to hire actors with reputations.

Nelson George, even though he had invested in the film, sensed Lee's tough road ahead: "There was no precedent for a black sex comedy. I knew all the other filmmakers in New York; they were all scrambling to get something going, but nothing was really happening. Hollywood was not interested in black subject matter for the most part; certainly not in black directors." But George, upon watching rough-cut footage of the film again, became even more convinced of its commercial possibilities. "[There] was a magic that people hadn't seen before." Lee finally had a rough cut of the whole film. He still had to raise more money to complete postproduction, but got NYU to allow him to host a screening. At the conclusion, he looked out over a group of potential investors. "I'm Spike Lee and I hope that you liked the film," he said. "I'll be calling you soon about becoming financially involved in helping us complete it." Faculty members who had watched the film had to admit—even if just to themselves—they had underestimated Lee's talents.

He finally did complete the movie, pleading with some members of the cast and crew to defer payments. They didn't complain; they'd become Spike believers. The MPAA forced Lee to delete some of the more aggressive sex scenes. The necessary cuts were eventually made to secure an R rating.

Lee had inserted a written prologue that appeared at the beginning of his movie. It came from Zora Neale Hurston's *Their Eyes Were Watching God*:

> *Ships at a distance have every man's wishes on board. For some they come in with the tide. For others they sail forever on the horizon, never out of sight, never landing until the watcher turns his eyes away in resignation, his dreams mocked to death by time. That is the life of men. Now, women forget all those things they don't want to remember and remember everything they don't want to forget. The dream is the truth. Then they act and do things accordingly.*

Word began seeping out about *She's Gotta Have It*. Lee and his film got invited to the 1986 San Francisco International Film Festival, the festival that had helped launch Melvin Van Peebles's *Sweet Sweetback* years earlier. The festival organizers, among them Peter Scarlet—who had a soft spot for Lee, having screened *Joe's Bed-Stuy Barbershop* in 1983—were excited to be hosting him again. The screening took place inside the eleven-hundred-seat Palace of Fine Arts. The fest always did ample publicity, and Lee's Friday-night premiere quickly sold out. (Among the attendees was Danny Glover, a Black actor who appeared on the big screen in 1985's *Witness, Places in the Heart,* and *The Color Purple,* a trio of appearances representing a rare burst of big-screen activity for a Black character actor.) Lee walked into the theatre wearing a dapper double-breasted suit. The film started, and then disaster struck: All the lights and power went out. The theatre was in darkness. "Folks, please sit tight," Scarlet told the crowd. "I'm gonna go outside and try to find out what's going on." The city had been plunged into an electrical-power outage. The police showed up and instructed everyone to leave the theatre. But the crowd soon saw lights around them blinking back on, and they all returned to their seats. At the movie's end, the crowd stood and cheered, their applause washing over a smiling Lee. Things moved quickly from there; a coveted invite to the Cannes International Film Festival soon followed.

Spike Lee had to borrow money to fly to France, but he arrived in a jubilant mood. It was clearly a coup for a young Black filmmaker to be invited to Cannes. The French didn't mind Lee's seeming rudeness, the way he could stare down someone who had asked a question that to him seemed mindless. He wanted to talk about film, but he wanted the French to understand the lack of attention given to Black filmmakers by those in power in America. He left Cannes with the 1986 Prix du Jeunesse Award, given to the best new director.

Island Pictures signed a distribution deal, and Spike Lee's full-length feature debut opened on August 8, 1986. Michael Wilmington, writing in the *Los Angeles Times,* called the movie "a joyfully idiosyncratic little jazz burst of a film, full of sensuous melody, witty chops and hot licks." He added: "Lee is an impudent original with a great eye and flair for humor and eroticism." From Gene Siskel, in the *Chicago Tribune:* "Featuring an all-black cast, this little film is a revelation, primarily because it provides Black faces with the most natural dialogue they've had in years." Siskel went on: "The other great pleasure of the picture is that it is simply funny. There's a series of quick cuts about various lines men use to romance women that applies to all men. And director Lee, playing a pushy little nerd, gets a laugh every time he's on camera with his insistent manner of repeating himself until he gets what he wants." *The New York Times* never mentioned the race of white filmmakers in their reviews, but they referred to Lee as "the young black film maker." The *Chicago Reader* critic felt that Lee's film "posed him as a rival to Woody Allen, nearly equaling him in psychological authenticity, perhaps bettering him in virtuosity and sheer creative glee."

The movie opened at New York City's Cinema Studio 1, and the lines of mostly young Blacks kept forming week after week. There were also long lines in Detroit, Atlanta, L.A., Houston, Chicago. Favorable reviews in alternative weekly publications around the country began appearing. Whites began filling theatre seats. *She's Gotta Have It* came to gross a whopping—given its $175,000 budget—$7.1 million. That was the kind of proof that drew the attention of Hollywood. Spike Lee hadn't simply given his film over to the public, he had also presented himself as an entrepreneur. He stood in front of Manhattan theatres that were playing his film, hawking merchandise: *She's Gotta Have It* T-shirts and hats and other knickknacks. Those coming out of the theatres often mistook Lee for a common street vendor, then, upon further gazing, realized it was the director himself. It was Mars Blackmon! Please, baby, please, baby, baby, baby, please. Lee had long thought that his father's jazz career was stifled because he didn't know how to market himself. The weekly *Village Voice* got a kick out of Lee's marketing prowess. They put him on the cover: "Birth of a Salesman," the headline crowed. When Michael Jordan saw *She's Gotta Have It,* he howled at the sex-starved Mars Blackmon and his sweet desperation—not to mention his fetish for basketball sneakers. Jordan mentioned Lee's movie to Phil Knight, the CEO of Nike. The advertising agency Wieden & Kennedy came aboard. Soon, Lee was filming Nike ads with Jordan while reprising his own Mars Blackmon persona. The reaction—Jordan flying to the rim, Mars Blackmon in his ear—was among the hippest advertising in years.

With one widely released film, Lee had galvanized Blacks, drawn the attention of cinéastes everywhere, and rushed to the forefront of American independent filmmakers. Hollywood called, practically ordering him to come out to the West Coast, to "take meetings." Their silky arrogance annoyed Spike Lee. He suggested to the Hollywood executives that they come to his base of operations—Brooklyn.

New York City's boroughs of Queens, the Bronx, Brooklyn, and Staten Island had an undeniable cultural richness. But that richness did not put a dent in the tribalism of the neighborhoods or the politicians who served their residents. By the mid-1980s, the overwhelming majority of politicians throughout the city and its boroughs remained white men. The political hierarchy was rooted in local clubhouses, smoke-filled rooms where leaders anointed the candidates they wished to support. Those leaders could be ruthless men who brooked very little dissension. They also played to racial factions. Italians, Jews, whites, and Blacks all had their political allegiances. Throughout the years, residents of New York City kept hardening themselves when it came to housing and neighborhood segregation. When critics of the renowned builder Robert Moses told him in the 1940s and 1950s that he was laying out the city with new bridges and highways in a manner that would promote racial segregation into the future, he scoffed. Theirs was a familiar lament from many Southerners moving into Northern cities in the post-civil-rights era, who were seeing segregation as entrenched as anything they had seen in the South.

Spike Lee's mother had worried more than a little during her lifetime about keeping her children safe in the environs of New York City. There were two events in the 1980s that would have shaken the nerves of any mother of a young Black male. Both involved murderous white mobs.

William Turks, a resident of Queens, worked the late shift in a Sheepshead Bay maintenance yard fixing subway cars for the Coney Island Transit Authority. He routinely left work around eleven-thirty at night, often accompanied by his work friends Dennis Dixon and Donald Cooper, all in their early thirties. On June 22, 1982, they climbed into Dixon's station wagon to head home. As usual, they made a stop at a nearby Brooklyn bagel shop to get something to drink and eat. When they emerged from the bagel shop, two young white men began yelling racial slurs. The three Black men made it to Dixon's car. Having heard the racial slurs, they decided it was wise to get out of the area. Just as Dixon began to drive away, however, his car stalled. And, just that quick, a group of whites—police later cited the number as being about twenty—who had been hanging out in a nearby schoolyard joined the first two white men and began pulling the occupants from the car. Dixon and Cooper escaped from the car and fled into the night. Turks was viciously beaten, his skull bashed. Cooper was able to wave down a police car, which rushed to the scene. The white gang scattered, but a badly beaten and bloody Turks lay prostrate on the pavement. He died hours later at Coney Island Hospital. Mayor Ed Koch expressed outrage; a team of twenty-five investigators were sent to work the case. Black citizens rose up anew to protest the city's racial climate. Three suspects were eventually charged. Gino Bova was sentenced to five to fifteen years for second-degree manslaughter. Paul Mormando received consecutive one-year terms for misdemeanor assault. Joseph Powell—on the run for two years until he surrendered—received a sentence of three to nine years.

———

On the night of December 19, 1986, another trio of Black men left a stalled car and unwittingly found themselves in Howard Beach, Queens, an Italian stronghold. The Black men were Michael Griffith, Cedric Sandiford, and Timothy Grimes. A fourth man, Curtis Sylvester, remained with the vehicle. The trio stopped at a Howard Beach pizzeria. They asked to use the phone to call for help; the owners refused. So they sat and ordered slices of pizza. Within minutes, the police showed up. Someone had called them, believing the Black men looked "suspicious." The police arrived, found nothing to be concerned about, and left. But word had raced around a nearby block about the three Black men. "There's niggers on the boulevard, let's go fucking kill them," Jon Lester was later reported to have said, instigating what happened next. When the trio left the pizzeria—nearing 1:00 a.m.—they encountered a group of angry white toughs wielding baseball bats and broken tree limbs. Grimes, the fleetest of the trio, escaped. But Griffith and Sandiford were viciously assaulted. Griffith—who lived in Brooklyn—was finally able to tear himself away and bolted. He ran onto the nearby Belt Parkway and was hit by a car. The impact killed him. The white attackers then scattered.

The news of the assaults spread quickly. The outrage in the Black community began boiling. Within twenty-four hours, there were demonstrations in front of the pizzeria, led by Rev. Al Sharpton, a Falstaffian figure who had found a following among local Blacks based on his past association with singer James Brown and an ability to dominate a microphone. Politicians condemned the beatings and the death of Griffith. But the Black community wanted more than apologies; they wanted justice.

Within days, the police arrested three high-school students—Jon Lester, Jason Ladone, and Scott Kern—charging all with second-degree murder. Blacks didn't trust John Santucci, the Queens district attorney, who was having a hard time convincing eyewitnesses to step forward. The charges against the original three suspects were dropped, reinforcing the validity of Blacks' mistrust. Governor Mario Cuomo appointed a special prosecutor, and in February 1987, twelve men were indicted, including the original three suspects. A variety of sentences were eventually handed out, ranging from five to thirty years.

Offscreen, the Black mothers of New York were crying. The pain was hardly over.

On the evening of April 19, 1989, Trisha Meili, who worked in finance at Salomon Brothers, left her Manhattan apartment and went for a jog in Central Park. She was viciously attacked, raped, and left for dead. Her eventual recovery was miraculous and hailed around the nation. Five young Black men—Yusef Salaam, Korey Wise, Kevin Richardson, Antron McCray, and Raymond Santana, Jr.—were arrested and charged with various crimes in the case; during their trial, an army of white demonstrators massed around the courthouse. All five men were convicted and sentenced to prison. Donald Trump took a full-page ad urging the death penalty for all five men. Only they were not guilty. The real attacker, Matias Reyes, was discovered years later, using irrefutable DNA evidence. The case exposed the tragedy of false confessions and the rush to judgment against Black defendants by the New York Police Department. The five Black men were finally released from prison, having served between seven and thirteen years. In late 2002, the convictions of the Central Park Five were vacated by a New York State Supreme Court justice. There were substantial monetary settlements. Trump never backed down from his rush to judgment, even when filmmakers shed light on the mystery of how it all happened: Ken Burns produced a documentary, and Ava DuVernay a highly praised television miniseries.

The horrors of the Turks and Griffith killings—heightened by other racial incidents and allegations of police brutality in New York City—seared into Spike Lee's consciousness. More than most filmmakers, he was intensely attuned to America's civic discourse—and lack thereof when it came to race. As a filmmaker, he was also angling for originality; he knew that too many films were but knockoffs of other films.

Spike Lee was an admirer of Robert De Niro, who was married to a Black woman. Lee asked the Italian American De Niro if they could meet to discuss the Griffith murder, and De Niro agreed. Lee had a movie idea percolating, and De Niro found it intriguing. Lee imagined a film, set in his beloved Brooklyn, about the cultural battle between a group of Blacks in the community and the Italian family that owns a local pizzeria, inspired by the Turks and Griffith murders. Lee knew the action would take place on an extremely hot day. De Niro liked the idea, but couldn't play a part in the film because of previous commitments. Lee went to work on the script anyway, and scrawled the word "Heatwave" on the title page. Happy with the final result, he began showing it around. Universal Pictures came aboard. Lee changed the title from *Heatwave* to *Do the Right Thing*. He signed up an eclectic cast: Ossie Davis, Ruby Dee, Danny Aiello (recommended by De Niro), John Turturro, John Savage, Bill Nunn. Mookie, a vivid character in the script, would be played by Lee himself.

Lee decided to film in Brooklyn on a one-block stretch of Stuyvesant Avenue, a worn-down street with omnipresent remnants of the crack epidemic. The film crew transformed the block and even built Sal's Pizzeria. Lee decided to host a block party before filming began, a move that set area residents at ease about the disruptions the filming could cause. Shooting began on July 18, 1988. On the day of a crucial scene, a confrontation between Sal (the pizza shop owner, played by Aiello) and Buggin Out (an emotional Black character played by Giancarlo Esposito), Lee told both actors they could improvise some of the insults. "I heard things from [Aiello's] mouth I hadn't heard in years—insulting things that broke my heart—and he heard the same from me," Esposito recalled. The $6.2-million-budgeted film wrapped production on September 14.

On May 19, 1989, Lee's film screened to a rapturous reception at the Cannes Film Festival, followed by a black-tie premiere at the Palais des Festivals. Universal secured Lee a suite at the Carlton. He had moved on up: when he was in Cannes years earlier for *She's Gotta Have It* he'd had to share a room with seven others. Roger Ebert confessed he had emerged from the Cannes screening "with tears in my eyes." Ebert felt that Lee had "made a movie about race in America that empathized with all the par-

Spike Lee, on the set of *Do the Right Thing* (1989). The gifted Antagonist.

ticipants." But the feel-good aura of Cannes was soon dimmed by articles in *Newsweek* and *The Village Voice* stating that the movie had the potential to cause violence when it opened on June 30. Lee sensed a not-so-subtle racial ploy at play. Universal stuck by their filmmaker, feeling they had a special movie ready to enter the marketplace. (Paramount's cadre of white executives had passed on the movie, voicing fears to Lee that the film might indeed ignite urban mayhem. Such thinking, Lee noted, was never uttered regarding the films of Clint Eastwood or other white directors.)

When *Do the Right Thing* opened, it was met not with violence but with the kind of reviews that would make any director swoon. Writing in the *Los Angeles Times,* Sheila Benson proclaimed Lee a "director working with absolute assurance and power." Terrence Rafferty of *The New Yorker* called the thirty-two-year-old Lee "the most prominent Black director in the American movie industry," adding that the filmmaker "probably feels as if he were sprinting downcourt with no one to pass to and about five hundred towering white guys between him and the basket." From Vincent Canby of *The New York Times:* "'Do the Right Thing' is a big movie. Though the action is limited to one more-or-less idealized block in Bed-Stuy, the scope is panoramic. . . . It has the heightened reality of theatre, not only in its look but also in the way the lyrics of the songs on the soundtrack become natural extensions of the furiously demotic, often hugely funny dialogue." (In Chicago, a young law-firm associate by the name of Barack Obama took Michelle Robinson, an attorney, on a first date to see the film.)

Spike Lee had not only shaken up Hollywood with his propulsive and racially themed movie, he had shaken up worldwide cinema. He now seemed bolder and more fearless than any filmmaker working. He also had the touch of gold: *Do the Right Thing* grossed thirty-seven million on its six-million-dollar budget. Danny Aiello (Supporting Actor) and Lee (for Screenplay) received Academy Award nominations. They also received—along with the film—Golden Globe nominations. A host of film critics and critics' associations either named *Do the Right Thing* the best film of the year, or placed it in their top ten. Blacks, however, continued to chart their progress—or lack thereof—in the motion-picture industry by tabulating Academy Award attention. The 1990 Academy Award telecast saw more Black nominees than usual, with Morgan Freeman (*Driving Miss Daisy;* Best Actor nominee) and Denzel Washington (*Glory;* Best Supporting Actor). Neither Freeman nor Washington believed the Academy would give two acting awards to Black performers on the same night.

They were right: Washington took home a statuette, but Freeman lost out to Daniel Day-Lewis in *My Left Foot. Driving Miss Daisy,* with its Black costar, did win Best Picture. "If you look at the movies Oscar-nominated as Best Picture in 1990—*Driving Miss Daisy, Born on the Fourth of July, Dead Poets Society, Field of Dreams, My Left Foot*—there isn't one of them," the critic David Thomson said, "I'd rather see than *Do the Right Thing.*" Thomson added: "What can you say when a lace doily of a movie wins Best Picture and *Do the Right Thing* doesn't get nominated, except that the Academy is a club where people can get very sentimental over how good they are to their chauffeurs."

Joe Klein of *New York* magazine, and Janet Maslin of *The New York Times,* were but two white writers who assailed Lee's *Do the Right Thing* before it had opened nationally. Lee asked a pertinent question regarding such critics: did they heap such pre-release scorn upon white films that had far more violence than his film? Lee knew they did not.

———

James Baldwin fit perfectly riding shotgun alongside Spike Lee. Understand Baldwin, you understand Lee. Both were lively students of Hollywood, of its lineage and its hypocrisy. Baldwin—a sometime film critic—could pontificate endlessly about Lana Turner or Bette Davis; Lee could do the same regarding Akira Kurosawa or Francis Ford Coppola.

In 1968, Baldwin hopped a plane for L.A. He was going to write a screenplay based on *The Autobiography of Malcolm X* for the producer Marvin Worth. Baldwin and Malcolm X seemed a match made in Black cinema heartbreak heaven, and it was: Baldwin was soon crying. Worth had matched him with a "collaborator," Arnold Perl. The scenes Baldwin wrote were handed to Perl and rewritten. Baldwin found his work twisted, the cultural juice zapped from the scenes. This went on until Baldwin had knots in his stomach. "I simply walked out," he allowed, "taking my original script with me—but the adventure remained very painfully in my mind, and, indeed, was to shed a certain light for me on the adventure occurring through the American looking glass."

For years and years, Baldwin's Malcolm X "script" simply languished.

Worth held the rights to Malcolm's story. He had first gotten to know Malcolm in Detroit when both were young men hanging around jazz clubs. "It's such a great story, a great American story, and it reflects our society in so many ways," Worth said. He produced a documentary film that received a stellar reception and an Academy Award nomination. (The documentary opened with Billie Holiday singing "Strange Fruit.") Over the years, directors who had enough muscle to be taken seriously—white directors—would inquire about the Baldwin screenplay, credited to Baldwin and Perl, in hopes that Worth would allow them to direct a feature film. In 1990, Worth took a meeting with Norman Jewison and liked Jewison's pitch. Jewison was a highly respected filmmaker, with decades-long credits; among his films were *In the Heat of the Night* (1967), *Rollerball* (1975), and *A Soldier's Story* (1984). But when Spike Lee heard that Jewison was going to direct a Malcolm X picture, he expressed his displeasure loudly. Jewison—who had already begun discussions with Denzel Washington to portray Malcolm—had also already engaged Charles Fuller, writer of the play and film script for *A Soldier's Story*, to pen the Malcolm X screenplay. Lee felt a Black director had to direct the film. He said that Francis Ford Coppola brought more cultural awareness to the *Godfather* films because he was Italian, like many of the characters in them. Same for Scorsese with *Mean Streets* and *Raging Bull*. "White Americans will never know what it feels like to be an African-American in this country," Lee said. "This is a story of Malcolm X whose life you might say is very symbolic of the whole African-American experience in this country."

Lee arranged a meeting with Jewison, who stepped aside from the film. Worth quickly turned the reins over to Lee. Then yet another issue erupted. Some ad-hoc organizations in New York City—led by the poet and Black nationalist Amiri Baraka, a spokesman for the United Front to Preserve the Legacy of Malcolm X—began attacking Lee, questioning his bona fides. "We will not let Malcolm X's life be trashed to make middle-class Negroes sleep easier," Baraka told an anti-Spike rally held in Harlem. The poet implored the gathering to write Lee about their misgivings. Spike Lee was hardly going to take the bubbling contretemps silently. He directed much of his ire toward Baraka: "Where's his book on Malcolm?" Lee asked. "When Malcolm was of this earth Amiri Baraka was LeRoi Jones running around the Village being a beatnik. He didn't move to Harlem until after Malcolm X was assassinated. So a lot of these guys—not all—weren't even down with Malcolm when he was around. . . . I was seven years old so I had an excuse. I had to be home by dark."

Lee busied himself with rewriting the Baldwin-Perl script. Baldwin's name was eventually removed, and the script credited to Lee and Perl. Warner Brothers began budget negotiations with Lee. They finally agreed on twenty million dollars, and Lee raised another fifteen million on top of that. In between *Do the Right Thing* and the start of *Malcolm X,* Lee directed and released two other films: a jazz drama, *Mo' Better Blues,* starring Denzel Washington, Wesley Snipes, and John Turturro; and *Jungle Fever,* an interracial romance starring Snipes and Annabella Sciorra. Both films made money. *Jungle Fever* was a notable box-office hit; on a fourteen-million-dollar budget, it grossed forty-four million. It also elicited quite a bit of discussion about Black-white relationships, especially among Black women.

While still planning his Malcolm X film, Lee made a visit to Whittier College in California. College students had begun looking upon him as a hipster, largely because of the Michael Jordan–Mars Blackmon pairing in the Nike ads and his *Do the Right Thing* soundtrack, with its rap anthems. Spike was crossing over to the mainstream. A Whittier student raised his hand during the question-and-answer session and asked whether the characterizations of Moe and Josh Flatbush, the Jewish nightclub owners played by John and Nicholas Turturro in *Mo' Better Blues,* were stereotypes. Lee's response: "Why is it that there can be no negative Jewish characters in films? . . . [Yet] why do we have Black pimps and Black drug dealers . . . ?" Lee had a fearless penchant for wading into thorny issues. Men of Jewish heritage, for the most part, ran the Hollywood studios. Others might be frightened of a healthy debate about the genesis and dictates of Hollywood, but Lee could not be counted among them. Still, the debate caught John Turturro by surprise: "I was shocked by the reaction," he said. "My wife is Jewish. There have always been Jewish managers of clubs, and that is a natural antagonistic relationship, between an artist and a financier-owner. We never made an issue of it. It was the media that called the Flatbush brothers 'cheap bastards.'"

Over the years leading up to Norman Jewison's involvement in *Malcolm X,* the names bandied about to play the lead had included Billy Dee Williams and Richard Pryor. By the time Jewison—and then Lee—had taken on the project, it appeared a foregone conclusion that there was one actor above all others who should play the role.

Denzel Hayes Washington was born in 1954 in Mount Vernon, New York. His mother worked in a hair salon; his dad was employed by the New York City Water Department. When his parents divorced, Washington, fourteen years old, began running with a suspect crowd. His mother fretted, and finally sent him off to the Oakland Military Academy in New Windsor, New York, for his high-school years. At Oakland, he played football and baseball, played in the band, yakked a lot about the world, wore nice clothes. "The first time I saw patent leather shoes, he was wearing them," recalled his classmate Andrew Penny. Washington entered Fordham University and expressed an early interest in journalism. Poor grades forced him to take a break from school, but when he returned, it was with a fierce determination to succeed. Professors encouraged him to tackle drama. He got cast in Fordham productions; an agent saw him in *Othello* and then *Emperor Jones,* and signed him, a big break for a young actor. In 1977, he played a small role in *Wilma,* a Bud Greenspan–directed television movie about the Olympic track star Wilma Rudolph. In 1981, Washington went to New York and met Woodie King, Jr., founder of the Henry Street Settlement's New Federal Theater, and found the stage role that would define his early career: Malcolm X. Laurence Holder had written *When the Chickens Came Home to Roost,* a one-act play about a confrontation between Malcolm X and Elijah Muhammad. Washington was cast alongside Kirk Kirksey, who played Muhammad. "He was extremely developed mentally," remembers King of Washington. "He did such careful research. It's a deep, deep understanding of who he is playing. When he walked onto the stage, they thought Malcolm walked onto the stage." In the drama, Malcolm comes to the office of Muhammad to confront him about paternity suits lodged against him, which is actually what ignited the split between the two men. "It's much to the credit of Denzel Washington's firm, likeable performance that this Malcolm is honorable and altruistic without ever becoming a plaster saint," Frank Rich wrote in *The New York Times.* It was far more than just a physical likeness to Malcolm that Washington possessed; he gave a sly and erudite performance.

The young actor made his big-screen debut that fall in *Carbon Copy* alongside George Segal, a comedy about a white man who comes to realize he has a long-lost Black son. Hollywood was of the mindset that such revelations were profound. In 1982, Washington then began a multiple-year run as a doctor on television's ensemble drama *St. Elsewhere.* Acclaim in feature films soon followed: *A Soldier's Story* in 1984 (four studios passed on the film—telling the director Norman Jewison they didn't want to do a Black movie—before Warner Brothers signed on); Oscar-nominated for *Cry Freedom,* about the South African activist Steven Biko, in 1987; the Oscar win for the slave-turned-soldier in 1989's *Glory.* Many thought of him as the new Sidney Poitier, but his roles were far more complex and varied. Washington's name helped the filmmaker Mira Nair raise money for *Mississippi Masala,* which opened in February 1992; it told the story of a Black carpet cleaner who falls in love with an Indian woman. Nair later revealed that timid financial backers in America kept imploring her to change the lead from a Black man to a white man. She raised a considerable amount of the film's budget from foreign investors.

Just as there wasn't much debate about who would play Rhett Butler in *Gone with the Wind,* there was not much debate about who would play Malcolm X in Spike Lee's drama. Alongside Washington, Lee cast Angela Bassett, Delroy Lindo, Albert Hall, Lonette McKee, Debi Mazar, Al Freeman, Jr., and Wendell Pierce. More than three hundred actors were cast in the film. Filming took place in Boston, Harlem, and Newark, and overseas in Egypt, South Africa, and Mecca, Saudi Arabia. Production costs ballooned, and Lee—as usual—became financially creative. He gave a substantial part of his own three-million-dollar salary to keep production in motion. He needed additional help in the home stretch and was forced to ask Black celebrities, among them Oprah Winfrey, Prince, Michael Jordan, and Janet Jackson, for money, which they gave. During filming, cast members were awed by Washington's work; even when he ad-libbed as Malcolm, it appeared so organic that Lee did not complain. When production on the film wrapped, Lee announced that he had "an epic picture . . . on the scale of the great films that David Lean did." Lean had directed, among others, *Doctor Zhivago* and *Lawrence of Arabia.*

Less than two months after Lee's film wrapped, a trial began, anchored to a 1991 case in which four white police officers were seen on a videotape viciously beating a Black motorist, Rodney King, after an auto chase. King suffered a skull fracture, brain damage, broken bones, and other injuries. It was a ghastly beating. The nation saw white cops, with savage grins, swinging their batons on an unarmed, helpless Black man. But the California jury—on which there was not a single Black—acquitted the police. Following the decision, Los Angeles erupted in searing spasms of violence over a period of six days. There were sixty-three deaths and about twelve thousand arrests. Buildings and stores were burned and looted.

Even before the release of the videotape, the Black residents of Los Angeles were weary and angry. A week before the riots, Latasha Harlins, a fifteen-year-old Black girl, walked into a Korean grocery store in South Central Los Angeles. She put a bottle of orange juice in her backpack, apparently to walk it to the counter; she was holding the money to pay for it in her hand. But an argument ensued between her and the store owner, Soon Ja Du, who shot the young girl in the back of the head, killing her instantly. Looking at the videotape—and taking statements from two eyewitnesses—police concluded that Harlins had intended to pay for the orange juice and that Du had murdered her. She was convicted of voluntary manslaughter. The jury decided she should receive the maximum sentence, sixteen years in prison. But the judge overruled them and sentenced Du to probation and community service. Blacks were outraged, and that outrage erupted after the Rodney King videotape emerged. Two of the L.A. officers involved in the King beating were eventually convicted in a federal trial, but sentenced to less than three years each in prison. King later settled a multimillion-dollar lawsuit against the LAPD.

Those who saw advance screenings of *Malcolm X* immediately began heaping praise on Denzel Washington's performance. Warner Brothers announced that the movie would open nationally on November 18, 1992. But they—along with Lee—had to listen to concerns from the LAPD that violence might erupt around the film's release. Lee sought to take the offensive. Wielding a report from the American Society of Newspaper Editors showing that fewer than 5 percent of journalists in newsrooms across the country were Black, Lee announced he would like to be interviewed by Black journalists. Warner Brothers and the newspaper editors were flummoxed. Expressing a lack of diversity in newsrooms was important to Lee, but his requests were delicately ignored. The Ku Klux Klansman David Duke then announced that everyone should boycott *Malcolm X*. Lee was getting plenty of free publicity, even if controversial, which of course he considered a positive.

The opening of Lee's film showed the burning of the American flag that crumpled to form an "X." That was followed by images of the Rodney King beating and protests. What followed were three hours of a fierce view of Malcolm X's passage through his American life, dominated by Denzel Washington's blistering performance. *The New York Times* opined that the movie was "not exactly the equal or even the equivalent of the book, but it's an ambitious, tough, seriously considered biographical film that, with honor, eludes easy characterization." From Roger Ebert: "Walking into 'Malcolm X' I expected an angrier film than Spike Lee has made. This film is not an assault but an explanation, and it is not exclusionary; it deliberately addresses all races in its audience. White people, going into the film, may expect to meet a Malcolm X who will attack them, but they will find a Malcolm X whose experiences and motives make him understandable and finally heroic." Kenneth Turan of the *Los Angeles Times* had never been one of Lee's ardent supporters. Yet: "The unexpected aspect of this forceful, purposeful work by a director with a reputation for being an in-your-face polemicist and provocateur is just how careful and classical a film it finally is." Turan went on to call the film "a grand epic for people of color, an African-American counterpart to 'Gandhi' that aims to move a controversial thinker and doer who has not been much revered outside of the black community into the heart of the American mainstream." In *Entertainment Weekly,* Owen Gleiberman began his review by taking issue with Lee's ongoing public spats with Hollywood. "Now, though, Lee's war may have ended. Malcolm X . . . is a triumph, an intimate and engrossing biographical saga that is also one of the most passionate political films ever made in this country." Included in the film's coda is a scene of Nelson Mandela standing in a Soweto classroom, teaching young kids about Malcolm X. Mandela hadn't been long released from prison, after serving twenty-seven years for taking on South Africa's brutal apartheid regime. Lee was the rare filmmaker who sensed the symmetry between Malcolm and Mandela.

Malcolm X's family announced they were delighted with the movie. And, once again, Black America awaited the Academy Award nominations. The nominees for Best Director were Neil Jordan, Robert Altman, James Ivory, Martin Brest, and Clint Eastwood. Spike Lee did not make the list. The nominees for Best Picture were *Unforgiven, Scent of a Woman, Howard's End, A Few Good Men,* and *The Crying Game.* Denzel Washington, however, did receive a nomination for Best Actor alongside Robert Downey, Jr., Eastwood, Al Pacino, and Stephen Rea. And Ruth Carter received a nomination for Costume Design. Lee made a prediction: Washington would win the Best Actor prize for his towering *Malcolm X* performance. "If he doesn't win," Lee said, "we'll burn the Academy down."

It was Al Pacino who took home the Best Actor prize. Sidney Poitier remained the only Black actor to win for Best Actor. That had happened in 1964, and its distance in the rearview mirror was getting longer—and, to Blacks, harder to stomach.

# The Blackout That Haunted a Decade

A MERICANS HAD BEEN WILDLY ADDICTED to the triumphs and downfalls of entertainers and musicians—of celebrities—for ages. Throughout the 1960s, 1970s, and 1980s, three magazines rode the crest of that interest: *Life, Look,* and *Ebony.* Their stories on the world of film often made the covers and were accompanied by lavish photos. In the late 1960s, *Life* asked Richard Burton to write something up about Liz Taylor, his wife. The two stars were, at the time, the most famously recognizable acting duo in the world. "I think we were and still are very good for each other," Burton wrote in the magazine. "My smattering of scholarship has darted off onto her and a smattering of her honesty onto me. The quality in her that appealed, and still appeals, to me most is her blazing honesty. She cannot tell a lie." The public simply couldn't get enough of their life—the comings and goings; the jewelry; the spats! They divorced, remarried, and divorced again. The magazines—especially *Life* and *Look*—had ample budgets to cover what they needed to. Advertising was quite good. Their writers and photographers traveled the world. But some of the execs who ran the magazines could see the beginning of the waning of advertising dollars. It was high time to start thinking of other ventures. Andrew Heiskell had been *Time*'s top executive; before that, he had been publisher of *Life.* Heiskell came up with the idea for a new weekly magazine, with a smaller-sized format than either *Life* or *Look.* The magazine would be an exposition of Americana, unique stories about interesting people. It intended to set most of its gaze upon Hollywood. Heiskell gathered some *Time* and *Life* veterans for the undertaking, and they went to work creating *People* magazine. "We're getting back to the people who are causing the news and who are caught up in it, or deserve to be in it," proclaimed Richard Stolley, the first managing editor of *People*.

The first issue sold for thirty-five cents per copy and hit the stands March 4, 1974. It featured the actress Mia Farrow, who was appearing alongside Robert Redford and Bruce Dern in the latest movie version of F. Scott Fitzgerald's *The Great Gatsby*. The magazine caught on. Three months after its initial issue, the editors decided to put the actress Cicely Tyson on its cover. Tyson had starred in *The Autobiography of Miss Jane Pittman*, which aired on CBS on January 31, 1974. She played a onetime slave who lived into freedom and exercised the right to vote. She also had been recently Oscar-nominated for her performance in *Sounder*.

Before training as an actress, in the 1950s, Tyson had worked as a secretary in Manhattan. One day, she stood up from her seat, looked around the office, and boldly announced: "I'm just sure God didn't put me on the face of this earth to bang on a typewriter the rest of my life." Her co-workers wondered if she was having a nervous breakdown. She proceeded to walk out of the office and away from the job. Soon she was studying with Paul Mann, an esteemed acting teacher. She caught a very early break in 1955, cast in *Carib Gold*, an interracial crime drama released in 1956, starring Ethel Waters and set in Key West, Florida. The picture also marked the credited film debuts of Diana Sands and Geoffrey Holder. It opened exclusively in Key West in September 1956, at two theatres on Duval Street. White patrons attended the Strand Theater; Blacks had to see *Carib Gold* at the segregated Monroe Theater. After a three-day showing there, the movie was pulled from both theatres without explanation. There never was a wide national release, although it did have a very brief run in New York in 1957 and one in Los Angeles in 1958. Then something strange happened: *Carib Gold*—just like some of Oscar Micheaux's films and *Porgy and Bess*—went missing. For decades, cinema detectives looked for prints without luck. It was finally discovered in 2009. There have since been intermittent showings at small film festivals. Tyson, playing the wife of a shrimp-boat mate, looks beautiful in the film, her budding acting gifts quite apparent.

After filming, Tyson returned to New York. She continued studying and found stage roles. George C. Scott spotted her in a Broadway play and cast her in *East Side/West Side*, his 1963 weekly CBS television drama about social workers. She played a secretary, but one who got involved in the show's weekly dramatic arc. Her role was viewed as the first noncomedy role for a Black actress on weekly television. "For the first time," she

Ethel Waters in 1957. Sassy and underrated.

said, "a black person of either sex was given a regular TV role of some dignity." The show, however, never found sufficient advertising revenue; CBS knew it was because the show regularly dealt with racial issues. A scene showing George C. Scott's character dancing with a Black woman was deleted before airing. The show lasted barely a season. Tyson continued her drive to eke out a living as an actor—and then *Sounder* came along, followed by *Jane Pittman,* for which she won an Emmy. Even though it was a television movie, she was invited to the Cannes Film Festival for a showing. "I know that Claudette Colbert, Ann Sheridan and Barbara Stanwyck always had a lot of good roles to choose from," she said. "And of course I have no illusion about how much more difficult it is for a Black woman to become a star."

The editors of *People*—which had offices in New York and L.A.—prided themselves on keeping a bead on the movie business. They had heard the grumblings, mostly from the NAACP, about the lack of opportunity for Black actors and actresses. The civil-rights organization was making noise about leading a boycott of Hollywood studios to protest the situation. "We hoped the film industry would become racially mixed in its employment policies after [*Roots*]," said Collette Wood, executive secretary of the Beverly Hills/Hollywood branch of the NAACP. "But it didn't happen. There has been a steady decline in Black employment in the industry since 1975." When the magazine editors took a look at the results of Academy Awards for the previous four years, they were alarmed to see that between 1978 and 1982 there had been no films nominated directed by a Black, no films nominated that featured a Black actor or actress in a leading role, and no films nominated written by a Black writer. There were breakthroughs in the Best Supporting Actor category: Howard E. Rollins, Jr., was nominated for *Ragtime* in 1981, and Louis Gossett, Jr., was nominated and won in 1982. But those two actors—and a single win—hardly counted as progress. The revelations convinced the *People* editors they should assign a story about Blacks in Hollywood. A team of reporters descended into the film community. Their findings were astonishing, published (though not as the cover story) in the May 17, 1982, edition. "The day of Stepin Fetchit is past," the article began. "It is hard to imagine a movie today in which a Black man shuffles along in a haze of lethargic stupidity, as Fetchit did to great acclaim in a string of movies in the '30s. The Grinning Minstrel in blackface, the Grateful Slave, the Gibbering African, the Watermelon Baby—all the conspicuously racist stereotypes have vanished. Yet Black actors and actresses in Hollywood aren't rejoicing: They, too, are fast disappearing from American films." What was most jarring to the magazine's reporters was that not a single studio chief wished to be quoted discussing the matter. Dolores Robinson was one of the few Black personal managers working in Hollywood at the time. Black actresses fared the worst, she felt: "If you're beautiful, you can play a prostitute; if you're fat, you can play a mother; if you're ugly, you can play a maid." She lamented that she had started shooing away potential Black clients. "There are no jobs," she told them. "I'm not a miracle worker." Hollywood's NAACP executives were quite aware of the experience of the filmmaker Sylvester Stallone. Stallone, who had starred in *Rocky,* a box-office smash in 1976, wanted to cast his Depression-era drama, *Paradise Alley,* with a mostly Black cast. But his financiers objected. "They said a black movie could only gross a certain amount of money and never had a chance to go into megabucks," Stallone said. One of the few white producers to talk to *People* about the issue was Robert Radnitz, who had produced *Sounder.* "The feeling in the motion picture community reflects an enormous backlash in this country," Radnitz said, referring to the rising conservative climate. "The cop-out is, 'We're just reflecting the times, the mores of the country.' Well, my opinion has always been that the real artist, the real person does not just reflect—you try to do a little leading."

The NAACP threats to boycott the film industry never gained traction. Films stayed white and—in front of the camera as well as behind the camera—were getting whiter. Lawrence Kasdan's film, *The Big Chill*, premiered in 1983. It revolved around a group of eight friends gathered together after another friend's suicide. Black Motown music played in the movie's background scenes and on its soundtrack, but the friends in the film were all white. There was not a single major Black in the entire cast. This was a movie in tune with Black music, but no Black acquaintances were among its so-called hip cast. "We're becoming invisible again," Richard Roundtree had said earlier.

The Hollywood studios turned to Jack Valenti to deal with the *People* magazine story. In 1966, Valenti became president of the Motion Picture Association of America. It was his job to represent the studio chiefs before the public at home and as a lobbyist in Washington. Valenti had been a trusted aide to President Lyndon Johnson, and was by Johnson's side as he sought to heal the nation's racial wounds by shepherding and signing into law the 1964 and 1965 civil-rights bills. Valenti soon realized that dealing with domestic legislation in Washington and studio chiefs in Hollywood were two completely different challenges, especially when it came to race. Not unexpectedly, he sided with the studio chiefs and their outlook regarding Black actors. "Producers want to make the best movies possible," Valenti said, "so they'll hire the best people, regardless of color." Valenti sounded as if he was questioning the availability and quality of Black talent. When he bragged in 1982 to the NAACP that "Black and Hispanic" speaking roles amounted to 10 percent of speaking roles in all movies, the NAACP scoffed. They knew better, and accused him of adding Hispanic numbers just to bolster the Black statistics. Furthermore, the NAACP was quick to remind him that Blacks made up a third of the ticket-buying, moviegoing public. Leroy Robinson, president of the Black Motion Picture and TV Producers' Association—and with the blessing of the NAACP—shared with Valenti his group's own diagram. By their calculations, there were 299 major films released between September 1979 and April 1982, and Blacks played less than 3 percent of all speaking roles.

By the dawn of the 1990s, it had been a full three decades since Harlem congressman Adam Clayton Powell, Jr., had launched an investigation into the issue of Black employment in Hollywood. His investigation began in the aftermath of the formation of the Committee for the Employment of Negro Performers, a group founded in 1962 in New York by a trio of Black actors—Godfrey Cambridge, Charles Gordone, and Hugh Hurd. First elected to Congress in 1944, Powell languished for years, often battling race-baiting Southern congressmen. But with President Kennedy's election, he ascended to chairman of the Education and Labor Committees. The chairmanship gave Powell his first real legislative power. He had an interest in Hollywood because his wife, the jazz pianist Hazel Scott, was a sometime actress and often told him about the demeaning maid roles she had been offered. Powell gave his 1962 hearings into Hollywood a title: Investigation of Discrimination Practices in the Performing Arts. He invited Hollywood studio chiefs—or their representatives—to appear before his committee, but none showed. An array of Black actors and actresses—among them Hilda Simms, Sidney Poitier, Diahann Carroll, and Ossie Davis—arrived in New York (where the hearings were held) to testify about the hardships they faced in Hollywood. "I think it is 13,000 Screen Actors Guild members, I being the only Negro to earn a living in the motion picture industry," Poitier told the committee in 1962. "I have been working in pictures about 13 or 14 years. Often I am the only Negro on the set. That includes technicians, actors, extras." No one in Hollywood, however, paid attention to Powell's committee findings and revelations that the film industry practiced discrimination, like—as Poitier said—the nation at large.

It was becoming painfully apparent to Blacks in the motion-picture industry that no one was coming to aid their cause or concerns. The politics of the nation had taken a rightward shift, a shift that had actually been going on for years. Between 1968 and 1988, Republicans lost only one presidential election, in 1976, and that was a very close vote in favor of Democrat Jimmy Carter. The long-gestating racial backlash against the civil-rights movement had caught the Democratic Party—who had a loyal base in the Black voter—off guard. Many Democrats, particularly in the South, had long been bolting the party to join the Republican Party. Suburbia had become a GOP stronghold. "These white Democratic defectors express a profound distaste for blacks, a sentiment that pervades almost everything they think about government and politics," a pollster reported about the political shift.

In early October 1991, the United States Senate ushered in hearings for the U.S. Supreme Court nominee Clarence Thomas, chosen to replace the legendary Thurgood Marshall, who was retiring. After Thomas's hearings concluded, the Senate received a report that he had sexually harassed a former colleague. Women senators demanded that Senate Judiciary chairman Joseph Biden reopen the hearings. The accuser, Anita Hill, agreed to testify. In tones both somber and even, she laid out a pattern of Thomas's alleged harassment, which included a lot of office talk about pornography and his sexual fantasies. Thomas boiled as he listened to the graphic testimony, and demanded an opportunity to return to the committee and defend himself. Thomas and Hill were now suddenly positioned as two Black combatants before a national audience. It was the kind of large-scale drama—involving Blacks—that Hollywood could hardly have imagined. And there was a riveted coast-to-coast TV audience. In his opening statement, Thomas boldly upended the *To Kill a Mockingbird* dynamic, casting himself as his own Atticus Finch: "This is not an opportunity to talk about difficult matters privately or in a closed environment," he told the committee, glaring. "This is a circus. It's a national disgrace. And from my standpoint, as a black American, it is a high-tech lynching for uppity blacks who in any way deign to think for themselves, to have different ideas, and it is a message that unless you kowtow to an old order, this is what will happen to you. You will be lynched, destroyed, caricatured by a committee of the U.S. Senate rather than hung from a tree." America—white America—had never seen anything like it. This was a conservative Black man with no allies, Black or white, from the civil-rights movement, who used fiery race talk to pin the conscience of many whites to the fence post. The strategy—theatrical and dramatic—had an effect. Thomas was confirmed to the court by a vote of fifty-two to forty-eight. Seven months after the Thomas hearings came the Los Angeles riots. And a little less than two years after those uprisings came yet another racially charged, nation-shaking drama, this one right in the neighborhood of many of Hollywood's most powerful people.

On June 12, 1994, Nicole Brown Simpson and a male friend, Ron Goldman, were discovered murdered outside her Brentwood condominium. It was a ghastly scene: both had been stabbed multiple times, leaving bone-deep knife wounds. Simpson was the ex-wife of O. J. Simpson, a football star turned actor. He was also the first Black celebrity to be a crossover advertising icon, appealing equally to Blacks and whites in a series of memorable commercials for Hertz Rent-a-Car. Acquaintances of Nicole immediately suspected her ex-husband, who had been known to abuse her physically. Simpson gave weight to those suspicions when, days later, he fled in a white Bronco down a California freeway, television cameras airing the bizarre unfolding scene. It was, indeed, like something out of a movie. Simpson was arrested and charged with two counts of murder. The arrest unleashed torrents of gossip and conjecture about the tribulations of interracial marriage. Victim-rights advocates warned this was a simple act of jealous rage leading to violence, and had nothing to do with race. Simpson retained Johnnie Cochran, an attorney with a reputation for getting lucrative settlements in L.A. police-brutality cases. In a months-long trial that gripped Hollywood—and the world—Simpson, despite overwhelming circumstantial evidence, was acquitted. But he later lost a multimillion-dollar civil lawsuit filed by Nicole's family. As well, in late 2008, Simpson was sentenced to a term of thirty-three years for a Las Vegas hotel robbery in which he claimed he was trying to retrieve memorabilia that had been stolen from him. He served nine years of the sentence before being paroled.

In a space of less than three years, the troika of Clarence Thomas, Rodney King, and O. J. Simpson—in varying ways—had exposed a psychic pain across the Black landscape. Black men seemed to be in society's bull's-eye. There was, as the freelance journalist Jimi Izrael wrote in an opinion piece for NPR at the time, a "perceived perpetual failure of black manhood." Many Blacks felt that whites would further stereotype Black men, just as they had over the issue of Willie Horton. Horton, a Black man, was serving a Massachusetts prison sentence for murder when, in 1986, he received a weekend furlough. He disappeared. Ten months later, he raped a Maryland woman and beat her fiancé with a gun. In the 1988 presidential campaign, George H. W. Bush repeatedly mentioned the Horton case to white audiences; it was also played up in a controversial TV ad for Bush, orchestrated by Lee Atwater. Bush's opponent in the presidential race was Governor Michael Dukakis, who was in office during the time of the Massachusetts furlough program. *Reader's Digest,* one of the most mainstream magazines in the country, ran a big story about the Horton incident. In some corners of white America, Black men were being presumed—and seen—as menacing figures, almost boogeyman-like apparitions. It was all unsettling to large portions of Black America, including Louis Farrakhan, the Chicago-based Nation of Islam leader.

Farrakhan began thinking of an event that would bring Black men together in a positive light, that would show their unity and pride. He joined forces with Benjamin Chavis, a former NAACP executive director, and a plan was hatched to have an epic march of Black men on Washington. It was meant to evoke the large-scale human rights marches of the past, only this one would be the largest ever, a desired goal of a million Blacks, dwarfing the 250,000 who marched on Washington in 1963. Some in the Black community, though intrigued, took a cautious approach. Their concerns revolved around Farrakhan and Chavis.

In 1960, Benjamin Chavis was the first Black in the small town of Oxford, North Carolina, to get a local library card. He was twelve years old. After college, he became involved with various civil-rights organizations. In early 1971, Chavis, now with the Southern-based Commission for Racial Justice, arrived in Wilmington, North Carolina, to protest Klan intimidation and support a Black boycott of schools. On February 6, 1971, someone set fire to Mike's Grocery in Wilmington, a white-owned store. Chavis and nine others were arrested and charged with arson. At a sham trial, all were sentenced to prison terms ranging from fifteen to thirty-four years. Their case became a cause célèbre; Amnesty International called them political prisoners. In 1980, an appeals court threw out the sentences and they were freed. In 1993, Chavis became executive director of the NAACP. A year later, he was fired for agreeing to settle sexual-discrimination lawsuits against the NAACP, moves that the board said they knew nothing about and that were ill-advised, inasmuch as the organization was in debt. In one lawsuit, the NAACP employee Harriet Diles accused board member Gentry W. Trotter of sexual harassment. In another, Chavis's own personal assistant filed a sexual-discrimination lawsuit; in that legal case, it was never made clear who was the accused.

Louis Farrakhan had started his adult life as a calypso singer. He later became enamored of the Muslim religion. But he was one of the Muslim leaders charged with fomenting a climate of distrust toward Malcolm X, a climate many believe helped lead a pathway to his murder. The Anti-Defamation League also came to accuse Farrakhan of anti-Semitism because of inflammatory statements he had made over the years.

But now Farrakhan asked Chavis to join his crusade, and the two men found common ground. The march took place on October 16, 1995. Even though there were wild variations in estimations of the attendance (the ABC television network cited more than eight hundred thousand), the event was considered a genuine success. Black men and their sons arrived in Washington from around the country, demanding respect. They were fathers and grandfathers, uncles and nephews; Black men who had known segregation; Black men who had risen high in law firms; Black doctors and schoolteachers. And though it was called the Million Man March—a title some feminists objected to—a small number of women were there. Two renowned women, Rosa Parks and Maya Angelou, were given speaking slots. Among the main speakers—aside from Farrakhan and Chavis—were Dick Gregory, Jesse Jackson, and Martin Luther King III. The speeches were about fatherhood, responsibility, discipline, and love.


Bill Borden had produced several movies, among them *Alien Nation, A Midnight Clear,* and *Desperado.* Borden was impressed with the Million Man March; he thought there might be a film in it. He phoned Reuben Cannon, a friend and casting agent. "What if we did a movie about a group of men taking a trip from Los Angeles to Washington, D.C., for the Million Man March?" Borden asked Cannon. Cannon, a Black man, was intrigued. "What appealed to me about the idea," Cannon recalled, "was that it would provide an opportunity to show diversity in black men in a way that we rarely see." Cannon was not sold on Borden's idea to shoot it on the extremely low budget of seven hundred thousand dollars. He felt he could raise more money than that, and also had a director in mind: Spike Lee. It had long been known in Hollywood that Lee, unlike many directors, was courteous enough to return phone calls. Lee listened to Cannon's pitch. "There may be something there," Lee told Cannon before the conversation ended. But fifteen minutes later Cannon's phone rang again. It was Lee. "The more I think about it," he told Cannon, "I really like it. But if we do it . . . we should do it in the spirit of the march, and the money should come from black men." Lee told Cannon they needed to raise $2.5 million. He also told Cannon that—given their pedigree and film contacts—if they couldn't raise that amount of money, "they should be shot."

Reuben Cannon was a rare Black individual who had made it up from a studio mail room. He had arrived in Los Angeles from Chicago in 1970 and got a job in the mail room at Universal. Not long after, he became a trainee in the casting department. The higher-ups were impressed with his work ethic and determination. In 1974, he was named casting director. Warner Brothers pulled him away in 1978 and made him their TV casting director. In 1979, he formed Reuben Cannon & Associates, and went on to cast major motion pictures, among them *What's Love Got to Do With It, Trespass,* and *Who Framed Roger Rabbit.* He thought it important to cast

Black actors in roles they were not traditionally thought of for: "There's no shortage of good black actors," he said, "there's just a shortage of imagination in the industry in using black actors."

Following his conversation with Spike Lee, Cannon flew to New York with Borden and Barry Rosenbush—a producing partner of Borden's—all to meet with Lee, who had agreed to direct the film. By the time the trio landed, Lee had drawn up his filming plans: he wanted the movie to be in theatres within a year of the march's first anniversary. Such a time line would mean a grueling production schedule. Many movies, from inception to arrival in theatres, take at least five years. Lee also told the group he thought the route to go with fund-raising was tapping into professional Black athletes around the country. They all thought it was a novel concept; Cannon was made point man for the fund-raising. He drew up a prospectus, had Lee's name prominently displayed, and began sending it out.

Lee went to work on his end, looking for a scriptwriter. He had known Reggie Rock Bythewood, a young screenwriter who had attended the Million Man March—and been extremely moved by it—and asked him if he wanted to write the script. Bythewood, who had TV script credits, was excited to come aboard. He had taken a bus from New York to D.C. for the March, and now took another bus trip, this time from Los Angeles to Washington, to inspire him to imagine and create characters for his script.

Reuben Cannon, however, was encountering problems with fund-raising. Most of the Black athletes had white money managers, and those managers balked at their clients' investing in the movie. "Well," Cannon explained to one money manager about his client, "maybe he'd like to do it because there's a cultural connection that you can't understand?"

"I don't care 'bout his culture!" the man snapped. "I care 'bout his portfolio!"

Cannon decided to change direction and contact successful Black businessmen—men who could write their own personal checks without any oversight. He didn't know enough women in high positions. He needed men who had plenty of money in their bank accounts. Olden Lee, a vice-president at Taco Bell/Pepsi, phoned Cannon. "I've read your prospectus," he said. "I like what I hear about you. I like the idea and the concept. Where do I send my check?" The momentum began to pick up.

Yet, by February, Cannon had still only raised $1.5 million of the needed $2.5 million budget. At this point, Bythewood turned in a first draft of his script. It needed work, but everyone liked it. Lee went about casting the film. He got commitments from Ossie Davis, Richard Belzer, Albert Hall,

Wendell Pierce, and Joie Lee. Columbia Pictures was impressed that the Cannon-led team had brought the movie to the starting gate—without studio help of any kind—and were about to commence principal photography. "If this project had been brought to us," an executive there said, "we'd still be in development." The studio came aboard and agreed to buy the film and distribute it. The filmmakers realized they could definitely have the movie in theatres by the fall of 1996. Bythewood's nuanced script was more than just a road movie. The Black men on the bus were a group of disparate characters—straight, gay, old, young, liberal, conservative. Throughout the journey, they discussed Republican versus Democratic politics, history, racism, self-reliance in the Black community, police brutality, anti-Semitism, and the meaning of the Million Man March itself. Lee shot the movie in three weeks; it was guerrilla-style filmmaking, which for him was par for the course. Before the movie was scheduled to open, Reuben Cannon let the media know it had been financed by fifteen Black men (among them Johnnie Cochran)—a point of pride.

Columbia opened *Get On the Bus* on October 16, 1996. *Variety* was full of praise: "A vital regeneration of a filmmaker's talent as well as a bracing and often very funny dramatization of urgent sociopolitical themes." Roger Ebert, in the *Chicago Sun-Times,* called the movie "extraordinary": "I have always felt Lee exhibits a particular quality of fairness in his films. *Do the Right Thing* was so even-handed that it was possible for a black viewer to empathize with Sal, the pizzeria owner, and a white viewer to empathize with Mookie, the black kid who starts the riot that burns down Sal's Pizzeria." From *Newsweek*'s David Ansen: "The wonder of this funky, heartfelt film is that its humanity easily eclipses its didacticism." In February 1997, *Get On the Bus* had a showing at the forty-seventh annual Berlin International Film Festival and came away with an Honorable Mention prize. Against its $2.5 million budget, the movie grossed $5.5 million in the United States, not much of a financial reward, but all involved were proud of what the movie proved to Hollywood: that Black men could get a film to the theatres and have it be a critical success. "When the credits rolled," Reuben Cannon recalled, "and it said, 'This film was completely funded by fifteen African-American men,' and their names came up on the screen at the premiere . . . that got the biggest ovation of all."

One of the most acclaimed film performances in the mid-1990s was turned in by Don Cheadle in *Devil in a Blue Dress.* The 1995 film, directed by Carl Franklin and based on Walter Mosley's film-noir novel, told the story of the Los Angeles detective Easy Rawlins and his efforts to solve a byzantine crime wrapped in murder and blackmail. Easy is played by Denzel Washington, who gives his usual knowing and soulful performance. But it was Cheadle's Mouse—Easy's trigger-happy and psychotic sidekick—who walked off with the picture. "Cheadle," proclaimed *Rolling Stone*, "is a knockout as this gold-toothed, baby-faced killer." Kenneth Turan, in the *Los Angeles Times*, concluded that Cheadle had given a performance of "picture-stealing bravado." Every time Cheadle stepped into a scene, it popped like a firecracker. Franklin's direction also drew critical praise. "He comes straight out of a tradition of straightforward narrative cinema that reaches back to Howard Hawks and John Huston, yet with a realistic social consciousness that gives his movies even greater depth and relevance," *The Washington Post* said. "Right now, he's right up there with the best." It seemed to bode well for the director, being mentioned in the company of Howard Hawks and John Huston.

In 1995, several Black comic dramas made money (*Friday, Bad Boys, Waiting to Exhale*) but only *Devil in a Blue Dress* was in the Oscar conversation. Cheadle won the Los Angeles Film Critics Association and the National Society of Film Critics awards. He received nominations from a slew of prestigious organizations—the Screen Actors Guild among them—as well. Such recognition made Cheadle a confident bet for a Best Supporting Oscar nomination. The Black press—*Jet* and *Ebony* magazines, *The Chicago Defender*, the *Los Angeles Sentinel*—was trumpeting not only Cheadle, but also Washington's lead performance and Carl Franklin's direction. The Academy was also known for its affinity for period costume design, so it was hoped that Sharen Davis, costume designer for *Devil*, might gain a nomination as well.

On February 13, 1996, the denizens of Los Angeles awoke to hear the announcement of the Academy Award nominees. The Best Picture nominees were: *Apollo 13, Babe, Braveheart, Sense and Sensibility*, and an Italian film, *Il Postino (The Postman)*. *Devil in a Blue Dress* had been overlooked. The Best Actor nominees: Nicolas Cage, Richard Dreyfuss, Sean Penn, Massimo Troisi, and Anthony Hopkins. Nothing for Denzel Washington. The Best Supporting Actor nominees: James Cromwell, Ed Harris, Brad Pitt, Tim Roth, and—the final nominee—Kevin Spacey. No Don Cheadle. Blacks across the nation began fuming. "The fact that Cheadle didn't get a nomination is deeply, deeply disturbing," said the Black filmmaker Warrington Hudlin. "Not only should he have been nominated, he should [have won]." Now overlooked Black performances were thrust into the spotlight. The Academy had long shown an appreciation for actors pulling off Shakespeare performances, so it grated that Laurence Fishburne's praised performance of *Othello* was also overlooked. What of Kenneth "Babyface" Edmonds and the highly praised *Waiting to Exhale* soundtrack? When the entire list of nominees had been unspooled—a total of 166 nominations—only a single Black, Dianne Houston, had been nominated, and that was in the far-below-marquee category of Short Films. (Houston shared her nomination with Joy Ryan on their film, *Tuesday Morning Ride*; the Black nominee only got half a nomination.)

Rev. Jesse Jackson encouraged Blacks to avoid watching or attending the ceremony. "It doesn't stand to reason that if you are forced to the back of the bus," he offered, "you will go to the bus company's annual picnic and act like you're happy." Jackson also announced he was encouraging a boycott of ABC affiliates, the station that broadcast the Oscar ceremony. "We are going to open up the consciousness of America," he vowed. Peter Bart, editorial director of *Variety,* had previously worked in the film business as a producer and studio head. Bart—still quite aligned with the power brokers in Hollywood—took issue with Jackson's position. He wrote a letter, directed to Jackson, saying that "protests and picketing are passé." Bart had more to say: "Johnnie Cochran and his client, O. J. Simpson, have sharply reduced the number of good souls around who will go out on a limb to extend a helping hand." The NAACP and many in the Black community were aggrieved by Bart's letter, feeling that he was subtly maligning them for a legal saga that had nothing to do with Blacks or the film industry.

Landon Jones was executive editor of *People* magazine at the time of the 1996 announcements. The lack of Black nominees disturbed him, and he immediately thought of the Oscar ceremony he had attended a year earlier: "First of all, the audience was entirely white," he said. "Then I remembered that the seat-fillers were entirely white." (Seat-fillers were people who filled seats when someone went to the stage, so the TV cameras didn't show any empty seats.) Jones told some staffers that they needed to do a story on Hollywood's profound lack of diversity and recognition of Black talent. It was definitely time to launch an investigation, but he also knew it would be an unusual undertaking. "There was," Jones recalled decades later, "the thought that if we did a big story about Blacks in Hollywood, it would sell poorly. I was basically paid on how well a cover story sold."

But he began laying out his plans anyway. One benefit that Jones had was that few magazines took on the workplace situation in Hollywood. "I was fairly driven," he says. "I wanted to do serious stories. We [*People*] didn't really have competition. There were no competitors. I could just do what was morally right." Jones, based in New York, held long discussions with the magazine's L.A. bureau. There was nary a *People* staffer on either coast who wasn't involved in working on some facet of the story.

In 1996, reporters did not have the benefit of IMDb, the Internet tool now used to look up a photo or short biography of anyone associated with the film industry. The magazine's staffers were obviously aware of the racial background of high-profile nominees—Pitt, Roth, Penn. But they were at a disadvantage with nominees whose names they did not recognize. So Jones, the editor, tasked every reporter working on the story to phone every single nominee—Costume, Sound, Art Direction, Music—and ask them an all-important question: "It's embarrassing now to even say this," Jones says, "but the reporters had to ask: Are you Black?" And when the survey results came back, the results of the 166 Academy Award nominees were stunning, with Houston the sole Black nominee. That fact alone would make the looming magazine issue seem prescient. The magazine, with a blistering cover-story headline, "HOLLYWOOD BLACKOUT," hit the newsstands on March 18, 1996, just days before the March 25 Oscar ceremony. On the cover were these words: "The film industry says all the right things, but its continued exclusion of African-Americans is a national disgrace."

Jones knew that a *People* cover story often got wide attention, drawing commentary on TV as well as radio. "The big deal with the *People* cover was that the magazine was in every grocery store in America." Jones himself came up with the title. "It was right in your face," he says. He went on CNN's *Reliable Sources* to talk about the story.

Among the statistical findings of the *People* investigation: there were fewer than two hundred Black members in the 5,043-strong Academy of Motion Picture Arts and Sciences, the body that actually votes on nominations; there were only 2.6 percent of Blacks in the Writers Guild; and less than 2 percent in Local 44, the union for set decorators and property masters.

Both the Los Angeles chapters of the National Urban League and the NAACP once again jumped into the fray. "The continuing reality is that if you're an African-American, it's still a good ol' boys club," said John Mack, president of the Los Angeles chapter of the Urban League.

Black actors and actresses and their agents and managers often heard the cry about P & L—profit-and-loss—statements. (It was impossible to decipher, but *Devil in a Blue Dress* may well have been punished by Academy voters for its weak box office: against a $27 million budget, it only grossed sixteen million.) Studios held up the P & L statements when negotiating with agents and managers, but those numbers seemed to be used more harshly when it involved Black actors who appeared in under-performing films. Agents wondered how their clients could show their profit-making abilities if they were rarely cast in films that were certain to turn into blockbusters. It was the conundrum of being trapped in a Catch-22 scenario. The filmmaker Reginald Hudlin proclaimed that the "levels of segregation [in Hollywood] would not be accepted in IBM or American Express."

The brouhaha about Blacks and the film industry was enough to attract the attention of Gilbert F. Casellas, chairman of the U.S. Equal Opportunity Commission. He arranged a meeting with studio representatives and civil-rights organizations. "Some of the grievances I have been told about are blatant and egregious," he said, following the meetings.

What was ultimately surprising to Landon Jones was how little attention the "BLACKOUT" issue received beyond film and media circles. "It sold poorly," he says, "but I'm really proud of it. Maybe the public wasn't ready to hear about the problem." Nevertheless, the story got wide notice, because there were newer outlets—like cable TV—that paid attention to it.

Seven days after the *People* issue hit the newsstands, the Academy Award ceremony took place. Rev. Jesse Jackson had asked attendees to wear ribbons of protest in support of Black grievances in the movie industry. Whoopi Goldberg hosted the ceremony. Her presence illuminated the racial brouhaha that had descended upon Hollywood. "Look," she announced from the stage at the beginning of the evening, "I want to say something to all the people who sent me ribbons to wear, you don't ask a Black woman to buy an expensive dress and cover it with ribbons." There may have been chuckling in the overwhelmingly white audience, but not out there in Black America.

When Landon Jones went on CNN's *Reliable Sources*, a questioner called in and asked how come the *People* story hadn't appeared in magazines that traditionally covered hard news. Howard Kurtz, the host of the program, offered this theory to the listening audience: "One of the reasons you don't see this in magazines like The Atlantic or The New Republic is that some of those magazines have almost no black staffers themselves. They might be reluctant to make an issue of this."

Louis Gossett, Jr., was now going on his third decade of working in Hollywood. He was delighted to see that *People* had exposed the real problems facing Blacks in Hollywood. "We got a little attention," he recalled. "It let the air out of the balloon a little."


Theodore Witcher very much liked watching movies. "The thing that influenced me were the 1970s movies," he says. "I would see *The Godfather, The French Connection, All the President's Men, Apocalypse Now.*" He and his father went to see Kurosawa's *Ran:* "It blew my mind." Witcher graduated from Naperville Central High School, outside Chicago. In 1991, he received his film degree from Columbia College in Chicago. The milieu of moviemaking fascinated him. "I remember walking down Michigan Avenue," he said, of watching something being filmed, "and asking a friend, 'How do you do this?'" With a film degree in hand, he knew he needed to find some kind of work in film production. He was hired by *The Jerry Springer Show,* a reality-TV show that highlighted couples yelling and fighting. Amid the show's on-air bedlam, Witcher, who is Black, always kept an eye on Brian Gardner, one of the show's Black directors. "He was supercool. I mean, so calm. He was able to exude that to the crew." He decided that when he became a director he'd appropriate some of Gardner's style. In his leisure time, Witcher hung out with friends in Chicago's downtown poetry scene. They'd talk about great poets and recite their own poems onstage while jazz floated in the background. It was a world of cool Black people, of strivers and dreamers.

Meanwhile, he began writing screenplays. "My mom suggested I write a letter to all the chairmen of all the studios and introduce myself," he says. "It seemed insane and ridiculous to me." Finally, to appease her, he did. He got a single response, from the office of Mike Medavoy, at TriStar Pictures. The query fell to Rick Hess, another executive, who phoned Witcher. "He said, 'You got something I can read?'" Witcher sent Hess some of his scripts, even if they were works-in-progress. Hess was impressed enough that he connected Witcher with an agent and a manager. In quick order, Witcher was hired to write a screenplay for Allen and Albert Hughes, twin brothers who together directed 1993's hit *Menace II Society* and 1995's *Dead Presidents,* urban-set films with largely Black casts that marked the arrival of major filmmakers. Witcher's script was to be a sequel to *Menace II Society*. After he wrote it and sent it off, he left Chicago for L.A.

Nothing prepared him for what happened next:

"The day I arrived," he recalls, "I got fired." There was no explanation given, only that the producers no longer like the script. But he was there, in L.A., where he wanted to be, and had no intention of going back home. The town was still abuzz about the devastating *People* article. He got some meetings. At one of them, he met Helena Echegoyen, an executive at New Line Cinema. Echegoyen had been part of the producing team for 1994's *House Party 3* and 1995's *Friday;* the latter starred Ice Cube, Chris Tucker, and Nia Long, and on a budget of $3.5 million made an impressive twenty-seven million. Echegoyen asked Witcher what he was thinking about writing next. When he told her he had an idea about a romance between a photographer and an artist set amid the Black spoken-word poetry scene of Chicago, her eyes brightened: "Drop everything! Because I want you to write that." Echegoyen felt the reason for the deficit in Black cinema was that Black movies weren't given the chance to relax, and be sublime, and quiet; they were not given a chance simply to luxuriate in characters' lives. "Whites," she says, "had a larger experience of making movies about 'nothing.' " She felt Black movies were often burdened with having to take on the world and solve a litany of woes. In Echegoyen's mind, Witcher was going off to write a movie "about young people finding themselves."

New Line Cinema had financed *Menace II Society;* they had made it for $3.5 million, and it grossed twenty-eight million. It was a disturbing movie with extravagant violence: some moviegoers were upset by it. Gang fights erupted outside some theatres showing the film. The conservative columnist George Will weighed in, and with a rather surprising interpretation: "In a nation saturated with violence, can a portrayal of violence be valuable because it is therapeutic? The answer may be: Yes, if the portrayal is so relentlessly realistic that it nearly sickens viewers and strengthens their resolve to enforce domestic tranquility."

Echegoyen was happy that her colleagues at New Line were willing to consider making a much quieter film than *Menace II Society*. "I have to give Bob Shaye and New Line credit," she says, referring to the company's founder.

Witcher holed up in his tiny Koreatown apartment. "There was no light," he says. "It was dark and cramped." Alone in L.A., not knowing many people, he had nothing to do but concentrate on writing his screenplay. He'd dash out to get groceries, then dash back to his work. At the end of six months, he had a script, something he was calling, in the lowercase fashion of e. e. cummings, *love jones*. When Helen Echegoyen read Witcher's script, she was moved and touched; she convinced her bosses at New Line to purchase it. The twenty-six-year-old Witcher was ecstatic, but he wanted more: he wanted to direct the film. Surprisingly, New Line executives agreed to his request. They allowed him a seven-million-dollar budget. For a first-time director, it was a fine start.

The *love jones* cast came together with a cadre of young Black film actors: Larenz Tate, Nia Long ("She was like an 'it' girl for black people at the time," Witcher says of Long), Lisa Nicole Carson, Isaiah Washington, and Bill Bellamy. "I remember the first day of filming, and the van picks me up," Witcher recalls. "The line producer, Jeremiah Samuels, said, 'Are you ready to have a hundred thousand volts of electricity wired to your testicles?'" There was nervous laughter. The last thing Witcher wanted to do was appear nervous to the cast and crew. "When you show up to do something you've never done before," he says, "it's not confidence. It's bravado." It took him time to get used to the long days and nights of filming, of being in charge. "I remember waking up after three weeks of shooting. I had never been that tired in my life. I remember staring up at the ceiling and saying, 'I'm not going to make it.' Then you pass that moment."

Filming was completed in seven weeks. If there was a model for Witcher, it was the journey taken by Steven Soderbergh and his 1989 film (also with a lowercase title) *sex, lies, and videotape,* an independent film that caught the cinema world by surprise. It was wildly applauded at the 1989 Cannes Film Festival, winning the Palme D'Or. The film also won the Audience Award at the Sundance Film Festival. And against a $1.2 million budget, Soderbergh's film grossed twenty-four million in the United States and a total of thirty-six million worldwide. The success of the movie catapulted Soderbergh into the formidable rank of young directors on Hollywood's radar.

When Theodore Witcher got the call that *love jones* was accepted at Sundance, "I said to myself, 'The plan is working.'" Then, just as had happened for Soderbergh, he won the Sundance Film Festival Audience Award. "That was a surprise," Witcher says. (The movie was also a Sundance Grand Jury Prize nominee.) All this positive pre-release reception confirmed in Julia Chasman, another producer who worked on the movie, her original feelings about Witcher's script: "It was the first script," she said, "that I had seen that was attempting to show the lifestyles of a whole sector of young African-American artists—the sort of striving artist that we were so used to seeing in white movies."

The movie opened March 14, 1997, on 825 screens, which was fairly wide for a Black film. "This slickly made romance will be touted as something new in modern black films," crowed the *Variety* review, "a look at smart, middle-class urbanites without a gun or homeboy in sight, and pic's fresh feel, along with a sultry jazz and R & B soundtrack, look to push it to sharp B.O. returns." The *New York Times* reviewer had some caveats, but liked the movie: "Theodore Witcher, who wrote and directed his first feature with a sure hand, brings nothing of Spike Lee's political awareness to this frankly sultry and entertaining date movie. Yet if he doesn't examine his characters' ideas closely, neither does he reduce their love story to the crass, garish level of 'Waiting to Exhale.'" From *Entertainment Weekly*: "With its quick-witted portrait of contemporary black bohemia, love jones, like Spike Lee's She's Gotta Have It, offers the slight shock of something that shouldn't, by now, be nearly so novel: the sight of middle-class African-Americans hanging out in a movie just the way white people do—playing pool, flirting, joshing each other with home truths."

Film executives know fairly early if a movie will succeed or not. When the returns for *love jones* began coming in, the mood inside New Line grew somber. It made a little under four million dollars its opening weekend. Two weekends later, the gross had dropped 34 percent. The final tally in its theatrical run was twelve million dollars. In the statistical tabulations of Hollywood, it is commonly thought that a movie has to make two and a half times its budget before it can start showing a profit, so *love jones*'s box office came up very short. If he is to keep going, a director's films have to make money. As the Hollywood quip went: No business, no show.

Witcher was in a tough and wobbly situation. His movie had been well received. Critics liked it. But not enough people actually purchased tickets to see it. It never found a white audience. It never "crossed over." "Perhaps in the end," he says, "maybe it was a bit too novel at the time." In the years that followed, Witcher wrote other scripts, took many meetings. "The fact that [my] movie won an Audience Award at Sundance," he says, "doesn't come into play when you are pitching a movie. If your movie didn't make money, the attitude in those meetings is: 'Why am I having a meeting with this person?'" As much as he tried looking ahead, he couldn't help looking back. "I know audiences liked the movie if they saw it. We couldn't get enough people to buy in." Five years rolled by, then ten—now he was inching up on his late thirties—and he hadn't been able to get another movie to the screen. He had spent years writing an ambitious romantic drama set in the world of musicians. No one was interested. Thoughts came and went about a *love jones* sequel. But nothing came of that, either. "After you cool off," he says, "the town looks at you like you're the problem." He started becoming a fascinating cinema curiosity. Cinéastes began asking, Whatever happened to Theodore Witcher? But, as happens with certain movies over time, *love jones* began rising from the ashes. Young Black writers on film magazines rediscovered it and began writing articles and trumpeting its unique 1990s vibe. He found himself with invitations to museums and cultural centers to screen the film and reflect on its unique take on young Black romance. Witcher was undeniably gifted, but not at all productive. He was like Harper Lee, who only wrote and published one novel during her lifetime. As 2020 began, however, Witcher was hard at work on a romantic drama for Amazon—a project that stalled when the pandemic hit.

One young Black director who didn't have Witcher's problem was John Singleton, who had grown up in South Central Los Angeles. A twenty-three-year-old wunderkind—a mere year removed from USC's film school—he had directed *Boyz n the Hood,* which garnered electrifying high praise at the 1991 Cannes Film Festival. His film told of three friends in South Central trying to keep their friendship together amid gang violence. The Cannes praise was no fluke. *The Hollywood Reporter* called the film "a knockdown assault on the senses, a joltingly sad story told with power, dignity and humor. No mere studio genre piece preening as social significance because its characters are black, Boyz is straight from the neighborhood . . . and straight from the heart." Gene Siskel, writing in the *Chicago Tribune:* "What Singleton does so well is what Martin Scorsese accomplished in 'Mean Streets'—take us inside a closed neighborhood and open up its rituals. 'Mean Streets' was an Italian-American film of the night; 'Boyz n in the Hood' is an African-American film of bright sunlight." *The Christian Science Monitor* referred to Singleton as a "stunningly gifted newcomer" and called his film "complex and nuanced." Singleton made history by becoming the first Black director in Hollywood filmmaking ever to be nominated for a Best Directing Oscar. (Not a single other Black was nominated for one of the marquee Academy Awards that year, but Singleton was greeted with two nominations, for directing and writing. Jonathan Demme won the directing award for *Silence of the Lambs* and Callie Khouri the writing award for *Thelma & Louise*.) Singleton went on to direct many other movies, among them *Poetic Justice, Higher Learning,* a *Shaft* remake with Samuel L. Jackson, and *Baby Boy.* He also directed episodes of TV series, among them *American Crime Story, Empire,* and *Billions.* When he died from complications of a stroke on April 28, 2019—at the age of fifty-one—his death received front-page coverage in newspapers across the country.


Other young Black directors emerged during the 1990s, among them Leslie Harris, who directed *Just Another Girl on the IRT;* Darnell Martin, who directed *I Like It Like That;* Ernest Dickerson, who directed *Juice;* and Matty Rich, who directed *Straight Out of Brooklyn.* None of the films were wildly successful, but they drew fine reviews and exhibited promise. There were stories in national magazines about the advent of Black filmmakers, but all of those Black filmmakers had a difficult time getting their desired follow-up feature off the ground. Harris says: "I had a script about a female executive. What I heard was that it was just hard to get a Black actress in a movie, with me being a Black woman director, producer and writer." Darnell Martin had every right to feel exuberant about the response to her romantic comedy, *I Like It Like That.* Martin received the New York Film Critics Circle Award for Best New Director, and the film won the Film Independent Spirit Award for Best First Feature. But just as quickly, Martin was saddled with the label of being difficult: "As an African-American woman who speaks up and fights against things that are racist or misogynistic, I felt a very big backlash. If I had a penny for every time I was blacklisted and somebody told me, 'You will never work again,' I'd be super, super wealthy." Ernest Dickerson became so frustrated with a lack of opportunities on the big screen that he turned to television work. Matty Rich moved to Paris. Theodore Witcher pulled up yet another chair on another stage, there to talk about all the love being bestowed on his one and only film, years after it had opened to disappointing box office. "White people," Witcher allowed, "get more bites of the apple. That's just true. You can fail three, four times and still have a career. But if you're black, you really can only fail once."

From 1996 to the end of the decade—and across eighty total nominations for Best Actor, Best Actress, Best Supporting Actor, Best Supporting Actress—there were only three nominations and only one Academy

Award bestowed to Black actors, the latter a Supporting Actor statuette for Cuba Gooding, Jr. When you factor in other Academy categories—art design, cinematography, directing, writing—the statistics were even more grim, further exposing the near-impenetrable fortress of Hollywood unions that kept the industry almost all-white.

# 18

# [An Interlude]

## The Ghost of Sidney

H E HOVERED OVER THE TOWN STILL, after all these years. It was because of the ground he had plowed, becoming the first Black actor to win a Best Actor statuette, in 1964 for *Lilies of the Field*. That was also the year when Black America—with a lot of other things on its mind—seemed to come alive to the possibilities of what could happen in Hollywood. No one talked much about Hattie McDaniel anymore and her historic win back in 1940 because, though groundbreaking, her performance was very difficult to watch with modern eyes, a cinematic lesson in stereotyping and racism. Mammy—even with what she had to endure—was a relic. But Poiteeaayy—as his name was still reverently uttered in the American Black and Caribbean communities—was a tall-as-timber legend. The film industry decided to honor him again, at the 2002 Academy Awards ceremony, this time with an Honorary Oscar, to be given, in the words of the Academy, "for representing the industry with dignity, style, and intelligence." No one could deny he had done so.

The year before, there was, yet again, not a single Black among the major nominees. But this year's slate showed a rare and quite welcome diversity: Denzel Washington was nominated for Best Actor for *Training Day*, as was Will Smith for *Ali*—two Black men, and one portraying a Black icon who fought against racism!—along with Russell Crowe, Sean Penn, and Tom Wilkinson. Halle Berry was nominated for Best Actress for *Monster's Ball*, along with Judi Dench, Nicole Kidman, Renée Zellweger, and Sissy Spacek. It had been six years since that explosive *People* magazine issue about the lack of opportunities for Blacks in Hollywood. Now there were segments and newspaper stories on the number of Black nominees. Still, the NAACP wasn't sidelined by the burst of noticeable inclusion and was quick to point out the historical tabulations: up to the eve of the 2002 Awards, there had been 1,369 actors and actresses nominated overall for Academy Awards; of that number, only thirty-nine were Black, and of that number, only six had won. For the civil-rights organization, the residue of the *People* article still hung heavily in the air.

The Oscar ceremony took place on March 24, 2002.

Deep into the show, Julia Roberts opened the envelope for Best Actor. "I love my life," she said as she smilingly glanced at the winner's name. It seemed a hint of her affection for Washington, with whom she had appeared in *The Pelican Brief;* she often bemoaned the fact he had missed out on the Best Actor prize in the past. "Denzel Washington!" she announced. At the lectern, Washington raised his Oscar in the direction of Poitier, who was seated in the balcony. "For forty years I've been chasing Sidney," he said. "I'll always be chasing you, Sidney."

Russell Crowe had the honor of announcing the Best Actress winner. Many saw Kidman, nominated for *Moulin Rouge,* as the odds-on favorite. She had already won a Golden Globe for her performance. Berry received Golden Globe and BAFTA nominations for her *Monster's Ball* role, but won neither. A Black actress had never won a Best Actress prize. Crowe opened the envelope. When he announced "Halle Berry," the camera quickly panned to her. There was a look of genuine astonishment upon her face. "This moment," Berry said at the microphone, "is so much bigger than me. This moment is for Dorothy Dandridge, Lena Horne, Diahann Carroll. . . . It's for every nameless, faceless woman of color who now has a chance because this door tonight has been opened." She cried—sometimes almost uncontrollably—throughout her speech.

Two heights had been scaled in one night inside the thirty-three-hundred-seat Kodak Theatre on Hollywood Boulevard. And the spiritual godfather to every Black in the film industry, the lion of Black Hollywood, was a smiling witness to it all.

It wouldn't take long, however, for many Blacks to wonder if too much significance had been ascribed to the night.

# 19

# The Reckoning

FROM THE 1940S THROUGH THE 1980S, many Blacks had not been emotionally glued to the public perception or reaction to the Academy Awards. There were simply too many other weightier societal concerns. But now it was becoming painfully clear to many Blacks that they deserved to be in the Hollywood conversation. It was hardly a secret that even when Hollywood chose to make a Black-themed film, it was appropriating Black life with very little Black cultural input. The writers and producers and directors were overwhelmingly white. The Black actor in Hollywood was up against whatever notions of Black life those writers and producers and directors brought to the production. Too often, they were skewed or stereotypical assessments. James Baldwin recognized this dilemma: "What the black actor has managed to give are moments—indelible moments, created, miraculously, beyond the confines of the script: hints of reality, smuggled like contraband into a maudlin tale, and with enough force, if unleashed, to shatter the tale to fragments."

In 1987, the Chicago-born actor and comedian Robert Townsend wrote, directed, and starred in *Hollywood Shuffle*, a ribald and autobiographical look at what Black actors went through during the audition process for roles. Townsend cobbled together a hundred thousand dollars to make his film. His biggest role before *Shuffle* had been a small but noticeable part in 1984's *A Soldier's Story*, opposite Howard Rollins, Jr., and Denzel Washington. "I told my agent," he recalled after that film had opened, "I want to do more movies like this. My agent was like, 'Robert, they only do one black movie a year. You just did it. Be happy.'" Townsend had been auditioning for roles on the East and West Coasts since the early 1980s. But

*Hollywood Shuffle* gave his career a serious boost. In one dreamlike scene, Townsend's character is at a session of Black Acting School, where a white instructor tells him how to *act* Black. "Consider the trained black actor in today's Hollywood," Sheila Benson wrote in her 1987 review of Townsend's film, "auditioning desperately for the chance to read lines like 'Why you gotta pull a knife on me? I be got no weapon.'" Benson adds: "Somehow, the humiliating limitations with which Hollywood has hogtied black actors have not eroded Townsend's bedrock sweetness." The Samuel Goldwyn Company released *Hollywood Shuffle.* The hundred-thousand-dollar movie was a hit, grossing five million at the box office.

In the year following the Washington-Berry double win, only one Black, Queen Latifah, received an Academy Award nomination, for her supporting role in *Chicago.* Catherine Zeta-Jones took home the statuette in that category for the same film. The following year, an African actor, Djimon Hounsou, was nominated for Best Supporting Actor for *In America;* he lost to Tim Robbins in *Mystic River.* The year after that, the 2005 show was a high mark for Blacks and Oscar nominations: Don Cheadle (*Hotel Rwanda*) and Jamie Foxx (*Ray*) were nominated for Best Actor; Foxx even received two nominations, his other was for Best Supporting Actor opposite Tom Cruise in *Collateral.* Morgan Freeman (*Million Dollar Baby*) won that category. Sophie Okonedo, a Black British actress, received a Best Supporting Actress nomination for *Hotel Rwanda.* Foxx took home the Best Actor Award.

Then, in August of that year—just as many studios were plotting their next Academy Award campaigns—the water came.

When the heavily Black city of New Orleans was struck by Hurricane Katrina, the disaster quickly exposed the world of indifferent politics and the ongoing plight of poverty in Black America.

For many years, critics of the Army Corps of Engineers had been trying to bring attention to what they perceived as structural flaws in the levees and flood walls that had been constructed to protect New Orleans from fierce hurricanes. But those complaints fell upon deaf ears. The levees in the eastern and western parts of the city were especially worrisome, and those were the levees that had to protect the areas where mostly poor and Black residents lived. On August 23, 2005, meteorologists began spotting severe hurricane potential in the Bahamas. A tropical depression had begun forming, and it looked to be headed right for the Gulf Coast—with Mississippi, Alabama, and especially Louisiana in its path. By August 28, the National Weather Service had begun issuing evacuation orders. But it was estimated that one in four residents of New Orleans did not have a car. A good many of them were living below the poverty line. Many were trapped.

Before landing, the hurricane circled out at sea, whirling and twirling like some kind of angry monster, building momentum. City officials rolled around the city, pleading through bullhorns for lingering residents to leave right away. As officials began realizing that a good many residents simply had no way to flee, they announced that the New Orleans Superdome would be opened to shelter them. Thousands began a trek there, flailing through water that kept rising around them, screaming for loved ones. On the morning of August 29, 2005, the hurricane struck New Orleans with a Biblical force. Trees and cars flew through the air. Winds yanked rooftops from homes. Snakes and alligators slithered down streets. The drowning began, souls gulping for air then disappearing beneath the torrents of water. The entire Ninth Ward, home for much of the city's Black populace, was underwater. The wealthy and the middle class had long made it out of the city, to Baton Rouge or farther, to Houston and Atlanta. Now only the helpless remained. It was a real-life horror movie. The American government seemed frozen and was late to mobilize. When government military units, along with FEMA, finally sprang into action, television audiences watched in stunned disbelief as throngs of mostly Blacks took to rooftops, holding up signs—"PLEASE HELP"; "WHERE IS THE USA?"; "WE NEED FOOD." Mothers were seen holding infants, both wailing. Old Black men and women walked the streets in hospital gowns, carrying bags of clothing and their medicine. The Superdome filled to capacity; the supplies inside were scanty. Fights broke out. Television viewers squinted, hard, when they thought they spotted the actor Sean Penn helping people through the muck. Was it really him? Yes, it was. He looked like an action hero.

When people left the Superdome in search of food, they sometimes attempted to cross bridges leading away from the city. White police officers sometimes fired at them because they didn't want them to enter other jurisdictions. (Some of those officers were later arrested.) The horrors seemed endless. The flood ultimately claimed the lives of eighteen hundred people; the estimated cost of the damage approached a hundred billion dollars. In the aftermath, state politicians blamed one another. President George W. Bush's administration would never recover from the inadequate federal response. The United States Congress demanded an investigation of the lack of governmental preparation. Civil-rights leaders insisted that such a lackluster rescue effort would not have been allowed to happen to whites. Members of the Congressional Black Caucus kept highlighting the true anger at the overwhelming loss of life. Among its many duties, the caucus was especially involved with issues of racial fairness and justice. Beginning in 2005, the Congressional Black Caucus welcomed another member to its body—United States senator Barack Obama, from Illinois.

America—white America—had never seen anything like him. But Black America had long known of gifted Black sons, highly educated young men, thinkers like Du Bois, Martin Luther King, Jr., Whitney Young. Men with high dreams. It pained the young men when those dreams were undercut through no fault of their own. Barack Obama was born in Honolulu to a white mother and African father. At Columbia University, the young Obama was introduced to Harlem, where he listened to jazz and read James Baldwin. Baldwin had such a stylish way of introducing anyone to America—the America that wasn't on television, or at the movies. After Columbia, Obama found work as a community organizer in Chicago. He was making thirteen thousand dollars a year. It was good work, hard and soul-satisfying. But there were other dreams. In 1988, Obama left Chicago and entered Harvard Law School. When he was named editor of the *Harvard Law Review,* the first Black editor, the national press came calling. He married Michelle Robinson, another lawyer. Then came the itch to enter politics. He was elected to the Illinois State Senate in 1996. He was also a fine writer; his book *Dreams from My Father* had been published the year before. It was a tender book, full of insight and honesty, and also an exploration of race in America, and racial attitudes around the world. In 2000, he ran for the U.S. Congress—and lost. Back working in the State Senate, he got his name on notable pieces of legislation, some involving the police and racial profiling. In the 2004 Illinois primary, Obama became the Democratic nominee for the United States Senate. This turned him into a seemingly overnight wonder: There were, at the time, no other Blacks in the Senate. He received ceaseless speaking invitations. He had the gift of captivating audiences.

Senator John Kerry, the 2004 Democratic nominee for president, invited the U.S. Senate candidate Obama to give the Democratic Convention keynote address in Boston that summer. The world didn't know the man who took the Fleet Center stage that evening. Obama stood there, cool, smiling, confident, and delivered less a speech and more a sermon, a tutorial, about where America had been and where he hoped it could go. His words—"there is not a liberal America and a conservative America—there is the United States of America"—seemed to fly like miniature hawks beyond the television screens, landing everywhere. The crux of his speech was simple: He believed in America. And if he—a Black man whose people had been dragged through endless trials—could believe in America, then why couldn't everybody else? It was stirring oratory, filled with visions of unity. At the conclusion of his speech, there was thunderous applause, as well as tears and hugs.

John Kerry went down in defeat that November, but Barack Obama won his Senate seat. It didn't take long to see that there were klieg lights wherever he went. He was Harry Belafonte and Sidney Poitier; he was Paul Newman and Robert Redford; he was James Baldwin–literate; he was cooler than a Miles Davis album. He had done that tricky thing for a Black man in American life—he had crossed over. He made white America feel comfortable coming to him with their hopes and dreams. Two years later, the noise about running for president kept rising. Harry Reid, the Democratic Senate minority leader, summoned Obama to his office and warned him that he would ultimately grow bored in the Senate. Reid, cagey, smart, told him to set his sights on the presidency.

On February 10, 2007, Barack Obama stepped to a lectern in Springfield, Illinois—thousands arrayed before him, cheering, with American flags festooning buildings in the distance—and talked about hope, and audacity, and the wounds that America had reached down over the years to try to heal in order to survive. Then he announced to the gathering what they had come to hear: he was running for president of the United States of America. There had been so many—revered Black politicians among them—who thought it was all just crazy, that it was all so quixotic, that he was taking this audacity thing a bit too far.

A Black man in the White House? Back in 1972, Hollywood thought the idea of such a thing so unbelievable that they made a fictional movie about it: *The Man,* starring James Earl Jones as the nation's first Black president. It flopped.

———

Irving Wallace was born in Chicago but spent his formative years in Wisconsin. He was interested in writing and talented enough to sell a few stories to magazines, though he was a college dropout. After his service in World War II, Wallace tried his hand at screenwriting. Among other films, he was part of a trio of writers who penned *The West Point Story,* a 1953 musical based on Wallace's story that starred James Cagney, Doris Day, and Virginia Mayo. But Wallace grew tired of Hollywood and soon concentrated on writing novels. His breakout book, *The Chapman Report,* published in 1960, revolved around two sex psychologists interviewing women about their sex lives. Wallace's publisher, Simon and Schuster, believed the book would draw favorable comparisons to *Peyton Place,* Grace Metalious's 1956 bestseller, which became a popular 1957 movie and later a television series. Wallace's novel did well, if not *Peyton Place* well, and it was turned into a 1962 film directed by George Cukor and starring Efrem Zimbalist, Jr., Jane Fonda, Shelley Winters, and Claire Bloom. Wallace soon went to work on quite an ambitious novel, called *The Man,* about a Black United States senator named Douglass Dilman. Through a series of strange and impossible-to-believe incidents, Dilman—without being elected—becomes the nation's first Black president. Wallace pleaded with President John F. Kennedy to allow him to spend time roaming the White House to get background material for his novel, and Kennedy agreed. Wallace also read a lot of Abraham Lincoln and Frederick Douglass. In his novel, white racists conspire against Dilman. There is both an assassination attempt and an impeachment trial. *The Man* became a *New York Times* bestseller and was bought as a film by ABC Films and Lorimar Productions. The idea of a Black man as president—in a nation that had only outlawed segregation eight years earlier—seemed far-fetched to many reviewers. They mostly ignored writing about the film. *The New York Times* did weigh in: "About halfway through 'The Man,' one comes to realize that, in its own unwitting way, the film is much more interested in contemplating incompetence than in presenting any ideas about politics, race relations, international diplomacy, personal ambition, courage or what have you." The low-budget film never found an audience.

---

Barack Obama's presidential campaign began to catch fire. He convinced his supporters to turn the word "hope" into something messianic. It became a gospel chant. The faster the weeks on the calendar swirled, the more the campaign's confidence soared. The lions of the civil-rights movement—aging now—boarded the crusade. A nation ripped by race had never seen so many multiracial gatherings. An elderly Black lady named Elise Martin laid her hand on Obama's chest and said: "I am a 93-year-old woman working the polls because you are running. Never give up because I know you can win." Many Blacks had a tender spot for Hillary Clinton, but Obama vanquished her, and his locomotive roared on. On Election Night, the states began falling his way: Virginia, Ohio, North Carolina. And they kept falling. At 11:00 p.m., the television announcers began telling the world: Barack Obama was going to become the forty-fourth president of the United States of America. In a nation where Black men had been lynched in the bright daylight, where his own father had been denied service at restaurants in the nation's capital, a Black man had been elected president. Having rewritten the American narrative, he spoke that night from the stage in Grant Park in Chicago.

Now, against the new cultural landscape—one of undeniable possibility—even Hollywood would have to rethink its positioning: a Black man had ascended to the highest position in the world. He was higher than any Hollywood CEO. The scripts and screenwriters would have to start reflecting a new reality: The cultural weight of Black America meant something and could no longer be ignored. If Hollywood did not alter its landscape, it would appear simply out of step with the times.

President Barack Obama: The Man.

———

In 2013, against all the cultural energies of the Obama era—and his 2012 re-election—the appearance of a set of five films in particular could hardly be seen as coincidence.

The noise began with 42, the Chadwick Boseman–Harrison Ford drama about the rise and life of the baseball legend Jackie Robinson. This Brian Helgeland film opened April 12, 2013, to commemorate the beginning of baseball season. The film had perhaps too many Disney-like moments, redolent of the general shyness American filmmakers often adopted when seeking to make virulent racism palatable to an American mainstream audience. But the cumulative reviews leaned toward the positive, with Boseman, as Robinson, consistently praised for his performance. *The New York Times* called the movie "blunt, simple and sentimental, using time-tested methods to teach a clear and rousing lesson." *Time* magazine liked the movie, but the critic wondered if there were too many "white-washing" scenes with the intended aim of "affording the white audience a comforting distance" from the ravages of racist brutality. Wesley Morris, a Yale man, reviewed 42 for *Grantland* and felt the film focused too much on the Branch Rickey character played by Ford. "So 66 years after Robinson became the first black major league baseball player, here we are with 42, which has been made with such reverence for Robinson's importance that Robinson is barely there."

———

Early in the morning of New Year's Day, 2009, Oscar Grant III, a twenty-two-year-old Black man, was rousted, along with hundreds of others, from a train as it pulled into the Fruitvale Station in Oakland, California. Police had gotten reports of celebratory noise from an unruly crowd; there was also a report of possible gang confrontations. Grant—who had a young daughter—had been telling relatives that he was turning his life around. He had spent time in jail, but now he wanted to become a barber and be a good father. He was thinking of marriage. And, on this Oakland night, all he wanted to do was celebrate New Year's. Johannes Mehserle, a police officer with the Bay Area Rapid Transit System (BART), was on duty as the train—carrying Grant and many others—pulled into the Fruitvale Station. For some reason, Mehserle seemed agitated and, as later reported, was raising his voice in a disturbing manner. His loudness caused many of the train riders to reach for their cell-phone cameras. Youth in many American cities—particularly minority youth—had long been wielding their phones as weapons against wrongdoing, especially by the police. Anthony Pirone, another BART officer on duty, viciously kneed Grant and took him to the ground. Then Grant was handcuffed. The videos had already started recording. Mehserle stepped into view and, in a motion so quick and so eerie and so inexplicable, pulled his gun and shot Grant dead. There were immediate gasps and yelling. A white officer had shot a Black unarmed—and handcuffed—youth in the back, in front of hundreds of bystanders. This could not be covered up or talked away in police verbiage or departmental legalese.

Mehserle told his superiors he thought he was firing his stun gun into Grant, a claim many thought preposterous. Twelve months later, he was charged with second-degree murder. On July 8, 2010, Mehserle was found guilty of involuntary manslaughter. He served less than a year in prison.

Ryan Coogler was a young Black filmmaker living in the Bay Area—where he had grown up—at the time of Oscar Grant's killing. Coogler, who

went through college on a football
scholarship, went to grad school at
the respected USC School of Cinema
Arts. He began to pay special attention
to the craft of screenwriting. Between
2009 and 2011, Coogler made three
short films, all of which showed promise. He was so affected by the killing at
the train station that he reached out
to the Grant family and told them he
wanted to make a film focused mostly
on the last day of Oscar's life. The
family embraced the young Bay Area
filmmaker. Coogler began writing a
script. It attracted the attention of the
producer Nina Yang Bongiovi, who
headed the Academy Award–winning
actor Forest Whitaker's production
company. Whitaker had long taken
an interest in young filmmakers who
might be stymied by the traditional

Forest Whitaker in 2007, accepting
an Oscar for *The Last King of
Scotland* (2006). Both a leading
man and a dazzling character
actor.

Hollywood system. He and Bongiovi signed on as producers to raise the
necessary money and shepherd Coogler's script to the screen.

For the role of Oscar Grant, Coogler cast Michael B. Jordan, a young
actor who had a role on the TV series *Friday Night Lights.* Octavia Spencer
agreed to play Grant's mother. Funding of independent films always posed
a challenge, and Spencer joined in the effort. (One of the investors was
Kathryn Sockett, author of *The Help,* which Spencer had starred in.) With
the necessary money raised, Coogler convinced BART officials to allow
him to shoot pivotal scenes at the Fruitvale Station.

Ryan Coogler's debut film had its first showing on January 19, 2013,
in Park City, Utah, at Sundance. Coogler won an Audience Award and a
Grand Jury Prize at the festival. The director seemed genuinely awed in
accepting the awards. "At the end of the day, when I first made this project,"
he told the audience, "it was about humanity, and how we treat the people
we love most and the people we don't know. To get this award means that it
had a profound impact on the audience that saw it, on the people that were
responsible for picking it up." He went on: "And this goes back to my home,
to the Bay Area, where Oscar Grant lived, breathed, slept, loved, fought,

had fun and survived for twenty-two years." Coogler's film went on to win an award at the Cannes Film Festival, among many others.

The movie opened on July 12, 2013. *The Guardian*'s Peter Bradshaw called it a "bold act of imagination and compassion." Bradshaw also thought the film deserved to be compared to the works of Ken Loach, Charles Burnett, and Michael Roemer. *Rolling Stone*'s Peter Travers had seen the movie at Sundance and had been praising it ever since. In his review he wrote: "*Fruitvale Station* is a gut punch of a movie. By standing in solidarity with Oscar, it becomes an unstoppable cinematic force." Bob Mondello of NPR referred to the movie as "Greek tragedy": "*Fruitvale Station* doesn't have anything shattering to say about the case, or the man, really. But it may well leave you shattered by his story." From *The Washington Post*'s Ann Hornaday: "*Fruitvale Station* isn't just a great film about a timely subject but a great film, period—a study in character and atmosphere every bit as urgent and expressive as the Italian neo-realists or Cassavetes and Scorsese in their prime." The year 2013 was at the halfway point. "*Fruitvale Station*," reported the New Orleans *Times-Picayune,* "is only the first in a string of civil-rights minded movies set to hit theatres this year—contributing to what could be the most racially conscious award season in recent memory."

———

Black Americans still carried painful memories of Hollywood's recent civil-rights-themed movies. They always had a white protagonist, and went about diluting the bravery displayed by Blacks in the South. No movie had stung like Alan Parker's 1988 *Mississippi Burning*. The film told the real-life story of the three civil-rights workers who had gone missing in Mississippi in 1964. They were found murdered, and Mississippi law-enforcement officers had done the killing. The film starred Gene Hackman and Willem Dafoe as the FBI agents looking for the vanished trio. Parker, the director, was British, and his unfamiliarity with the reality of America's racial history skewed his movie in a strange direction. In Parker's cinematic telling, the white FBI agents emerged as heroes solving the case. The case was actually cracked with the help of an informant, who was given a thirty-thousand-dollar reward. In truth, the FBI stifled Black progress, playing a minimal role in the South during the heightened civil-rights battles, all on orders from FBI director J. Edgar Hoover. The blowback upon the film's opening was swift. Civil-rights historians—as well as those who themselves were in the 1960s battles—assailed Parker and the film. Julian Bond, the Atlanta civil-rights figure who had worked alongside Martin Luther King, Jr., and the *Mississippi Burning* actor Gene Hackman went on ABC's *Nightline* to discuss the film in the wake of the controversy. "It's just wrong," Bond said about the approach of the film. "These guys [FBI] were tapping our telephones, not looking into the murders of Goodman, Chaney, and Schwerner." Hackman seemed uncomfortable on the program. "I don't feel the film needs defending," he said. Mike Medavoy, who headed Orion Pictures, the studio that made the movie, told the *Los Angeles Times*, "This is the first broadly acceptable film any studio has made on this subject. I'm proud of it, and I didn't see Bill Cosby or Eddie Murphy making it."

Hollywood had become hooked by the white-savior theme in films purportedly about Blacks. In 1989, Euzhan Palcy became the first Black woman to direct a major Hollywood (MGM) studio film. She was given the reins to adapt André Brink's novel *A Dry White Season,* set in apartheid South Africa. The well-intentioned film, which starred Donald Sutherland, Susan Sarandon, Zakes Mokae, and Marlon Brando, was about a white family and its inner turmoil when confronted with the horrifying conditions in which Blacks lived in South Africa. "Recent dramas," *The Washington Post* noted in reviewing Palcy's film, "such as 'Cry Freedom' and 'Mississippi Burning' have been criticized for emphasizing the white role in what is essentially a black struggle, and thereby garnering a greater audience." The review went on to state that Palcy's "authentically portrayed black characters are much more than victims, if still not the sole protagonists in their story." The following year, 1990, Whoopi Goldberg and Sissy Spacek starred in the drama *The Long Walk Home.* It told the story of the Montgomery Bus Boycott, which took place in 1955 Alabama. That boycott turned Martin Luther King, Jr., and Rosa Parks into marquee figures of the burgeoning civil-rights movement. But *The Long Walk Home*—narrated by a white character—focused on the turmoil of the white character played by Sissy Spacek.

When it came to civil-rights history and films, Hollywood was reimagining what had actually taken place.

———

In the same week as Barack Obama's 2008 election, an article appeared on the front page of *The Washington Post* about the life of Eugene Allen, a

Black man, a longtime White House butler who served eight presidents, from Harry Truman to Ronald Reagan. He was born in 1919 in a log cabin in Virginia. He never for certain knew his birth father, but speculation always centered on the plantation's white overseer. (Large farms still kept the identity of being "plantations" many years after slavery had ended.) Allen left Virginia and made his way to Washington, D.C., where he worked in country clubs, establishing a reputation as a dependable worker with excellent manners. Starting in 1952, during the waning days of the Truman administration—doing menial duties such as setting tables and washing dishes as a pantry man—Allen rose through the ranks during three decades to a position of maître d', the highest-ranking position on the White House service staff. During his service, Allen met a long list of luminaries—Martin Luther King, Jr., Frank Sinatra, Pablo Casals, Sammy Davis, Jr., James Brown, and Elvis Presley among them—and witnessed many of the history-altering White House events from his unique perspective. When Laura Ziskin, a successful Hollywood producer known for the highly successful *Spider-Man* films, read the article, she was immediately convinced it should be a movie.

Ziskin set her planned film up with Amy Pascal, the head of Sony Pictures. Danny Strong, an actor and gifted screenwriter (Emmy nominee for TV's 2008 *Recount* and Emmy winner for *Game Change* in 2012), came aboard to write the script. Sony eventually let the picture go, but Ziskin and her producing partner, Pam Williams, only grew more enamored of it. Strong reimagined the film so it became an epic look at the civil-rights movement with a White House butler—loosely modeled on the real Eugene Allen—spinning around at the center of the story. Steven Spielberg and Denzel Washington expressed interest, but their schedules could not be worked out. It was now 2011. Spielberg, who was keeping an eye on the project, told Ziskin he felt it was important to get the movie in motion—in case Obama lost the 2012 election. The filmmaker thought a loss might dilute the film of some of its power.

Lee Daniels had made a very dramatic splash in Hollywood in 2009 when he became the first Black director to have a motion picture (*Precious*) nominated for a Best Picture Oscar. The film told the story of a Black teenager abused by her mother and raped by her father. Daniels also became just the second Black director—after John Singleton seventeen years earlier, in 1992—to be nominated for a Best Director award. He also made history when he became the first Black filmmaker nominated for a Directors Guild of America award for *Precious*. Daniels, of late, had been trying to get a drama about Martin Luther King, Jr., and the march across the Edmund Pettus Bridge off the ground. But no major studio stepped forward to finance the project. Ziskin approached Daniels about directing Strong's screenplay. "When I first read Danny Strong's screenplay," Daniels said, "I knew I had to direct this film." In the summer of 2011, Ziskin, who had suffered from breast cancer, took a turn for the worse. Her stamina waned; she'd nod off on the phone while pleading with potential investors to help finance the film. On June 12, 2011, she died. On her deathbed, Ziskin made those around

Lee Daniels in 2010. His movies won awards and carved his place in Hollywood history.

her promise to get the film made. She believed in the project so deeply she left money in her final will to ensure that it would stay on course to get made. Sheila Johnson, one of the founders of Black Entertainment Television (BET) and an investor in the movie they were now calling *The Butler*, adopted a page from the Oscar Micheaux game plan: she recruited a cadre of investors to raise the remaining needed funds. It was a multi-racial assemblage—athletes, financiers—and it worked. Finally, they had raised thirty million dollars.

Lee Daniels recruited an astonishing array of talent for his film: Forest Whitaker played the butler; Oprah Winfrey the butler's wife; David Oyelowo and Elijah Kelley sons of the butler; Lenny Kravitz and Cuba Gooding, Jr., additional White House butlers. Others in a cast laden with Oscar winners included Jane Fonda, Vanessa Redgrave, Robin Williams, Terrence Howard, and James Marsden. The actors told the press they were eager to work with Daniels because he was "an actor's director." Filming took place in and around New Orleans in the summer of 2012. Daniels found his shooting schedule exceeding the film's budget, and at times during filming retreated to his trailer, picked up the phone, and relentlessly scrounged up more money to finish. Various studios got an early look at a rough cut. They began offering bids to distribute and market the film. The Weinstein Company won out and announced the movie would open on August 16, 2013.

Oprah Winfrey and Terrence Howard. Oprah came out of "retirement" from movies to star in *The Butler*.

Weeks before its planned opening, *The Butler* found itself mired in a bizarre arbitration motion filed by Warner Brothers. The studio revealed to the Motion Picture Association of America (MPAA) that they had a 1916 silent short film titled *The Butler,* and since they owned the rights to that title, they didn't want anyone else to use it. The flap had roots in some unnamed film-negotiation skirmish between Warner and the Weinstein Company. In the end, the contretemps was settled. A fine was levied upon the Weinstein Company, and there was a name change. It was now officially called *Lee Daniels' The Butler.*

A. O. Scott wrote, in *The New York Times,* "A brilliantly truthful film on a subject that is usually shrouded in wishful thinking, mythmongering and outright denial." He added, "The genius of 'The Butler' lies in the sly and self-assured way it connects public affairs to private experience." *Entertainment Weekly* heaped praise on the performances of Oprah Winfrey ("a beautifully nuanced Oprah Winfrey") and Forest Whitaker ("As Cecil, Whitaker is mesmerizing. The actor seems to shrink into his imposing frame, summoning a performance of quiet, bottled up force"). Framing his review against the backdrop of *Mississippi Burning,* Peniel Joseph, on *IndieWire,* wrote: " 'Mississippi Burning' sparked rightful outrage from activists and historians for willful dissemblance in changing the heroes of Mississippi's 1964 Freedom Summer from black students and white volunteers to FBI agents. In contrast, 'The Butler' presents a depiction of civil rights era violence that's powerful and moving." He went on: "It's also unusual, since Hollywood has studiously avoided a film that accurately explores racial violence during the 1960s." Theatres quickly began reporting sellouts. Church groups from rural Southern communities began booking whole theatres. When the receipts came in for the first week, it showed *The Butler* sitting atop the box office, with a twenty-five-million-dollar haul. It remained there for two more weeks, surprising box-office analysts. At the end of its North American run, *The Butler* had a domestic gross of $116.6 million, and another $51.1 million in foreign markets, bringing its worldwide take to $167.7 million.

---

For a Black man in pre–Civil War America, Solomon Northup led a life he was proud of. He lived as a free man in Hebron, New York, with his wife, Anne, and their three children, Alonzo, Margaret, and Elizabeth. Everyone pitched in with farm chores. Northup was willing to move around to find more financially rewarding work so he could better provide for his family. He did so in 1832: "With one cow, one swine, a yoke of fine oxygen I had lately purchased of Lewis Brown, in Hartford, and other personal property and effects," he recalled, "we proceeded to our new home in Kingsbury. That year I planted twenty-five acres of corn, sowed large fields of oats, and commenced farming upon as large a scale as my utmost means would permit." There was another element of life that made Solomon Northup happy: he was a musician, and played the fiddle at small villages in upstate New York. "Throughout the surrounding villages," Northup wrote, "my fiddle was notorious." His musical talents added to the family's finances. Another move, in 1834, saw the Northup family settle in Saratoga Springs, New York. He worked as a carriage driver during the next two years, while Anne worked mostly as a hotel cook. He still played his music whenever he could.

Slavery wasn't legal in New York State, but slave owners could still travel into the region with their slaves. Northup frequently ran into slaves in Saratoga Springs. They engaged him in furtive conversations about their longing for freedom. Their stories of bondage horrified him. He was thankful that his family was far removed from the nightmare of slavery. White strangers also struck up conversations on the street with Northup, often to compliment his musical skills. So it was no surprise to him when two white men approached on the street in Saratoga Springs in March 1841. They immediately complimented him on his musical ability, which put him at ease. The two men told Northup they were with a Washington, D.C., circus and wished to employ him for his fiddle playing. The men were well dressed, sounded reputable, and offered wonderful wages. Northup rushed home and packed. Soon he found himself seated in a carriage with the two businessmen, rumbling toward points south. They first stopped in New York City, which Northup thought was the final destination. But the men told him that an even better opportunity and more money awaited him in Washington, D.C. Northup knew Washington was a slave territory and thus dangerous for him. The men quieted his worry by taking him to get "free papers," documents that verified his legal freedom. Northup trusted the men and agreed to go on with them. Once there, he was given cash, which eased his concerns, told again that the circus was going to be happy to employ him, and plied with booze. A blurry night passed by, and when he woke up his head was pounding, and men were telling him he surely needed medical attention. It was likely more than just alcohol Northup had consumed; something had sickened him. He recalled in his memoir being dragged down a hallway, and days of foggy reality—"but when consciousness returned I found myself alone, in utter darkness, and in chains."

Solomon Northup had been kidnapped. He was ensconced in a Washington slave pen, shaking and delirious with fear. A slave owner approached and told him that he was now his property, and that he would be going to New Orleans—as his slave. The self-proclaimed circus employers were con artists and slave kidnappers. To prepare him for his journey farther south, he was stripped naked and beaten on the spot. Northup was then transported to Louisiana, lost to his wife and children, terrified daily, a kidnapped Black man turned slave. The hard, brutish years on cotton plantations and sugar plantations—1841 to 1853—rolled painfully by, twelve years in all. "My great object always was to invent means of getting a letter secretly into the post office, directed to some of my friends or family at the North," he later wrote. "The difficulty of such an achievement cannot be comprehended by one unacquainted with the severe restrictions imposed upon me. In the first place, I was deprived of pen, ink, and paper."

One day in 1852, Northup—long existing under the name "Platt"—overheard a conversation between a slave master and an itinerant white carpenter by the name of Bass who hailed from Canada. It was obvious from the conversation that Bass opposed slavery. Northup began wondering if he could trust Bass to deliver a letter for him, letting his family in the North know he was alive and needed immediate rescue. When the two finally engaged in conversation, Bass believed Northup, was astonished at his plight, and quietly agreed to help him.

It took weeks still, but once the letters got to Northup's family members and judges in New York, a concerted effort to free him was put in motion. No one on the Louisiana plantation where Northup was enslaved suspected a thing. Armed men on horseback with official documents arrived to free him. They met no resistance. The horrifying nightmare was finally over. When Solomon Northup finally reached his family in New York, his son was away still trying to earn money to buy back his father's freedom.

Solomon Northup wrote of his kidnapping in *Twelve Years a Slave*, published in 1853, the year of his rescue. He dedicated the book to the author of *Uncle Tom's Cabin*, Harriet Beecher Stowe. He worked for abolitionist causes, but then, not long after his rescue, vanished completely. No one could confirm a sighting of Northup in the intervening years. There were those who believed he had returned South to rescue slaves because he had been so haunted by his own ordeal. It was believed that he died sometime between 1864 and 1875. In the succeeding years, Solomon Northup's book receded from view. It was finally resurrected in 1968, republished by the Louisiana State University Press.

––––––––

The psychological grip of colonialism lay so heavy upon British life that there was no such thing as a Black film industry in Britain. There was not the wickedness of segregation laws, as in America. Yet British cinema, for the most part, simply ignored Black life. The first Black British film star wasn't even a Brit. It was Paul Robeson, who had left America to work in the British film industry in the 1930s and '40s. Blacks in Britain who knocked on the doors of the film industry went unheard.

It was supposed to be different for Johnny Sekka. Born in Gambia, Sekka arrived in London in 1952. He was handsome and soon pointed in the direction of the theatre, training at the prestigious Royal Academy of Dramatic Art. Sekka began appearing in films: *East of Sudan, Khartoum, The Last Safari*. In the early 1960s, he was being compared to Sidney Poitier. But Sekka's career just as quickly leveled off. "Sean Connery, Terry Stamp, Michael Caine, Tom Courtenay, John Hurt. I started out with these people," he told *The Times* (London) in 1969. "Today they are stars. I'm not jealous. But why the hell not me? I have the same talent and ability."

A young Black aspiring to the film industry in England had to have both pluck and vision. Steve McQueen started going to films in the 1980s, thrilled by the art of cinema. It was better than the drudgery of school life. "School was painful because I just think that loads of people, so many beautiful people, didn't achieve because no one believed in them, or gave them a chance, or invested in them," he said in a 2014 interview with *The Guardian*. "A lot of beautiful boys, talented people, were put by the wayside. School was scary for me because no one cared, and I wasn't good at it because no one cared."

McQueen landed at art school. There were more movies to see. He saw something special in the films of Jim Jarmusch, Martin Scorsese, and the young Spike Lee. And since they all had links to New York University, that's where he wanted to go. His parents supported his trek across the pond, but the NYU experience wasn't fortifying. He returned to London, where he began making experimental films.

Some were shorts, only a few minutes in length, but they were artsy and attention-grabbing. McQueen was fascinated by the 1981 hunger strike staged by Irish Republican prisoners and set out to make a feature-length film about it. The film, *Hunger,* was brilliant and powerful, an extraordinary feature debut. It starred Michael Fassbender and had its premiere at the 2008 Cannes Film Festival. McQueen became the first British director to receive the Caméra d'Or at Cannes, a prize given to a first-time director. *Hunger* picked up other prizes along the way from the Sydney Film Festival, the Toronto International Film Festival, and the Los Angeles Film Critics Association. On the hustings he'd talk about the need for filmmakers to challenge themselves. He made *Shame,* a film about a sex addict. And then McQueen turned to the evils of slavery.

His wife handed him Solomon Northup's *Twelve Years a Slave*. McQueen was ashamed he knew nothing about the story. He had long held a view that American filmmakers were afraid to tackle the subject of slavery. McQueen was hardly the only Black filmmaker who felt that with the election of President Obama, Hollywood's eyes might widen. He rounded up financing. Brad Pitt's production outfit, Plan B Entertainment, joined the film, along with Arnon Milchan and Anthony Katagas. John Ridley, a Black writer, wrote the screenplay. McQueen cast Chiwetel Ejiofor as Northup. Others in the cast were Fassbender, Benedict Cumberbatch, Sarah Paulson, and a newcomer, Lupita Nyong'o.

Filming of Northup's harrowing story took place in Louisiana during the summer of 2012. McQueen was determined to stretch his modest twenty-two-million-dollar budget as much as possible. Some of the scenes were filmed near where some of Northup's slave years were actually spent. Both McQueen and his crew were in awe of the ground they were filming on. "Everything I've done," McQueen said in 2019, speaking with the *Evening Standard,* "I've made it my job to fail, and I've been fortunate not to. If you do something about a hunger striker, do something about slave addiction, do something about slavery . . . it's taking the hard road."

The early film-festival showings for *Twelve Years a Slave* created a loud buzz. "Stark, visceral, and unrelenting, *Twelve Years a Slave* is not just a great film, but a necessary one," wrote *The Guardian*'s Paul MacInnes during the Toronto Film Festival. The film's distributors decided to "platform" the film, opening it slowly around the country, in hopes of building word of mouth, good interviews, and momentum. The plan worked; the reviews were electric. Writing in *Entertainment Weekly,* Owen Gleiberman called it "a new movie landmark of cruelty and transcendence" as well as "a movie about a life that gets taken away, and that's why it lets us touch what life is." In her *New York Times* review, Manohla Dargis felt that "the genius of 'Twelve Years a Slave' is its insistence on banal evil, and on terror, that seeped into souls, bound bodies and reaped an enduring terrible price."

The critic Steve Boone weighed in: "2013 seems to be the year of settling up accounts with American racism and white supremacy at the movies." There seemed to be a sudden rush by Black filmmakers to get their diverse stories in front of financiers and studio chiefs. The question hung in the air: Would Hollywood be so receptive after Obama departed the White House?

If there had been a box-office curse on movies about slavery, Steve McQueen's *Twelve Years a Slave* vanquished it. It earned a respectable fifty-six million dollars from the United States box office and an eye-popping $131 million internationally, a worldwide gross of $187 million. And even though there was a white heroic figure in the character of Bass, there was no doubt that the true hero of the film was the fiddle-playing gentleman from New York who had disappeared into an American nightmare. "I needed to see them," McQueen told *The Guardian* in 2014, referring to the images of slavery throughout his film. "It's very important. I think that's why cinema's so powerful."

———

Filmgoers in 2013 were treated to yet one more major Black film before year's end. On November 29, *Mandela: Long Walk to Freedom*—about the rise of the South African anti-apartheid leader—opened, with a cast led by Idris Elba and Naomie Harris.

Nelson Mandela had been largely unknown to many Americans until the anti-apartheid movement swept from Europe into the United States in the 1980s. Mandela, born in 1918, had studied and practiced law in South Africa. When the white government instituted laws designed to brutalize Blacks and began a series of oppressive actions, along with unchecked police powers, Mandela and the African National Congress (ANC) began protesting to force the government to change. When they sensed the government's intransigence, they went underground. There were bombings and civic disruptions. Mandela, pursued by the government, became known as the Black Pimpernel, a takeoff of the Scarlet Pimpernel, the English fictional character who performed good deeds during the French Revolution. In 1962, Mandela was captured at a roadblock and sentenced to life in prison. Throughout the years, international pressure ignited by the British government intensified to have him released. Americans came late to the rallying cry, but when they did, it became a cause on college campuses. The efforts lasted twenty-seven years.

Mandela emerged from prison in 1989 as a worldwide hero. The movie about the South African, directed by Justin Chadwick, was stately and stodgy. "At times, *Mandela* lurches from event to event, in the way that movies do when filmmakers are covering lots of history," the *San Francisco Gate* critic wrote. "This results in some moments of awkwardness, but they are a small price to pay when the overall effect is enlightening and inspiring." From *The Washington Post*: "'Mandela' . . . does a worthy job of honoring both its subject and its audience. It can feel, at times, both overlong and oversimplified, but the story propels itself along while awakening in viewers some profound emotions."

The prestigious Screen Actors Guild (SAG) nominees are usually good predictors of Oscar nominations. On December 11, 2013, the SAG nominations were announced. The five nominees for Outstanding Performance by a Cast in a Motion Picture (the equivalent of Best Picture): *American Hustle, Twelve Years a Slave, August: Osage County, Lee Daniels' The Butler,* and *Dallas Buyers Club.* The nominees for Outstanding Performance by a Male Actor in a Leading Role were: Bruce Dern (*Nebraska*), Tom Hanks (*Captain Phillips*), Forest Whitaker (*The Butler*), Matthew McConaughey (*Dallas Buyers Club*), and Chiwetel Ejiofor (*Twelve Years a Slave*). The nominees for Outstanding Performance by a Male Actor in a Supporting Role were: James Gandolfini (*Enough Said*), Michael Fassbender (*Twelve*

*Years a Slave*), Daniel Brühl (*Rush*), Barkhad Abdi (*Captain Phillips*), and Jared Leto (*Dallas Buyers Club*). The SAG nominees for Outstanding Performance by a Female Actor in a Leading Role were: Cate Blanchett (*Blue Jasmine*), Sandra Bullock (*Gravity*), Judi Dench (*Philomena*), Meryl Streep (*August*), and Emma Thompson (*Saving Mr. Banks*). The nominees for Outstanding Performance by a Female Actor in a Supporting Role were: Jennifer Lawrence (*American Hustle*), Julia Roberts (*August*), Oprah Winfrey (*The Butler*), Lupita Nyong'o (*Twelve Years a Slave*), and June Squibb (*Nebraska*). Prognosticators were now putting *Twelve Years a Slave*, *Fruitvale Station*, *The Butler*, *42*, and *Mandela* in the Best Picture Oscar conversation. (The eventual winners for the SAG awards were *American Hustle*, McConaughey, Leto, Blanchett—all white—and Nyong'o.)

The 2014 Academy Award nominations (for 2013 films) were announced on January 16. There was an immediate and fierce eruption of painful, heated discussion about all the Black-themed movies that were denied nominations: zero nominations for *Fruitvale Station*, *The Butler*, and *42*. *Mandela* did receive a single nomination, for Best Original Song. The only Black-themed film that received multiple nominations was *Twelve Years a Slave*, which received an impressive nine. The *Twelve Years* marketing team had coined a phrase that was emblazoned on the film's ads: "It's Time." The words were a pointed reminder that a picture directed by a Black director had never, in the long history of the Academy Awards, won the Best Picture prize.

———

The comedian Ellen DeGeneres hosted the 86th Academy Awards telecast. Toward the end of her opening monologue, she said there were two possibilities that would be remembered about the night: One, that *Twelve Years a Slave* would win Best Picture. "And possibility two: you're all racists." The laughter was of a nervous kind. But *Twelve Years a Slave* did win three Academy Awards that night: Best Picture, Best Adapted Screenplay (John Ridley), and Best Supporting Actress (Nyong'o). McQueen did not win Best Director, a category that no Black had ever won. But it was nevertheless a glorious night for the filmmaker. In the months ahead, he would announce plans to make a series of small-screen films about racial incidents that had long haunted his native Britain and been for the most part ignored by filmmakers.

· **20** ·

# The Front Page

THE YEAR 2015 WAS THE CENTENNIAL of 1915's *Birth of a Nation* and its screening at President Woodrow Wilson's White House. In succeeding decades, American presidents—well aware of the Wilson cinematic brouhaha—kept their movie watching at the White House rather tame. President Franklin D. Roosevelt enjoyed watching documentaries, although Winston Churchill suggested he take time to watch *Mrs. Miniver,* a World War II film with Walter Pidgeon and Greer Garson, which he did. President Eisenhower liked Westerns; one of his favorite films was the homespun all-white musical *Oklahoma!* In November 1963, President Kennedy watched *From Russia With Love* at the White House. The day after the viewing, he departed on his fateful trip to Dallas. President Johnson would fall asleep during screenings at the White House. At the end of a movie, he'd pop up, turn to the gathering, and blurt, "Did ya'll like it?" But there was one film that LBJ loved so much that it was screened eighteen times at the White House. (He sat through twelve of those screenings!) It was a documentary titled *The President's Country,* narrated by Gregory Peck, and it was about one of Johnson's favorite people in the whole wide world: himself! President Jimmy Carter would brag to friends how astounded he was that he could simply express an interest in a brand-new film and a Hollywood studio would send it right to the White House. His favorites were noncontroversial films, nothing that would upset mainstream (white) society. There hadn't been much racial diversity across the decades in the films screened at the White House. But all that changed with President Barack Obama and First Lady Michelle Obama.

President Obama was renowned for his appreciation of cinema. His

Harlem congressman Adam Clayton Powell, Jr., and President
Lyndon Johnson in 1965. Powell was the first politician to hold
hearings about discrimination in the film industry.

White House movie screenings were coveted invitations. The films the
Obamas screened were eclectic, veering from animation to the socially
conscious. Never had so many Black actors and actresses been seen
inside the White House during any previous administration. In 2012, the
Obamas hosted *Lincoln*, Steven Spielberg's film about the Great Eman-
cipator. The film won an Oscar for Daniel Day-Lewis's towering performance. Also that year, the Obamas hosted a showing of *Beasts of the
Southern Wild*, a fantasia of a movie about a six-year-old Black girl who
goes by the name of Hushpuppy, played by newcomer Quvenzhané Wallis, surviving in a post-apocalyptic New Orleans. Wallis was so stunning
in the movie that she received a Best Actress nomination, and the film
a Best Picture nomination. (The independently produced *Beasts,* made
for $1.8 million, reaped twenty-three million in worldwide box office.)
In 2013, the Obamas hosted screenings for *Mandela: Long Walk to Freedom* and *42*, the Jackie Robinson biopic. In the summer of 2013, Obama
watched *The Butler* on his summer vacation. "I teared up thinking about
not just the butlers who worked here in the White House," he confided to
the radio host Tom Joyner, "but an entire generation of people who were
talented and skilled. But because of Jim Crow and because of discrimination, there was only so far they could go."

Filmgoers in 2013 had experienced richly diversified cinema offerings;

many—especially those in the Black community—were hoping for more of the same in 2014. But the lineup of films with Black performers in major roles was markedly less robust that year.

It wasn't until May 2 that American audiences were treated to a film with a Black leading role that elicited awards talk. *Belle* had its roots, however, in England. Dido Elizabeth Belle was a Black child born into slavery in the British West Indies in 1761. Her father, Sir John Lindsay, a naval officer, secreted her (he had found her living in wretched conditions) back to England; her mother was a slave whom Lindsay had impregnated. Lindsay allowed the child to be raised by other family members, principally a cousin, the well-heeled William Murray, First Earl of Mansfield, and his wife, Elizabeth, the countess of Mansfield. It was a fairy-tale turn of events for young Dido. She would remain in the sumptuous living quarters of Sir John Lindsay's palatial Kenwood House for three decades. The family had stipulated in their will that "Belle," the name many called her by, would be granted her freedom. She eventually married a Frenchman and died at the age of forty-three, in 1804. Because of the unique turns of her life, Belle became the subject of paintings, plays, novels, and short films. She was a heroine to Blacks in Britain.

The young filmmaker Amma Asante became interested in Belle's legacy and began putting together her film in 2010, with the help of a consortium of British production companies. A Black woman who had grown up in London, Asante was an actress before turning to directing. The first film she directed, *A Way of Life,* appeared in 2004. It told the story of an Asian family dealing with racism in England. For *Belle,* Asante had to convince producers she could handle the task of directing a bigger movie—in budget and scope—that was also a period piece. She cast Gugu Mbatha-Raw—a product of the Royal Academy of Dramatic Art, who had recently been appearing on episodic British television—as Belle. Others in the cast were Miranda Richardson, Tom Wilkinson, Matthew Goode, and Penelope Wilton. When the film opened, May 2, 2014, it earned praise for its acting and directing from a wide range of critics, but it may have been too sedate for American audiences, earning ten million dollars, and another six million abroad. On a budget of ten million, it could hardly be classified as a profitable film. Nevertheless, both Gugu Mbatha-Raw and Asante garnered attention from Hollywood.

With the release of *Belle,* two Black British directors—Asante and Steve McQueen—had taken on subjects set in the antebellum era, which American directors were still shying away from.

Just over eight weeks after the premiere of *Belle,* a gruesome attack took place in New York City that was devastating to Black America.

A man by the name of Eric Garner was lolling about on Bay Street in the Tompkinsville section of Staten Island. He was a large Black man, harmless, a Ralph Ellison character—invisible to much of white society but at home among his Black friends in the streets. It was three-thirty on the afternoon of July 17, and Garner had just played Good Samaritan by breaking up a street fight. His friend Ramsey Orta—like others nearby—was happy to see that Garner had deescalated a skirmish. The commotion, however, drew the attention of two police officers. Sidling up to the huffing and puffing Garner, they looked up and down the street, trying to assess things, and saw nothing amiss. The officers knew Garner from past encounters, which Garner had previously called harassment. They told him they suspected him of selling loose cigarettes, considered a minor infraction of New York State law (because loose cigarettes could not be taxed). Garner told them they were wrong. The officers, indeed, had no proof. Voices were raised. "Every time you see me, you want to mess with me," Garner complained. "I'm tired of it." One of the officers reached for Garner, and he swatted the officer's arm away, upon which they jumped him. Garner crumpled to the ground. As bystanders suddenly howled, one of the officers, Daniel Pantaleo, put Garner in a chokehold. "I can't breathe," Garner said, "I can't breathe." He uttered those words eleven times. Pantaleo—his arms thick and muscled—continued his vise-grip around Garner's neck. More officers appeared. Orta, Garner's friend, had pulled out his cell phone and was recording the mêlée. Garner fell unconscious. Hours later, at the hospital, he was pronounced dead. The outrage was swift—another Black man dead at the hands of white law enforcement. Surely, with the existence of the horrific Orta video, there'd be an indictment. But a grand jury refused to indict Daniel Pantaleo, and he walked free. "This one," the comedian Chris Rock reminded the country after the decision, "was on film."

The words "I Can't Breathe" began showing up on posters, on the sides of buildings, on warm-up shirts worn by NBA players before their games got under way—in arenas where white fans overwhelmingly outnumbered Blacks.

There was one genre of Black film that American film directors continued to embrace: the twisting tales of famous music performers who rose, fell, rose again, and sometimes fell again. For years, the journey of the singer James Brown had entranced directors and producers, but it had been difficult to get a project in motion. Brown's life constituted an attractive and dramatic storyline. He was born in Depression-era South Carolina in 1933; at the age of fifteen, he was sent to the Georgia Juvenile Training Institute with an eight-to-sixteen-year sentence for car theft. While incarcerated, he honed his self-taught music skills, and when he was released, in 1952, he started singing, formed a band, and began making records. He melded the rhythm-country-blues genres, his sound enhanced by a thumping, rocking band. They were known as James Brown and the Famous Flames, and their tunes ("Try Me," "Think") cracked the charts. In 1963, his *Live at the Apollo* album crested at number two on *Billboard*. He was singing and screaming, and making money, and becoming rich; he wasn't rock-and-roll superstar rich, but it still made for a mighty sweet lifestyle. Then, amid all the pain and blood and crying of 1968, came his song "Say It Loud, I'm Black and I'm Proud," and he suddenly seemed to be singing right through the rampaging fires. Teens and adults screamed the song's new slogan: the anthemlike song rocked its way to become a top-ten hit. His admirers called him the Godfather of Soul. The honors rolled in: a Grammy Lifetime Achievement Award in 1992, a Kennedy Center Honors in 2003. But there were actually few nights that James Brown found gentle; there were demons that stretched back to his childhood. He was paranoid; he heaped abuse on other singers, particularly women; he began taking the hallucinogenic PCP. In September 1988, Brown decided that someone was using the bathroom in his offices without proper permission. He showed up with a shotgun at an insurance company adjacent to his office, yelling, spitting indecipherable words, waving the shotgun. The employees screamed; he retreated, hopped into his pickup, and hit the gas pedal. He could soon see in his rearview mirror that the law was riding hard up on him. It turned into a wild chase. Finally arrested, he served three years in a South Carolina penitentiary. There were concerts after he got released, the aging singer with his musicians from the days of yore. But there were also more run-ins with the police, more fines, more news stories about his erratic behavior. On Christmas Day, 2006, the seventy-three-year-old funk master died of pneumonia.

The Rolling Stone Mick Jagger—wowed when he saw Brown in 1964 at Harlem's Apollo Theater—had long been interested in producing a James

Brown movie, but navigating the maze of music licensing had proved a nightmare. Finally, the matter seemed settled in 2012. A script by Jez and John-Henry Butterworth persuaded Jagger and Brian Grazer, another producer on the project, that it was time to proceed. Spike Lee was in discussion to direct, but the parties couldn't come to an agreement and Lee left the *Get On Up* project. Jagger and Grazer turned to Tate Taylor, who directed *The Help*, which had been a huge hit. They thought it important to have a director with Southern roots; Taylor is a Mississippian. But his hiring renewed a roiling debate: white directors continually got the important jobs directing Black films—Taylor Hackford on *Ray*, Bill Condon on *Dreamgirls*, Taylor on *Get On Up*. "Hollywood," said *Slate* magazine about the lack of opportunities for Black directors helming Black biopics, "needs to do better."

When Taylor came aboard, he thought it important to have an actor with Southern roots. He and the producers cast Chadwick Boseman, the star of the Jackie Robinson film *42* and himself a native of South Carolina. Others hired to join the cast of *Get On Up* were Viola Davis, Jill Scott, Dan Aykroyd, Octavia Spencer, and Nelsan Ellis.

Boseman dived into practicing the patented Brown dance moves—the splits, the strutting. Jagger shared his own memories about seeing Brown perform in the 1960s. Special attention was paid by the production crew to Brown's colorful wardrobe (capes, pants with flared leggings) and his hair, which Brown seemed obsessive about: "Make it higher," Brown instructs a hairstylist in the script. "Hair rising up to the lord like a flame."

There were equally high hopes for the thirty-million-dollar film when it premiered. Critics were in agreement about Boseman's performance. The actor gave a "startling and galvanic performance," according to *The New Yorker*. From *Rolling Stone*: "Boseman tears into the role like a man possessed. You can't take your eyes off him." *The Hollywood Reporter* opined that Boseman's performance "transcends impersonation and reverberates long after the screen goes dark." *Variety* concluded that nothing Boseman does in the film "smacks of mimicry." But *Get On Up* failed abysmally at the box office. Against that thirty-million-dollar budget, it grossed only $30.1 million. Boseman's praised performance aside, there was a jaggedness to the narrative, summed up by *Newsday*'s comment that the movie played "tricks with chronology and reality." Movies that are "authorized"—meaning that the subject's family can weigh in and sanitize the picture's direction—often sacrifice a certain amount of texture, depth, and honesty. It was a complaint heard about *42* with the Jackie Robinson heirs. "Maybe the [James] Brown family input," offered *Rolling Stone* about *Get On Up,* "inspired the reticence. Maybe the Brown biopic Spike Lee envisioned making with Eddie Murphy would have cut deeper."

———

Comedy and satire had always been wise ways for Black performers to make the issue of race and racism digestible for large segments of the white populace. The practice, of course, dated from the earliest days of vaudeville. For decades, segregation (legal and de facto) had been so much a part of the American grain that it was unusual—save at certain sporting venues and jazz festivals—to see whites and Blacks even sitting in close proximity. The reality of the phenomenon hit Justin Simien when, in 2001, he left Houston, Texas—where "you see Black people everywhere"—to enroll at Chapman University in Orange, California. "By and large," Simien recalled, "that part of the country is very white, Republican, and there are just people who honestly had never met a Black person before." Blacks were 2 percent of the student population when Simien entered Chapman. He found it awkward and peculiar when white students wanted to touch his Afro, or belabor him with questions about Black athletes—as if his intellectual orbit were confined to sports. One of the courses that stood out for Simien was titled Fear and Evil in Film and Fiction.

After college, Simien worked in and around the film industry in Los Angeles. He began writing, working on a script that was thinly based on his college experiences. One character in Simien's script has a YouTube channel, and he dispenses advice: "Dear white people, dating a Black person to piss off your parents is a form of racism"; "Dear white people, the number of Black friends required to not seem racist has officially been raised to two. Sorry, but your weed dealer doesn't count."

Simien worked and reworked his script over a five-year period. He made a demo reel of what his film might look like. It got attention, and he eventually signed a deal with Code Red Films. He let it be known to his financiers that he wanted to direct the film, and they agreed. The director and his largely unknown cast—the exception being Dennis Haysbert—began filming *Dear White People* in Minnesota in the fall of 2013. The shoot was completed in nineteen days.

Few films set on a college campus involved any kind of racial dynamic, and the films that dared touch upon the subject were often sports dramas. As buzzy word filtered through the film community about Simien's debut film—with a plot that sprang from a "blackface gangsta party" thrown by whites that backfires—it was clear that it had touched a cinematic nerve. Simien came away from the January 2014 Sundance Film Festival with a Special Jury Prize for Breakthrough Talent. "If it ultimately feels modestly edgy rather than shocking or dangerous, 'Dear White People,'" *Variety*'s Justin Chang wrote from Sundance, "nonetheless provokes admiration for having bothered to ask some of the hard questions without pretending to know any of the answers." Simien's film hit theatres nine months later. "It's true that satire is the perfect weapon of reason," Ann Hornaday would write in *The Washington Post*, "and Justin Simien deploys it with resourcefulness, cool assurance and eagle-eyed aim." From Owen Gleiberman, writing for the BBC: "Dear White People beautifully satirizes the superficially progressive yet stifling PC style that's come to dominate US college life in the swirling racial stewpot of the 21st Century. It portrays the goings-on . . . as a microcosm of the Obama era, in which haughty postures too often pass as enlightened. These characters show that you can be too busy trying to do the right thing to actually do it."

Simien's film was a minor box-office success—grossing $5.4 million on a one-million-dollar budget—and he kept garnering awards, among them a 2015 Spirit Award for Best First Screenplay. The director's writing—witty, edgy, insightful, comedic—was uniformly praised.

———

Edmund Pettus loved the South. In his mind, there was no more noble cause than firing his rifle and rattling his saber against Union soldiers. Pettus had become wealthy through his family's Alabama cotton sales and slave labor. A trained lawyer, he was eager to join the Confederate Army; he abhorred Lincoln and the efforts to end slavery. By 1863, Pettus had been elevated to brigadier general. He presided over five regiments, battling from Tennessee to Georgia, until he was seriously wounded in battle and captured. After the war, Pettus went into Alabama politics; he was elected to the United States Senate in 1896. He died in 1907, during his second term. In 1940—thirty-three years after his death—Selma officials christened their new bridge the Edmund Pettus Bridge. And twenty-five years after that moment, Alabamans woke up to see a phalanx of Blacks and whites marching across that bridge on behalf of civil rights. It took them three attempts to get across the bridge without bloodshed (and rampaging horses charging at them), but the Martin Luther King, Jr.–

led marchers finally made it from Selma to the Alabama State Capitol in Montgomery on March 25, 1965, singing, holding hands, and battling the ghosts of Edmund Pettus and all he stood for. It became one of the signal and dramatic events of the American civil-rights movement.

When his life in Britain working in the petrochemical industry began to bore Paul Webb—who had previously worked as a schoolteacher—he convinced himself he should try his hand at writing scripts. In 1999, he had his first play, *Four Nights in Knaresborough,* produced in London. The drama told the story of Archbishop Thomas Becket, who was assassinated in 1170, and Webb sold the screen rights. "It all happened so quickly, I thought that's the way it works," he said. Hollywood began calling him for screenwriting jobs. Steven Spielberg hired him to write a draft of *Lincoln.* (The film made it to the screen in 2012 with a script credited to Tony Kushner.) Webb wrote other scripts that attracted name directors, but the projects went nowhere. He finally decided he wanted to tackle an idea about the behind-the-scenes battle between Martin Luther King, Jr., and President Lyndon Johnson, leading up to the final Selma march. Webb's script, *Selma,* made the 2007 Black List, a list of the best unproduced scripts that routinely grabs the attention of producers and studio executives. A British film company, Pathé UK, put up seed money to develop Webb's script. It was a move in stark contrast to the American film industry, which still resisted backing films about civil rights.

And then *Selma,* the movie, stalled.

Pathé UK couldn't find other financiers. The script was considered worthy and the story powerful, but Hollywood studios and production companies kept passing. Finally, Oprah Winfrey's Harpo Films and Brad Pitt's Plan B came aboard, joining forces with Pathé, Cloud Eight Films, and Ingenious Media. A twenty-million-dollar budget was approved. Lee Daniels wanted to make the film and had tried to put it together during its long march to the screen. But when progress dragged, Daniels went off to make *The Butler.* David Oyelowo, a British actor, was cast as Martin Luther King, Jr. Oyelowo had previously starred in *Middle of Nowhere,* a small independent film directed by Ava DuVernay. Oyelowo praised her talents and brought her to the attention of *Selma's* producers.

———

After getting her undergraduate degree from UCLA and working for a brief period in broadcast journalism, Ava DuVernay began working in publicity at Twentieth Century–Fox. In 1999, she founded her own public-relations agency. She went on to work on Hollywood productions: *Lincoln* for Spielberg; *Dreamgirls* for Bill Condon; *Collateral* for director Michael Mann. She had an epiphany while working on the Mann film: "I just remember," she recalled, "standing there in the middle of the night in East L.A. and watching Michael Mann direct and thinking, 'I have stories.'" She started making documentary films, focusing on intimate Los Angeles tales and characters. In 2011, having cobbled together fifty thousand dollars, DuVernay directed her first fictional feature film, *I Will Follow,* about how a family death affects other family members. It drew plaudits on the independent-film-festival circuit; Roger Ebert proclaimed it "one of the best films I've seen about coming to terms with the death of a loved one." DuVernay's follow-up film, *Middle of Nowhere,* brought her national attention. The film—focused on a Black woman dealing with the pain of having her husband serving a prison stretch—garnered a Best Directing Award at the 2012 Sundance Festival. She was the first Black woman to receive this prize. *The New York Times* called the film "a plaintive, slow-burning, quietly soul-stirring drama" that was without "dreary stereotypes."

Despite the glowing reviews, DuVernay was not approached by the studios with offers, as previous Sundance prizewinners had been. She was quite intrigued when the producers of *Selma* approached her. When finally offered the job, she went about rewriting parts of the script. Since the King family would not authorize use of his historic speeches, she wrote original speeches for the film. Joining Oyelowo in the cast were Tom Wilkinson as LBJ, Tim Roth as Governor George Wallace, Carmen Ejogo as Coretta Scott King, Common as James Bevel, Colman Domingo as Ralph Abernathy, André Holland as Andrew Young, and the producer Oprah Winfrey as the activist Annie Lee Cooper. The cast and crew went to Selma to meet up with the rattling ghosts of Edmund Pettus and his ilk.

DuVernay's reworked script gave a heightened presence to women and their bravery in the civil-rights orbit. And because she felt Webb's original script had a little too much of the "white savior" syndrome, DuVernay was intent that Martin Luther King, Jr.—and not President Johnson—be the focal point of the film.

Not long into the filming, a decision was passed down by the conservative majority of the U.S. Supreme Court: in *Shelby County v. Holder,* it was ruled that two key provisions of the 1965 Voting Rights Act no longer needed to be enforced. DuVernay called the decision "a violent dismantling of something that was there to ensure freedom." She grew weary: "I don't even know how you make this film about the crafting and creation of [the Voting Rights Act], because by the time it comes out, the thing is basically dead and it's meaningless." She nevertheless steeled herself and managed to keep her filming schedule on track.

*Selma* opened on Christmas Day, 2014. "Joining an already crowded field of Great Man movies about the likes of Stephen Hawking, Alan Turing, J. M. W. Turner, and Louie Zamperini . . . is Ava DuVernay's rousing biopic of slain civil rights leader Dr. Martin Luther King Jr.," the *Entertainment Weekly* critic wrote. The magazine concluded: "Not only has she made one of the most powerful films of the year, she's given us a necessary reminder of what King did for this country—and how much is left to be done." The *New York Times* review stretched across the top half of its Arts section. " 'Selma' is not a manifesto, a battle cry or a history lesson," A. O. Scott wrote. "It's a movie: warm, smart, generous and moving in two senses of the word. It will call forth tears of grief, anger, gratitude and hope. And like those pilgrims on the road to Montgomery, it does not rest." From Ann Hornaday of *The Washington Post:* " 'Selma' carries viewers along on a tide of breathtaking events so assuredly that they never drown in the details of the despair, but instead are left buoyed."

DuVernay's drama stormed right into the Oscar sweepstakes. She and David Oyelowo were nominated for Golden Globe Awards, as was *Selma* itself. In the glow of the film's success, DuVernay and members of the cast could hardly stop talking about two particular memories they held dear: The first was the time they had spent on the film set with Congressman John Lewis and Andrew Young, confidants of Martin Luther King, Jr. The second was the evening of the New York premiere. They wanted it to be more than just another glitzy affair, so they all donned black T-shirts printed with "I Can't Breathe" on the front, a tribute to Eric Garner. It made them all feel closer to the spirit of Martin Luther King, Jr.

No Black woman had ever been nominated for a Best Director Oscar. There was a strong feeling that Ava DuVernay might finally burst through that wall.

On Thursday, January 15, 2015, Academy of Motion Pictures president Cheryl Boone Isaacs, the directors J. J. Abrams and Alfonso Cuarón, and the actor Chris Pine gathered to announce the annual Oscar nominations. Abrams and Cuarón led off the early-morning program from Los Angeles by naming largely the technical nominees, such as best song (the theme from *Selma*, "Glory," was nominated), editing, sound editing, production design. Isaacs and Pine then appeared at the lectern to announce the acting and directing nominees. No one from *Selma* was named in the Best Supporting Actor category. Nor was anyone from *Selma* named in the Best Supporting Actress category. No one from *Selma* was named either when it came to costume design, cinematography, or screenplay. The nominees for Best Director were Richard Linklater for *Boyhood*, Bennett Miller for *Foxcatcher*, Wes Anderson for *The Grand Budapest Hotel*, Morten Tyldum for *The Imitation Game*, and Alejandro G. Iñárritu for *Birdman*. Ava DuVernay did not make the list. Now *Selma*'s hopes rested with David Oyelowo and his galvanizing performance as Martin Luther King, Jr. DuVernay was confident that Oyelowo would land on the list. Richard Brody of *The New Yorker* had considered Oyelowo "a well-deserved lock" for the nomination. Then the nominees were announced for Best Actor: Bradley Cooper for *American Sniper*, Michael Keaton for *Birdman*, Eddie Redmayne for *The Theory of Everything*, Benedict Cumberbatch for *The Imitation Game*. The remaining slot went to Steve Carell for *Foxcatcher*. Every acting nominee was white. Cheryl Boone Isaacs, the Black president of the Academy, had known the outcome in the predawn hours. "I saw the pamphlet with the nominees, and my assistant kept staring at me," she recalls. "My heart went down to my stomach. Ava didn't get nominated. And David didn't get nominated." *Selma* did make the list of eight films for Best Picture: "But it was still like 'Oh God,'" Isaacs says of the *Selma* snubs and the all-white acting nominations.

The backlash against the six-thousand-member Academy was swift. The statistics started tumbling out again: 98 percent of the producers in the Academy were white; 98 percent of the writers, white; 99 percent of the Best Actress winners had been white. A Black woman director had still never been nominated. The absence of Oyelowo in the Best Actor category was what seemed to jar the sensibilities of Black America the most. His performance was so stupendous that passing him over seemed an act of willfulness. It also seemed a slap in the face to the man he was portraying—Martin Luther King, Jr.

When *Selma* opened in Britain, Oyelowo's performance was again widely praised, but that did not stop the BAFTA voters from ignoring him as well. "However one chooses to read it, the absence of David Oyelowo from the Bafta and Oscar best actor roll-calls strikes a jarring note," Mark Kermode wrote in London's *The Guardian.*

The cast of *Selma* remained quiet during the uproar. But something haunted Oyelowo. The *Selma* producers had received a call from a representative of the Academy of Motion Picture Arts and Sciences the day after the cast and director appeared at the premiere wearing their "I Can't Breathe" shirts. Oyelowo recalled: "Members of the Academy called in to the studio and our producers saying, 'How dare they do that? . . . We are not going to vote for that film because we do not think it is their place to be doing that.'"

On Friday, January 16, the day following the Academy announcements— also the day after Martin Luther King, Jr.'s birthday—members of *Selma*'s cast and crew appeared at a gala screening of *Selma* at Obama's White House. The man in the White House made them all feel very appreciated.

Several years after the *Selma* imbroglio, on the morning of June 26, 2020, readers of *The New York Times* woke up to an essay in the newspaper titled "You Want a Confederate Monument? My Body Is a Confederate Monument." It was written by Caroline Randall Williams, a Black woman and a poet. She wrote: "I am a black, Southern woman, and of my immediate white male ancestors, all of them were rapists. My very existence is a relic of slavery and Jim Crow. . . . I am more than half white, and none of it was consensual. White Southern men—my ancestors—took what they wanted from women they did not love, over whom they had extraordinary power, and then failed to claim their children. . . . I don't just come from the South. I come from Confederates. I've got rebel-gray blue blood coursing my veins. My great-grandfather Will was raised with the knowledge that Edmund Pettus was his father. Pettus, the storied Confederate general, the grand dragon of the Ku Klux Klan, the man for whom Selma's Bloody Sunday Bridge is named."

On the morning of the 2015 Academy Awards nominations, April Reign, a middle-aged Black woman, was sitting in her family room at home in the Washington, D.C., area, with her eyes glued to the television. She was a huge fan of the Oscars. She didn't hear the name David Oyelowo called. She didn't hear Ava DuVernay's name announced. She was stunned; from category to category, every nominee was white. As she was getting ready to go to work—she worked in campaign finance reform—and putting breakfast on the table for her boys, she couldn't stop thinking of the pain she felt about the announcements. What did it matter that a Black man was sitting in the White House if something like this could unfold? She decided she wanted to do something, to make a statement in hopes that someone might respond and feel the same way she did. She had become attuned to the ways of Twitter, so she picked up her phone—it was 9:56 a.m.—and tweeted out the words "#OscarsSoWhite they asked to touch my hair," and then she went to work. The words in her tweet were bunched together and affixed with a hashtag and a frowning face. By the time she got to work, her one tweet was trending internationally. It was trending wildly. Black actors and actresses were retweeting her words. Her phone started ringing like crazy. During the next days, weeks, and months, April Reign found herself in the decades-long conversation of race and Hollywood. The phrase "OscarsSoWhite" began swirling around the canyons of Hollywood as if shot out of a rocket.

The woman announcing the all-white Oscar nominees in 2015 was not only a Black woman but was Cheryl Boone Isaacs, president of the Academy of Motion Picture Arts and Sciences. Bette Davis, the first woman, elected in 1941, quickly became fed up with the governing body when they refused all of her suggestions for change. "It was obvious that I had been put in as president merely as a figurehead," she said. Davis's tenure lasted less than two months. Fay Kanin, a screenwriter and producer, served as president from 1979 to 1983. Cheryl Boone Isaacs was working with the director and producer Reginald Hudlin to diversify the Academy's membership, but their efforts had not yet been felt. It was the pre-2015 membership—white, male, and aging—who were responsible for the 2015 nominations.

Cheryl Boone Isaacs may have risen to the top of the AMPAS, but she was not the first person in her family to make a splash in Hollywood. That distinction belonged to Ashley, her older brother.

When the Boone children were growing up in Springfield, Massachusetts, their parents—postal worker, stay-at-home mom—had one phrase for them if they complained about the unfairness of life and the trials of being Black in New England: "Get above it." It was drilled into the

Boone children that they were as good as, if not better than, anyone else. Ashley graduated from Brandeis University, where he studied economics. He dreamed of someday working at the World Bank. But someone with Brandeis connections introduced him to Bob Benjamin, cochairman of United Artists. Benjamin was quite impressed with the young man, and Ashley Boone soon found himself in the publicity department—as a trainee—in the New York office of United Artists. There were no other Blacks around to learn from, but he knew what he had to do: get above it. Boone began rising in the publicity ranks. There was an opportunity to market movies for foreign distribution. "The [foreign marketing] department was in such bad shape," he later recalled, "that they said, 'You're a bright kid. You can't be any worse than the guy who's doing it. Why don't you go for it?' So I did." In that capacity, Boone formed alliances with Sidney Poitier, Berry Gordy, and Quincy Jones. "There is a picture of Ashley between Poitier and Berry Gordy," says his sister. "Ashley would point to it and say, 'Now there's real Black power.' "

Ashley Boone shepherded the overseas rollout of some of the most celebrated pictures of the late 1960s and early 1970s: *Lilies of the Field, Sounder,* the James Bond films, *Tom Jones. The Pittsburgh Courier* called Boone "perhaps the most knowledgeable black man in America when it comes to national and international distribution of motion pictures." In the mid-1970s, when he was thirty-eight, Boone moved to Fox Studios. There he met a young filmmaker who had just completed a film about heroes and villains in outer space. The filmmaker was George Lucas, and his film was *Star Wars.* Boone was integral to the decision to open *Star Wars* at midweek instead of on the usual Friday, and also planned a good part of the marketing campaign. "Time-worn methods of selling movies are getting a shake-up by a new generation of marketers," the Associated Press reported, "and one of those leading the revolution is Ashley Boone." *Star Wars* would end up grossing $776 million (the equivalent of $3.3 billion in 2020 dollars), and, of course, launched one of the most iconic series in movie history. When Alan Ladd, Jr., departed Fox, Boone and another executive were chosen to split the duties of running the studio; Boone served as president of distribution and marketing. But he left after only four months on the job, after some of his duties and responsibilities were suddenly curtailed. "Reports abound about why Fox—which is in an enviable financial position because of the success of 'Star Wars'—should want to rock the boat so soon after appointing Ashley Boone as president of distribution," *The New York Times* wrote. For a brief shining moment, Ashley Boone was the highest-ranking Black in Hollywood studio history.

After starting his own consulting firm, Boone bounced back into the studio system, first at Columbia, then at Lorimar. Playing musical chairs was simply a part of that system. He joined an effort in the mid-1980s to urge the studios to disinvest from South Africa because of its apartheid policy. Secrets were also a big part of the Hollywood system. And Boone had his—he was gay. It's unclear if that had any part in his nomadic career.

Boone died on May 1, 1994. He was fifty-five years old. There was much bitterness by many Blacks in the film business because Boone was overlooked in the "In Memoriam" tribute at the following Oscars telecast.

———

After she graduated from Whittier College, in 1971, Cheryl Boone Isaacs became a flight attendant. Often, when she was between flights on the West Coast, she'd accompany her brother to film premieres. Through his eyes, she saw how much hard work it took to make the glitter of Hollywood seem fun and exciting. After a few years, she followed her brother into the film world, starting out in publicity at Columbia. Over the next few years, she worked on publicity campaigns for—among many other films—*Close Encounters of the Third Kind, The Right Stuff, Once Upon a Time in America, Forrest Gump,* and *Braveheart.* At New Line Cinema, she became the first Black woman to oversee a studio marketing department. As she continued her rise up Hollywood's ladder, the power brokers at the Academy of Motion Picture Arts and Sciences took note. They were looking for a new president. Cheryl Boone Isaacs knew movies, knew how to market movies, had been around the Academy for years. "The day I was elected president," she recalls, "I had an out-of-body experience. Everybody went into a meeting afterward. I can't even remember what I said."

Isaacs and Reginald Hudlin were hoping—going into the 2015 movie year—there would be enough quality films to heave a spotlight on the best Black performances. They knew all too well it would come down to the Academy's voting bloc. And that bloc still remained overwhelmingly white and male.

The 2015 movie season promised another *Star Wars,* another *Mission Impossible,* another James Bond film, and another *Jurassic Park.* There was also another *Hunger Games* (*Mockingjay, Part 2*), and another *Fast and*

*Furious* film, titled *Furious 7.* The Obama years were coming to a close, and Hollywood's appetite for films by Black directors, or with Black leading men and women, seemed to be waning noticeably.

While film executives were preparing their summer-2015 releases, on the opposite end of the country, Dylann Roof was planning his own event.

––––––––

On the evening of June 17, in Charleston, South Carolina, Dylann Roof, a slender twenty-one-year-old, calmly walked into the Emanuel African Methodist Episcopal Church. Those already inside were attending their weekly Bible-study gathering. The church's Black congregation was quite proud of its history, which stretched from slavery and Reconstruction and through the 1960s civil-rights protest era. One of its cofounders had been Denmark Vesey, who, in 1822, had plotted the slave uprising in the city. One hundred and ninety-three years later, it did not raise an eyebrow among the congregants when Roof, the white visitor, entered the church just after 8:00 p.m.; all were welcome. He had floppy brown hair and was wearing a gray sweatshirt and jeans. The white supremacist was also concealing a loaded Glock handgun. He sat down and proceeded to insert himself into the Bible discussion. His fervent nodding was followed by an "Amen" here, an "Amen" there. Then the amens suddenly stopped. He pulled out his handgun and started firing. There were screams; old and young began falling, and the last thing they heard was his racist rants about white women being raped. He reloaded and continued firing. It was unimaginable horror, six endless minutes. When the shooting stopped, eight congregants lay dead; another would die at a hospital. The dead were Cynthia Hurd, Susie Jackson, Ethel Lance, DePayne Doctor, Tywanza Sanders, Daniel L. Simmons, Sharonda Coleman-Singleton, Myra Thompson, and Rev. Clementa Pinckney, who was also a state senator. It was another indelible branch added to the Southern tree of horror. President Obama delivered the eulogy. Worshippers—and much of the country—wept.

Dylann Roof eventually received a federal death sentence. He said he had no reason to feel remorseful or to apologize.

––––––––

In the mid-1980s, the fever of gangsta rap demanded to be taken seriously. One of its main creative purveyors was N.W.A (Niggaz Wit Attitudes), a

Compton, California–based group consisting of Ice Cube, Dr. Dre, Eazy-E, MC Ren, DJ Yella, The D.O.C., and Arabian Prince. They wore baseball caps and bulky clothes, and riffed, in their rap songs, about racism, corrupt police, and police brutality. If politicians would not talk about police brutality—and they would not—then N.W.A certainly would. They used their own run-ins with the police to fuel their songs. There was also a powerful whiff of misogyny in some of their songs, but they did not care about niceties. This was not soft, genteel Motown. This was diving over the cliff: their mission was to expose corruption at the highest and most meaningful level, all against a thumping rap beat! They were fearless and loud. The group's first album, *Straight Outta Compton*, arrived in 1988. It sold millions, crossing over from the inner cities to the white suburbs and college campuses. Among the song titles "Gangsta Gangsta," "Express Yourself," and "Fuck the Police." A second successful album, *Niggaz4Life*, released in 1991, featured "Alwayz into Somethin'" and "Approach to Danger." These were musicians and provocateurs and rebels with causes. Across the years of the group's existence, there would be breakups, threats, reunions, fights, letters from the FBI about their incendiary lyrics. All of it was ripe for a film. So Hollywood decided to get in business with the Niggaz Wit Attitudes.

———

F. Gary Gray was a director who had directed members of N.W.A in music videos. The group, after agreeing to the idea of having a film made about them, felt comfortable with Gray. He was given a script about the group's genesis, written by Andrea Berloff and Jonathan Herman, and signed on. Universal came aboard to finance and distribute. Filming was not without its typical N.W.A problems—there were threats of violence from real-life gang members—but Gray finished on time, and the movie was released on August 14, 2015.

Many whites routinely dismissed rap as abrasive music, but the reviews of *Straight Outta Compton* disagreed. " 'Straight Outta Compton' is epic, baby, an explosively entertaining hip-hop biopic," Peter Travers wrote in *Rolling Stone*, "that raps home truths about race and police brutality as timely now (think Ferguson) as they were during the 1980s in Compton, California." Travers proclaimed that Jason Mitchell's portrayal of Eric "Eazy-E" Wright was "award-caliber." *The Washington Post*'s Ann Hornaday praised the film and hoped its viewership stretched wider than the expected core base: "Thanks to eerily on-point timing and adroit direction . . . this classic star-is-born story manages to transcend its own tight focus." From the Memphis *Commercial Appeal*: "Arriving when the battle cry of 'F*** Tha Police' has been superseded by the equally urgent if more palatable slogan 'Black Lives Matter,' the film opens a window onto a re-created recent past that doubles as a reflection of the outraged present."

The film's first weekend's box-office tally was an eye-popping $60.2 million. It became the highest-grossing R-rated movie ever to open in August. The majority of ticket buyers were Black, but nearly a quarter of those who purchased tickets were white. The film eventually grossed $161.2 million in North America, and another forty million in foreign markets. It became the highest-grossing movie with a Black director. Given its commercial success and brilliant acting ensemble, *Compton* jetted itself right into the awards-season conversation. Universal held a screening for Oscar voters. "Universal is said to be bullish about the film's awards prospects and, based on the audience it drew and reception it received at its official Academy screening on Saturday night," *The Hollywood Reporter* noted, "it's hard to disagree."

Three months after the release of *Compton,* Ryan Coogler's follow-up to his *Fruitvale Station* arrived in theatres. *Creed* was an extension of the Sylvester Stallone *Rocky* franchise, one that many believed had become tiresome. In carrying the story forward—with Stallone's blessing, after two years of pleading by the young director—Coogler shifted the lens to Apollo Creed's son, Adonis. Apollo Creed had been played by Carl Weathers; Michael B. Jordan, the star of *Fruitvale Station,* was cast as Adonis "Donnie" Creed. As in most boxing movies, there is the fighter's doubt, downfall, romantic pangs, a deeper downfall, and, finally, ring triumph. "It's an invigorating piece of nostalgia that fuels a bigger adrenaline rush with its climax than any big budget blockbuster could provide," *The Atlantic* said. *Variety* opined that Coogler had made a "smart, kinetic, exhilaratingly well-crafted piece of mainstream filmmaking," and allowed that Jordan had taken "yet another substantial stepping stone on his climb to stardom." Writing in *Vanity Fair,* Katey Rich was so impressed with the film that she saw Oscar nominations in its future, stating that *Creed* could be "the next emotional boxing drama to win over the public and the Academy alike." The film traveled well in foreign markets. "In this revival," came the sentiment of Spain's *El País,* "there is not only talent, but also affection and intelligence." *The Irish Times* proclaimed, "There's an earthiness and street quality that we haven't witnessed since the 1976 original." The Coogler-Stallone-Jordan collaboration proved potent at the box office. Against a budget of thirty-five million dollars, it reaped $109.8 million in North America, and another $63.8 million in overseas markets, for a worldwide gross of $173.6 million. And the awards talk showed no signs of abating. IndieWire announced that the film's success had "spurred Oscar murmurs for stars Michael B. Jordan and Sylvester Stallone."

If the first half of 2015 had been lackluster as far as showcasing Black talent, the season had now caught fire. F. Gary Gray and Ryan Coogler had directed two of the most critically acclaimed and financially successful films of the year. Actors from those two films—Michael B. Jordan, Tessa Thompson, Phylicia Rashad (*Creed*), Jason Mitchell, O'Shea Jackson, Jr. (*Compton*)—were being singled out for their performances. In accepting praise for their work while out on publicity tours, many of the actors felt compelled to address the recent Charleston church shooting. "We'd like to take a moment to send out prayers and strength to our people in Charleston, South Carolina, who have endured but are prevailing over a horrific act of domestic terrorism," Michael B. Jordan said from Los Angeles.

———

Christmas Day was always a big day for opening a film with awards potential. And Will Smith, one of Hollywood's most bankable stars—Black or white—was waiting in the wings.

Born in Philadelphia in 1968 to a mother who was a school administrator and a father who was a refrigerator engineer, Will was a precocious child, gifted academically and quite creative. His counselors at Overbrook High sensed he had the talents to succeed at an Ivy League college, but he ignored them, wanting instead a career in music. It happened fast, and while Smith was still in high school: He and Jeffrey "DJ Jazzy Jeff" Townes, a friend and fellow rapper, got a record deal and cut a song, "Girls Ain't Nothing but Trouble," which became a hit. By the late 1980s, Smith, now known as the Fresh Prince, and Townes had become teen sensations. In 1989, they received a Grammy for Best Rap album. Two years later, they released "Summertime," a jumpy and jangly pop tune that netted another Grammy. Their rap was different from West Coast rap, free of profanity and political messaging. It was bubble-gum rap, the kind that white parents didn't mind their teenagers playing; it was crossover rap. And it caught the attention of Hollywood.

In 1990, the predominantly white executives at NBC cast Smith in a sitcom called *The Fresh Prince of Bel-Air.* It revolved around a rapper (Smith) who goes to live with rich relatives in Bel-Air, the wealthiest enclave in L.A. There are hijinks, class differences, and minimal racial insight, a concoction that poured from TV screens into living rooms with ease. The show ran for six seasons, and Smith became a television star. He made his big-screen film debut in 1992 in *Where the Day Takes You,* about teenage runaways in Los Angeles. It bombed at the box office. Then there was 1993's *Six Degrees of Separation;* he played a con man hustling a white family, making them think he's Sidney Poitier's son. It was Smith's next film, however, 1995's *Bad Boys,* that catapulted him to the upper echelons of Hollywood; the nineteen-million-dollar-budgeted film, costarring Martin Lawrence, grossed sixty-five million in North America and more than that overseas. He went on to a string of huge box-office hits—*Independence Day; Men in Black; I, Robot; The Pursuit of Happyness; Hancock.* There were a few exceptions—*Ali, The Legend of Bagger Vance*—but Smith grew into the number-one box-office attraction in the world. His roles were seldom race-specific, and he mostly avoided social dramas. He stood right in the center of the billion-dollar juggernaut of mainstream moviemaking. One of his most interesting choices was *Concussion,* the story of Dr. Bennet Omalu, a Nigerian-born forensic pathologist based in Pittsburgh, Pennsylvania. Omalu studied the early deaths of professional football players, discovering brain injuries directly related to the repeated blows they'd taken to the head on the playing field. He called the disease chronic traumatic encephalopathy (CTE). *Concussion* got so-so reviews and had a lackluster performance at the box office. On a thirty-five-million-dollar budget (some estimates claimed higher), it brought in only $48.6 million. But Smith's reviews were superb, and he was nominated for Best Actor in the Golden Globes. (Leonardo DiCaprio won for *The Revenant.*) Admirers of Smith's performance thought the Globe nomination boded well for his chances of an Oscar nomination.

———

There was more than the usual hyperkinetic attention paid to the 2016 Academy Award nominations because of the backlash over the previous year's all-white slate. Expectations were high—especially emanating from urban radio—that various people from the cast and crew of *Straight Outta Compton, Creed,* or *Concussion* would be nominated. All three films had already done well on the awards circuit. And if there were to be any nominee surprises—as there often were—there was building chatter that Idris Elba, playing a warlord in *Beasts of No Nation,* might squeeze into the mix. Elba's riveting performance had netted him a slew of honors: Golden Globe, BAFTA, and Screen Actors Guild nominations for Best Supporting Actor (the last of which he won).

————

Cheryl Boone Isaacs rose in the wee hours of the morning on January 14 to get ready for the Oscar announcements. She arrived at her office at 2:30 a.m. The directors Ang Lee and Guillermo del Toro would be making the first round of announcements, followed by Boone and the actor John Krasinski for the second round. It was the second round of nominees that grabbed the most attention. After del Toro and Lee wrapped up their announced nominees—cinematography, documentary, sound, makeup, and the like—Boone and Krasinski walked to the lectern. The names of the Best Supporting Actor nominees rolled forth: Christian Bale, Tom Hardy, Mark Ruffalo, Mark Rylance, and Sylvester Stallone. All white. That was the category *Compton's* producers were most hopefully eyeing. The nominees for Best Supporting Actress: Jennifer Jason Leigh, Rooney Mara, Rachel McAdams, Alicia Vikander, and Kate Winslet. All white. The Best Director nominees were Adam McKay, George Miller, Alejandro Iñárritu, Lenny Abrahamson, and Tom McCarthy. Fifteen nominees, fifteen white men and women. The announcements continued. The Best Actress nominees: Cate Blanchett, Brie Larson, Jennifer Lawrence, Charlotte Rampling, and Saoirse Ronan. They, too, were all white, as were the Best Actor nominees: Bryan Cranston, Matt Damon, Leonardo DiCaprio, Michael Fassbender, and Eddie Redmayne. Like all the 2015 nominees, every one of the 2016 Academy Award nominees was white. April Reign was livid; phones were ringing and ringing across Black America. News producers knew they had another angle of the nominations to report.

Cheryl Boone Isaacs had had to stand there with a poker face; she had known the results hours earlier. As Boone recalls of the moment, "I knew this was not going to be a good day."

By the time daylight rose across California, the news had spread throughout the nation like a wildfire, on radio, TV, and the front pages of newspapers. Civil-rights leaders, Black politicians, and Black radio commentators appeared outraged. To make matters worse, the Boone-led Academy had arranged what Reginald Hudlin would refer to as "the

Blackest Oscars ever." Hudlin and Boone, of course, were Black, and they had engaged Chris Rock to host the ceremony. "We get Chris Rock to host," Hudlin said, "then we get an all-white slate of nominees!"

One year of all-white nominees might have been seen as unfortunate and coincidental, but two years in a row struck the Black community as downright nefarious.

Reginald Hudlin thought it wise to call a Board of Governors meeting immediately. "I said to the board, 'Look, this is a different day. We are dead in the water. We can't even book presenters for the show because of this." Hudlin—along with Boone—convinced the board that aggressive measures must be taken. Plans were put in place to increase minority membership—since it was the overwhelmingly white voting bloc that was responsible for the slate of nominees. April Reign, of OscarSoWhite, was back in the spotlight. "White folks are the gatekeepers," she says. "It's not until the head of studios say, 'Okay, I get it,' that things will change."

Black actors and actresses threatened to boycott the upcoming ceremony. Jada Pinkett Smith, aggrieved that her husband, Will Smith, did not receive a nomination, was one of the first to announce her boycott. She felt that "begging for acknowledgement, or even asking, diminishes dignity and diminishes power." Spike Lee—long an Academy antagonist—announced he also would not attend. Ice Cube, one of the producers of *Compton,* had a sanguine reaction. "I'm not surprised," he said. "It's the Oscars. They do what they do." It wasn't, however, a total washout: The screenwriters for *Compton,* Andrea Berloff and Jonathan Herman, received an Original Screenplay nomination. Sylvester Stallone received a Best Supporting Actor nomination for *Creed.* But critics of the Academy—though acknowledging the talents of those three nominees—also pointed out they, too, were all white.

On February 28, 2016, Chris Rock walked out on the stage of the Dolby Theatre and commenced hosting the 88th Academy Awards. "Well," he said, grinning and scanning the audience, "I'm here at the Academy Awards. Otherwise known as the White People's Choice Awards. You realize, if they nominated the host, I wouldn't even get this job! Y'all would be watching Neil Patrick Harris right now."

By the evening's end, the writing nominees for *Compton,* and the sole acting nominee for *Creed,* all went home empty-handed.

# Moving in the Moonlight

A T THE BEGINNING OF 2016, the klieg lights were turned hard in the direction of politics and a presidential prize. And, for all the country to see, racial dynamics were very much at play. Republican Donald J. Trump, a New York real-estate figure and the former host of *Celebrity Apprentice*, a reality-TV show, had fueled his campaign with the birther movement, a hodgepodge of innuendo and bizarre accusations that President Barack Obama was not born in America. The birthright clause, in Article 2 of the U.S. Constitution, stipulates that an individual must have been born in the United States to become president. The Trump narrative implied that America's first Black president may have somehow sneaked into America after his birth in a foreign land. Barack Obama was, in fact, born on August 4, 1961, at the Kapiʻolani Medical Center in Honolulu, Hawaii. The hospital actually produced official—and unassailable—records of the president's birth. But the birther movement remained glued to Trump's racist and false campaign. Billboards across America stared down at drivers: "WHERE'S THE BIRTH CERTIFICATE?" Trump—stoking insults (against Mexicans, Blacks, those with physical infirmities) throughout his campaign—stormed from city to city, wearing a blue Wall Street suit while unlocking closet doors and sending racial skeletons rattling across the landscape. He seemed a close cousin of Bill Starbuck, the grinning con man who promised relief from a dried landscape in *The Rainmaker,* the 1956 Burt Lancaster film. Trump's white followers felt aggrieved, lost, unwooed, in a land that, in their minds, had dried up on their dreams and left them and their once-Great America behind. Trump's scars—bankruptcies, marital affairs, political inexperience, federal lawsuits alleging racial discrimination against Blacks in his housing complexes, his calling for the execution of the innocent Central Park Five—meant nothing to them. He somehow convinced them that their grievances were his grievances, and they voted him to victory, stunning many, and leaving Hillary Clinton vanquished.

———

It is the most poignant kind of fate: two Black boys growing up in the same tough public-housing project in Miami, Florida, both of whom came to take on American filmmaking with astounding success. But if Barry Jenkins, born November 19, 1979, and Tarell Alvin McCraney, born eleven months later, on October 17, 1980, were to make it out of Florida, they'd have to survive Miami's Liberty City itself.

Liberty City was a sprawling archipelago of apartments on the north end of the city that grew out of official segregation policies in the 1930s. Much of America knew little if anything about the public-housing project; it was actually an official "city" only in the mindset of its Black residents. One reason for that mindset: throughout the 1960s and 1970s, Liberty City, like much of Black America, was subject to the whims and actions of an overwhelmingly white police force. And on the early morning of December 17, 1979, four of those white officers interrupted Arthur McDuffie's American Dream.

McDuffie was a handsome thirty-three-year-old former Marine. He worked as an insurance agent and was happy about his recent plans to remarry his ex-wife, Frederika. He drove a Kawasaki Z1 motorcycle all around Liberty City, and when he ran a red light, he heard the police siren but chose to keep going. When he stopped, it was 2:00 a.m. Police officers—apparently angered by the chase—handcuffed McDuffie and began beating him with batons and their fists. Other officers came upon the scene and joined in the beating. "Easy, one at a time," one of them instructed. Their fury was wretched; McDuffie died four days later at a local hospital. In their reports, the officers claimed McDuffie crashed his motorcycle, ran from them, and, when caught, attacked them. They also stated that his grievous head-gash resulted from his having tripped and fallen. An investigation revealed that the officers had, top to bottom, lied; one of the officers, granted immunity, testified and told the tale of wanton beating, choking, and kicking—with McDuffie never raising a hand—followed by a massive cover-up. Four of five white officers were indicted for manslaughter and tampering with evidence. A fifth officer received an acquittal before trial. Because of pretrial publicity, their trial was moved to Tampa. Five months later, on May 18, 1980—despite overwhelming evidence and testimony from an eyewitness about the savage beating—an all-white, all-male jury acquitted the white officers. Miami and Liberty City erupted. Protests and riots lasted three days. Parts of Liberty City burned; so did parts of Overtown, Brownsville, and West Coconut Grove. The National Guard were sent in. There were eighteen deaths, and more than six hundred were arrested.

———

Barry Jenkins's mother, trying to keep herself together in Liberty City, would often fall into despair. There were problems with drugs. She had multiple children, who had multiple fathers. "There were seven or eight of us in a two-bed apartment," Barry Jenkins recalled. "There was usually food, but sometimes not. The lights usually worked, but sometimes not." Despite being small for his size, Jenkins played sports in high school. He leaned heavily into academics and performed well enough to get into Florida State University. While there, he began to study film. He made a short student film, *My Josephine,* with a provocative premise: it revolved around the aftermath of the 9/11 terrorist attacks and the Arab American owners of a Laundromat who choose to make American flags—for free. The film gave Jenkins confidence in his ability. Other film students came from well-heeled backgrounds; he came from Liberty City. "I said, 'I can place my feelings about being a Black man in the south into this.' And it . . . worked. I thought, 'This is what I am going to do for the rest of my life.'" The L.A. film world sucked him west after school. Initially, he found work at Harpo, Oprah Winfrey's production company, then got work as a director's assistant. But the cliquish, it's-who-you-know world of film dismayed him, so he fled the city. Young Barry Jenkins turned into Jack Kerouac, roaming the country, riding trains, often eyeballed by curious police officers.

He settled in San Francisco and got a warehouse job, loading and unloading boxes. Then he started thinking of filmmaking again. In 2006 he began writing a screenplay about a young Black hipster couple in San Francisco who meet at a party, have an affair, and ruminate about the mostly white city, their discussions bouncing from gentrification to Black politics to life in America. Jenkins cobbled together enough money—fifteen thousand dollars—to make his debut independent film, *Medicine for Melancholy.* The film caught the attention of the South by Southwest and the Toronto International film festivals. After success on the festival circuit, the film was released in January of 2009. "Clearly, here is a young filmmaker who wants to tell stories rather than deliver shocks and sensation," announced *The Hollywood Reporter. Variety* thought the film "charming and stylish," and Roger Ebert called it a "very assured" film. Jenkins drew enough praise to convince himself he could continue to make films.

Jenkins and Tarell McCraney did not know each other during their childhoods. But they shared many similar traits: family adults with addiction woes; surrogates who cared about them; their own inner drive; the rampaging crack epidemic they had to sidestep; and the ghostly figure of Arthur McDuffie summoned by adults when they felt a need to frighten young Black boys about the dangers of corrupt police. McCraney was precocious enough to excel at the New World School of the Arts in downtown Miami. Then he went off to DePaul University in Chicago. In one of his classes, the students were asked to write a scene about a happy childhood memory. McCraney didn't care if his fellow students—"white and privileged"—snickered; he was going to write the truth, and the truth involved an adult friend by the name of Blue: "So, I wrote about the time a drug dealer got off his crate and taught me how to ride a bike." At DePaul, McCraney began work on a screenplay. It was semi-autobiographical, about growing up Black and queer in Liberty City, a hybrid of a play and a screenplay. He titled it *In Moonlight, Black Boys Look Blue.* He put the screenplay away and enrolled in the Yale School of Drama.

Theatre professionals became enamored of Tarell Alvin McCraney's gifts and knew he had a future. Barry Jenkins, after his first film, had been procrastinating on his follow-up; friends pleaded with him to get to work on a new project. A Miami arts-community group found it astonishing that Jenkins and McCraney had never met, and connected the two of them. There was warmth and laughter and Black-cats-talking chatter about Liberty City, about fate, and having made it out of a place to come to love it more because of all the memories. They wanted to collaborate on something, and Jenkins felt that *In Moonlight, Black Boys Look Blue* was worthy of a film treatment. Jenkins—an admirer of James Baldwin—did a Baldwin-like move and jetted off to Brussels to write the script.

When he returned, Jenkins attended the 2013 Telluride Film Festival. He showed around his finished script, based on McCraney's work. Executives at Plan B, the production company overseen by Brad Pitt, Dede Gardner, and Jeremy Kleiner, took the project on, and later joined with A24, another film company, to finance and produce it. Jenkins assembled an eclectic cast, known and unknowns. The producers were now betting that this film—the title changed to just *Moonlight*—with a Black cast, told in a three-act manner, about a bullied gay youth's coming of age in an American ghetto, could resonate with the public. The best-known actors in the cast were Mahershala Ali, Janelle Monáe, and Naomie Harris. Jenkins took *Moonlight* to the Telluride Film Festival in September 2016. Hours before the screening took place, he confided that he hoped the movie would have a universal appeal. "There are people who don't see themselves in arts and letters who want to see themselves, and yes, this is for them," he said. "But I also want other people who do see themselves to see these people. This movie was made for anybody who has ever felt other, or like they can't be themselves and be accepted in society."

Beyond the festival circuit, *Moonlight* was slated to open on October 21, 2016, in a relatively small number of theatres, and then spread slowly on a wider release. The reviews from the festivals were very strong. Now, with the film out in the world, they were rapturous. From *Rolling Stone*: "It's impossible to pinpoint exactly how . . . Moonlight gets inside your head and makes you see the world with new eyes. But it does—and then it owns you. This is a game-changer, the kind of movie that defies glib categorization." *The New York Times*: "a disarmingly personal film and an urgent social document." From Hilton Als in *The New Yorker*: "Did I ever imagine, during my anxious, closeted childhood, that I'd live long enough to see a movie like 'Moonlight,' Barry Jenkins's brilliant, achingly alive new work about Black queerness? Did any gay man who came of age, as I did, in the era of Ronald Reagan, Margaret Thatcher, and AIDS, think he'd survive to see a version of his life told onscreen with such knowledge, unpredictability, and grace?" And from *The Guardian*: "It is the kind of film that leaves you feeling somehow mentally smarter and physically lighter. Love, sex, survival, mothers and father figures are its themes, the last one foregrounded by the poignant absence of the fathers themselves."

The oncoming awards-season chatter for *Moonlight* was inevitable. But, so often left at the altar, Black America had the jitters about making Oscar predictions—even when a film had received overwhelming critical praise and achieved financial success. *Moonlight* had a four-million-dollar budget. It grossed twenty-seven million domestic, and thirty-seven million overseas.

There were other Black-themed films in 2016 that caught the wide attention of filmgoers. The smallest, and most poignant, of those films was *Loving*, based on the interracial marriage—and arrest—of Richard and Mildred Loving and the legal aftermath. Ruth Negga and Joel Edgerton turned in searing, quiet performances as the Loving couple, under the direction of Jeff Nichols. Reviews were strong, but the box office was lackluster. Then, during the Christmas season, two other films, *Fences* and *Hidden Figures*, were released.

––––––––

Denzel Washington had long been enamored of August Wilson's work and had spent years trying to convince the studios to bring his plays to the screen. Wilson, born in Pittsburgh to a German father and a Black mother, had ascended to the top ranks of American playwrights with a series of plays that told of Black life in a multidimensional and poetic manner. The plays—*Jitney, Ma Rainey's Black Bottom, Fences, Joe Turner's Come and Gone, The Piano Lesson, Two Trains Running, Seven Guitars*—stunned and mesmerized theatregoers and critics. "I think my plays offer [white Americans] a different way to look at black Americans," Wilson said. "For instance, in *Fences* they see a garbageman, a person they don't really look at, although they see a garbageman every day. By looking at Troy's life, white people find out that the content of this black garbageman's life is affected by the same things—love, honor, beauty, betrayal, duty. Recognizing that these things are as much part of his life as theirs can affect how they think about and deal with black people in their lives." Washington had appeared on Broadway in *Fences* in 2010. Six years later, the film debuted, with Washington directing and starring. His costars were Viola Davis, Mykelti Williamson, Russell Hornsby, and Stephen McKinley Henderson. The critics appeared divided, praising the performances but feeling the play hadn't transferred from stage to screen in a completely satisfactory manner. But when it came to the box office, *Fences* acquitted itself nicely, collecting sixty-four million dollars against a twenty-four-million-dollar budget.

––––––––

It was difficult enough to find a story with dominant Black characters and engineer it to the motion-picture screen. To find one that involved outer space and true-life Black characters seemed unimaginable. But Margot Lee Shetterly did just that.

When she was growing up in Hampton, Virginia, in the 1970s, it was drummed into little Margot that Blacks were far more gifted than society gave them credit for. She only had to look around the dinner table for proof: Her father was a scientist at the Langley Research Center—one of NASA's field centers—and her mother taught literature at the well-thought-of Hampton University. The soirées at the Lees' house often included scientists and mathematicians; the Black female mathematicians particularly fascinated Margot Lee. She heard them talk about things they had done when the country had legal and devastating segregation—they were setting the mathematical templates for astronauts to go into outer space, and safely return to earth. Margot Lee would go on to graduate from the University of Virginia and start a career in investment banking. But she never forgot about those Black women mathematicians. In 2010, she started writing a book about them, focusing primarily on the trio of Katherine Johnson, Mary Jackson, and Dorothy Vaughan. Her book, *Hidden Figures: The American Dream and the Untold Story of the Black Women Mathematicians Who Helped Win the Space War*, was published in 2016 and received fine reviews. Donna Gigliotti, an Oscar-winning (for *Shakespeare in Love*) film producer who had been working in Hollywood since the 1980s, had already purchased the film rights to Shetterly's book, prepublication. It mattered little that two other films about math geniuses—*Good Will Hunting* and *A Beautiful Mind*—had been quite profitable at the box office and also won Oscars, because Gigliotti knew making *Hidden Figures* would be an uphill climb. "Many people," she said, "thought I was crazy for even thinking that there was a movie in a story where the three leads were African-American women, and the story was fundamentally about math."

Gigliotti ran an independent film company, which meant she had leverage and a bit of house money. She brought in two other production companies and set about making *Hidden Figures* on a twenty-five-million-dollar budget. Ted Melfi—who co-wrote the *Hidden Figures* screenplay with Allison Schroeder—was also hired to direct. The cast quickly came together: Taraji P. Henson, Octavia Spencer, Janelle Monáe, Glen Powell, Kevin Costner, and Mahershala Ali. The film opened on Christmas Day. Many reviews praised the fact that it was, basically, an untold story, and the cast was universally lauded. But, as was common with films touching upon civil rights and Jim Crow America, scenes depicting brutish racist attitudes were softened—or laden with ill-timed chuckling—as if to stem the guilt that might be expected to swirl across some white audiences. Richard Brody of *The New Yorker* caught the dynamic:

> Melfi and Schroeder [screenwriters] are white; perhaps they conceived the film to be as nonthreatening to white viewers as possible, or perhaps they anticipated that it would be released at a time of promised progress. Instead, it's being released in a time of . . . unabashed racism. The time for protest has returned; for all the inspired celebration of hitherto unrecognized black heroes that "Hidden Figures" offers . . . I can only imagine the movie as it might have been made, much more amply, imaginatively, and resonantly, linking history and present tense, by Ava DuVernay or Spike Lee, Julie Dash or Charles Burnett.

Burnett and Dash had made films that were heaped with critical praise, though not box-office success. As independent Black filmmakers in the early phase of that movement, their careers never got the boost from Hollywood that might have granted them more opportunity and financial rewards.

Above all, however, the *Hidden Figures* filmmakers had unmistakably produced a crowd pleaser. Against that twenty-five-million-dollar budget, the film grossed $169.6 million in America and Canada, and another $66.3 million worldwide.

And now, early in 2017, it was time to announce the Oscar nominees. On January 24, those announcements came, delivered by Cheryl Boone Isaacs and a multiracial group of actors and actresses. The *New York Times* headline revealed: "Oscar Nominations 2017: 14 for 'La La Land,' and 6 for Black Actors." Those six were Viola Davis, Denzel Washington, Naomie Harris, Ruth Negga, Octavia Spencer, and Mahershala Ali. *Fences, Moonlight,* and *Hidden Figures* all received Best Picture nominations. Barry Jenkins was nominated for Best Director. And in the Adapted Screenplay category, Allison Schroeder and Theodore Melfi for *Hidden Figures,* Barry Jenkins and Tarell Alvin McCraney for *Moonlight,* and—most poignantly—August Wilson, who had died in 2005, for *Fences.* A notable and dramatic change had taken place.

At the Academy Awards ceremony, hosted by the late-night TV host Jimmy Kimmel, Casey Affleck won Best Actor for *Manchester by the*

*Sea,* Mahershala Ali Best Supporting Actor for *Moonlight,* Emma Stone Best Actress for *La La Land,* and Viola Davis Best Supporting Actress for *Fences.* Barry Jenkins and Tarell Alvin McCraney won Best Adapted Screenplay for *Moonlight.* The Academy decided they wanted Hollywood royalty to announce the Best Picture winner. They chose Warren Beatty and Faye Dunaway, the stars of Beatty's classic 1967 *Bonnie and Clyde,* which Beatty also produced. Throughout her career, Dunaway was notorious for her temperament. "I saw Faye the day before the Oscars at the Sally Hershberger salon on La Cienega," Lisa Taback, an Academy consultant for that year's ceremony, recalled. "She'd been driving the staff crazy for the past three days, trying to get her blond hair just right. When I walked in, the staff was ready to throw her out the window." The show had been proceeding smoothly up until the Best Picture announcement. Beatty and Dunaway walked out onstage. Beatty opened the envelope. It said, "Emma Stone, *La La Land.*" He paused—the audience on edge—and squinted. Sensing something awry, Beatty handed the envelope to Dunaway. Her eyes zeroed in on the words "*La La Land*" and she quickly announced "*La La Land!*" as the Best Picture winner. There was immediate jubilation from the cast and crew of that film. But, backstage, the Price Waterhouse accountants—who had memorized the winners in the event a snafu occurred—knew that *La La Land* was not the winner. Beatty had been handed the wrong envelope; Dunaway never looked at the outside of the envelope, only the card announcing the winner; it was Emma Stone's card for Best Actress. A Price Waterhouse accountant immediately piped into his microphone that Dunaway had read from the wrong envelope! But the *La La Land* producers and cast members were already onstage and making their acceptance speeches. Pandemonium began building. Academy staffers maneuvered through the onstage crowd, causing concern and confusion. "I felt like someone had been hurt," *La La Land*'s star Ryan Gosling said later. "I thought there was some kind of medical situation." Security also appeared onstage. Then Jordan Horowitz, one of the *La La Land* producers, reached the microphone. "There's a mistake. Moonlight—you guys won best picture. This is not a joke." Horowitz proceeded to hold up the correct card: "*Moonlight,* best picture." The *Moonlight* cast and crew rose from their seats and rushed to the stage. A wowed Jenkins—in comments that were brief because of time constraints—offered thanks to those who told him he couldn't abandon the project when doubts had begun to set in. The *Moonlight* cast and crew left the stage in a state of delirium.

. . .

A couple of weeks after the Oscars, Barry Jenkins was at a South by Southwest film event in Texas to give an address. He knew the audience expected him to talk about his double Oscar win. He told the gathering there were a lot of Chirons—the gay Black boy in his film—throughout America, and that he wanted them to endure and to dream. "We are that boy," he said of himself and McCraney. "And when you watch 'Moonlight,' you don't assume a boy who grew up how and where we did would grow up and make a piece of art that wins an Academy Award. I've said that a lot, and what I've had to admit is that I placed those limitations on myself, I denied myself that dream."

Jenkins and McCraney returned to Liberty City together later that year to celebrate and be celebrated. Among the celebrants that day were relatives of Arthur McDuffie. It is hard these days to be in Liberty City and not be reminded of McDuffie. In 2003, the city of Miami christened Arthur Lee McDuffie Avenue, near the site of his fatal encounter with police.

––––––––––

For decades, melodramas and comedies had been the major themes of Black filmmaking, evidence of Hollywood's reluctance to allow certain filmmakers to stretch their talents. Pure horror—as opposed to horror mixed with comedy, spoofing the genre—was an area into which Black filmmakers very rarely ventured. In 2017, Jordan Peele upended that dynamic.

Peele had made a reputation in sketch comedy as half of the duo Key & Peele, with Keegan-Michael Key. With a go-for-broke, no-holds-barred rambunctiousness, they were political, socially aware, sometimes angry, but always funny. Peele veered into moviemaking in 2016, scripting *Keanu*, a comedy about a missing cat. But he had loftier ambitions. The Obama presidency and the countrywide racism in reaction to it were often on his writing mind. "The notion of bringing up racism was almost thought of as perpetuating it," he said of the post-racial mindset that swept parts of the white populace after Obama's election. Peele, biracial, then wrote a script about a young Black-and-white couple who venture to upstate New York to visit the girlfriend's parents. The parents, unleashing streams of post-racial mumbo-jumbo, are actually concealing a host of secrets—racism, hypnosis, kidnapping, and debauchery. It's a Rubik's Cube–like screenplay, with many sides, and all those sides playing against and into the racial stereotypes threaded into the American psyche. Peele cobbled together a modest $4.5 million budget. *Get Out,* starring Daniel Kaluuya, Allison Williams, LaKeith Stanfield, Catherine Keener, Betty Gabriel, and Bradley Whitford, opened February 24, 2017. "The film," wrote the *New York Times* critic, "is an exhilaratingly smart and scary freak out about a black man in a white nightmare, the laughs come easily and then go in for the kill." *The Guardian*'s critic opined that the film "finds the still grinning ghoulish skull of age-old servitude and exploitation unveiled during a rollercoaster ride into a very American nightmare." And from *The New Yorker:* "The film is a major achievement, a work that deserves, in its own way, to be viewed alongside Barry Jenkins's 'Moonlight' as a giant leap forward for the possibilities of black cinema; 'Get Out' feels like it would have been impossible five minutes ago." The critics raved; but Peele had made more than just a critical darling. His film was a blockbuster, pulling in $255 million worldwide.

Jordan Peele, in his film, exposed a living, breathing, and quite spooky entity: American racism, a thing of true horror. Rising above that racism, his movie earned a slew of nominations and awards, among them the 2018 Best Original Screenwriting Academy Award.

———

Horror was not the only genre Hollywood shied from when it came to Black filmmakers. The superhero phenomenon was also off limits. The Marvel superheroes who reached the screen—Hulk, Iron Man, Captain America, Spider-Man—were always white. They flew through the air, defeated dangerous enemies, and had great swagger. The films broke worldwide box-office records, making mind-boggling sums of money for the studios, filmmakers, stars, and, of course, the creator of the comic books, Marvel. Their superhero films, in total, had grossed over thirteen billion dollars. Since 1966, there had been a Black superhero in the shadows. The Black Panther first appeared in the Marvel *Fantastic Four* comic. Eleven years later, in 1977, he got his own comic strip. "I came up with the Black Panther because I realized I had no Blacks in my strip," Jack Kirby, the Panther's co-creator, said in 1990. "I had a lot of black readers . . . and here I was ignoring them because I was associating with everybody else."

The Black Panther storyline was set in Wakanda, a fictional nation known for its independence and ability to avoid the wickedness of colonization. The superhero king of Wakanda is known as T'Challa.

———

Nate Moore, a Marvel Studios executive, was keen on making a stand-alone Black Panther film. It was time.

Growing up in California's San Joaquin Valley, Moore loved reading comic books, saving his allowance to purchase more and more of them. As a Black kid, however, he never saw the Black superhero figures he read about—Luke Cage, the Falcon, the Black Panther—up on the movie screen. When he became a Marvel executive—the only Black producing executive in Marvel's film division in 2016—he was delighted to find that the studio was plotting a Black Panther movie. Kevin Feige, Marvel Studios' president, had been making noises about diversifying the Marvel figures on-screen. Feige and Moore knew they needed just the right actor to play the lead role, and they decided on Chadwick Boseman, who had drawn wide praise for his portrayals of Jackie Robinson and James Brown. Boseman was on the James Brown press tour in Switzerland when Feige caught up with him by phone. The brief conversation was deceptively simple: "Hey Chadwick. It's Kevin Feige here. We want to know if you want to be the Black Panther."

In 2016, Marvel introduced the Black Panther on-screen in *Captain America: Civil War*. It was a cameo, just a tease, but Marvel fans swooned.

The studio spoke to many directors for its stand-alone film. Feige and Moore finally settled on Ryan Coogler, the acclaimed young director of *Fruitvale Station* and *Creed*. In some ways, it was a bold choice to hand the young director a two-hundred-million-dollar-budgeted picture. No Black director had ever been given such a large amount of money to make a film. But Ryan Coogler's confidence had grown. He believed in his talent. As excited as he was to be given the reins, he had something he needed to clarify with Feige and Moore: "You realize that this movie is going to be a predominantly Black cast?" Feige's response: "That's why we're doing it."

Coogler's *Panther* cast was a mixture of both new and veteran Black talent. Joining Boseman were Michael B. Jordan, Lupita Nyong'o, Danai Gurira, Forest Whitaker, Angela Bassett, Winston Duke, and Daniel Kaluuya. Also in the cast were Martin Freeman, Andy Serkis, and Isaach De Bankolé. Coogler chose three gifted Black women for jobs as well, jobs they might not have gotten from a white director: Hannah Beachler was the production designer, Ruth E. Carter was the costume designer, and Rachel Morrison was hired as cinematographer. Filming got under way in January 2017, in Atlanta. Part of the filming took place at Tyler Perry Studios, a 320-acre complex that Perry, a formidable figure in Black entertainment circles, had built. Much of the other location shooting took place in South Korea.

On August 11, 2017, a group of white supremacists gathered in Emancipation Park in Charlottesville, Virginia. Carrying and waving Confederate and Nazi flags, they were protesting the planned removal of the statue of the slave owner and Confederate general Robert E. Lee. A rival group was there to protest the Nazi presence. The following day, a mêlée broke out. Protesters began attacking one another. Around one forty-five that afternoon, the white supremacist James Fields, Jr.—who had driven from Ohio in a 2010 Dodge Challenger to attend the rally—drove his car into a crowd of anti-Nazi protesters. Bodies bounced off his car; flesh tore from bodies. At one point, Fields put his car in reverse and gunned the engine, ramming even more peaceful protesters. Nearly two dozen people were admitted to hospitals. Heather Heyer, a thirty-two-year-old anti-Nazi protester, died from her injuries. Most Americans expected President Trump to condemn the Nazi-fueled bloodshed and offer healing words for a nation once again rattled by racial bloodshed. He did not: "You had some very bad people in that group, but you also had people that were very fine people, on both sides." His statement drew wide condemnation. Such insensitive and incendiary racial talk hadn't been heard from a sitting American president in anyone's recent memory.

———

*Black Panther* flew onto American movie screens on February 16, 2018, with a riveting cinematic force. For all filmgoers to see, it was unabashed Blackness on screen, a kind of cultural bildungsroman, a race of people showcasing—flaunting!—their own ingenuity and resilience. The box-office results immediately began to break records; the reviews were rapturous. "Delivered through Coogler's judicious eye," stated *Wired* magazine, "[*Black Panther*'s] existence alone generates a counter-history in film and mass media—first by scraping whiteness from its narrative core, then by making Black people and Black self-determination the default." The *Guardian* review referenced writers from history: "It's an action-adventure origin myth which plays less like a conventional superhero film and more like a radical Brigadoon or a delicious adventure by Jules Verne or Edgar Rice Burroughs." The crossover film represented more to Blacks than just its appearance as a blockbuster; it was an emotional journey. "There are no signs of the excitement abating, either," opined *Vox,* "as the conversation about the film has evolved from discussions about the importance of representation into something grander: a rather groundbreaking celebration of black culture." From *Vanity Fair:* "Black Panther champions, and makes champions of, underserved demographics in a way that's somehow both casual and defiant, a statement of strength that proudly insists it needed no stating to begin with." Manohla Dargis, in her *New York Times* review, had special praise for Coogler: "There are sequences in 'Black Panther' that may make you cry because of where they go and what they say, but also because of the sensitivity he brings to them. He makes some savvy story choices too." Dargis added: "Race matters in 'Black Panther' and it matters deeply, not in terms of Manichaean good guys and bad but as a means to explore larger human concerns about the past, the present and the uses and abuses of power."

*Black Panther* amassed a whopping worldwide gross of $1.3 billion. Its opening weekend—$201 million—had box-office chroniclers doing double takes. It sat atop the box office for five straight weeks, longer than any other Marvel superhero movie. Hollywood—for decades the creator of stereotypes and Catch-22 roadblocks when it came to Black cinema—was forced to heed such success. "The revolutionary thing about *Black Panther,*" Jamil Smith wrote in *Time* magazine, "is that it envisions a world not devoid of racism but one in which black people have the wealth, technology and military might to level the playing field—a scenario applicable not only to the predominantly white landscape of Hollywood but, more important, to the world at large."

Attracting ticket buyers across races, cultures, and nations, Marvel and its cadre of young Black talent had stunned the world. Marvel may well have been a part of Hollywood, but it pushed aside the old and timid mindset of Hollywood. It had let Blackness—at least for one movie—strut its stuff on the big screen. It appreciated the enthusiasm of the Black executive Nate Moore. It had hired a Black director and Black cast and let them both honor Hollywood tradition—in many ways, the film is a traditional, thrilling, superhero movie—and, simultaneously, inject it with an unyielding cultural force. "All hail the new king," crowed *The Atlantic* about *Black Panther*.

Chadwick Boseman had amassed the kind of career that would have been the envy of any Hollywood actor. So his death—at the age of forty-three—shocked the entertainment world. Such had been the impact of *Black Panther* that there were page one tributes to the actor from around the country. One of his final roles was as the musician Levee in the Denzel Washington–produced *Ma Rainey's Black Bottom*, from the August Wilson canon.

———

No one was more delighted than Spike Lee to witness the rise of new young Black filmmakers. For many, Lee had been their lodestar. He still held tight his Captain Ahab persona, firing his harpoon at the big white whale of Hollywood. Ever since his student days at New York University, Lee had been pondering a cinematic treatment of the 16th Street Church bombing in Birmingham, Alabama, by Klansmen. It was a dramatic, gut-wrenching story—four little girls blown to pieces, and the subsequent lengthy search for their killers—but Hollywood wouldn't touch it. So Lee took his cameras to Birmingham, got a room at the Tutwiler Hotel, and convinced family members of the four girls to tell their stories. Lee's documentary, *4 Little Girls*, premiered in 1997. *The New York Times* called the documentary "remarkable," and credited Lee with "making the girls unforgettable and eliciting the long-buried emotions of those who loved them." The film won a host of awards, and was nominated for an Oscar as Best Documentary Feature.

The racial traumas of America kept fueling Lee's creative juices. In 2005, Hurricane Katrina's flooding of New Orleans savagely exposed the fault lines between Black and white America and governmental inaction when it came to that city's impoverished Black populace. "The residents of the Gulf Coast were not a priority for [the Bush] administration," Lee felt. "Actions speak louder than words, and two times . . . with earthquakes and tsunamis the United States of America have gone more than halfway around the world and was there in two days. And it took the same government four days to reach New Orleans." Lee's documentary, *When the Levees Broke: A Requiem in Four Acts*, premiered on HBO in August 2006. "What breaks your heart is the film's accumulated firsthand stories of New Orleans residents who lost everything in the flood," Stephen Holden wrote in *The New York Times.* Lee filmed a sequel, *If God Is Willing and da Creek Don't Rise,* which arrived in 2010. This sequel involved the ongoing efforts of city officials to restore New Orleans to some form of livability. It also had to deal with the April 10, 2010, BP oil spill, which poured sixty thousand barrels a day into the Louisiana Gulf. "It's about justice, it's about right and wrong," Lee said of the sequel. "I love this country, and these people are just screwing it up over greed. It's a disgrace. What we stress is that eleven people died on that oil rig over a company's decision to cut corners."

Lee's big-screen fictional film career remained in motion, seesawing between commercial hits and flops. He directed Denzel Washington in *Inside Man* in 2006, a twisty bank-heist movie. On a budget of forty-five million dollars, it made $186 million worldwide. In 2008, he directed *Miracle at St. Anna,* based on James McBride's novel. On an estimated forty-million-plus budget, it only reaped a total gross of nine million dollars worldwide. Lee had wanted to make *Miracle* as a corrective to Clint Eastwood's two 2006 films, *Letters from Iwo Jima* and *Flags of Our Fathers.* He was incensed that Eastwood had not honored the role of Black soldiers in those films. Lee showed no hesitancy in criticizing Eastwood: his harpoon was flying through the air again. "In my opinion, it doomed the movie," says McBride, also *Miracle's* screenwriter, of Lee's public criticism

2017 Nazi March in Charlottesville. The Nazi and Confederate flags were echoes of *The Birth of a Nation.*

of Eastwood. "The press just didn't like it. Spike has always been an outsider. Spike and I were always aware that the mythology of World War II never included Black people."

There were more Lee movies (*Red Hook Summer, Oldboy, Da Sweet Blood of Jesus*) that under-performed. But in 2017—with the involvement of the director of *Get Out,* Jordan Peele—a most unusual project landed on Lee's desk. It was the story of Ron Stallworth, a Black Colorado Springs police officer who went undercover in the late 1970s to expose criminal activity in the Ku Klux Klan. Stallworth dealt with the Klan by telephone; when person-to-person meetings were required, a white officer replaced him. Lee co-wrote and directed the film. *BlacKkKlansman* landed at the Cannes Film Festival in May 2018 and left with the coveted Grand Prix award. The film contained scenes from *The Birth of a Nation* and *Gone with the Wind*—Spike Lee's ongoing ding at America's cinematic history. It opened in America on August 10, 2018, and garnered some of the best reviews of his formidable career. The flamboyantly gifted Spike Lee, according to the critics, was back. In reality, he had never gone anywhere. *BlacKkKlansman,* on a fifteen-million-dollar budget, totaled a worldwide gross of ninety-three million. Lee's movie ended with a haunting tableau of the Charlottesville Nazi demonstration and bloodshed. It included a picture of Heather Heyer, whose death struck Lee as an "American apple pie act of terrorism."

―――――

By 2018, there seemed to be no American writer more relevant and of the moment—even though he had died in 1987—than James Baldwin. With a nation whiplashed by racist- and Nazi-fueled demonstrations—and a Donald Trump White House less racially diverse than any in recent memory—Baldwin's currency kept rising. Against a country's hard shift to the right, commentators were more and more referencing Baldwin; essayists were quoting his work. In Baldwin's mind, the racial problems that haunted America all his life could be traced to whites' willful ignorance about the tragedies of America's racial history—and their lack of love. "White people in this country," Baldwin wrote, "will have quite enough to do in learning how to accept and love themselves and each other, and when they have achieved this—which will not be tomorrow and may very well be never—the Negro problem will no longer exist, for it will no longer be needed."

James Baldwin in 1963. He held nothing back when talking of Hollywood.

Even with Baldwin's literary output, and his acclaim, Hollywood had ignored adapting the author's works. He had, however, been on the mind of Barry Jenkins. With the success of *Moonlight,* Jenkins had some currency to choose his next project. He turned his attention to Baldwin's 1974 novel, *If Beale Street Could Talk.* The novel is a Harlem-set story about Fonny and Tish, two young lovers engaged to be married. The drama unfolds with the realization that Tish is pregnant. No sooner has the couple expressed a determination to make a life together than Fonny is falsely accused of rape. He is sent off to jail, with the assistance of a crooked police officer. The tragic corruption of the criminal-justice system sends the couple into a tailspin, testing the depths of Black love. Jenkins assembled a cast including Regina King, Colman Domingo, Michael Beach, Dave Franco, and, as the young lovers, Stephan James—a Canadian-born actor who played Jesse Owens in *Race*—and the newcomer Kiki Layne.

*If Beale Street Could Talk* opened on December 14, 2018. "This isn't a happy film but it isn't a hopeless one, either," Odie Henderson wrote for

RogerEbert.com. "The most striking thing that you'll take with you is that Baldwin's novel was written 44 years ago, but it's just as timely now."

Jenkins had introduced the great James Baldwin to filmgoers in a way Baldwin had never been introduced. For decades, Hollywood had perpetuated and, by extension, taught the myth of the leathery cowboy, the ruthlessness of the Great Plains Indian, the wisdom of the corner cop—but all too rarely had it taught and cinematically shown the true weight of injustice when it came to Blackness. On a twelve-million-dollar budget, *If Beale Street Could Talk* crested at a disappointing twenty million. But, lackluster box office aside, America seemed in genuine need of a dose of Baldwin. Jenkins's film reaped nominations and awards. Regina King won a Golden Globe for her performance, and the film earned Globe nominations for Best Picture and Best Adapted Screenplay.

The Academy Award nominations were scheduled to be announced on January 22. Spike Lee had never received a competitive Oscar. (He did have an honorary one, bestowed in 2015.) There was no denying that *BlacKkKlansman* had hit the zeitgeist and proved quite profitable, so many thought this would finally be his year.

The actors Tracee Ellis Ross and Kumail Nanjiani gathered to announce the nominations. *The Favourite* and *Roma* led all films with ten nominations apiece. Lee received nominations for both directing and screenwriting. *Black Panther, Green Book,* and Lee's *BlacKkKlansman* all received Best Picture nods. Regina King was nominated for her turn in *If Beale Street Could Talk.* There were multiple nominations as well in technical categories for *Panther, Green Book,* and *BlacKkKlansman;* many of those were for Black technical talent—design, costume. (Although she wasn't Oscar-nominated for *Black Panther,* Rachel Morrison, that film's cinematographer, had been nominated for *Mudbound,* making her the first woman to receive an Oscar nomination in cinematography.)

It is commonplace for an aggrieved segment of the moviegoing public—sometimes aided by film critics—to zero in on a particular nominated film, finding flaws and putting a bull's-eye upon that film. Among the 2019 nominees, that film was *Green Book,* which is nominally about a Black character, only to have that character's storyline overwhelmed by a white character. The film, starring Viggo Mortensen and Mahershala Ali, told the story of Don Shirley, a jazz pianist, and his 1962 tour dates through the South while being driven by Frank "Tony Lip" Vallelonga, a white man of Italian descent. The title of the movie stems from a real-life pamphlet—*The Negro Motorist Green-Book*—first published in 1936, that highlighted Black establishments where Blacks could stay and eat throughout a segregated nation. "You will find it handy on your travels, whether at home or in some other state, and [it] is up to date," the small booklet advertised. "Each year we are compiling new lists as some of these places move, or go out of business and new business places are started giving added employment to members of our race."

Vallelonga's son, Nick, had been trying to get producers interested in the story for years. Finally, Peter Farrelly decided to direct it. From *The Guardian:* "Green Book's approach to race is at best naïve and at worst jaw-droppingly ill-judged." Harry Belafonte and Quincy Jones, however, announced their admiration of the film, believing that at least it introduced Don Shirley—largely unknown outside of precious jazz circles—to a wider audience.

The Oscars ceremony took place on February 24. The highly debated *Green Book* won Best Picture, and Mahershala Ali won for Best Supporting Actor; Spike Lee won his first competitive Oscar for Adapted Screenplay, sharing it with Charles Wachtel, David Rabinowitz, and Kevin Willmott; Regina King won her first Oscar; Ruth Carter (Costume Design) and Hannah Beachler (Production Design, shared with Jay Hart), two Black women, won their first Oscars for *Black Panther,* which also won for Original Score.

It had been a remarkable year for Black talent, and they received their just rewards. But, as always, questions remained: Would studio projects continue to have multiracial casts? Would more Black writers be hired? Would studio chiefs think as broadly as Marvel's Kevin Feige and Nate Moore had done? Would other production companies rise up and attempt to emulate what Brad Pitt's Plan B had done in seeking out actors and directors of color? And, perhaps most important: Would the real world accept and emulate Hollywood's progress? Would reality take the lead from purveyors of fantasy? The answer was a resounding and horrifying no.

The year 2019 saw some progress, or, at least, an attempt to keep Black actors and technicians and filmmakers working and relevant. Spike Lee found an interesting home at Netflix rather than the traditional Hollywood studios. "At the other places, there are no Black people in the room," he said. Focus Features/Universal made *Harriet,* a box-office success about the courageous life of Harriet Tubman, directed by a Black woman, Kasi Lemmons. Cynthia Erivo, who played Harriet, was the sole Black actor to receive an Oscar nomination. There was *The Last Black Man in San Francisco,* about home displacement and gentrification; *Queen & Slim,* about two Black characters on the run from the police. But none of the films released in 2019 had anywhere near the impact of a 2020 video that was shot on an iPhone. That film energized and possibly changed the world.

# The Scourged Back

T HE MEN WHO INVENTED THE CAMERA—which grew into the movie camera—might well have been challenged imagining the multiple uses it would come to have across the reach of humanity. In the life of Black Americans, photographs and moving images would come to be quite significant, illustrating both hardship and brutality. The camera might be adjusted or angled by any photographer, but it rarely could be manipulated to lie. It dealt in visual facts and specific moments of time.

In 1863, a slave by the name of Gordon, living on the John and Bridget Lyons Plantation, eighty miles from Baton Rouge, figured he'd die if he remained on the plantation much longer. He'd been recently whipped and beaten—again—about the back. "I was two months in bed sore from the whipping," he said. Eight weeks before Christmas, Gordon fled. He crawled through swamps and dodged alligators. He ran and ran. He rubbed his body with onions to throw off the bloodhounds giving chase, pulling the slave catchers with them. He rested when he could, which was not often. He prayed. And ran on. On the tenth day of his trek, he finally reached a Union Army camp—and freedom. Army surgeons tended to him, aghast at the scarring on his back, a gruesome sight of jagged and bumpy lines left by the whip's lashings. A photographer at the camp was also stunned at the sight of the escaped slave's wounds. He took a photograph of Gordon sitting with his exposed back to the camera and decided it was important for others around the country to see. *Harper's Weekly* printed the photograph on July 4, 1863. It was given a title, *The Scourged Back*. Men and women who cared about freedom shook their heads in disgust when eyeing the photo and were revolted that human beings were chained and whipped like animals. Many wept.

The visual impact of the photograph inspired many Blacks to join the Union Army. The ex-slave Gordon was later seen carrying a rifle and wearing Union blue, marching off with fellow soldiers to engage in battle with the Confederates. As was true of so many former slaves, however, the latter years of his life went undocumented. The photo of Gordon has gone on to hang in museums and exhibits around the world. In 2020, Will Smith and the director Antoine Fuqua—bypassing the traditional Hollywood studio system—joined forces with Apple to announce plans to make *Emancipation,* a movie of Gordon's escape from the plantation where he was brutalized. A film shoot was planned for Georgia. But when Governor Brian Kemp signed what many felt was a restrictive voting law that would hurt Blacks, Fuqua and Smith announced they would not be filming their $100-million-budget movie in the state. It was the kind of political-cinematic clout that Sidney Poitier and Harry Belafonte never possessed.

All through history, the plight of the Black American has been fitfully captured in the camera lens. The 1960s civil-rights uprisings and marches were documented in photos and newsreels. The images stunned many whites who lived in the same country but in a different world. Segregation

George Floyd protests. Hollywood—like the rest of the world—couldn't ignore the public killing of George Floyd.

and racial abuses had long been ignored throughout America. But when technology evolved—cell phones, then the magic of cameras affixed to cell phones, then video cameras built into cell phones—anonymous citizens did not just become witnesses to all manner of evil, they filmed it. The camera did not lie.

On the afternoon of February 23, 2020, Ahmaud Arbery, a twenty-five-year-old Black man, went out for a jog, running along Holmes Road in the small Southern town of Brunswick, Georgia. At one point, he stopped and sauntered into an opened home under construction, looked around without touching anything, left, and continued on with his jogging. He had been a high-school athlete; staying fit was important to him. William Bryan, a white town-resident, spotted Arbery jogging—and there went his adrenaline. Bryan phoned Travis McMichael and his dad, Gregory—also white—and told them there was a "suspicious" Black man jogging down the road. There had been reports of house break-ins. Although those reports had come months earlier, the McMichael father and son grabbed their loaded guns, hopped into their pickup, and roared off down the road. Bryan also gave chase in his truck. Arbery, hearing engines, quickly sensed the commotion—pickup trucks going fast, then slowing down, voices being raised at him. He began zigzagging in his running, trying to avoid being hit. Gregory McMichael yelled at him to stop; the frightened Arbery didn't know why he should or would stop but now had a truck in front of him that was slowing down and blocking him, and a truck in back of him, driven by Bryan, that was crowding him. Bryan rammed his truck into Arbery, shocking the young runner, who was now hurt and bleeding. Arbery ducked into a shallow ditch and found himself cornered. Travis McMichael hopped out of the truck and neared the stunned and heavily breathing Arbery. McMichael pointed the shotgun. Arbery, petrified, grabbed the barrel. In a flash, McMichael shot him in the chest, then the shoulder, and finally the wrist. The young Black man tumbled over, dead. Bryan, in his pickup, recorded the whole thing on his phone. "Fucking nigger," Travis McMichael said, standing over Arbery's body. Thereafter, everything turned Faulknerian. A small Southern town, its white power structure firmly in place, saw two layers of district attorneys refuse to charge the McMichaels or Bryan with any crime. They determined that the killing—of an unarmed man—was done in self-defense. They all knew the McMichael family quite well. Gregory McMichael had even worked for years as an investigator for the local police department.

Ahmaud Arbery was laid to rest amid his sobbing family. Nothing that had happened made sense to Wanda Cooper-Jones, his mother. She needed more details, so she kept making calls to the police department. It did not matter who recused themselves; whenever the case went up the chain of command, the same answer came back: no charges would be filed. But the Black citizens of Brunswick—unable, as of yet, to draw national attention to the case—would not be deterred. They began to march. William Bryan, the driver of the second truck, had videotaped the whole thing, and, strangely, decided that if the video were seen it could exonerate everyone—certainly himself, since his name had filtered out into the community as being a participant in, or at least a witness to, the killing. Bryan gave the video to his attorney, who turned it over to a local radio station. Station managers, on May 5, posted it online. The visual imagery showed Arbery running, cornered, then shot dead. It quickly went viral, and the country realized what they were seeing was another ghastly cold-blooded murder of a Black man. Governor Brian Kemp—realizing the public would now refuse to accept decisions made by the local prosecutors—quickly ordered the Georgia Bureau of Investigation to take over the case. It took only two days for them to gather enough evidence to arrest the McMichaels, charging them with felony murder, malice murder, aggravated assault, and false imprisonment. Bryan was arrested two weeks later and charged with felony murder and criminal attempt to commit false imprisonment. A special prosecutor was soon appointed to prosecute the case.

White America, according to multiple surveys, still regarded the word of police officers as sacrosanct: the police were never to be doubted, or, at the very least, must always be supported. Black America did not hold the same view.

Then America—and the world—saw what happened on May 25, 2020.

On that day in Minneapolis, George Floyd, a Black man, went into a convenience store to make a small purchase. One of the clerks suspected that Floyd passed a counterfeit twenty-dollar bill, an accusation never proved. Nevertheless, police officers soon arrived. Floyd was questioned, handcuffed, and seated in the back of a police car. More police officers arrived, among them Derek Chauvin, a veteran Minneapolis cop. Numerous complaints about the use of unnecessary force had been filed against Chauvin over the years, but the department, for the most part, ignored them; he was thought so highly of that he even became one of the department's training instructors. Chauvin pulled the handcuffed Floyd out of the first car and walked him over to another police car. He then—assisted by fellow officers—placed Floyd on the ground, on his stomach. Some of the officers sat atop the still-handcuffed Floyd, pinning him. Then only Chauvin was left atop the helpless Black man, his knee settled upon Floyd's neck. A young Black teenager began filming the scene on her cell phone. Her name was Darnella Frazier, and she was still in high school. Floyd lay grimacing, in obvious pain. At one point he said, "I can't breathe." Two minutes turned to three minutes. Floyd—just as Eric Garner had done—cried out, "Mama . . . I'm through!" The teenager kept recording. An ambulance arrived. Chauvin finally rose and nonchalantly sauntered off to his squad car. The unconscious Floyd was taken to the hospital, where he was pronounced dead. Floyd had been pinned for a little more than nine minutes. The Minneapolis police department quickly misled the public about Floyd's death, and so the teenager, Frazier, posted her video to let the world know the truth.

Another image of yet another tortured or dead Black man was burned into the annals of American history: *The Scourged Back;* fourteen-year-old Emmitt Till in the casket; the 1930s and 1940s lynching photos. Against cries for justice over the public murder of George Floyd, Minneapolis began to burn. Then other cities began to burn. Then the burning stopped, and peaceful marching began. All around America, Blacks and whites marched side by side across bridges, down Main Street, U.S.A. Waves and waves of marchers. Nothing like it had been seen before, not even in the sixties. "BLACK LIVES MATTER" signs appeared at rallies, on lawns, on banners. "*Say his name*" was chanted across the country. The multiracial coalitions—of a size never seen before in American history on behalf of African American justice—stunned the politicians who pulled the levers of power and who had ignored systemic racism for so long. The marches continued in Houston, in Miami, in New York City, in Atlanta, in New Orleans, in Washington, D.C., in Portland, Oregon. Politicians believed—or hoped—that it would quickly wane; that the populace would rally behind the men and women in blue, the police. But the politicians were wrong. Marchers in foreign lands were also on the move for Black justice: they marched in Montreal, in Hong Kong, in London, in Paris, in Beijing, in Sydney, Australia. There were worldwide demands to investigate the systemic racism that had affected all walks of American life—schools, medical care, universities, the arts, sports, and cinema.

In June 2020, the ever-busy Spike Lee entered the fray, releasing a short film, 3 *Brothers—Radio Raheem, Eric Garner and George Floyd*. It bracketed newsreel footage from the murders of Floyd and Garner with the fictional murder of Radio Raheem from Lee's *Do the Right Thing.* It's an eerie film, as if Lee, in his 1989 movie, had been able to see into the dark side of the American future: that the police chokehold would come to be as devastating and racially catastrophic as the lynch rope.

Other stories, which hadn't received as much attention as the Arbery and Floyd killings, emerged: On March 13, 2020, Louisville police officers had, without announcing themselves, busted through the door of Breonna Taylor, a Black woman, and shot her dead in the hallway outside her bedroom. They had come to the wrong address. None of them were charged with murder. The single charge filed: one officer was charged with endangering one of Taylor's neighbors because he had fired a shot into that neighbor's house.

Not long after Floyd's murder, on June 12, a white Atlanta cop shot Rayshard Brooks, a Black man, in the back, killing him. It, too, was captured on video. That cop was arrested and charged with murder.

Four officers were finally arrested and charged with the murder of George Floyd. On April 21, 2021, Derek Chauvin, the first officer to be tried in the death of Floyd, was found guilty of murdering him. The names of other Blacks killed in recent years at the hands of law enforcement—or those closely identifying with policing—resurfaced: Eric Garner, Trayvon Martin, Philando Castile, Tamir Rice. "I call the young people who grew up in the past twenty-five years the Trayvon Generation," Elizabeth Alexander would write in *The New Yorker* soon after the Floyd murder. "They always knew these stories. These stories formed their world view. These stories helped instruct young African-Americans about their embodiment and their vulnerability. The stories were primers in fear and futility. The stories were the ground soil of their rage." She went on: "They watched these violations up close and on their cell phones, so many times over. They watched them in near-real time. . . . They watched them on the school bus. They watched them under the covers at night."

A lone white Marine veteran, in full uniform, stood in front of the Utah State Capitol, wearing an "I CAN'T BREATHE" face mask.

The mayor of Washington, D.C., ordered "BLACK LIVES MATTER" to be stenciled in the largest of letters on a street near the White House.

Confederate statues—monuments that honored white men who had terrorized and attempted to destabilize a nation over the issue of Black freedom—began to fall.

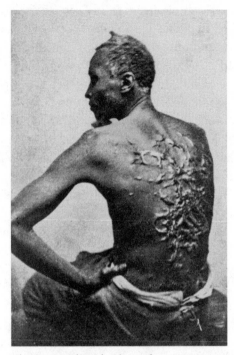

*The Scourged Back.* The enduring pain.

A California couple, Nicole Anderson and David Nelson, were arrested and charged by the Contra Costa District Attorney's Office for scrubbing away a "BLACK LIVES MATTER" mural that had been approved by the city. They were charged with a hate crime.

Conversations began about systemic racism in America, a kind that had never before taken place in white society. The idea of militarized police departments was suddenly being debated. The history of juries' refusing to convict police officers for killing unarmed Blacks flowed through communities.

In 2020, America's scourged back was exposed to the world.

On June 22, a collage by Kadir Nelson of Black figures murdered throughout history and into the present, *Say Their Names,* appeared on the cover of *The New Yorker.* The faces were pressed against the large visage and outline of George Floyd. In the lower right-hand corner of the drawing sat Gordon, the runaway slave who had bolted into the Louisiana swamps all those years ago.

They kept marching. They marched down Highland Avenue in Hollywood, old and young and Black and white and Hispanic and Asian. The

Hollywood marches turned attention to Hollywood itself. McKinsey and Company, a giant management consulting firm, issued a report that stated Hollywood's anti-Black bias resulted in the loss of at least $10 billion in yearly revenues. Black actors and actresses became part of an initiative, Hollywood4BlackLives, and wrote a letter to the industry:

> Hollywood has a privilege as a creative industry to imagine and create. We have significant influence over culture and politics. We have the ability to use our influence to imagine and create a better world. Yet, historically and currently, Hollywood encourages the epidemic of police violence and culture of anti-blackness. The way that Hollywood and mainstream media have contributed to the criminalization of Black people, the misrepresentation of the legal system, and the glorification of police corruption and violence have had dire consequences on Black lives.

In November 2020, a president and vice-president who refused to utter the words "BLACK LIVES MATTER" before the public were voted out of office. President Joseph Biden and Vice-President Kamala Harris (the first woman of color to hold the vice-presidency) took office January 20, 2021. Five months after the inauguration, the Pulitzer Prize board announced that Darnell Frazier—the young videographer—would receive a special Pulitzer citation for her courage in filming the Floyd video.

———

A lot of it, when it came to Hollywood, whipped back to the beginning, to the showing of *The Birth of a Nation* in Woodrow Wilson's White House, and to Wilson himself. None of it—like slavery—could be squeezed back into a bottle.

In November 2015, a group of student activists at Princeton University staged a sit-in in the office of the university's president, Christopher Eisgruber. They were demanding that the school remove Wilson's name from campus buildings because of his well-documented racism. In April 2016, the university agreed to undertake some changes to foster more inclusion on the campus, but would not agree to remove Wilson's name from any of its buildings. In late June 2020, the university had a change of mind. "The board," President Eisgruber announced, "reconsidered these conclusions this month as the tragic killings of George Floyd, Breonna Taylor,

Ahmaud Arbery, and Rayshard Brooks drew renewed attention to the long and damaging history of racism in America. . . . Wilson's racism was significant and consequential even by the standards of his own time. He segregated the federal civil service after it had been racially integrated for decades, thereby taking America backward in its pursuit of justice. He not only acquiesced in but added to the persistent practices of racism in this country, a practice that continues to do harm today." Eisgruber went on to say that the building bearing Wilson's name would bear his name no more. That same year, Princeton announced that a residential college on the campus would be named after Mellody Hobson, a highly successful Black businesswoman and 1991 Princeton graduate. Hobson College will sit on the site of what was formerly known as Wilson College. (Hobson's husband is the filmmaker George Lucas.)

Film had rested for so long on the front brim of pop culture, with the wounds ever present. In early 2021, on the eve of the Hollywood Foreign Press Association's 78th annual awards ceremony, it was revealed that the HFPA, which administers the Golden Globes, hadn't had a Black member in its ranks for twenty years.

Across more than a century's time line, it came to pass that the spiritual sons and daughters of Oscar Micheaux were still grappling with the weight of cinematic history, a history that had dived into the psyche of a segregated land with a potent force, creating storylines that its white arbiters deemed digestible to white audiences. Black artists have struggled, since movies first began, to grab hold of the storyline, investing in, when they could, a more honest narrative. But even the most creative minds could not have imagined the potency of the films of slain victims of police brutality, seen by the entire world when movie theatres were shuttered because of a health pandemic. In their own way, those homemade films swept into the silt of a restless world. Now, at long last, *The Scourged Back* was being turned around—as if on a split screen—demanding of a nation that it look, full on and unblinkingly, at what it had done, good and bad, with the magic of its camera machinery.

# Acknowledgments

Like the evolution of most cultural entities in America, the world of cinema began as a segregated undertaking. Movie-theatre owners, in keeping whites from having to interact with Blacks, would assign special days for Blacks. Absent special days, they would direct Blacks to sit in the balcony. When it came to racial integration and filmmaking, the movie industry evolved in a painfully slow manner—often notably slower than the rest of the country. When I mentioned to Peter Gethers, my editor, that it would be interesting to tell the story of America intertwined with filmmaking and racial dynamics—in a kind of triptych, all under the covers of one book—he expressed delight at the idea. We met in New York City at the Algonquin Hotel—a nostalgic hang-out for actors and writers (the Roundtable)—to discuss it further. I'm very grateful that Peter, who grew up in the environs of Hollywood, was my editor yet again. We are on the same wavelength. This is our fifth book together.

Also at Knopf, I would like to thank Tatiana Dubin, Kathy Zuckerman, Amy Hagedorn, Julianne Clancy, Victoria Pearson, and Maggie Hinders. Thanks also to the keen-eyed copy editor, Terry Zaroff.

Esther Newberg at ICM has been my literary agent on all nine of my books. I thank her immensely for her steadfast support of my work through these years.

Miami University, in Oxford, Ohio, has given me a home away from home. It gives me great pleasure to be affiliated with the Department of Media, Journalism, and Film there. Among those at the university whose support and friendship I am appreciative of are Gregory Crawford, Bruce Drushel, Chris Makaroff, Phyllis Callahan, David Sayler, Darrell Hedric, Kathy Squance, Richard Campbell, Jason Osborne, Jack Owens, Ted Pickerill, James Tobin, Patty Newberry, Dawn Tsirelis, and Ron Scott.

There are others who have given moral support—and abided my conversations about movies these past few years, sometimes offering wonderful leads that aided this endeavor—and they must be mentioned: Greg Moore, Tina Moody, Michael Coleman, Bob Miller, Larry James, Paul Hendrickson, Peter Guralnick, Donna James, Steve Flannigan, Larry Young, Charles Allen, Mary Jo Conte, Marty Anderson, Wonda Haygood, Ceil Hendrickson, Bill Orrico, Ben Bradlee, Jr., Tony Stigger, Rick Momeyer, Naomi Shavin, Sue Momeyer, Paula Stanley, Shane Cagney, Al Edmondson, Diane Stigger, and Faness Haygood. Robert Lewis kept me smiling as he recalled memories of the blaxploitation film era. Lynn Peterson was gracious—as she ever is—in sending along films and books I may well have missed.

# Notes

Aside from interviews over the past several years with directors, actors, producers, screenwriters, and Academy of Motion Picture Arts and Sciences officials, I am also grateful to the staff at Howard University's Moorland-Spingarn Research Center in Washington, D.C. Their collection of entertainment-oriented periodicals, stretching from the 1930s onward, helped shed a light on the history of Blacks working in American cinema.

It helps to understand the rhythm of moviemaking if one can spend time on a movie set watching a film come together. I am very grateful that the director Lee Daniels and producer Pamela Oas Williams invited me to Montreal in 2019 to watch, over the course of several days, the filming of his movie *The United States vs. Billie Holiday,* which Daniels directed and for which Andra Day received a Best Actress Oscar nomination. I have tried to infuse this book with insight into how filmmakers craft their films, and Daniels greatly aided my effort.

The following granted me interviews and have my gratitude: James McBride, Michael Schultz, Woodie King, Jr., Louis Gossett, Jr., Cheryl Boone Isaacs, Reginald Hudlin, Ann Slider, Nelson George, Helene Echegoyen, Theodore Witcher, April Reign, Robert Hooks, Cliff Frazier, and Landon Jones.

It was Pamela Oas Williams with whom I first discussed the idea of this book years ago. We met in the aftermath of my writing about White House butler Eugene Allen. Her insights about the world of filmmaking proved invaluable.

I would like to point out four books that proved particularly valuable to my understanding of the world of Oscar Micheaux, and also the temperature around the making and release of *The Birth of a Nation.* The books are: *Oscar Micheaux: The Great and Only,* by Patrick McGilligan; *With a Crooked Stick—The Films of Oscar Micheaux,* by J. Ronald Green; *Straight Lick: The*

*Cinema of Oscar Micheaux,* also by Green; and *The Birth of a Movement,* by Dick Lehr.

**CHAPTER 1** MOVIE NIGHT AT
WOODROW WILSON'S WHITE HOUSE

3  "some deprivation of": *Princeton Alumni Weekly,* March 3, 2011.

3  "superior to those": Ibid.

5  "The only place": Evans, *The American Century,* p. 130.

6  "politically the most": quoted in Michaeli, *The Defender,* p. 48.

7  "Nothing could be": Litwack, *Trouble in Mind,* p. 104.

9  "revolutionizing motion picture": quoted in Lehr, *The Birth of a Movement,* p. 115.

9  "It hit me": quoted in ibid., p. 117.

9  "I could just": quoted in ibid.

10  "mix the two": Ibid., p. 123.

10  "It hasn't been": Ibid., p. 127.

10  "I could see": Ibid., p. 128.

10  "The Klan at": Ibid., p. 133.

11  "I told him": Ibid., p. 150.

11  "I assured him": quoted in ibid.

11  "If we could": quoted in ibid.

13  "There were 500": quoted in ibid., pp. 155–56.

13  "I was gratified": quoted in ibid., p. 156.

14  "calculated to arouse": quoted in ibid., p. 172.

14  "unloosen the energy": quoted in ibid., p. 283.

14  "It hurt me": quoted in ibid., p. 154.

15  "I would like": quoted in ibid., p. 187.

15  "most enthusiastically received": quoted in ibid., p. 199.

15  "The more the": quoted in ibid.

15  "I cannot describe": quoted in ibid.

16  "I am quite": quoted in ibid.

17  "We won't leave": quoted in ibid., p. 216.

17  "As a racial": quoted in ibid., p. 222.

18  "Within one year": quoted in ibid., pp. 226–27.

18  "I sympathize with": quoted in ibid., p. 234.

18  "nauseating": quoted in ibid., p. 238.

18  "a splendid thing": quoted in ibid.

19  "What should we": quoted in ibid., p. 251.

19  "not to accept": quoted in ibid., p. 255.

19  "There was general": quoted in ibid.

19  "decided the license": quoted in ibid., p. 265.

19  "BIRTH OF A": quoted in ibid.

19  "Months of frantic": quoted in ibid., p. 277.

20  "Under a blazing": quoted in ibid., p. 278.

20  "I had to": McWhirter, *Red Summer,* p. 70.

**CHAPTER 2** THE RARE AND
EXTRAORDINARY SIGHTING OF
A BLACK FILMMAKER

23  "About the only": quoted in McGilligan, *Oscar Micheaux,* p. 11.

24  "The mornings I": Micheaux, *The Conquest,* p. 40.

24  "Two hundred miles": quoted in McGilligan, *Micheaux,* p. 30.

24  "It had been": Micheaux, *Conquest,* p. 41.

26  "The fifth day": Ibid., p. 44.

26  "You can't find": quoted in McGilligan, *Micheaux,* p. 41.

26  "At first I": Micheaux, *Conquest,* pp. 56–57.

28  "Isn't it enough": quoted in McGilligan, *Micheaux,* p. 69.

29  "My head ached": quoted in ibid., p. 86.

30  "The book has": quoted in ibid., p. 94.

31  "operated and owned": quoted in ibid., p. 108.

31  "We are always": quoted in ibid.

32 "I expect to": quoted in ibid., p. 121.

32 "the largest theatres": quoted in ibid.

32 "Aside from the": quoted in ibid.

33 "Writing it caused": quoted in ibid., p. 123.

34 "Every Race man": quoted in ibid., p. 129.

34 "I can see": quoted in ibid., p. 130.

35 "Every detail of": quoted in ibid., p. 131.

35 "Many scenes, stated: quoted in ibid.

36 "the biggest protest": quoted in ibid., p. 140.

36 "*The Birth of*": quoted in ibid., p. 144.

37 ". . . beg to advise": quoted in Green, *With a Crooked Stick*, p. 25.

37 "creating a sensation": quoted in Green, *Straight Lick*, p. 244.

38 "What American literature": quoted in Driskell, et al., *Harlem Renaissance*, p. 63.

38 "In Harlem," the writer: quoted in Lewis, *When Harlem Was in Vogue*, p. 103.

39 "Moving pictures have": quoted in McGilligan, *Micheaux*, p. 156.

39 "See the Ku": quoted in ibid.

40 "holds the interest": quoted in ibid., p. 167.

42 "Michaux [sic] made storm": quoted in ibid., p. 206.

42 "A magnificent combination": quoted in ibid., p. 217.

42 "Beautifully photographed": quoted in ibid.

42 "Oh boy!": quoted in ibid.

42 "In Houston are": quoted in ibid., p. 220.

43 "He could get": quoted in ibid., p. 237.

43 "one of the": quoted in ibid., p. 238.

43 "well worth seeing": quoted in ibid., p. 237.

44 "persistent vaunting of": quoted in ibid., p. 245.

45 "Some good acting": quoted in ibid., p. 255.

45 "a portrayal of": quoted in ibid., p. 256.

46 The critics were: Ibid., p. 281.

46 "Nothing makes a": quoted in *New York Times*, Aug. 12, 2019.

47 "I'm leaving the": quoted in *Time*, Feb. 4, 2008.

47 "We may come": Ibid.

47 "Publishing a book": quoted in Green, *With a Crooked Stick*, p. 31.

48 "A preposterous, tasteless": quoted in McGilligan, *Micheaux*, p. 340.

48 "faulty, to say": quoted in ibid., p. 341.

**CHAPTER 3** THE IMITATION GAME

51 "long hours outside": quoted in Kroeger, *Fannie*, p. 10.

51 "There is nothing": quoted in ibid., p. 19.

51 "That picture of": quoted in ibid., p. 22.

52 "on the edge": quoted in Lewis, *When Harlem Was in Vogue*, p. 116.

53 "There is something": quoted in Boyd, *Wrapped in Rainbows*, p. 61.

53 "Zora Neale Hurston": quoted in ibid., p. 99.

54 "lived laughingly": quoted in Kroeger, *Fannie*, p. 122.

55 "a triumph of": quoted in ibid., p. 198.

55 "one of the": quoted in ibid.

56 "I won't be": Hurst, *Imitation of Life*, p. 149.

57 "so full of": quoted in Kroeger, *Fannie*, p. 208.

57 "old stereotype of": quoted in ibid., p. 207.

57 "I knew that": quoted in ibid., p. 208.

57 "fall short or": quoted in ibid., p. 211.

58 "shot through with": quoted in ibid., p. 260.

60 "We are sick": quoted in Haygood, *King of the Cats*, p. 227.

60 "Asia and Africa": quoted in ibid.

61 "Sammy Davis, Jr.": Gossett, interview by author.

63 "If you're not": *Los Angeles Times*, July 9, 2000.

63 "That was a": Ibid.

68 "I thought Lana": Ibid.

68 "the secondary plot": *Variety*, Dec. 31, 1958.

69 "holding a looking": quoted in Boyd, *Wrapped*, p. 268.

**CHAPTER 4** A MOST PECULIAR KIND OF FAME

72 "Mrs. Stowe betrays": Stowe, *Uncle Tom's Cabin*, p. xvi.

72 "A round, black": Ibid., p. 24.

72 "A cook she": Ibid., p. 25.

75 "They desired no": *Atlantic*, May 31, 2013.

75 "in memory of": Ibid.

75 "faithful colored mammies": Ibid.

76 "In Grateful Memory": Ibid.

78 "a tiny woman": quoted in *Morning Call*, July 17, 1986.

81 "I knew that": quoted in Watts, *Hattie McDaniel*, p. 31.

81 "Imagine a person": quoted in ibid., p. 40.

83 "We greet you": quoted in Haygood, *In Black and White*, p. 63.

83 "Hattie McDaniel, blues": quoted in Watts, *McDaniel*, p. 51.

83 "I never had": quoted in ibid., p. 75.

84 "There is a": quoted in ibid., pp. 103–4.

85 "In my opinion": quoted in Buckley, *The Hornes*, p. 135.

86 "would probably want": quoted in Watts, *McDaniel*, p. 155.

86 "I visualized myself": quoted in ibid., p. 176.

87 "Tonight we want": quoted in ibid., p. 169.

87 "It is the ultimate": quoted in ibid., p. 173.

87 "one of the screen's": Ibid., p. 173.

88 "I pointed out": White, *A Man Called White*, p. 199.

89 "He reminded the": Ibid., p. 201.

89 "But I am": quoted in Watts, *McDaniel*, p. 226.

90 "I am sorry": quoted in Jearl-Chara Bohan Nix, "Reaching Across the Color Line: Margaret Mitchell and Benjamin Mays, an Uncommon Friendship," in Scholar Works @ Georgia State University, 2013, pp. 127–31.

90 "Recently our colored": quoted in ibid.

91 "The only Negroes": quoted in Buckley, *The Hornes*, p. 156.

93 "It was as if the": *Hollywood Reporter*, Feb. 19, 2015.

**CHAPTER 5** [AN INTERLUDE–1933] *Baby Face and Chico*

96 "Despite efforts to": *Women and Hollywood*, Aug. 15, 2011, online publication.

**CHAPTER 6** [FLASHBACK] *The 1939 Academy Awards*

100 "It is with": quoted in Watts, *Hattie McDaniel*, p. 179.

100 "It makes me": quoted in ibid.

101 "I sincerely hope": quoted in ibid.

101 "They said it": "Finding the Oscar," *Howard Law Journal*, no. 55, 2011, p. 35.

**CHAPTER 7** DANGEROUS LOVE *Starring Inger Stevens, Sammy Davis, Jr., James Edwards, Ike Jones, and Dorothy Dandridge*

103 "It was about": *Washingtonian*, Nov. 2, 2016.

104 "He was good": quoted in Haygood, *In Black and White*, p. 133.

105 "She's a nice": quoted in ibid., p. 135.

106 "The white woman": quoted in ibid., p. 254.

106 "the proverbial quality": quoted in ibid., p. 257.

107 "Sammy and Kim": quoted in ibid.

107 "They were very": quoted in ibid., p. 258.

107 "He was so": quoted in ibid.

107 "I grab him": quoted in ibid., p. 259.

107 "The names of": quoted in ibid., p. 261.

108 "I know the": quoted in ibid., p. 263.

108 "Harry Cohn wanted": quoted in ibid., p. 264.

108 "The gossip," Sammy's friend: quoted in ibid., p. 267.

108 "Whites in the": quoted in ibid., pp. 268–69.

110 "She kept saying": *Washingtonian*, Feb. 9, 1988.

110 "The whole thing": *New York Times*, March 29, 1953.

111 "He really was": Belafonte, *My Song*, p. 122.

111 "What I wanted": Ibid.

111 "Dorothy," he believed: Ibid., p. 123.

112 "All he ever": quoted in Alpert, *Porgy and Bess*, p. 274.

112 "Preminger directs with": *Variety*, Dec. 31, 1953.

112 "a big musical": *New York Times*, Oct. 29, 1954.

113 "If I seem": The Oscars, video telecast, viewed at Legacy.com Nov. 9, 2015. online.

115 "The defendant [Denison]": quoted in *Sepia*, Jan. 1963.

115 "I thought that": quoted in *Sepia*, Dec. 1965.

115 "When I touched": quoted in ibid.

115 "borne the disappointments": quoted in ibid.

116 "No matter how": quoted in ibid.

119 "He told me": quoted in ibid., p. 14.

120 "This was breaking": quoted in ibid., p. 17.

120 "When I was": quoted in Deane, *James Edwards*, p. 11.

121 "Don't be discouraged": quoted in ibid., p. 22.

121 "This comparatively inexpensive": quoted in ibid., pp. 24–25.

121 "In the role": *New York Times*, May 13, 1949.

121 "It is hard": Deane, *Edwards*, p. 24.

121 "It is something": quoted in ibid., p. 29.

121 "abashes the white": quoted in Bogle, *Toms, Coons, Mulattos*, p. 204.

121 "Let no smug": quoted in ibid.

122 "Home of the": quoted in Deane, *Edwards*, p. 26.

122 "Film's leading box office": quoted in *Cinema Journal*, Fall 2004.

122 "Lana loved Black": Gossett, interview by author.

123 "in terror": quoted in Deane, *Edwards*, p. 64.

123 "It has been said": quoted in ibid., p. 65.

123 "one of the most dangerous": quoted in Friedrich, *City of Nets*, p. 299.

124 "well-dressed and well-poised": quoted in Deane, *Edwards*, p. 70.

124 "Of all the": *Sepia*, March 1970.

125 "All young Negro": quoted in ibid.

125 "It is axiomatic": *Los Angeles Times*, Sept. 24, 1999.

126 "could turn out": quoted in Belafonte, *My Song*, p. 176.

**CHAPTER 8** THE PRICEY BLACK MOVIE THAT VANISHED AND HOW IT CAME TO BE

129 "Our people now": quoted in Goodwin, *Team of Rivals*, p. 347.

129 "to sustain the": quoted in ibid., p. 348.

130 "Negroes in long": quoted in Alpert, *Porgy and Bess*, p. 22.

131 "Samuel Smalls, who": quoted in ibid., p. 17.

131 "For fear and": *Virginia Quarterly Review*, Autumn 1930.

131 "an unfortunate race": quoted in Haygood, *In Black and White*, p. 281.

131 "Hush, little baby": quoted in ibid., p. 282.

132 "The best novel": quoted in Alpert, *Porgy*, p. 39.

132 "Of a beauty": Ibid., p. 39.

132 "a literary advance": quoted in ibid.

132 "illuminating chronicle of": quoted in ibid., p. 67.

133 "To hear the": quoted in ibid., pp. 67–68.

133 "In 'Porgy,'" opined: quoted in ibid., p. 67.

134 "I'd like to": Smithsonian.com, Aug. 8, 2010.

134 "It is still": quoted in Alpert, *Porgy*, p. 73.

134 "I shall never": Smithsonian.com, Aug. 8, 2010.

135 "an eager student": Ibid.

135 "I felt about": quoted in Alpert, *Porgy*, p. 100.

137 "George," he whispered: quoted in ibid., p. 111.

137 "When the cries": quoted in ibid., p. 112.

137 "one of the": quoted in ibid., p. 116.

137 "If the Metropolitan": quoted in ibid., pp. 114–15.

137 "admiring it will": quoted in ibid., p. 118.

137 "elements that have": quoted in ibid.

139 "The box-office champion": Ibid., p. 169.

139 "She gave it": quoted in ibid., p. 169.

140 "A superlative cast": quoted in ibid., p. 171.

140 "They kept up": quoted in ibid., p. 174.

140 "One sits in": quoted in ibid., p. 175.

140 "The Most Sensational": quoted in ibid., p. 178.

140 "It is life": quoted in ibid.

141 "I admired his": quoted in ibid., p. 225.

141 "For fifteen years": quoted in ibid., p. 233.

141 "came from its": quoted in ibid.

142 "We ain't got": quoted in Kluger, *Simple Justice*, p. 4.

143 "We are sick": quoted in Haygood, *King of the Cats*, p. 227.

143 "the most insulting": quoted in Alpert, *Porgy*, p. 181–82.

143 "Instead they are": quoted in ibid., p. 182.

144 "The black community": quoted in ibid., p. 183.

145 "In a period": quoted in Haygood, *In Black and White*, p. 285.

145 "If I refuse": Poitier, *This Life*, p. 211.

145 "Swear on your": quoted in Haygood, *In Black and White*, p. 479.

146 "a man who": quoted in Berg, *Goldwyn*, p. 485.

147 "Choruses march and": quoted in Alpert, *Porgy*, p. 276.

147 "One can praise": *Saturday Review*, July 4, 1959.

147 "He is a": Ibid., p. 278.

148 "We object to": quoted in ibid., p. 279.

148 "We do not": quoted in ibid.

148 "If he will": quoted in ibid.

149 "What is also": Report of the U.S. Commission on Civil Rights (Washington, D.C.: U.S. Printing Office, 1959).

149 "a white man's": Baldwin, *The Price of the Ticket*, p. 179.

150 "History has thrust": quoted in Haygood, *In Black and White*, p. 292.

150 "They did something": *Hollywood Reporter*, Feb. 23, 2017.

**CHAPTER 9** TWO COOL CATS WITH CARIBBEAN ROOTS DISRUPT HOLLYWOOD

152 "There was a": quoted in *Chicago Tribune*, Jan. 31, 1988.

152 "There was no": Poitier, *This Life*, p. 12.

152 "Miami was awful": Ibid., p. 50.

153 "When I hear": Ibid., p. 64.

154 "Actors Wanted by": Ibid., p. 84.

155 "In one stupendous": Ibid., pp. 104–5.

156 "Sidney Poitier," the *New York*: *New York Times*, Aug. 17, 1950.

156 "You're going to": quoted in *Vanity Fair*, Feb. 1, 2017.

156 "The Army wouldn't": quoted in *Senses of Cinema,* no. 83, Feb. 2006.

156 "I am invisible": Ralph Ellison, *Invisible Man* (New York: Vintage, 1995), p. 3.

157 "I will bend": Poitier, *This Life,* p. 150.

158 "Keep this in": Ibid., p. 155.

158 "We were doing": Ibid., p. 156.

158 "Sidney Poitier is": *Variety,* Dec. 31, 1951.

158 "The particular interest": *New York Times,* Jan. 24, 1952.

159 "I know much": *Look,* July 23, 1968.

161 "Poitier captures all": *Variety,* Dec. 31, 1957.

161 "He starts off": Ibid.

161 "Mr. Poitier stands": *New York Times,* Sept. 25, 1958.

161 "American racism helped": *New Yorker,* May 2, 1959.

162 "Sidney, Claudia, and": Gossett, interview by author.

162 "Mama, it is": Hansberry, *To Be Young, Gifted and Black,* p. 109.

162 "has vigor as": *New York Times,* March 12, 1959.

162 "gives a heroic": Ibid.

163 "What is relevant": quoted in Hansberry, *To Be Young,* p. xii.

163 "I'm thrilled, and": *New Yorker,* May 2, 1959.

163 "We've violated every": *New York Times,* July 17, 1960.

163 "write off most": Ibid.

164 "a critical juncture": *Daily Variety,* March 28, 1961.

164 "Here, for the first": *Saturday Review,* March 25, 1961.

164 "Sidney Poitier . . . rises": Ibid.

166 "Many factors combine": *Variety,* Dec. 31, 1962.

166 "The element of": *Hollywood Reporter,* July 23, 1963.

166 "The industry is": *Look,* July 23, 1968.

167 "The next time": Ibid.

167 ". . . If you'd been": *Vanity Fair,* Jan. 1, 2017.

168 "The Blacks in": Gossett, interview by author.

168 "By the time I started": Belafonte, *My Song,* p. 45.

168 "How about Negro": *Time,* March 2, 1959.

168 "There is bigotry": Ibid., 3-2-1959.

169 "there was a": Ibid.

169 "Why don't you": Belafonte, *My Song,* p. 53.

169 "Both Sidney Poitier": Ibid., p. 58.

169 "We listened in": Ibid, p. 64.

170 "I couldn't believe": Ibid., p. 80.

171 "raw, gritty, American": Ibid., p. 94.

171 "One of the": quoted in ibid., p. 99.

171 "Belafonte," noted *Variety*: quoted in ibid., p. 102.

172 "From the top": quoted in *Time,* March 2, 1959.

172 "As was the": *New York Times,* June 13, 1957.

172 "Harry scared Hollywood": Gossett, interview by author.

172 "under the hammer": *Time,* March 2, 1959.

173 "I need your": Belafonte, *My Song,* p. 149.

174 "That must be": Ibid., p. 7.

174 "When Sidney and": Ibid., p. 8.

174 "I am thirty-seven": Ibid., p. 9.

175 "a drawn out": *New York Times,* Feb. 28, 1967.

175 "I found my": quoted in *Life,* Feb. 4, 1966.

175 "Never, not ever": Ibid.

176 "A lot of": quoted in *Chicago Tribune,* Jan. 31, 1988.

176 "In the early days": quoted in Stevens, *The Great Moviemakers,* pp. 445–46.

**CHAPTER 10** [FLASHBACK]
*The 1964 Academy Awards*

178 "I would like to think": *Cinephiled,* March 2, 2014, online.

178 "In the present": *Guardian,* April 12, 1964.

179 "If the actor": *Cinephiled,* March 2, 2014.

**CHAPTER 11** THE HUSTLERS, DETECTIVES, AND PIMPS WHO STUNNED HOLLYWOOD

181 "The caricature of": quoted in Harris, *Pictures at a Revolution,* pp. 159–60.
181 "The implicit moral": quoted in ibid., p. 160.
182 "The city, state": *Ebony,* July 1971.
183 "I thought they": Van Peebles, online interview by Stax Records, 2019.
183 "I discovered there": *Filmmaker,* July 29, 2018.
184 "Van Peebles," Johnson felt: San Francisco Film Festival brochure, 1967, online.
185 "If an American": "Radio & Television Report to the American People on Civil Rights," June 11, 1963, JFK Presidential Library.
185 "Tarzan is a": *The Hollywood Palace* (TV variety show), Nov. 12, 1969.
186 "He can con": quoted in *New York Times,* Sept. 12, 1976.
186 "falls crashingly flat": *New York Times,* May 28, 1970.
186 "Not much of": quoted in Howard, *Blaxploitation Cinema,* p. 221.
190 "The certainty of": quoted in Haygood, *Showdown,* p. 267.
190 "The Negroes of": quoted in ibid., p. 264.
191 "As a black": Brattle Theater Film Notes, July 13, 2018, *Main Slate,* online.
191 "No one had": quoted in *Baadasssss,* documentary, 2003.
192 "No man spoke": *Life,* April 19, 1968.
193 "It was beyond": *Baadasssss* documentary.
193 "As a businessman": quoted in *New York Times,* Aug. 20, 1972.
193 "the radicalization of": quoted in *New York Times,* Sept. 12, 1976.
194 "Alas!—I mean": *New Yorker,* June 19, 1971.
194 "third and worst": *New York Times,* April 24, 1971.
194 "shallow characterizations": quoted in *Ebony,* Sept. 1971.
194 "revolutionary nor black": Ibid.
194 "A technically fancy": *New York Times,* Sept. 12, 1976.
195 "the first truly": quoted in Guerrero, *Framing Blackness,* p. 87.
195 "presents the need": quoted in ibid., p. 88.
195 "Lynch me—if": *New York Times,* Aug. 20, 1972.
196 "There is not": *New York Times,* Aug. 7, 1969.
196 "a black man": promotional material for Ernest Tidyman, *Shaft* (Mount Laurel, N.J.: Dynamite Entertainment, 1970).
196 "could give Black": Parks, *Voices in the Mirror,* p. 362.
196 "exhaustive search": Ibid., p. 363.
196 "I just knew": quoted in ibid.
196 "I think I've": Ibid.
197 "I'm dropped off": quoted in *New York Times,* June 17, 2019.
197 "It has to": quoted in Parks, *Voices,* p. 364.
197 "Richard Roundtree," Parks recalled: Ibid., p. 365.
198 "Dad, you've got": Ibid.
198 "The line was": Ibid.
198 "And to kids": quoted in *Sepia,* July 1972.
198 "has a kind": *New York Times,* July 3, 1971.
198 "In his second": *Variety,* June 16, 1971.
198 "Hollywood," *Time* magazine: *Time,* June 15, 2018.
199 "You wouldn't see": Young, interview by author.
200 "But he has": *New York Times,* Aug. 5, 1972.
201 "Its story of": *New York Times,* April 4, 1979.
201 "At present," he said: *New York Times,* Dec. 17, 1972.

203 "any dumb ox": quoted in *Sepia,* July 1972.

204 "walk woodenly through": *Boston Globe,* June 17, 1972.

204 "shows definite acting": *New York Times,* May 18, 1972.

204 "90 percent of": quoted in *Variety,* July 26, 1972.

204 "I'm a badass": *Torontoist,* Feb. 12, 2015.

205 "[Cleveland] is the only": quoted in Zirin, *Jim Brown,* p. 83.

205 "handles himself well": *Variety,* Dec. 31, 1963.

205 "We were trying": quoted in Zirin, *Jim Brown,* p. 172.

205 "The filming of": quoted in ibid.

206 "The acting of": *New York Times,* March 27, 1969.

206 "The eagerness of": *Atlantic,* Aug. 1977.

**CHAPTER 12** FOXY BROWN ARRIVES, VANISHES, AND GETS RESURRECTED

207 "Where is Lena": quoted in Buckley, *The Hornes,* p. 242.

208 "beautiful tenderness": review, Oct. 21, 1970, RogerEbert.com.

209 "Ossie was just": Frazier, interview by author.

209 "If you do": Ibid.

209 "There are more": *New York Times,* Jan. 2, 1972.

210 "A gritty, hearty": *Variety,* Dec. 31, 1973.

210 "Claudine," stated *The New*: *New York Times,* March 23, 1974.

210 "an engrossing and": *Los Angeles Times,* May 12, 1974.

210 "a sweet-spirited": *New Yorker,* April 29, 1974.

210 "It spoke with": Frazier, interview by author.

211 "a pleasant, loose": *Variety,* Dec. 31, 1976.

211 "Money ran out": Frazier, interview by author.

213 "Not yet," Warsuma: quoted in Givhan, *Battle of Versailles,* p. 154.

214 "These women impacted": Grier, *Foxy,* p. 38.

214 "Police in riot": Ibid., p. 57.

215 "There are lots": Ibid., p. 73.

215 "if things don't": Ibid., p. 74.

216 "We would stage": Ibid., p. 79.

218 "It was the age": quoted in Howard, *Blaxploitation Cinema,* p. 36.

219 "To me," Jack Hill: quoted in ibid., p. 34.

219 "It was common": Grier, *Foxy,* p. 126.

220 "*Foxy Brown* is": *Monthly Film Bulletin,* March 1975.

220 "*Foxy Brown* is selling": *Chicago Tribune,* April 17, 1974.

221 "To me," Grier remarked: Grier, *Foxy,* p. 126.

221 "Although many moviegoers": *Chicago Tribune,* April 4, 1975.

222 "are the only": *Ms.,* Aug. 1975.

222 "This is one": *New York Times,* Dec. 26, 1975.

222 "Grier has some": *Variety,* Dec. 31, 1974.

223 "When I came": quoted in *Sepia,* March 1973.

223 "Up until very": Ibid.

223 "A white friend": *Chicago Tribune,* Feb. 19, 1969.

224 "I conceived of": *Sepia,* March 1973.

224 "Ladies don't have": quoted in *Ebony,* Nov. 1973.

224 "Tamara Dobson," wrote *Variety*: *Variety,* Dec. 31, 1972.

224 "The movie seems": *New York Times,* July 5, 1973.

225 "My mafia is": quoted in *Washington Post,* July 3, 1999.

226 "When I realized": Coppola, *The Godfather Notebook,* pp. 20–24.

227 "That was like": quoted in Mario Van Peebles, *Baadasssss* documentary, 2003.

228 "His long brown": Grier, *Foxy,* p. 237.

228 "I'm writing a": Ibid.

229 "Bridget Fonda is": Ibid., 238.

229 "[Tarantino's] affection for": *Rolling Stone*, Dec. 25, 1997.

229 "restored to star": *Washington Post*, Dec. 26, 1997.

229 "The picture is": *Entertainment Weekly*, Jan. 9, 1998.

229 "It's never too": *Salon*, Dec. 25, 1997.

**CHAPTER 13** [FLASHBACK]
*The 1972 Academy Awards*

232 "I don't think": *Dick Cavett Show*, downloaded, YouTube, Nov. 12, 2018, plus other downloads.

**CHAPTER 14** BERRY GORDY DARES TO MAKE MOVIES

234 "I said, 'Smokey'": White, *Motown*, p. 48.

235 "Your Big Daddy": quoted in ibid., p. 70.

235 "When he came in": quoted in ibid., p. 71.

236 "My parents," he said: Ibid., p. 79.

236 "In Cincinnati": quoted in ibid., pp. 79, 85.

237 "Motown hadn't released": quoted in ibid., p. 168.

238 "We were convinced": quoted in ibid., pp. 136–37.

238 "We here at": quoted in ibid., p. 366.

239 "Our youth are": quoted in ibid., p. 277.

240 "We kept hanging": quoted in *Sepia*, Sept. 1970.

241 "I'm putting you": quoted in White, *Motown*, pp. 118–19.

241 "Barney," she asked: quoted in ibid., p. 139.

242 "Listen, it's important": quoted in ibid., p. 143.

242 "a performance the": quoted in ibid., p. 151.

242 "It was like": quoted in ibid., p. 147.

244 "a minor without": quoted in Blackburn, *With Billie*, p. 8.

244 "I have been": quoted in ibid., p. 198.

245 "He was magic": Gossett, interview by author.

246 "The cast, all": quoted in Hughes and Meltzer, *Black Magic*, p. 239.

246 "But Berry rushes": Williams, "Behind the Scenes," *Lady Sings the Blues* DVD.

247 "The fact that": *Chicago Tribune*, Oct. 27, 1972.

247 "When the movie": *New Yorker*, Nov. 4, 1972.

247 "an actress of": *New York Times*, Oct. 19, 1972.

247 "For the bulk": *Variety*, Oct. 18, 1972.

247 "one of the truly": *Los Angeles Times*, Oct. 25, 1972.

248 "It's very clear": quoted in *Vanity Fair*, Dec. 13, 2008.

249 "thinking of me": quoted in *Ebony*, Oct. 1975.

249 "an unholy alliance": *Chicago Sun-Times*, Jan. 1, 1975.

249 "squandering one of": TIFF.net, Dec. 21, 2017.

249 "pretty silly any": *New York Times*, Oct. 26, 1975.

250 "We had this": *Chicago Sun-Times*, Oct. 26, 1975.

250 "A star is": *Time*, Aug. 23, 1970.

251 "The Black Gable": Ibid.

251 "It was Poitier": quoted in *Chicago Sun-Times*, Oct. 26, 1975.

251 "What I present": Ibid.

251 "When I was": *Georgia Straight* [Canadian publication], Feb. 26, 2019.

252 "He delighted in": Schultz, interview by author.

253 "My thinking at": Ibid.

253 "What I thought": Ibid.

253 "you don't have": *Variety*, Dec. 31, 1974.

254 "has used the": quoted in *AFI Catalog*, July 6, 1976.

254 "What do you": Cohen, *Original Sin* interview, online, March 5, 2018.

255 "Billy Dee Williams": *Chicago Tribune*, Sept. 27, 1977.

255 "Williams is fine": *Variety*, Dec. 31, 1976.

255 "The fact is": *New York Times*, June 20, 1978.

256 "There is an almost": *Washington Post*, Oct. 25, 1978.

256 "'The Wiz' is": *New York Times*, Nov. 26, 1978.

257 "It's torrentially syrupy": *New Republic*, Nov. 11, 1978.

257 "A huge budget": quoted in *Washington Post*, Oct. 25, 1978.

257 "The only guy": *Chicago Tribune*, July 14, 1989.

258 "I'm a leading": Ibid.

258 "If I'm trying": Ibid.

258 "a kind of featured": Ibid.

258 "Well, the unfortunate": Ibid.

259 "A lot of people don't": Ibid.

**CHAPTER 15** KUNTA KINTE SEIZES THE MOMENT

260 "With the assistance": Marable, *Freedom*, p. 20.

260 "For generations African-American": Ibid., p. 26.

261 "Fugitives fording the": Ibid., p. 29.

261 "Beginning in 1890": Ibid., p. 53.

261 "Between 1882 and": Ibid., p. 59.

262 "The squadron was": Ibid., p. 199.

262 "Colored entrance of": Ibid., p. 226.

263 "Dr. Martin Luther": Ibid., p. 265.

263 "Sit-in demonstration": Ibid., p. 278.

263 "Wallace's conflict with": Ibid., p. 311.

264 "The speech carefully": Ibid., p. 326.

264 "Is this America": Ibid., p. 356.

265 "Us ole Alabama": quoted in *Reporting Civil Rights*, vol. 2, 1973, p. 841.

267 "Grandparents," Alex Haley would: quoted in *Los Angeles Times*, Feb. 14, 1986.

268 "You can call": United States Coast Guard Historian's Office, available online.

269 "its dead-level": quoted in Marable, *Malcolm X*, p. 466.

269 "brilliant, painful, important": quoted in ibid., pp. 465–66.

270 "The condition of": *New Yorker*, Feb. 6, 1977.

270 "'Roots,'" he wrote: *New York Times*, Sept. 26, 1976.

271 "If people perceive": quoted in *Mother Jones*, June 2, 2016.

272 "It was like *A Raisin*": Gossett, interview by author.

274 "They couldn't realize": Ibid.

274 "By the eighth": *Baltimore Sun*, Feb. 11, 1992.

274 "Vistas of jungleland": *Variety*, Jan. 21, 1977.

274 "absorbing, beautifully acted": New York *Daily News*, Jan. 23, 1977.

274 "a crime so": *Time*, May 26, 2016.

274 "'Roots' is best": *New York Times*, Feb. 27, 1977.

274 "so compellingly unique": *Washington Post*, May 30, 2016.

275 "American actors, whose": *Hollywood Reporter*, Jan. 21, 1977.

275 "They gave us": Gossett, interview by author.

275 "We were so fabulous": quoted in *Mother Jones*, June 2, 2016.

275 "deep depression": quoted in ibid.

275 "I put my soul": Gossett, interview by author.

276 "Somewhere, somebody gave": quoted in *New York Times*, Dec. 15, 1978.

276 "Thank God for": Gossett, interview by author.

**CHAPTER 16** AIMING A CAMERA IN BROOKLYN

278 "I was the firstborn": Lee, *That's My Story and I'm Sticking to It*, p. 4.

279 "Oh God," she wrote: quoted in ibid., p. 8.

279 "We got in": quoted in *Atlanta Journal-Constitution*, Oct. 23, 2019.

280 "Film allowed him": quoted in Lee, *That's My Story*, p. 11.

280 "such people were": quoted in ibid.

280 "We cannot have": quoted in *Atlanta Journal-Constitution,* Oct. 23, 2019.

280 "He ran all": Lee, *That's My Story,* p. 14.

281 "no way . . . a": *Cornell Daily Sun,* Sept. 22, 2019.

281 "At NYU," he found out: Lee, *That's My Story,* p. 14.

282 "I don't think": quoted in *New Yorker,* Sept. 15, 2008.

282 "He was trying to solve": quoted in ibid.

282 "So they wanted": Lee, *That's My Story,* p. 16.

283 "It's a slap": quoted in *New York Times,* Dec. 17, 1983.

283 "It's a drama": *New Yorker,* Jan. 15, 2019.

285 "What do you think": Lee, *That's My Story,* p. 27.

286 "Spike lived around": George, interview by author.

286 "At first I": Ibid.

286 "There was just no": quoted in Lee, *That's My Story,* p. 39.

287 "[There] was a": quoted in ibid.

287 "I'm Spike Lee": MTV News, July 26, 2013.

287 "Ships at a": Hemenway, *Zora Neale Hurston,* p. 3.

288 "Folks, please sit": *IndieWire,* online, May 16, 2018.

288 "a joyfully idiosyncratic": *Los Angeles Times,* Aug. 21, 1986.

288 "Featuring an all-black": *Chicago Tribune,* Sept. 12, 1986.

288 "the young black film maker": *New York Times,* Aug. 8, 1986.

288 "posed him as": Peter Keough, in *Chicago Reader,* online, n.d.

291 "There's niggers on": Frankie Bailey and Steven Chermak, eds. *Crimes & Trials of the Century,* p. 83.

293 "I heard things": quoted in *Hollywood Reporter,* Sept. 19, 2000.

293 "with tears in": RogerEbert.com, May 27, 2001.

294 "director working with": *Los Angeles Times,* June 30, 1989.

294 "the most prominent": *New Yorker,* July 17, 1989.

294 "'Do the Right Thing'": *New York Times,* June 30, 1989.

295 "If you look": Thomson, *Have You Seen . . . ?,* p. 235.

295 "I simply walked": Baldwin, *Price of the Ticket,* p. 620.

295 "It's such a": quoted in *New York Times,* Nov. 23, 1992.

296 "White Americans will": quoted in *Newsday,* Nov. 19, 1992.

296 "We will not": *Newsweek,* Aug. 25, 1991.

296 "Where's his book": Ibid.

297 "Why is it": quoted in *Los Angeles Times,* Feb. 26, 1992.

297 "I was shocked": quoted in Lee, *That's My Story,* p. 118.

298 "The first time": quoted in *Times Herald-Record,* Jan. 8, 2000.

298 "He was extremely": King, interview by author.

298 "It's much to": *New York Times,* July 15, 1981.

299 "an epic picture": quoted in *Orlando Sentinel,* Feb. 11, 1992.

300 "not exactly the": *New York Times,* Nov. 18, 1992.

300 "Walking into 'Malcolm X'": Roger Ebert.com, Nov. 18, 1992.

301 "The unexpected aspect": *Los Angeles Times,* Nov. 18, 1992.

301 "Now, though, Lee's": *Entertainment Weekly,* Nov. 20, 1992.

301 "If he doesn't win": *Los Angeles Times,* Feb. 26, 1992.

**CHAPTER 17** THE BLACKOUT THAT HAUNTED A DECADE

302 "I think we": *Life,* Feb. 24, 1967.

302 "We're getting back": *Time,* March 4, 1974.

303 "I'm just sure": quoted in *People,* June 3, 1974.

303 "For the first": quoted in ibid.

304 "I know that": Ibid.

304 "We hoped the": quoted in *People,* May 12, 1982.

305 "The day of": Ibid.

305 "If you're beautiful": quoted in ibid.

305 "They said a": quoted in ibid.

305 "The feeling in": Ibid.

306 "We're becoming invisible": Ibid.

306 "Producers want to": Ibid.

307 "I think it": Employment Practices in the Performance Arts, Hearings Before the Committee on Education and Labor, House of Representatives, 87th Congress, Oct. 29–Nov. 2, 1962, Govt. Printing Office, 1963.

307 "These white Democratic": *New York,* July 4, 2016.

308 "This is not an opportunity": Hearing of the Senate Judiciary Committee on the Nomination of Clarence Thomas to the Supreme Court, Oct. 11, 1991, Electronic Text Center, University of Virginia Library.

309 "perceived perpetual failure": Jimi Izrael column, Oct. 15, 2010, NPR online.

311 "What if we": quoted in Berry with Venise T. Berry, *The 50 Most Influential Black Films,* p. 253.

311 "There may be": quoted in ibid.

312 "There's no shortage": *Black Enterprise,* Dec. 1986.

312 "Well," Cannon explained: quoted in Berry, *50 Most Influential,* p. 254.

312 "I don't care": quoted in ibid.

312 "I've read your": Ibid., p. 255.

313 "If this project": quoted in ibid., p. 256.

313 "A vital regeneration": *Variety,* Oct. 7, 1996.

313 "I have always": *Chicago Sun-Times,* Oct. 18, 1996, RogerEbert.com.

313 "The wonder of": *Newsweek,* Oct. 27, 1996.

313 "When the credits": Berry, *50 Most Influential,* p. 256.

314 "Cheadle," proclaimed *Rolling Stone*: *Rolling Stone,* Sept. 29, 1995.

314 "picture-stealing bravado": *Los Angeles Times,* Sept. 29, 1995.

314 "He comes straight": *Washington Post,* Sept. 29, 1995.

314 "The fact that Cheadle": quoted in *People,* March 18, 1996.

315 "It doesn't stand": quoted in *New Republic,* Jan. 29, 2016.

315 "We are going": quoted in ibid.

315 "protests and picketing": quoted in ibid.

315 "Johnnie Cochran and": quoted in ibid.

315 "First of all": quoted in ibid.

315 "There was," Jones recalled: Jones, interview by author.

316 "I was fairly": Ibid.

316 "It's embarrassing now": Ibid.

316 "The big deal": Ibid.

316 "The continuing reality": *People,* March 18, 1996.

317 "levels of segregation": Ibid.

317 "Some of the": Ibid.

317 "It sold poorly": Jones, interview by author.

317 "Look," she announced: quoted in *New Republic,* Jan. 29, 2016.

317 "One of the": Ibid.

318 "We got a": Gossett, interview by author.

318 "The thing that": Witcher, interview by author.

318 "I remember walking": Ibid.

318 "He was supercool": Ibid.

318 "My mom suggested": Ibid.

318 "He said, 'You'": Ibid.

319 "The day I": Ibid.

319 "Drop everything!": Ibid.

319 "Whites," she says: Echegoyen, interview by author.

319 "In a nation": *Washington Post,* June 17, 1993.

319 "I have to": Echegoyen, interview by author.

319 "There was no": Witcher, interview by author.

320 "She was like": Ibid.

320 "I remember the": Ibid.

320 "I said to myself": Ibid.

320 "It was the first script": quoted in *Los Angeles Times*, March 14, 2017.

321 "This slickly made": *Variety*, Jan. 26, 1997.

321 "Theodore Witcher, who": *New York Times*, March 14, 1997.

321 "With its quick-witted": *Entertainment Weekly*, March 14, 1997.

321 "Perhaps in the": Witcher, interview by author.

321 "The fact that": Ibid.

322 "After you cool": Ibid.

322 "a knockdown assault": *Hollywood Reporter*, May 15, 1991.

322 "What Singleton does": *Chicago Tribune*, July 12, 1991.

322 "stunningly gifted newcomer": *Christian Science Monitor*, July 12, 1991.

323 "I had a script": quoted in *New York Times*, July 7, 2019.

323 "As an African-American": quoted in ibid.

323 "White people," Witcher allowed: quoted in ibid.

**CHAPTER 18** [AN INTERLUDE]
*The Ghost of Sidney*

325 "for representing the": this and all other quoted remarks are from the March 24, 2002, Oscar telecast.

**CHAPTER 19** THE RECKONING

327 "What the black": Baldwin, *Price of the Ticket*, p. 621.

327 "I told my": quoted in *Vanity Fair*, March 20, 2017.

328 "Consider the trained": *Los Angeles Times*, April 24, 1987.

332 "About halfway through": *New York Times*, July 20, 1972.

333 "I am a 93-year-old": Deborah Willis and Kevin Merida, *Obama: The Historic Campaign in Photographs*, p. 116.

333 "blunt, simple and": *New York Times*, April 11, 2013.

333 "affording the white": *Time*, April 12, 2013.

334 "So 66 years": *Grantland*, April 11, 2013.

335 "At the end": *AP/SFGate*, Jan. 26, 2013.

336 "bold act of": *Guardian*, June 5, 2014.

336 "Fruitvale Station is": *Rolling Stone*, July 13, 2013.

336 "Greek tragedy": NPR, July 11, 2013.

336 "Fruitvale Station isn't just": *Washington Post*, July 18, 2013.

336 "Fruitvale Station," reported: New Orleans *Times-Picayune*, July 26, 2013.

337 "It's just wrong": quoted in *South Florida Sun-Sentinel*, Jan. 20, 1989.

337 "I don't feel": Ibid.

337 "This is the": *Los Angeles Times*, Jan. 24, 1989.

337 "Recent dramas": *Washington Post*, Sept. 22, 1989.

339 "When I first": quoted in Haygood, *The Butler*, p. xi.

340 "A brilliantly truthful": *New York Times*, Aug. 15, 2013.

340 "a beautifully nuanced": *Entertainment Weekly*, Aug. 19, 2013.

340 " 'Mississippi Burning' sparked": Indie Wire.com, Sept. 16, 2013.

341 "With one cow": Northup, *Twelve Years a Slave*, p. 7.

341 "Throughout the surrounding": Ibid.

342 "but when consciousness": Ibid., p. 19.

342 "My great object": Ibid., p. 193.

343 "Today they are stars": *Sight & Sound, The International Magazine*, July 23, 2020.

344 "A lot of beautiful": *Guardian*, January 4, 2014.

345 "Everything I've done": *Evening Standard*, January 7, 2019.

345 "It's very important": *Guardian*, January 4, 2014.

345 "Stark, visceral and": *Guardian*, Oct. 26, 2013.

345 "a new movie landmark": *Entertainment Weekly*, Oct. 2, 2013.

345 "the genius of 'Twelve'": *New York Times,* Oct. 18, 2013.

345 "I wanted to": quoted in *New York Times,* Oct. 13, 2013.

345 "2013 seems to": Steve Boone, Aug. 15, 2013, RogerEbert.com, online.

345 "I don't think": *New York Times,* Oct. 13, 2013.

346 "At times, *Mandela*": *San Francisco Gate,* Dec. 24, 2013.

346 "'Mandela' . . . does a": *Washington Post,* Dec. 24, 2013.

**CHAPTER 20** THE FRONT PAGE

348 "Did y'all like": *Washingtonian,* Feb. 25, 2011.

349 "I teared up": quoted in *Hollywood Reporter,* Aug. 27, 2013.

351 "Every time you": CNN transcript, Dec. 8, 2014, online.

351 "I can't breathe": Ibid.

351 "This one," the comedian: *Vulture,* Dec. 3, 2014, online.

353 "Hollywood," said *Slate*: *Slate,* Nov. 2, 2012.

353 "Make it higher": quoted in *Los Angeles Times,* July 24, 2014.

353 "startling and galvanic": *New Yorker,* Sept. 5, 2014.

353 "Boseman tears into": *Rolling Stone,* July 31, 2014.

353 "transcends impersonation and": *Hollywood Reporter,* July 28, 2014.

353 "smacks of mimicry": *Variety,* July 28, 2014.

353 "tricks with chronology": *Newsday,* July 31, 2014.

354 "Maybe the [James]": *Rolling Stone,* July 31, 2014.

354 "you see Black": *The Undefeated,* April 29, 2017, online.

354 "By and large": Ibid.

354 "Dear white people": quoted in *Interview,* Jan. 28, 2014.

355 "If it ultimately": *Variety,* Jan. 19, 2014.

355 "It's true that": *Washington Post,* Oct. 16, 2014.

355 "Dear White People": BBC.com, Nov. 11, 2014.

356 "It all happened": *Variety,* June 8, 2008.

357 "I just remember": quoted in *New York Times,* Dec. 7, 2014.

357 "one of the": RogerEbert.com, March 8, 2011.

357 "a plaintive, slow-burning": *New York Times,* Oct. 12, 2012.

357 "a violent dismantling": quoted in *Guardian,* Dec. 17, 2014.

358 "I don't even": quoted in ibid.

358 "Joining an already": *Entertainment Weekly,* Dec. 25, 2014.

358 "'Selma' is not": *New York Times,* Dec. 25, 2014.

358 "'Selma' carries viewers": *Washington Post,* Dec. 23, 2014.

359 "a well-deserved lock": *New Yorker,* Jan. 22, 2015.

359 "I saw the pamphlet": Isaacs, interview by author.

359 "However one chooses": *Guardian,* Feb. 8, 2015.

360 "Members of the": *Entertainment Weekly,* June 5, 2020.

360 "I am a black": *New York Times,* June 26, 2020.

361 "#OscarsSoWhite": Reign, interview by author.

361 "It was obvious": quoted in *Hollywood Reporter,* Feb. 25, 2016.

361 "Get above it": Isaacs, interview by author.

362 "The [foreign marketing]": quoted in *Hollywood Reporter,* Feb. 6, 2020.

362 "There is a picture": Isaacs, interview by author.

362 "perhaps the most": quoted in *Hollywood Reporter,* Feb. 6, 2020.

362 "Time-worn methods": Ibid.

362 "Reports abound about": quoted in ibid.

363 "The day I": Isaacs, interview by author.

365 "'Straight Outta Compton'": *Rolling Stone,* Aug. 13, 2015.

366 "Thanks to eerily": *Washington Post,* Aug. 13, 2015.

366 "Arriving when the": Memphis *Commercial Appeal,* Nov. 6, 2015.

366 "Universal is said": *Hollywood Reporter,* Aug. 16, 2015.

366 "It's an invigorating": *Atlantic,* Aug. 24, 2015.

366 "smart, kinetic, exhilaratingly": *Variety,* Nov. 11, 2015.

366 "the next emotional": *Vanity Fair,* Nov. 18, 2015.

366 "In this revival": *El País,* Jan. 28, 2016.

366 "There's an earthiness": *Irish Times,* Jan. 14, 2016.

367 "spurred Oscar murmurs": *IndieWire,* Jan. 4, 2016.

367 "We'd like to": MTV news, June 29, 2015, online.

369 "I knew this": Isaacs, interview by author.

369 "the Blackest Oscars": Hudlin, interview by author.

370 "I said to": Ibid.

370 "White folks are": Reign, interview by author.

370 "begging for acknowledgement": BBC News, Jan. 19, 2016, online.

370 "I'm not surprised": *Entertainment Weekly,* Jan. 14, 2016.

**CHAPTER 21** MOVING IN THE MOONLIGHT

372 "Easy, one at": *Washington Post,* May 21, 1980.

373 "There were seven": quoted in *Guardian,* Feb. 7, 2017.

373 "I said, 'I'": Ibid.

374 "Clearly, here is": *Hollywood Reporter,* July 1, 2008.

374 "charming and stylish": *Variety,* May 13, 2008.

374 "very assured": RogerEbert.com, March 4, 2009.

374 "white and privileged": quoted in *New York Times,* Jan 4, 2017.

374 "So, I wrote": Ibid.

375 "There are people": quoted in *Los Angeles Times,* Sept. 4, 2016.

375 "It's impossible to": *Rolling Stone,* Oct. 19, 2016.

375 "a disarmingly personal": *New York Times,* Oct. 20, 2016.

375 "Did I ever": *New Yorker,* Oct. 17, 2016.

375 "It is the": *Guardian,* Feb. 16, 2017.

376 "I think my": *Paris Review,* Winter 1999.

377 "Many people," she said: quoted in *Los Angeles Times,* Feb. 12, 2017.

378 "Melfi and Schroeder": *New Yorker,* Dec. 23, 2016.

378 "Oscar Nominations 2017": *New York Times,* Jan. 24, 2017.

379 "I saw Faye": quoted in *Hollywood Reporter,* Feb. 26, 2018.

379 "I felt like": quoted in ibid.

379 "There's a mistake": Ibid.

380 "We are that": *Time,* March 12, 2018.

380 "The notion of": quoted in *Hollywood Reporter,* Nov. 21, 2017.

381 "The film," wrote: *New York Times,* Feb. 23, 2017.

381 "finds the still": *Guardian,* March 19, 2017.

381 "The film is": *New Yorker,* March 4, 2017.

381 "I came up": History Channel, online article by Ryan Mattimore, Feb. 15, 2018.

382 "Hey Chadwick. It's": *Undefeated,* May 17, 2016.

382 "You realize that": Ibid.

383 "You had some": quoted in *Washington Post,* May 8, 2020.

383 "Delivered through Coogler's": *Wired,* Feb. 16, 2018.

384 "It's an action-adventure": *Guardian,* Feb. 6, 2018.

384 "There are no": *Vox,* Feb. 23, 2018, online.

384 "Black Panther champions": *Vanity Fair,* Feb. 6, 2018.

384 "There are sequences": *New York Times,* Feb. 6, 2018.

384 "The revolutionary thing": *Time,* Feb. 19, 2018.

385 "All hail the": *Atlantic,* Feb. 16, 2018.

385 "making the girls": *New York Times,* July 9, 1997.

385 "The residents of": quoted on NPR, Aug. 13, 2006.

385 "What breaks your": *New York Times,* Aug. 21, 2006.

386 "It's about justice": quoted in *Los Angeles Times,* Aug. 23, 2010.

386 "In my opinion": McBride, interview by author.

387 "American apple pie": *Hollywood Reporter,* July 31, 2018.

387 "White people in": quoted in *Atlantic,* Jan. 9, 2019.

388 "This isn't a": RogerEbert.com, Dec. 10, 2018.

390 "You will find": Victor Green, *The Negro Motorist Green-Book,* a pamphlet published in New York by Green, 1940, p. 1.

390 "Green Book's approach": *Guardian,* Feb. 3, 2019.

391 "At the other": *New York Times,* July 5, 2020.

**CHAPTER 22** *THE SCOURGED BACK*

392 "I was two": quote from online article, undated, "Scars of Gordon, a Whipped Louisiana Slave, 1863."

397 "I call the": *New Yorker,* June 22, 2020.

399 "Hollywood has a": *Variety,* June 23, 2020.

399 "The board," President: Office of Communication, Princeton University, June 27, 2020, online.

# Selected Bibliography

Alpert, Hollis. *The Life and Times of Porgy and Bess.* New York: Alfred A. Knopf, 1990.

Baldwin, James. *Notes of a Native Son.* Boston: Beacon Press, 1955.

———. *The Price of the Ticket: Collected Nonfiction 1948–1985.* New York: St. Martin's, 1985.

Belafonte, Harry, with Michael Shnayerson. *My Song: A Memoir.* New York: Alfred A. Knopf, 2011.

Berg, Scott A. *Goldwyn.* New York: Alfred A. Knopf, 1989.

Berry, S. Torriano, with Venise T. Berry. *The 50 Most Influential Black Films.* New York: Citadel Press, 2001.

Blackburn, Julia. *With Billie.* New York: Pantheon, 2005.

Bogle, Donald. *Toms, Coons, Mulattoes, Mammies, & Bucks.* New York: Bantam, 1974.

Boyd, Valerie. *Wrapped in Rainbows: The Life of Zora Neale Hurston.* New York: Scribner, 2003.

Buckley, Gail Lumet. *The Hornes: An American Family.* New York: Alfred A. Knopf, 1986.

Burns, Sarah. *The Central Park Five.* New York: Vintage, 2012.

Chernak, Steven, and Frankie Y. Bailey, eds. *Crimes and Trials of the Century (Vol. 1): From the Black Sox Scandal to the Attica Prison Riots.* Westport, CT: Greenwood Press, 2007.

Coppola, Francis Ford. *The Godfather Notebook.* New York: Regan Arts, 2016.

Deane, Pamala S. *James Edwards.* Jefferson, NC: McFarland & Company, 2009.

Driskell, David, et al. *Harlem Renaissance.* New York: Harry N. Abrams, 1987.

Friedrich, Otto. *City of Nets: A Portrait of Hollywood in the 1940's.* New York: Simon & Schuster, 2005.

Gates, Henry Louis Jr., and Evelyn Brooks Higginbotham, eds. *African American Lives.* New York: Oxford University Press, 2004.

Givhan, Robin. *The Battle of Versailles.* New York: Flatiron, 2015.

Goings, Kenneth W. *The NAACP Comes of Age.* Bloomington: Indiana University Press, 1990.

Goodwin, Doris Kearns. *Team of Rivals: The Political Genius of Abraham Lincoln.* New York: Simon & Schuster, 2005.

Green, J. Ronald. *Straight Lick: The Cinema of Oscar Micheaux.* Bloomington: Indiana University Press, 2000.

———. *With a Crooked Stick: The Films of Oscar Micheaux.* Bloomington: Indiana University Press, 2004.

Grier, Pam. *Foxy: My Life in Three Acts.* New York: Springboard Press, 2010.

Guerrero, Ed. *Framing Blackness: The African-American Image in Film.* Philadelphia: Temple University Press, 1993.

Hansberry, Lorraine. *To Be Young, Gifted and Black.* New York: Signet, 1970.

Harris, Mark. *Pictures at a Revolution: Five Movies and the Birth of a New Hollywood.* New York: Penguin Press, 2008.

Harvey, James. *Movie Love in the Fifties.* New York: Alfred A. Knopf, 2001.

Haygood, Wil. *The Butler: A Witness to History.* New York: Atria, 2013.

———. *In Black and White: The Life of Sammy Davis, Jr.* New York: Alfred A. Knopf, 2003.

———. *King of the Cats: The Life and Times of Adam Clayton Powell, Jr.* New York: Houghton Mifflin, 1993.

———. *Showdown.* New York: Alfred A. Knopf, 2015.

Howard, Josiah. *Blaxploitation Cinema.* Surrey, England: FAB Press, 2008.

Hughes, Langston, and Milton Meltzer. *Black Magic.* New York: DaCapo Press, 1967.

Hurst, Fannie. *Imitation of Life.* Durham. NC: Duke University Press, 2004.

Hurston, Zora Neale. *Their Eyes Were Watching God.* Chicago: University of Illinois Press, 1991.

Kaplan, Carla. *Zora Neale Hurston: A Life in Letters.* New York: Doubleday, 2002.

Katz, Ephraim. *The Film Encyclopedia,* 3rd ed. New York: Harper Perennial, 1998.

Kluger, Richard. *Simple Justice.* New York: Alfred A. Knopf, 1976.

Kroeger, Brooke. *Fannie: The Talent for Success of Writer Fannie Hurst.* New York: Times Books, 1999.

Lee, Spike, as told to Kaleem Aftab. *That's My Story and I'm Sticking to It.* New York: Norton, 2005.

Lehr, Dick. *The Birth of a Movement: How* Birth of a Nation *Ignited the Battle for Civil Rights.* New York: Public Affairs, 2014.

Lewis, David Levering. *When Harlem Was in Vogue.* New York: Alfred A. Knopf, 1981.

Litwack, Leon F. *Trouble in Mind: Black Southerners in the Age of Jim Crow.* New York: Alfred A. Knopf, 1998.

Marable, Manning. *Malcolm X: A Life of Reinvention.* New York: Viking, 2011.

——— and Leith Mullings. *Freedom.* New York: Phaidon, 2002.

McCullers, Carson. *The Member of the Wedding.* Boston: Mariner, 2004.

McGilligan, Patrick. *Oscar Micheaux: The Great and Only.* New York: Harper, 2007.

McNeil, Alex. *Total Television.* New York: Penguin, 1996.

McWhirter, Cameron. *Red Summer: The Summer of 1919 and the Awakening of Black America.* New York: Henry Holt, 2011.

Michaeli, Ethan. *The Defender: How the Legendary Black Newspaper Changed America.* New York: Houghton Mifflin.

Micheaux, Oscar. *The Conquest: The Story of a Negro Pioneer.* IndoEuropean Publishing.com, 2019.

Mitchell, Margaret. *Gone with the Wind.* New York: Scribner (paperback), 2011.

Northup, Solomon. *Twelve Years a Slave.* New York: First 37 Ink / Atria, 2013.

Osborne, Robert. *85 Years of the Oscar.* New York: Abbeville, 2013.

Parks, Gordon. *Voices in the Mirror.* New York: Broadway Books, 2005.

Poitier, Sidney. *This Life.* New York: Alfred A. Knopf, 1980.

*Reporting Civil Rights Part Two: American Journalism 1963–1973.* New York: Library of America, 2003.

Stevens, George Jr. *Conversations with the Great Moviemakers of Hollywood's Golden Age.* New York: Vintage, 2012.

Stowe, Harriet Beecher. *Uncle Tom's Cabin.* New York: Barnes & Noble Classics, 2003.

Sullivan, Patricia. *Lift Every Voice: The*

*NAACP and the Making of the Civil Rights Movement.* New York: New Press, 2009.

Thomson, David. *The New Biographical Dictionary of Film.* New York: Alfred A. Knopf, 2002.

———. *"Have You Seen . . ."* New York: Alfred A. Knopf, 2008.

Wasson, Sam. *The Big Goodbye: Chinatown and the Last Years of Hollywood.* New York: Flatiron, 2020.

Watts, Jill. *Hattie McDaniel: Black Ambition, White Hollywood.* New York: Amistad, 2007.

White, Adam, with Barney Ales. *Motown: The Sound of Young America.* London: Thames & Hudson, 2016.

White, Walter. *A Man Called White.* New York: Viking, 1948.

Willis, Deborah, and Kevin Merida. *Obama: The Historic Campaign in Photographs.* New York: HarperCollins, 2008.

Wilson, Victoria. *A Life of Barbara Stanwyck: Steel-True 1907–1940.* New York: Simon & Schuster, 2013.

Zirin, Dave. *Jim Brown: Last Man Standing.* New York: Blue Rider Press, 2018.

# Index

Page numbers in *italics* refer to illustrations.

# ILLUSTRATION CREDITS

Wil Haygood is recognized as one of America's most notable biographers and journalists. The author of nine books, he has received writing fellowships from the Guggenheim Foundation, the National Endowment for the Humanities Foundation, the Alicia Patterson Foundation, and the C. V. Starr Center for the Study of the American Experience. A longtime national and foreign correspondent for *The Boston Globe*, where he was a Pulitzer finalist, and then a national reporter for *The Washington Post*, where he won multiple awards, Haygood—in his books and journalistic work—has told the sweeping story of American history from the angles of politics, entertainment, race, and sports. His quartet of biographies—Adam Clayton Powell, Jr.; Sammy Davis, Jr.; Sugar Ray Robinson; and Thurgood Marshall—has been widely acclaimed. Haygood also wrote the *New York Times* bestseller *The Butler: A Witness to History,* which was adapted into the award-winning movie *The Butler,* directed by Lee Daniels and starring, among others, Forest Whitaker, Oprah Winfrey, Jane Fonda, and Vanessa Redgrave. Haygood serves an appointment as Boadway Visiting Distinguished Scholar at his alma mater, Miami University, in Ohio.

A NOTE ON THE TYPE

This book was set in Minion, a typeface produced by the Adobe Corporation specifically for the Macintosh personal computer, and released in 1990. Designed by Robert Slimbach, Minion combines the classic characteristics of old-style faces with the full complement of weights required for modern typesetting.

*Composed by North Market Street Graphics, Lancaster, Pennsylvania*

*Printed and bound by Friesens, Altona, Manitoba*

*Designed by Maggie Hinders*